STAR TREK VISIONS
OF LAW AND JUSTICE

Edited by

Robert H. Chaires, JD, PhD

and

Bradley Chilton, PhD, JD, MLS

Adios Press
Law, Crime and Corrections Series – Volume I
Series Editor: Ona Barry

Published by
Adios Press
Dallas, TX

Publisher: John Stanley
Art Director: Barry Powell
Cover Design: Charlie McDonald

First edition
ISBN: 0-9668080-2-9
Library of Congress Catalog card Number: 2002102021

ACKNOWLEDGMENTS

Grateful acknowledgment is given to the authors for allowing their previously published articles to be included in this work.

Bradley S. Chilton, "*Star Trek* and *Stare Decisis*: Legal Reasoning and Information Technology," *Journal of Criminal Justice and Popular Culture* 8.1(2001): 25-36.

Robert Costanza. "Four Visions of the Future Ahead: Will it be *Star Trek*, Ecotopia, Big Government, or Mad Max?" first published in *The Futurist*, February 1999.

Paul Joseph and Sharon Carton. "The Law of the Federation: Images of Law, Lawyers, and the Legal System in *Star Trek: The Next Generation*" first published in 24 *U. of Toledo Law Revue* 43 (1992).

Michael Stokes Paulsen. "Captain James T. Kirk and the Enterprise of Constitutional Interpretation: Some Modest Proposals From the Twenty-Third Century" first appearing as an Albany Law School Enrichment Series Lecture and then published in 59 *Albany Law Review* 671 (1995).

Michael P. Scharf and Lawrence D. Robert. "The Interstellar Relations of the Federation: International Law and *Star Trek: The Next Generation*" first published in 25 *U. of Toledo Law Review* 577 (1994).

B. Grant Stitt. "The Understanding of Evil: A Joint Quest for Criminology and Theology" first published in *The Journal of Psychology and Christianity*, 6.3 (1987).

Robert H. Chaires dedicates this work to the Lentz family, William, Ed, and Sue, for their constant support and suggestions and his brother Michael Vucekovich for always being there for help and inspiration.

Bradley Chilton dedicates this work to his brothers Mitch and Patrick, B.C.

CONTENTS

Introduction

Star Trek - words that invoke and evoke images in minds all around the world. Science fiction, entertainment, philosophy, social criticism, media art, and prophetic visions are but a few of the images that come to our minds. The nearly universal understanding of the images of *Star Trek* in our diverse contemporary world is, in itself, an amazing phenomenon. But not all the images of *Star Trek* are complimentary; many are downright derogatory: sci-fi trash, cheap commercial exploitation, and a dangerous cult. What *trekkie* has not heard the slur, "get a life!"? Whatever the perception of *Star Trek*, there is one point that has passed from debate to fact; *Star Trek* is a phenomenon that has become an institution. To say that *Star Trek* was just a television show is akin to saying Shakespeare just wrote plays.

Because *Star Trek* has become an institution that is both trans-generational and international, the study of *Star Trek* has become legitimate in that most prudent of arenas: academe. "Prudent" may seem a strange word to use in a description of the contemporary campus, a place often associated with radical or experimental behaviors. But academe is prudent because there are often long and bitter battles before new ideas are accepted as legitimate fields of inquiry.

It should not surprise us, then, that a 1992 article in the *University of Toledo Law Review* on the legal issues of *Star Trek: The Next Generation* (republished in this book) triggered international attention. As another chapter in this book recounts, more than 175 newspapers in the U.S.A. ran special stories about the article. Additional media sensation was registered in numerous radio and television spots and other media. Of course, some of this is because the original *Star Trek* series, as well as *Star Trek: The Next Generation, Star Trek: Voyager* and now *Enterprise,* have captured high ratings as some of the most highly popular syndicated series on American television. And the series has been rated among the highest quality television viewing in America. The *Star Trek* series has been used to teach ethics on many college campuses at the undergraduate level. But this law review article was acclaimed for marking a new beginning for the study of *Star Trek,* a place in academe.

However, the scholarly study of the phenomena of Star Trek has faced three major problems in academe, making it into a study of something legitimate:

1. Academics are part of a bureaucracy that tends to prize incremental improvements on the known, rather than radical departures.

2. In many disciplines, especially the social sciences, a "blind peer review" process operates prudently to discourage publication of truly new ideas or approaches; "blind peer review" tends to results in acceptance of only those writings that are mainstream and widely accepted.

3. Academics are highly specialized and are not educated or rewarded to think broadly. While interdisciplinary "talk" is popular, the "walk" is often inhibited by 1 and 2.

Considering *Star Trek* as a legitimate field of academic study brings about a fourth problem – who owns it? Well, like law, no discipline can lay a claim to the study of *Star Trek* as an exclusive preserve. The interdisciplinary study of "popular culture" comes closest to being an overarching title to include the study of *Star Trek*, but there is more, much more, to *Star Trek*.

As one chapter author notes, Shakespearean advocates in the humanities like to point out that if one reads Shakespeare, he will find every <u>kind</u> of human being. Similarly, if one watches *Star Trek,* he will find every <u>known</u> problem of the human condition – and some not known until envisioned <u>in</u> *Star Trek*. This is the academic problem of *Star Trek*; it does not fit neatly into anything. It is extrapolation of hard sciences such as physics, biology, and chemistry. It is critical commentary on both social science and social history. It is a visual literature of philosophy, ethics, and art. *Star Trek*, at its best, can inspire people to aspire to be better at being human beings; it can be both bully pulpit and awe-inspiring poetry. It also can be, and quite often is, just plain soap opera entertainment.

So, should the study of *Star Trek* be relegated to English or mass media departments? Or should it be the subject of political science, sociology, philosophy, or even the new field of justice studies? Might the anthropological aspects of First Contact supercede the philosophic, legal, and moral dimensions of the Prime Directive? Could the discipline of philosophy claim that *Star Trek* is really only a philosophic extension to Locke's *Social Contract* or More's *Utopia?* Are not issues such as omnipotent beings and the evolution of humanity into super beings more the subject of theology or at least bioethicists? Do not the physicists and engineers and cosmologists have a right to declare *Star*

Trek is good or bad science?

Perhaps. The problem is there has been, relative to the size and duration of the phenomena, so little written about *Star Trek* that has actually entered the classroom and discourse of higher education. There has from the beginning been some reference, bits and pieces within academic articles—like references to classic literature. There has been, over the years, a few articles about *Star Trek* that have survived the academic process. There have been more than a few books about *Star Trek*. Some of these books have been serious scholarly works exploring issues such as the images of race and gender or critically exploring the "science" of *Star Trek*. Most writings, though, have been more in the line of "popular literature." Again, it must be considered that popular literature and popular culture are terms of consignment, places where many scholars put things with which they do not want to deal.

These chapters represent a view of *Star Trek* that is just beginning to take meaningful hold in academe: that there is much to learn from the various reincarnations of *Star Trek*. *Star Trek* has become a sort of "philosophy for the masses" that takes us back to the marketplace of ideas and embeds complex scholarly arguments within images and stories that are widely accessible across the lines of nationality, language, religion, generation, gender, and race/ethnicity. Thus, it deserves a legitimate place in the classroom and in more general scholarly discourse. A decade ago it probably would have been close to heresy to bring *Star Trek* into the classroom. Now, the editors, among others, teach courses with *Star Trek* themes, and, perhaps more importantly, the words "*Star Trek*" are now in the catalogs of course listings of several major universities. This book is intended to be a reader, a collection of works to supplement the perspective of a variety of disciplines and contexts.

Like the wide diversity of those who relate to and understand the *Star Trek* phenomenon, our book reflects a diversity of scholars and writing styles. For example, in reading this work, consider that law review articles written by legal scholars tend to be long. Legal academics generally prize detailed explanations and ample examples garnered from precedent. Social scientists tend toward brevity, but use a language and argument style that is often difficult to follow, with a focus on quantitative or qualitative empirical "proofs" of a thesis by the recitation of known "facts" as "proven" by past experimentation. Neither is a better way to do things, but seldom do legal and social science academics work well together. So, we challenge you to go where "few scholars have gone," and read all styles, to avoid one style of writing because it takes more time to read and consider is the mark of the perpetually naïve.

This work has been divided into three distinct areas. First, "*Star Trek* and

Law," presents a more traditional, legal scholarly perspective on the law presented in *Star Trek*, as well as comparisons to existing national and international laws. It is primarily written by legal academics. Second, "*Star Trek* and Justice" presents the disciplinary perspectives of scholars in the social sciences, including history, sociology, political science, public administration, education, theology, and so forth. Finally, "*Star Trek* Visions of the Future" goes beyond legal and social science disciplinary constraints to understand *Star Trek* issues through the interdisciplinary approaches of education, futuristics, information science, and phenomenology. It suggests an "applied *Star Trek*" that takes seriously the meanings we find within *Star Trek* as artifacts of our values and society, for both today and in our future.

Through this study of *Star Trek*, we hope to obliterate the idea that this is an area "where few scholars have gone before." In the end, we hope that you will understand what is scholarly is not just in the hands of the few; it is in ideas that we all share – a *Star Trek* marketplace of ideas. For we all can see, experience and think about the images of our *Star Trek* visions of law and justice.

SECTION ONE

Sᴛᴀʀ Tʀᴇᴋ ᴀɴᴅ Lᴀᴡ

When we think of law, often what comes to mind are restrictions; do not do this, or that, and most especially, never, never, engage in ....(fill in your own favorite). But law is only one form of social control. Families, communities, peers, schools, employers, and churches engage in other forms of social control. They may shame you, praise you, scold you, love you, and hate you; they may ostracize you or embrace you as one of "theirs." While there is not universal agreement, what makes law distinctive from other forms of social control is the specter of a penal sanction imposed by government. While in western societies, we generally divide law into two great spheres, criminal and civil, these divisions are not always so clear.

Criminal law is usually associated with penal sanctions such as fines, limitations on certain freedoms, as in probation, even deprivation of liberty in the form of confinement in a penal institution, a jail or prison. These, for want of a better term, are punishments by the government for violating law, law protecting the public good or at least some perspective of the public good. Civil law is more commonly seen as governing relations among private individuals, for example, the law of contracts, the law of torts, domestic relations law and corporate law. Indeed, while one will usually find in law school only three or four courses directly relating to the criminal, it is not uncommon to find more than 100 courses relating to civil law in a good-sized law school.

Yet, this division into the civil and criminal is misleading. For example, there is an area of law called administrative law that has characteristics of both civil and criminal. Individuals and corporations (which are "persons" in the eyes of the law) can be sanctioned in many ways for violating government regulations. A fine is only the least of the possible punishments. In a similar manner, all civil law, because it ultimately can be enforced by the government, carries very criminal law-like sanctions. Fail to pay child support and you can go to jail. Fail to comply with the court order to fulfill a contract and you can be fined, hugely, daily, and even go to jail. Here the punishment is for failing to comply with the commands of a branch of government, the courts. It is technically not a criminal punishment, but to the recipient, it can look and feel like one. It is important to understand that law is not always about stating what people, real and artificial, cannot do or must do. Quite often law restricts government by defining what the government may not do to people. This area of law, generically called constitutional law but involving much more than constitutions, places limits on the power of government to make law and to control, or compel, certain behaviors. It also places guidelines and limits on how government may conduct the law and gather evidence. In some areas, such as civil rights law, it provides for sanctions against the government for misconduct. Violating civil rights also may be a crime. While governments cannot be put in jail, government officials can be. Still, governments can be fined and forced to pay monetary damages to people.

Historically, a major issue of law has been that government has not protected all people equally, nor allowed all people equal access to law. Within this vein, the evolution of law can be seen as a continuing attempt to make law work for all. However, many hold that this evolution has never been largely successful. Further, an evolving idea is that of conflicts between *civil liberties* and *human rights*. Many view this conflict as one of *negative rights v. positive rights*. Civil liberties, the "negative rights" perspective, see the best government as not interfering in the human condition. Other factors, other social controls, the market place, the family, the schools, are best suited to define and control the human condition. The government that protects the individual by ensuring his civil liberties, maximum protection from government, is best. In contrast, the human rights or "positive rights" perspective holds that government must ensure some basic rights to equality, food, shelter, education, and medical care. Further, *interalia*, government must legislate controls that end abusive discrimination, patriarchy, sexual exploitation, economic oppression and fear of political oppression.

The future visions of life in *Star Trek*, at least in the Federation, are no longer greatly concerned with problems of civil liberties or human rights; they have faded away. Starfleet, in particular, appears to have reached a level of true equality, a future far different than the incremental improvements of the past. Or has it? Professors Paul Joseph and Sharon Carton suggest that not only has the law improved in the future, but so have the "lawyers" and the "process." People tend to trust both. However, professors Michael Scharf and Lawrence Robert see more continuity than change from our present to the world of *Star Trek*. As they point out, when we encounter "strange new worlds" many of the old laws, and conducts, of the 20th century still will apply. Professor Michael Stokes Paulsen takes a different track for *Star Trek*; he uses one episode to explain how too much attention to the "whole," too much deference to the courts interpreting law, can result in a dystopian future.

Law, Justice and Star Trek

ROBERT H. CHAIRES, JD, PHD AND BRADLEY CHILTON, PHD, JD, MLS

Law and justice! Like freedom, these two words are some of the most overused, and abused, words in history. In a very real sense, *Star Trek* exists because the meaning of law and justice has never been clear. Recorded history is full of attempts to *create* or *discover* law. There has been the law of God or gods, the law of kings and tyrants, the law of legislatures and "the people." Often, but not always intertwined, is the word justice. Like gods, kings – and people – justice can be absolute and harsh, fair and personal, full of bizarre ritual or difficult tests, such as trial by ordeal or inquisition. Cities and civilization have risen and fallen in the name of law and justice, and saints and sinners have died whispering, or screaming, *"Justice, justice."* There is only one indisputable fact we know about law and justice; its practice has never worked for everyone any place, even in the *Star Trek* universe of the 24th century.

The Federation and Starfleet, like any complex organization, are creatures of law. As Black (1976) relates, "Law increases in quantity as other forms of social control decrease in quality." While sociologists and legal scholars might argue whether a small, nomadic tribe actually had "law," it certainly had expectations and some form of sanction for failure to live up to those expectations. Cities have more hierarchy, more specialization, and more law (Black, 1976). Relations among cities, nations, worlds, require even more law. But law is not necessarily related to justice. In point, historically, and perhaps not so historically, law has been much more about maintaining the social order, the statuses, obligations, and privileges in societies and among societies where there is unequal distribution of resources, limitations on social and economic mobility—and perhaps most of all, inequitable access by individuals and groups to various means of achieving justice.

Joseph and Carton (1992:44) state about the law in *Star Trek: The Next Generation (ST:TNG)*:

> A legal system is not wholly separate from
> the general culture. It grows and changes in

response to growth and changes within the
society that creates and uses it. If the society
of the future has progressed and changed in
other ways, we would expect to see some
similar progress and change within the legal
system as well. Just as other areas of human
interaction are explored in the show, perhaps
the fictional setting of *ST:TNG* has something to say about what our legal system is or
could be.

In this vein, *Star Trek* has always been about law and justice, about our
aspirations to a better law, a better justice. The social and economic upheavals
of the 1960s were in large part the product of a growing recognition that great
inequities in social justice existed. Law, legislated and judicially created, was
perhaps the major vehicle by which attempts at reform were made. Indeed, it
was increased access to the means to law, the ballot box, the courtroom, and
even to public opinion via "reinterpretations" of the Constitution, most especially the 1st and 14th amendments, that generated a context for the original
Star Trek. Viewed from this perspective, the early *Star Trek* was about the failures of law and justice in America. *Star Trek*, without the background of those
failures, would have been just another television show. As Bernardi (1998:31-
32) relates, it would probably have become *Lost in Space*. Of course, these
were some people of color who the network brass at NBC would have preferred not having. In the 1960s, a multicultural vision of the future on television was still a strange, new land.

Thus, the law and justice of the original *Star Trek* (*ST*) was reflective of the
painful, explosive, turmoil of the '60s, of the Cold War, of nuclear
Armageddon. That the original *Star Trek* was overtly polarized, often simplistic
in its explanations of problems and solutions, was not surprising given the context. *Star Trek: The Next Generation* (*ST:TNG*) of the late 1980s and into the
1990s, along with the mid-1990s to early 2000s series *Deep Space 9* (*ST:DS9*)
and *Star Trek: Voyager* (*ST:V*), while occurring in probably no less polarized
social-political context, were usually more subtle in their presentations of that
future "just" society, but often no less simplistic in how law and justice were
presented. Simply put, in the "real" world, the basic issues of law and justice
had not changed. While 80 – odd years separated *ST* and *ST:TNG* in
Federation time, the 20 to 30 years of real time is not all that long. Most of the

"players" of the real life racial strife and international conflict embedded in *ST* were still alive.

In the 30 – odd years intertwined with the original series and the end of *Voyager*, real technology had leapfrogged, nations had fallen and risen, the civil rights revolution had been transformed from one of seeking legal equity to again declaring legal absolutes. Beneath the surface, for the poor, the disenfranchised, for people of color, things looked and acted very much the same, as they largely did in all the new versions of *Star Trek*. Arguably, because *Star Trek* has not substantially changed in its presentation of that utopian future, it has grown apart from the real future of the developing 21st century.

To explore change, or lack of it, in visions of law and justice in *Star Trek*, first some issues of technology, justice, and law will be presented. From there, an examination of three models of law and justice, absolute, equity, and due process, will be used to examine if *Star Trek* in all its manifestations truly has *gone where no one has gone before.*

Technology, Law and Justice

In the popular movie *Back to the Future, Part II*, which takes place in the near future, flying cars powered by "Mr. Fusions," small, commonly available fusion devices that run on garbage, are common. Yet, society and culture appear much as they do now. In reality (if it can be called that) much of society as we know it would disintegrate with just those two inventions.

> –Mr. Fusion by itself would destroy much of the economic and political stability (again if it could be called that) that exists in the world. In the economic dimension, the oil- and power-producing industries would collapse. Along with that collapse would come millions of lost jobs and probably a worldwide stock market crisis.

> –In the social justice dimension, Mr. Fusion, along with the flying car, would allow changes in residence locations and open up previously uninhabitable portions of the Earth. At the same time, with access to

unlimited, cheap power and transportation that does not require the building of vast infrastructures (i.e., roads, airports), what are now called "Third World nations" would be able to increase the living standard of its populations. If they did not, flying cars would render national boarders largely irrelevant.

–Politically/legally national economic powers such as Saudi Arabia would decline in geopolitical importance; no one would fight wars over oil. Similarly, the international and national political power of many major corporations would wither away. Without their enormous economic and political clout, many industries would be unable to sway legislation and judicial decisions in ways that benefit corporate interests over human interests, what Jerry Spence (1989) calls the choice of artificial people over real people. Entire fields of law would go the way of the buggy whip.

TECHNOLOGY AND LAW

One message of *Star Trek* is that technology will set you free. However, that is the facial message. The real message is that reasonably unrestrained access to the economic and social *benefits* of technology is a general pre-condition of a just society. In this direction, it can be argued that there is a human right to beneficial technology. And if there is a right, there is a duty to provide it and to protect it from abuses of powerful interest groups. This message contradicts American legal tradition.

The history of American law is largely one of conflicts about what is private and public. Things that were private were beyond the public law. Very simplistically put, what one owned, one controlled, totally. The role of government was to protect private property. That was justice. Claims that the ownership of one could cause misery to many were alien intruders into the law of property. Nothing in the law prohibited a man who owned a loaf a bread, or many loaves, from holding out for the highest price while many starved, or refusing to sell at all because he thought it better that the rabble starved. Victor Hugo in *Les Miserables* well presented this point of law and justice.

Star Trek, most especially *ST:TNG*, exposed vast numbers of viewers to fantastic new technology. While none of it was really "new" since virtually every "gadget" or system had been envisioned in some form by previous science fiction writers, there was an operating assumption in *Star Trek*; it was owned by mankind. No individual, private group or even government made a profit on it by exclusive control. Even information was "public" and freely available. Without a doubt, new technologies have the potential to change particular areas of law. Whether new technologies change the *behavior* of law, the tendency of law to benefit highly organized vested interests, is a different matter.

The law surrounding technology is about property – who owns it, who controls it, who profits from it. Always, the government, in the form of legislation and the courts, stands ready to enforce ownership of not only produced technology, but also of ideas. Vast systems of law, patent, trademark, intellectual property, commercial contract, product liability, trusts and estates, tax, are but a few *general* areas that deal with ownership of property. Is it really likely that in the future the Federation is going to give it away? Technology may not be bread, but in a technological universe it is the substance of life, and it requires substantial amounts of law even to give it away.

To explore this last point, **Table 1** portrays a simplistic relationship among technological advance, social and economic justice, and law.

It is perhaps of note that one biotechnology that currently exists has only received intermittent, and then only in negative formats, mention: genetic manipulation of humans. *ST* gave us the episode "Space Seed" and visions of supermen and genetic wars. *ST:DS9* references the illegality of genetic enhancement via the problems of Dr. Bashir. Arguably, that particular issue was, is, just too close in time and technology. Further, a genetically enhanced humanity, let alone Starfleet, would not present a "fair fight" to the universe, a point suggested in the opening episode of the new series *Enterprise* with the genetically engineered Suliban. If "human" values are to *go where no one has gone before* and prevail, then they must be true humans, not test tube ones.

Similarly, medical technology was never at the forefront of *Star Trek* pursuits. While Dr. McCoy, in one of his numerous forays into human past or contacts with nonwarp cultures, might bemoan working with instruments and technology not much above knives and leeches, none of the versions of *Star Trek* ever expanded on the obvious; transporter technology was the "magic bullet" to immortality. In the *ST:TNG* episode "Relics," Scotty from *ST* is found alive

Table 1: Law, Justice, and Technology

Technology	Economic Justice Implications	Social Justice Implications	Legal Arenas Impacted
Transporter	Costs of travel Place of employment Medical care	Place of living Longevity Political access	Immigration law Customs law Transportation law

Replicator	Distribution of
	  resources
	Basic needs
	Discretionary needs
	Money standard
	Employment
	  demands
	Medical care
		Wealth gap
		Status in wealth
		Time release to
		  pursue interests,
		  e.g., advanced
		  education
		Intrafamily goals
		Longevity
			Commerce law
			Monetary law
			Patent and
			  Trademark law
			Corporate law
			Tort law
			Contract law
			Health law
			Welfare law

Holotechnology	Health care	Entertainment
		Education
		Research
		Reintroduction of
		  servant class
			Constitutional
			  (human rights) law
			Entertainment law

after, as usual, finding a technological way to survive for almost 75 years by suspending himself in the pattern buffer of the transporter . While this is not real immortality, it is much different than the "cold sleep" of *ST*'s "Space Seed" (needed for interstellar travel) or *ST:TNG*'s episode "Neutral Zone" (survive until medicine advances). Clearly, the latter concept of temporarily suspending life functions for medical reasons was a common practice by the time of *ST:TNG* since it is done several times by placing people in "stasis fields." Whether this is true immortality is debatable. *Star Trek* avoided the issue. It appears that you got your five or six score years as a human (or seven score in the case of Dr. McCoy) and that was it. In *Star Trek,* immortality was an unfair advantage, and human members of Starfleet seemed never to be jealous of the long-lived or immortals.

Nevertheless, this interface of technology and law has seldom been explored in *Star Trek*, except in negative ways. The Federation, and most especially humans, "share, even give, technology," except were prohibited by the *Prime Directive*, a point to be discussed later. Those who profit from technology in purely monetary terms are usually portrayed in unflattering ways, e.g., the

Ferengi. Still, one must imagine a contemporary for-profit HMO with this technology. *Yes, we could reconstitute your pattern and remove your cancer and at the same time transfer your memory patterns to your 35-year-old body from an earlier storage. But your particular employee health plan does not provide for this.*

A MODEL FOR LAW AND JUSTICE IN STAR TREK

Predominantly, *Star Trek* presents an equitable view of law and justice. Simply put, usually *Star Trek* combines a humanistic view of sentient nature with a human rights perspective on law. A human rights perspective on the law can be perceived in terms of a continuing conflict among the ideas *negative rights* and *positive rights*. Negative rights theory is premised on the idea that individual rights are supreme and governments should not interfere with individual rights. Positive rights theory is premised on the idea that governments should ensure some minimal standards in a variety of areas (see, for example, Copelon, 1998).

Consider, for example, the areas of medical care and employment. Pure negative rights theory would hold these are private arenas in which providers of employment and medical services have a property right. The employer owns the business and should be free from government interference in salary, benefits, and conditions of employment because, of course, employees are individually free to "bargain" on these items. No employee is forced to take or keep a job. Similarly, providers of health care should be free to charge whatever the market will bear for services. Pure positive rights theory would hold that having employment under terms and conditions that support the health and welfare of the employee are fundamental rights to all that outweigh in substantial part (but not fully) individual property rights. Similarly, health care would be considered so fundamental a human right that everyone would have a right to it regardless of ability to pay.

At this time, different nations of the Earth have resolved these conflicts in different ways under varying political and economic theories, not without historical and contemporary conflict and even bloodshed. Within this vein of thought, *Star Trek* displays a future universe that is full of familiar discord, interspecies discord. And, as Scharf and Robert (1994) point out, the "Interstellar law" of the 24th century is remarkably similar to the International law of the 20th.

LEVELS OF LAW IN STAR TREK

As Scharf and Robert explain, there are really two sets of law displayed in *Star Trek*. Federation law is domestic in that it governs member planets and species of the Federation. By the term "federation," the United Federation of Planets is engaged in a power-sharing arraignment. However, the UFP is more akin to the strong internal federalism of the contemporary U.S., Germany and Canada than the weak federalism of today's United Nations. Thus, members of the UFP agree, as a condition of membership, to adhere to various constitutional limits on powers and to guarantee certain individual rights and liberties. That the Federation maintains a standing "military" arm, Starfleet, is a strong indication of the "strong federalism" in the balance.

In contrast, within this context, Interstellar Law governs relations between the Federation and nonmember planets and species. Not surprisingly, many other planetary associations are referred to in derogatory terms: Romulans, Klingons, and a host of others have "empires." As Scharf and Robert note, relations among the various autonomous others is governed by treaties and custom. Further, Starfleet is bound by the Prime Directive with its prohibitions against interference with the internal political operations of a planet and even contact with a pre-warp civilization. Yet, it appears that private citizens of the Federation are not so bound. For example, in the *ST:TNG* episode "Angel One," it is noted that the marooned men who are interfering with the matriarchal society have not committed a crime under Federation law because they are crew members from a private freighter. As such, they are not subject to the Prime Directive and cannot be forced by Starfleet to leave the planet.

While "Angel One" is one of the more contrived plots in *ST:TNG*, what Nemecek (1992:47) describes as a "one-note morality tale," it does point out a common law and justice theme in *Star Trek* – when the law is inconvenient it is disregarded or an exception is found. What can be seen here is that several sets of laws and theories of justice operate within *Star Trek*. As **Table 2** displays, there are four distinct arenas of law to consider.

Table 2. Levels of Law in Star Trek

Federation Law	Starfleet Law
Planetary Law	Ship Law

Federation law defines interplanetary relations among members, and Planetary law regulates intraplanet relations. In theory at least, the Federation would be responsible for enforcing various rights and liberties among all citizens of the Federation. Similarly, Federation law also would control commercial relations among planets. Indeed, it would seem the major role of the Federation would be the regulation and enforcement of civil matters. Not all planets have done away with money or commerce for profit, and issues of environmental damage, personal injury liability, and contract enforcement are sure to arise. Scharf and Robert (1992) address these matters and many others as they describe the complexities of a federalism that spans light years of distance.

Arguably, because the only viable model that exists for *Star Trek* is the United Nations, it is not surprising that it inconsistently appears. By the time of *ST:TNG*, where various technologies should have ended much of the underpinnings of conflict, the squabbling looks quite familiar. In this line of thought, Starfleet law, and the formal and informal adjudication of it seen in so many episodes, looks refreshing. But is it? Do ships' captains operate beyond the law? That answer is no. What is seen on *Star Trek* is the operation of equity law.

ABSOLUTE, EQUITY, AND DUE PROCESS MODELS

Blumenthal (1981) offers a useful model for examining law and justice. He relates that all theories, ideologies, and practices of law and justice fall into one of three major models: Absolute, Equity, and Due Process.

Absolute models are premised on an inviolate legitimacy of source. All people and situations are treated identically, and the result is always the same.

Equity models reject absolutes and are premised on the idea that justice can only occur when the particulars of the situation are considered. Thus, people in similar situations can and should be treated differently, and the fairness of the result is deemed more important than how the decision was made.

Due Process models reject absolutes as too simplistic, but also question whether people of sufficient intelligence exist to do "individualized justice." Thus, the fairness of the process of reaching a decision is stressed.

Within the various reincarnations of *Star Trek,* these models, paradigms if you will, of law and justice are seen in constant conflict. This conflict occurs at the macro level in the equitable/due process of the Federation vs. the absolute models of, say, the early Klingons, the Romulans, and the Ferengi, within the Federation among worlds, and most specifically as a constant thematic conflict within Starfleet via the "absolute" Prime Directive being in conflict with "equitable" considerations.

It is important not to equate Absolute models of law and justice as authoritarian or totalitarian systems of law and justice. They may be, however, an absolute model of law, and justice refers more to a system that has a predominant idea controlling all decisions and actions, for example, the Klingon warrior creed or the Ferengi *Rules of Acquisition*. An absolute model can exist even in what might be deemed an idyllic society.

An example of this point can be seen in the *ST:TNG* episode "Justice." Wesley Crusher is to be executed for a minor offense, essentially walking on flowers. While this may seem harsh, all Edos see this "any crime, one punishment" as essentially just; and few viewers would argue that the Edos were anything but a bunch of nice people in an idyllic (if soon boring) society. Captain Picard is caught in a conflict between the Prime Directive noninterference clause, an absolute, and his concept of a fairness that considers individual circumstances; Wesley is a juvenile and the punishment is disproportionate to the crime. Other members of the crew, especially Wesley's mother, voice both equity and due process arguments, each of which is refuted by the Edos: Wesley did not know; *ignorance of the law is no excuse*. Execution for minor crimes; *it works, and no one disobeys any law.* It is not fair to Wesley; *please do not do this to us. Look at our society.*

All of these points ring loud and long in Anglo-American legal history. For the most part, absolute law has been followed. For example, ignorance of the law and cultural defenses to criminal liability are usually not allowed in contemporary American courts. While we have some concept of proportionality of punishment, the Supreme Court has substantially upheld career criminal and "three strikes" laws that have had draconian applications (for example, *Solem v. Helm* 463 U.S. 277 [1983]). At the same time, federal and state courts have ratified laws that allow the execution of criminals who were impaired by mental illness or intelligence level and/or were juveniles at the time of their crimes (for example, *Stanford v. Kentucky*, 492 U.S. 361 [1989]).

Considering this, what can be seen in *Star Trek* is the continuing conflict surrounding law and justice that equates to two basic issues. The first is that *ST* expressed a 1960's view of law and justice via an anti-colonialist view of the Prime Directive, corruption of innocent society. That absolutist view extended to "any" interference with "natural development." For example, in *ST* "Return of the Archons" a self-aware computer, Landru, is destroyed (by logic) and the Starfleet personnel were left to guide the society "back to a more normal form" (Okuda and Okuda, 1996). Similarly, in the *ST* episode "The Apple," destruction of the computer god Vaal is justified because the culture was "stagnating." Thus, in an odd variation of the 19th century Monroe Doctrine which reserved the western hemisphere to nations in it, the Prime Directive of the '60s seems to have the flavor of an idea that all worlds were free to evolve, as long as they developed in a certain way.

The second is that *ST:TNG* expressed an absolutist view of the corruption of technology, that a society must grow socially and ethically before technology, lest it destroy itself. For example, in the *ST:TNG* episode "Arsenal of Freedom," the Minosians lose control of their weapons and are destroyed, and in the episode "Samaritan Snare," the Pakleds are deemed not intelligent enough to have the advanced technology of the Federation—even though they are well aware of the Federation's existence.

In *ST:TNG* the Prime Directive is sometimes carried to absurd levels. In "Pen Pals" Captain Picard is at first willing to let the planet Drema IV and its inhabitants be destroyed by geologic upheaval rather than use the technology of the *Enterprise* to save them and thus violate the Prime Directive. Data interferes and his actions are later ratified by Picard, but only after discourse that exposes the continuing internal conflicts many Starfleet members have about an absolutist version of the Prime Directive.

Table 3, which uses only episodes from *ST:TNG*, displays this point of internal conflict in individuals and societies regarding law and justice. These episodes are only representative. Because conflicts of law and justice are so thematic to *Star Trek*, the table would be pages long if a more exhaustive display was attempted.

Table 3: Conflicts of Law and Justice in *Star Trek: The Next Generation*

EPISODE	ABSOLUTE LAW & JUSTICE	EQUITABLE LAW & JUSTICE	DUE PROCESS LAW & JUSTICE
"Justice"	The Edos	Captain Picard	Dr. Crusher Commander Riker
"The Measure of a Man"		Captain Picard	Captain Louvois
"Pen Pals"	Captain Picard	Commander Data	
"The Offspring"	Admiral Haftel	Captain Picard	
"The Drumhead"		Captain Picard Commander Riker	Admiral Satie
"Half A Life "	The Kaelonians	Lwaxana Troi	
"The Outcast"	The J'naii	Commander Riker	
"The Perfect Mate"	The Kriosians Captain Picard	Dr. Crusher	
"Homeward"	Captain Picard	Dr. Rozhenko	

What emerges in **Table 3** is a simple point, what Captain Picard states in the closing of the episode "Justice": "There can be no justice as long as laws are absolute." Overwhelmingly, Ship's Law, or equity, is the dominant law of *Star Trek*. The members of Starfleet may encounter worlds and societies in which an absolute law is predominant. They may be subject to Federation and Starfleet law that is equally absolute in its demands or that entails due process procedures that are harsh and arbitrary, but, in the end, the model of law and justice that prevails will be an equitable one.

Indeed, in this context, it can be argued that the purpose of *Star Trek* is simple. It is a recognition that in a universe of infinite diversity, there can be no absolutes and that no set of laws and procedures can be defined and applied that will do justice in all circumstances. In short, above all, the *Star Trek* universe depends on ethical beings to do justice.

In the introduction to her wonderful and insightful work *The Ethics of Star Trek*, philosopher Judith Barad (2000: xi) states:

> One reason why *Star Trek* has endured from one generation to the next is that most of the stories themselves are indeed moral fables. Though the episodes are obviously self-contained, when taken as a whole they constitute a harmonious philosophy filled with hope. While our *Star Trek* heroes are far from perfect, they are nonetheless essentially decent beings whose interaction with "new life and new civilizations" is always guided by nobility and morality.

While "always" is perhaps too strong a word, it is appropriate when the context of learning from mistakes is considered. Unlike many figures associated with law and justice today, the characters of *Star Trek* are not afraid to admit mistakes. Indeed, it seems the major "sin" in Starfleet, or at least on the *Enterprise,* is not making a mistake, but failing to learn and grow from it. This especially extends to deliberate violations of law and Starfleet regulations. Unquestioning obedience to law is not a prized characteristic in *Star Trek*; looking into your heart to examine the purity of motive is.

CONCLUSION

Yes, the Federation and Starfleet may do unjust things in the name of justice. The darker visions of the Federation and Starfleet portrayed in *Deep Space Nine* are witness to the continuing point driven home in *Star Trek* - there will always be a dark side - evil done in the name of contingency.

Yes, as Scharf and Robert (1994) point out, the interstellar law of the future may look and act much like that of international law of today, reflecting a very imperfect system full of self-interest and acrimony. But, as Joseph and Carton (1992) relate, there is a difference in the future law portrayed in *Star Trek*. It places far less emphasis on strict adherence to due process and much more reliance on a basic faith in the innate ethical standards of shipboard decision-makers. The Federation and Starfleet may make bad law, implement unjust practices, but there is an abiding faith that when the cards are all down, people will do the just thing for the place and the moment, even if it costs them their careers, even their freedom and lives.

This may be the real story of law and justice in *Star Trek*. In that far future place they have evolved beyond a merely rational law, beyond ideas of the corporate good, beyond models of law that would hold that no one is above the law to an embedded belief that no one is beneath justice.

BIBLIOGRAPHY

Barad, Judith, with Ed Robertson (2000). *The Ethics of Star Trek*, New York: HarperCollins.

Bernardi, Daniel L (1988). *Star Trek and History: Race-ing Toward a White Future*, New Brunswick, NJ: Rutgers U. Press.

Black, Donald (1976). *The Behavior of Law.* New York: Academic Press.

Blumenthal, Murray (1981). These models of law and justice come from a series of lectures given by Professor Blumenthal at the University of Denver College of Law. It is unknown if they were ever published.

Copelon, Rhonda (1998). "The Indivisible Framework of International Human Rights," ind. Kairys, ed. *The Politics of Law*, 3rd ed. NY: Basic Books (216-239).

Joseph, Paul and Sharon Carton (1992). "The Law of the Federation: Images of Law, Lawyers, and the Legal System in *Star Trek: The Next Generation*," 24 *U. Toledo Law*. Rev. 43.

Nemecek, Larry (1992). *The Star Trek: The Next Generation Companion*, NY: Pocket Books.

Okuda, Michael and Denise Okuda (1996). *Star Trek Chronology: The History of the Future*, New York: Pocket Books.

Scharf, Michael P. and Lawrence D. Robert (1994). "The Interstellar Relations of the Federation: International Law and *Star Trek: The Next Generation*," 25 *U. Toledo Law Rev.* 577

The Law of the Federation:
IMAGES OF LAW, LAWYERS, AND THE LEGAL SYSTEM IN *STAR TREK: THE NEXT GENERATION*

PAUL JOSEPH, JD, LLM

AND

SHARON CARTON, JD, LLM

THE AUTHORS, WHO ARE PROFESSORS AT THE SHEPARD BROAD LAW CENTER OF NOVA UNIVERSITY, WOULD LIKE TO THANK CO-EXECUTIVE PRODUCER JERI TAYLOR, PRODUCTION ASSOCIATE TERRI MARTINEZ, MR. L.H. JOSEPH, JR., PROFESSOR MICHAEL RICHMOND AND STU-DENT RESEARCH ASSISTANTS RICHARD DeBOEST AND SHELLEY ZABEL FOR THEIR ASSISTANCE. STAR TREK, STAR TREK: THE NEXT GENERATION, AND U.S.S. ENTERPRISE ARE REGISTERED TRADEMARKS OF PARAMOUNT PICTURES CORPORATION.

Introduction

During the last 25 years, *Star Trek* and its progeny have come to occupy a unique place in American popular culture.[1] While the show began as a short-lived and marginally rated television series that survived only three seasons before final cancellation,[2] the *Star Trek* phenomenon did not end there. First, through syndication, the show gained a following it had never had as a network offering. *Star Trek* conventions provided gathering points for the faithful. A series of feature films updated and continued the story.[3] Books,[4] a cartoon series and merchandising spin-offs[5] helped to keep *Star Trek* in the minds of the public.[6] Fan pressure prompted NASA to name the first space shuttle *Enterprise* after the starship on the show. The humorous, late-night show *Saturday Night Live* twice parodied the show and its cult of hard-core adherents.[7]

Eventually, the continued popularity of the original *Star Trek* led to a second series, this time playing first-run in syndication, *Star Trek: The Next Generation* (*ST:TNG*).[8] More recently, a third *Star Trek* series, *Deep Space Nine*, has begun production. It is scheduled to premiere in January 1993.[9]

For most of its 25 year history, its original creator, the recently deceased

Gene Roddenberry,[10] exercised considerable control over the development of *Star Trek* in its various incarnations.[11]

Roddenberry's "vision of the future" remains a guiding light for the continuing *Star Trek* saga, says Rick Berman, executive producer of *Star Trek: The Next Generation*. "Gene felt strongly about the goodness of mankind," Berman says. "He knew there were rotten things also, but he liked to think of the future where wonderful things would continue and man could enhance the quality of his life."[12]

Today, Rick Berman fills much the same position.[13] Thus, there was a conscious effort to develop and examine certain ideas or themes,[14] and a greater consistency existed than there might otherwise have been without such a guiding vision.[15]

ST:TNG represents the best example to date of the themes of the *Star Trek* saga.[16] The basic concepts, set down in the original series, have been more fully developed and presented through the interaction of the characters.[17] This is probably because *ST:TNG* has survived longer than its predecessor and has achieved commercial popularity its predecessor never did during its initial run.[18] Thus, its production team has been able to develop its themes during a longer period of time, with larger budgets and with less interference than was true of the original series.[19]

The show takes place in the 24th century. Earth is united and part of an alliance, the United Federation of Planets, encompassing many species located on planets in numerous star systems. The show is set primarily on the flagship of that Federation, the *U.S.S. Enterprise*, a descendant of the craft featured in the original series and feature films. While technology and spectacular special effects are important components of the series, more important is the interaction among the ensemble cast and with various others, both friend and foe, whom they encounter.

The producers of the show take the view that they are telling human stories about today, not merely throwing around "gee whiz" technical gadgetry. While the stories are intended to present human issues and problems that we face today,[20] it is not intended that the people, their structures or their answers to problems be an exact duplicate of modern times. Rather, what is presented is a vision of a developed species, several steps closer to perfection than we are today.[21]

To accomplish their dual goals of telling stories relevant to our present[22] while presenting a vision of a positive future,[23] by necessity, the producers have had to create at least the outlines of the culture and society of the 24th century.[24] Thus, what is presented is not only what 20th century people do, but a vision of what we should do and who we should strive to become.[25] This makes *ST:TNG* an interesting prism through which to view 20th-century institutions, and it becomes reasonable to ask whether the *Star Trek* future has anything to teach us[26] about our present reality and the directions that our society should or should not take.[27]

A legal system is not wholly separate from the general culture. It grows and changes in response to growth and change within the society that creates and uses it. If the society of the future has progressed and changed in other ways, we would expect to see some similar progress and change within the legal system as well. Just as other areas of human interaction are explored in the show, perhaps the fictional setting of *ST:TNG* has something to say about what our law and legal system is or should be.

We had none of these thoughts when we began watching *ST:TNG*. We certainly never thought we would write about it. Yet, over time, we independently began to notice how often legal issues or ideas cropped up and how often they were worth a second look. What follows is our examination of the legal side of the 24th century as portrayed in *ST:TNG*. We first consider the legal system and then present various substantive legal issues.

Law and Society in the 24th Century

Neither Gene Roddenberry nor the *ST:TNG* production team ever sat down and designed a legal system. What they did was deal with legal problems on a case-by-case basis, while attempting to be consistent with the rest of what they had created.[28] Thus, it is useful to consider the show's 24th century in general to determine its operative principles, examine what has been presented concerning law and the legal system and then attempt to explain what a legal system would have to look like to be consistent. Only then can we ask whether it should be a model for our real, as opposed to our fictional, future.

We assume there is some relation between law and society such that a legal system will embody the history and cultural development of the people who created and use it.[29] Therefore, the legal system of the Federation will reflect, in some manner, the values, goals, needs and experiences of the 24th century as well as the process of historical development from our century to theirs.[30] Some of the features of their legal system will be familiar to us, but others could be quite different.

The *ST:TNG* writers/directors guide,[31] developed to present the basic framework of the show to those involved in particular episodes, explains something of the nature of the 24th century as envisioned by the creators and developers of *ST:TNG*. In addition, individual shows have established some elements of history leading up to the time period portrayed in the 24th-century milieu.[32] These are the starting points. The legal system must be consistent and in harmony with what is already known about *ST:TNG*'s 24th century.

The 24th Century Legal System – and Our Own

The fundamental ends of legal systems do not change, although the means of achieving those ends do. A system of law must settle disputes, give to each litigant that which he or she is due and do so with a process perceived by the participants, and the society at large, to be fair.

The 20th-century legal system may be characterized as one heavily influenced by conflict and distrust. Litigation is conceived of as a battle between hostile adversaries with truth and justice belonging to the victor.[33] Our distrust of each other (including government officials) makes us insist upon elaborate procedural formalities (e.g., evidence codes, rules of civil and criminal procedure, discovery rules, etc.) to assure fairness.[34] Decision makers (i.e., judge and jury) must be uninvolved, neutral persons, and there must be a multi-layered appeals process. It would be unthinkable to have a friend, employer or the superior officer of a litigant as the judge in the case.

Within the context of the *Star Trek* saga, it has been established that humanity went through a difficult time on the road to the 24th century. For example, one episode tells us that during a barbaric period following a nuclear war, the legal system established the rule that defendants were "guilty until proven innocent" and that lawyers were killed.[35]

The society of the 24th century, however, has evolved beyond the world we know and also beyond the time of troubles. "Most ... of the major problems facing the human species have been resolved;"[36] material want (the source of much 20th-century conflict) and money are no more.[37] People, while not perfect, appear to trust each other more, work together more harmoniously and feel a greater sense of community and mutual responsibility than people in 20th-century American society.[38]

These differences would not be expected to change the basic goals of the legal system, but they would be expected to change some of the ways in which these goals are achieved. It would be expected that a thoughtful presentation of future possibilities would reflect a system of law recognizable to us, but modified to reflect the changes in people and society that the show embodies. When we examined the legal system, as presented on *ST:TNG*, we found such changes.

Because people in the 24th-century trust each other more and are more willing to believe (until the facts show otherwise) that others will be fair, there is much less concern about legal formalities. Fundamental principles of justice are recognized and highly valued, but it is not generally necessary to insist on procedural formalities in order to obtain them. Thus, formal hearings with 20th-century trappings such as lawyers, professional judges and rigid procedural requirements are rare.

It appears the rights that we hold dear in the 20th century are still a part of the 24th-century legal system. "The Drumhead"[39] makes clear that accused persons are innocent until proven guilty, that there must be evidence of guilt to proceed against an accused[40] and that an accused cannot be forced to be a witness against himself.[41] We also learn that these (and other) fundamental rights are guaranteed in the Federation Constitution, the equivalent to our Bill of Rights.[42] In "The Measure of a Man," JAG officer Phillipa Louvois explains, "We have rule of law in this federation. You cannot simply seize people and experiment with them to prove your pet theories."[43]

In our time, we protect fundamental rights through detailed procedural rules and interpretive judicial decisions. This may be one reason laypeople criticize the system (especially the criminal part of it) as a "game," in which truth becomes subsumed to demands of procedural exactness. In an adversary system where even the neutral decision makers (i.e., judges) are elected or appointed as part of the ongoing political process, it is unlikely that, for example, criminal defendants, crime victims and the public at large would agree on informal methods of dispute resolution. In such a distrustful system, procedural regularity substitutes for trust.

In *ST:TNG*, formal invocations of rights are rare, even though the principles of fairness they embody often are referenced. The reason appears to be the litigants themselves generally neither demand such procedures nor see the benefit of them. Even people in conflict want to be fair and settle matters so that all parties are satisfied (if not happy) with the process and the results. It is rare that conflict reaches such a high level that informal resolution is not possible.

Most of the time, the legal system portrayed in *ST:TNG* is consistent with this analysis. Lawyers or judges are almost never seen, formal procedure is minimized and informality is the rule.[44] Even when conflict exists between individuals, the parties seem to retain the perspective that, as part of the societal group, they want the conflict resolved rightly, not just in their favor.

It would be unrealistic, however, to portray the 24th-century man or woman as perfected (as opposed to somewhat more evolved), and *ST:TNG* does not do this. Although it happens less often than today, people in the 24th century can lose their perspective. At times, even a 24th-century person may act like the worst kind of 20th-century person, e.g., unreasonable, grasping, unfair and unwilling to settle for anything less than the most he or she can possibly get.

Generally, it is in these situations that formal procedures mirroring 20th-century ones in many respects are invoked, usually by a participant who feels that he or she is being treated with gross unfairness. Thus, formal 20th-century procedures have not been wholly displaced, but they have been placed in a subordinate position. Their main function is to act as a "safety-net" when more informal processes of dispute resolution break down.

Of course, in some ways, this is a description of the 20th-century system as well. Litigation begins where conflict cannot be resolved other ways. Yet, what we find in *ST:TNG* is significantly different because even many of the "formal" mechanisms for dispute resolution are informal in the extreme by 20th century standards. It is a system that largely relies on the presumed goodness of the individuals within it.[45] Only in the most extreme cases are the formalities of "system" to be preferred over the goodness of the individual decision maker. Thus, *ST:TNG* is an argument for a system of "people not of laws," so long as the people are basically good.

We have taken to calling the *ST:TNG* legal system "dual tracked." The essence of it is that, as long as all parties agree, the "informal" system is followed. But, if a party insists, for whatever reason, he or she can invoke a more formal system of procedural safeguards with its historical roots in our own distrustful time.

Thus, in "A Matter of Perspective" the issue is whether Commander Riker will be extradited to a planet for trial under its legal system on a charge of murder. We are told that Starfleet regulations give Picard the authority to make the decision. However, Chief Investigator Krag, the official demanding that Riker be handed over, is dubious because he does not trust Picard to give a fair judgment in a case involving his first officer. He asks, "How can I expect a fair and impartial decision?"[46] For Picard, it is not enough that he has the authority to decide. Neither does his close relationship with Riker necessarily disqualify him from deciding. Rather, he promises fairness to Krag and offers a compromise in which re-creations of the events using the ship's holodeck technology will comprise much of the evidence. Krag accepts this, and Picard proceeds as "judge" in the case.

Under the dual-track approach, we assume that, had he demanded it, Krag could have forced a formal hearing at a starbase before a JAG officer. Similarly, Riker could have done so. If either had invoked these rights, a formal hearing (as portrayed in "The Measure of a Man") would have been held. Because both Krag and Riker became convinced they would receive a fair hearing before Picard with the holodeck re-creation procedure, the full-blown, formal trial procedure was not demanded or required.

The hearing actually held was an example of 24th-century informality balanced with a concern for fairness to the individual. Picard was clearly fair in dealing with all parties. Each witness was allowed to make a statement before giving testimony. Picard allowed hearsay testimony because it would be admissible under Tanugan law, but promised only to watch it and "weigh it accordingly."[47] Picard judged the case, but also took the lead in presenting evidence from Data and LaForge that Picard asked them to find in his role of captain.[48] Krag could be said to be the prosecutor, but also a judge of sorts. The proceeding was not ended until both Picard and Krag became convinced that Riker was innocent.[49] This sort of blending of roles and the fluidity of the proceeding would be unthinkable in the 20th century, but makes perfect sense in the 24th.

The "dual-track" structure fits the notion of a society slowly evolving beyond the need of 20th-century formalism. In the 24th century, most disputes can be settled informally with mutual presumptions of good faith, trust and fair dealing. Yet, older forms have not been totally abandoned and remain available for those rare litigants who still feel the need for them.[50]

Formal procedures would not be invoked merely because a litigant failed to prevail. Since there is always a disappointed party, this would mean that formal procedures would end up being invoked in nearly every case. Rather, it appears that the invocation of formal legal procedures would not occur so long as all parties felt fairly treated by the process. There would be a strong moral compulsion not to invoke such proceedings without a very important reason beyond mere personal gain.[51]

Thus, while we have seen formal trial-like procedures on *ST:TNG*,[52] they have usually been explained, within the context of the story, in ways consistent with our presentation of the legal system. Formal procedures are either invoked because a particular litigant is an atypical, untrusting sort or because some other special circumstance exists[53] that would justify a demand for unusual formality and more elaborate procedural safeguards. Two episodes, "The Drumhead" and "The Measure of a Man," serve to illustrate the point.

"The Drumhead" begins with an interrogation of a possible spy. There appears to be no need for lawyers or formal procedure.[54] Even when Admiral Satie arrives to aid in the investigation, the proceedings are very informal. Satie and Picard appear to share both investigative and judicial functions and the "suspect," J'Ddan, does not have legal counsel in the interrogation room. Later, at the interrogation of crewman Tarses, Picard notes that "if you would like counsel, it can be provided."[55] Tarses sees no need for this formality and questioning proceeds.

Later, Picard becomes increasingly troubled about the approach taken by Admiral Satie. Essentially, Picard is not sure Satie is being fair or objective. At this point, Picard, on his own motion, provides "counsel" for Tarses, but it is Riker, the ship's first officer, and not a lawyer who is provided. Picard says, "Mister Tarses, for your own protection, I have assigned a counsel to you in the person of Commander William Riker."[56] Tarses, who has not yet figured out that Satie is not behaving as a normal 24th-century person would, responds, "Thank you, sir, but I don't need protection. I have not done anything wrong."[57]

Finally, after Picard himself becomes the target of Admiral Satie's witch-hunt, Picard realizes that Satie is neither fair nor objective. Thus, more formalistic protection is required. Only then does he fall back on the rules of procedure. Only then are they necessary to ensure a fair hearing. Picard says, "I believe that Chapter Four, Article 12 of the Uniform Code of Justice grants me the right to make a statement before questioning begins."[58] The statement sounds stilted and strange because, in normal times, a 24th-century person would not have to quote chapter and verse to be allowed to speak. This would be granted routinely because it would be viewed as fair by all concerned.

The plot provides an explanation for Admiral Satie's bizarre behavior. Satie is distraught over the death of her father, and it has twisted her. In her grief, she has obsessively set herself on a quest for Federation enemies. She is unable to be either objective or fair due to her personal torment.[59] Indeed, this is exactly the kind of unusual situation that the 24th-century "safety net" of formal procedure is designed to catch.

A similar extraordinary situation requires a formal hearing conducted by a JAG officer in "The Measure of a Man." Here, too, however, we see a series of informal attempts at resolution. Only when these fail is the formal legal track invoked. By the time the conflict arises, Data has already been ordered to Starbase 173 and is not technically under Picard's command.[60] Normally, the commanding officer would decide disputes concerning subordinate personnel, but Data is not willing to trust Maddox, his new superior officer, to make a fair decision concerning him. There is an exchange between Maddox and Data in which we learn that Maddox voted against admitting Data to Starfleet Academy on the grounds that Data was not a sentient being.[61] Thus, Maddox has already made up his mind. Further, Data is convinced that Maddox does not have the knowledge to succeed in his experiment, thus putting Data's continued existence in jeopardy.[62]

It is also clear to Picard that Maddox must not be allowed to make this decision because, as he tells Phillipa Louvois, "I don't trust that man."[63] Picard views the transfer request as "unfair and unjust." Thus, both types of situations suggesting the invocation of the formal legal track are present. The decision maker (Maddox) is not trusted by the litigants, and the procedure (the transfer order) appears to be unfair.

Only at this point does Picard even begin to think about invoking the formal legal track. First, he calls up Starfleet regulations on transfers,[64] and, when they prove daunting, he consults Louvois about their legal significance.[65] Note two interesting points. First, Data's initial response to all this is not to invoke formal legal procedures and fight the transfer order. Rather, he resigns from Starfleet. While this probably has much to do with Data's personality, it is instructive to see that invoking formal legal procedure is not his first response to the situation. Second, the fact Picard consulted Louvois for advice to help Data did not prevent her from being a judge in the case once formal procedures were invoked.

Maddox asks for a decision from a more senior officer. Seeing Data about to elude him, he must act, yet, since the issue is whether he is or is not in command of Data, he cannot be both a litigant and judge in the matter without Data's consent. Maddox therefore requests a decision from JAG officer Louvois as to whether Data can resign. Even now, the formal legal track has not been invoked. Rather, an informal meeting between Maddox, Picard and Louvois is held. Data is not present. There are no lawyers, witnesses or formal procedure. Rather, Picard and Maddox state their positions, recognize that the issue is essentially legal and ask Louvois to research the law and make a decision.[66]

Finally, Louvois makes a decision based on her research. Data is property and cannot resign. Faced with this massive unfairness, Picard asks, "What if I challenge this ruling?" Louvois answers, "Then I shall be required to hold a hearing." Picard invokes the formal legal track: "Then I so challenge. Convene your hearing."[67] The formal legal track, once invoked, would normally require a 20th-century style court with lawyers. Because the starbase is new and such are not available, senior officers are used instead, but it is made clear that this is unusual once formal procedures are invoked. Thus, the following exchange takes place: Louvois states, "Captain, that [a formal hearing] would be exceedingly difficult. This is a new base. I have no staff." Picard replies, "Surely you have regulations to take care of such an eventuality." Louvois responds, "There are. I can use serving officers as legal counsel."[68] We see, then, that such a hearing would normally require actual lawyers.[69]

The informality of 24th-century proceedings is manifested in several ways:

1. Lawyers are seldom used. Generally, it is not even necessary to have anyone act for a litigant as an advocate.[70] When advocacy is deemed necessary, counsel is more likely to be a friend, colleague, shipmate or senior officer than a lawyer, unless a litigant demands one.

2. Professional judges are seldom needed. Senior Starfleet officers are empowered to judge most disputes, such as disputes between members of the crew that cannot be otherwise resolved, disputes arising on board the starship whether or not the disputants are Starfleet personnel and disputes involving an "away team."[71]

3. The strict 20th-century separation between investigators (police), defense counsel, prosecutors and judges is not the norm in the 24th century. Thus, Picard could properly investigate a problem, interview witnesses and "suspects" and judge the case. There would not be any problem with "ex parte communications" between himself and a litigant.[72] The presumption of integrity and honesty of all parties would make such acceptable unless a litigant objected.

4. Barring unusual circumstances, insistence on precise procedures would be rare. It is permissible to invent procedures for resolving disputes so long as they are fair and accepted by all parties. General principles of fairness, however, would be high on everyone's mind. Should an accused object to a procedure as being unfair, his or her concern should be treated with the utmost seriousness and respect. Seeing his or her objection treated seriously would, in most cases, satisfy the litigant, even if the decision on the point raised went against him or her.

20th Century Desires and the 24th Century Legal System

ST:TNG appears to present the case that a legal system that embodies a detailed and complex body of procedural rules, as ours does, is flawed and that such a system would be unnecessary if people were better and would agree to work together to solve problems. As humans evolve, such rule-bound legal systems will evolve away from formalism.[73] The better side of human nature, as it continues to develop, will allow us to solve legal-type problems without the formalities that are the hallmark of our present system.

This claim gives expression to longings felt by those both inside and outside the legal profession. The public is concerned that "legal technicalities" stifle justice and that the legal system is an expensive and time-consuming world of its own in which an obsessive focus on procedure becomes an end in itself.[74] Recent hesitant steps toward adoption of "alternate dispute resolution" procedures also speak to this concern.

These concerns also occur during a time of increasing skepticism about the nature of the legal system. Is it a system of rules or principles at all? Can legal rules have any objective meaning at all? Are rules neutral, or are they a mere smoke-screen for dominant political forces applying their own points of view?[75] Are judges confined by rules or are they really legislating, i.e., applying their own subjective view to cases as they arise? Should we care one way or the other?[76]

The legal system portrayed in _ST:TNG_ is one in which individual decision makers have much greater latitude in deciding cases than the 20th-century legal system's dominant theory permits. It substitutes good faith on the part of the participants for formalistic procedures as the primary source of fairness to litigants and to the discovery of truth.

One might argue that a system containing multiple layers of technical procedures and formalistic devices is made necessary solely because people have not yet evolved away from selfishness, greed and distrust. Should that day come, it could be argued, such a system would be unnecessary. In _ST:TNG_, we have a fictional vision of such an evolved time. Does the informal legal system work in _ST:TNG_'s setting? Would it work in our own?

How Well Does the 24th-Century Legal System Work?

ST:TNG creates a legal system in which formality has been replaced by informality and procedural safeguards have been replaced by trust. The setting for the show postulates and presents a better kind of person living within an evolved vision of society.

We have suggested that a legal system is created for certain purposes.[77] If it accomplishes these purposes, it will be considered a generally successful system. If it fails to accomplish these purposes, it will not. It is unlikely that a legal system will be able to carry out its primary missions unless it provides reasonably accurate processes for determining the facts of the case. This is especially true when facts are disputed. Unless the facts can be determined, litigants cannot be given what they are due. If there is no way to give them what they are due, it is unlikely the process of adjudication will be perceived to be fair. If the process is not perceived to be fair, it is less likely the dispute will actually be settled. Therefore, we think it very important to ask how well the *ST:TNG* legal system determines the facts in disputed cases.

An important episode in this regard is "A Matter of Perspective," in which the issue is whether Commander Riker is to be extradited to a planet to stand trial for murder. Since the local law assumes that a suspect is guilty until proven innocent,[78] the question of extradition is even more critical. As previously discussed, Picard uses the holodeck to provide three-dimensional re-creations of each person's statements.[79] This procedure serves very well to highlight the disagreements in the testimony between the parties. Yet, because there is no effective cross-examination, it is impossible to determine which story is true. Even with the help of Counselor Troi, whose Betazoid empathic abilities have determined that none of the parties are lying, it is impossible, merely by comparing the different honestly held beliefs, to arrive at the answer.[80] What does appear to be true is that there was enough agreement among all parties to point to Riker as a plausible suspect.[81]

Although the truth that clears Riker is eventually discovered, it is not the holodeck fact-finding process that discovers it. Instead, an independent investigation by Data, LaForge and Wesley of unexplained phenomena aboard the *Enterprise* eventually leads to the conclusion that the same cause destroyed the space station.[82] Thus, without the fortuitous fact that the cause of the space station explosion also caused problems on the *Enterprise*, the truth would never have been discovered, and Riker very likely would have been turned over for trial and almost certain conviction.[83]

The informal features of the 24th-century legal system did not provide an advocate for the accused or investigative staff. The defendant, Riker, through much of the episode, appeared to be so shocked at the accusation that he was a less-than-credible advocate on his own behalf.[84] Scientific investigation and the study of physical evidence, beyond the holodeck re-creation of witness recollections, were not a normal part of the proceedings. It appears to us that had Riker had a lawyer or other trained advocate who would have pressed opposing witnesses and conducted independent investigations, and if more formal procedures had been followed, the chance of an accurate determination of the facts would have increased. While the episode turned out all right, this result appeared to be more in spite of the informal procedures employed than because of them.

Another episode, "The Measure of a Man," explores the question of whether the android Lt. Commander Data is a being with rights or merely the property of Starfleet. The procedural progression from attempts at informal resolution to formal hearing has been discussed previously. For present purposes, the question is how well the formal as opposed to the informal procedures functioned to resolve the dispute. In our view, the "winner" is the formal adjudicatory procedures.[85] The informal mechanisms not only do not resolve the question but often appear to be unfair. This is especially true when the dispute involves persons outside the small and tightly supportive structure of the *Enterprise*.

At the start, Maddox comes on board having obtained ex parte orders from a superior officer allowing him to take Data with him and conduct experiments upon him against his will. Although Picard tries gamely to fight for Data (it is instructive that Data does not appear to have the clout to fight these higher-ups himself), the effort is a failure. Data attempts to resign from Starfleet (something he does not wish to do) as the only way he can see to escape from Maddox. The point here is that without formal procedures, the personalities become very important. This gives an unfair advantage to the powerful and the highly placed. It is "a system of men and not of law," which is the antithesis of our own system.

In "The Drumhead," although it becomes increasingly clear that something is wrong and unfair about the witch-hunting tactics of Admiral Satie, the informal dispute resolution track appears to provide a solution only to a person with great personal prestige, position and clout. First, Picard fights Admiral Satie using the leverage that Starfleet has ordered them to work together. When Satie then focuses her investigation on Picard, she is stopped only because an even more powerful admiral is convinced to order the hearings to cease.

In the story, it is Satie who brings Admiral Henry to the *Enterprise*, and she is undone when he witnesses her breakdown after Picard's impassioned speech invoking the name of Satie's dead father. It is possible Picard also might have been able to bring in the admiral himself. But could a simple crew member have done so? This seems very unlikely. One of the strengths of a system based on legal formalities is that the formalities become substitutes for personal status. In contrast, the informal system as generally portrayed on *ST:TNG* appears to work best when disputes arise within the context of a relatively small and homogeneous group in which there are authority figures known by the disputants to be fair and honest. Outside of this context, results are more problematic.

In contrast, the more formal legal track is shown as achieving correct results even when disputants do not trust each other.[86] In "The Measure of a Man," Picard eventually demands a formal hearing, which is held. Here the litigants are represented by others who make the strongest possible case for and against each side. There is cross-examination and presentation of witnesses and exhibits. The proceedings are closer to a 20th-century trial than most of the legal proceedings portrayed on *ST:TNG*.

Interestingly, it is through this more formal procedure that the issue is finally clarified and sharpened so that a correct decision can be reached. Picard says as much in a memorable speech:

> Your honor, a courtroom is a crucible. In it we burn away irrelevances, until we're left with a pure product-the truth-for all time. Now, sooner or later this man or others like him will succeed in replicating Commander Data. The decision you reach here today will determine how we will regard this creation of our genius. It will reveal the kind of a people we are, what he is destined to be. It will reach far beyond this courtroom and this one android. It could significantly redefine the boundaries of personal liberty and freedom, expanding them for some, savagely curtailing them for others. Are you prepared to condemn him and all who come after him to servitude and slavery? Your honor, Starfleet was founded to seek out new life. Well, there it sits ... waiting. You wanted a chance to make law, well here it is. Make it a good one.[87]

Our point is not that the system portrayed in *ST:TNG* is a bad one. We have noted that human rights are important and protected in Federation law and that formal procedures exist and can be demanded by litigants who require them. No system, including our own, infallibly produces the right results in all cases. Our point is, however, that the informal system of resolution does not work as well as might be expected. The fictional portrayal of the 24th-century legal system in *ST:TNG* requires us to confront the question of whether a legal system with only minimal procedural safeguards is likely to produce truth while protecting the rights of those subject to it. Even where the litigants and the administrators of the system are evolved people of good will, it appears that such a system is unlikely to systematically accomplish its goals.

The importance of procedure is not just that it controls the consciously evil impulses of humankind. Procedural safeguards may shield decision makers from the often powerful but subtle influences of emotional and personal information. They focus attention on the particular point in dispute rather than allowing an unfocused and diffused process. Where a fact question is crucial to a correct resolution, procedural requirements can help to assure that relevant facts are properly investigated and presented and that important points do not "slip through the cracks."

In taking the 24th-century legal system on its own terms, we find something of a cautionary tale for our own times. It suggests that we should be slow to dispense with "legal technicalities" and formalities because they play an important role in assuring that more fundamental goals of truth and justice are realized.

Conflict of Laws and Jurisdiction in the 24th Century

The United Federation of Planets appears to be a much looser federal system than our own. Individual planets or species retain sovereignty, giving up only limited powers to the Federation government. Federation citizens are protected from Federation overreaching,[88] but no such protection seems to be guaranteed as far as actions by planetary governments are concerned.[89] The Federation Prime Directive is non-interference with the internal affairs of others, and this appears to apply to Federation members and non-members alike.[90] *ST:TNG* gives the impression that commerce and cultural interaction are widespread. Both inside and outside the Federation, individuals from various planets often find themselves in the territory of some other planetary government.

For us, the facts of the *ST:TNG* universe immediately raise questions about conflict of laws and jurisdiction. The questions are particularly serious when dealing with Starfleet personnel who must function on many planets and who engage in a mix of scientific, diplomatic and military actions. When are Starfleet personnel subject to local laws? When conflicts exist between Federation law and local planetary law, to which are Starfleet personnel subject and under what conditions? Surprisingly, these issues have several times been central plot devices, but, from a legal perspective, the answers have not been completely satisfying.

The simplest answer seems to be that Starfleet personnel are subject to local law. Yet, it is not entirely clear either that this is the extent of the rule or that such an answer is a good one. Two problems with this answer are obviously apparent:[91]

> *1.* Traditionally, diplomats are not subject to foreign laws.[92] An important reason for this is to prevent diplomatic personnel

from being subjected to local criminal laws to gain political advantage. The sorry episode of the American hostages in Iran graphically makes this point. In *ST:TNG*, it is not just Federation ambassadors who engage in diplomacy. Starfleet personnel often exercise diplomatic responsibilities as part of their normal functions. Yet, it is not clear that diplomatic immunity extends to Starfleet personnel acting in diplomatic capacities.

2. Starfleet personnel appear to be needlessly put in jeopardy by subjecting them to local laws that violate basic norms of human rights. An example of this is "A Matter of Perspective," in which Riker is sent to a science research station in orbit around Tanuga IV to assess the progress of scientific research being conducted for the Federation. The scientist, Doctor Apgar, is killed when the station mysteriously blows up just as Riker is transported from it. When the cause of the explosion proves to be an energy blast within the station, Riker immediately becomes the prime suspect.[93] The show focuses on whether Riker will be extradited to stand trial for murder under Tanugan law. Although the captain is authorized to make the decision, there appears to be a presumption that extradition will occur if there is probable cause to believe Riker is guilty.[94] The problem for us is that Tanugan law presumes guilt. A criminal defendant is guilty until proven innocent. Yet, under Federation law, guaranteed by the Federation Constitution, a person is innocent until proven guilty.[95] It seems unacceptable that the Federation would subject its personnel to a system so clearly violative of human rights. It also seems implausible that there would not be clear rules outlining what is to be done in such a situation since it is bound to crop up over and over again.

The same problem can be found in "Justice," in which shore leave on Rubicun III turns nightmarish when Wesley Crusher inadvertently damages a flower bed only to discover the one and only punishment for all infractions is immediate execution.[96] Picard does not seem to have clear guidance about how to resolve the problem. While he pays lip service to turning Wesley over, it appears that this is a stall for time. Finally, he orders Wesley beamed off the planet even over the opposition of the inhabitants. Yet, Picard never seems to feel that he is on solid ground. He feels his way as if the problem had never come up before.[97]

The primary task of the *ST:TNG* team is to create interesting and entertaining television, not to construct a legal system. At times, consistency and realism must be sacrificed to the entertainment value of the series. Yet, it appears to us that an acceptable legal answer could have been found in both of these shows without sacrificing the entertainment and dramatic value of the shows.

With regard to "A Matter of Perspective," the problem could have been solved either by cutting the "guilty until proved innocent" line or by having Krag assure Picard that, as a Starfleet officer, Riker's trial would use Federation law (a very nice "choice of law" solution). In "Justice," we would have liked to hear some clear statement from Picard that he would not leave Wesley on the planet because Starfleet regulations do not require that their personnel submit to a legal system that is fundamentally unfair. Wesley's initial jeopardy was really a prelude to conflict between Picard and the powerful alien guardians of Rubicun III, and that same conflict would have existed whether Picard's decision to remove Wesley by force was based solely on his own judgment or was supported by Federation law.

In defense of the *ST:TNG* writing and production team, they are not lawyers, and issues such as choice of law and jurisdiction are less likely to occur to non-lawyers than to people like us. Still, part of the success of *ST:TNG* is that it generally creates a believable and consistent structure. Indeed, one of the central points in this article is that *ST:TNG* deals with legal issues with a high degree of consistency, inventiveness and accuracy. Thus, we feel we should also point out those areas in which some additional thought would improve the *ST:TNG* universe.[98]

Substantive Law in the 24th Century

For a show without any preconceived, unified legal framework, *ST:TNG* nonetheless espoused or implied a consistent approach on numerous jurisprudential fronts. By examining the series' evocation of current substantive legal issues, we hope to illuminate the social and legal mores of our own century.

Star Trek has attempted to confront problems in contemporary society by placing them in a futuristic context. This enables the viewer to gain new perspectives and insights into those problems by stepping back from their contemporary context. This has traditionally been characteristic of much of science fic-

tion, but it is particularly true of *Star Trek*, which reflects the utopian philosophy of Gene Roddenberry. *ST:TNG*, more so even than the classic series, has
attempted to serve this goal inasmuch as Roddenberry had more control over
the creation and early development of the new series than over the original.[99]

Moreover, *ST:TNG* provokes a substantial amount of viewer attention for
the manner in which the series handles substantive legal, moral and political
issues.[100] This massive viewer response suggests that the series' creators and contributors have successfully designed a different yet plausible future that would
make sense as an extension of our own. Thus, we care how they handle these
issues inasmuch as we believe that their approach has relevance for us today.

What is so superlative about *ST:TNG* is that, without setting out to create a
24th-century legal system or to expostulate 24th-century views on substantive
legal issues, the resulting doctrines that have emerged evidence a consistent
jurisprudence. Thus, from the existing five seasons of episodes, we can cull not
just a legal framework,[101] but also more detailed consideration of substantive
legal issues. These provide a futuristic perspective on problems and issues facing humanity as we face the fast approaching 21st century.

Sexual Orientation and Gender

Gene Roddenberry's vision of a more nearly perfect society in the 24th century extended to areas of gender equality. It is implicit that Starfleet embodies
legal equality for all. In addition, in its non-legal aspects, the show attempts to
include images of equality by including a diverse group of characters. Also, the
show has taken the lead in exploring matters of customs and mores that so
often provide the background for legal and political disputes. Eulogizing
Roddenberry, one commentator noted that *ST:TNG* "moves several years ahead
of the original series in the area of sexual equality. No longer are characters
strictly token contributors whose talents are never fully realized (namely, Lt.
Uhura), nor do they serve as the captain's 'Galactic Play Toy of the Week.'"[102]

The diversity of the *ST:TNG* characters did suffer a blow with the death of
the aggressive and physical Tasha Yar. It has been noted that this left *ST:TNG*
with a quorum of soft, nurturing females-Troi, Dr. Crusher and Guinan.[103] The
appearance of the sharper, more militant Ensign Ro in the fifth season may be
seen as a promising development, one in keeping with the stereotype-breaking
model of *Star Trek*.

Early *ST:TNG* efforts at lambasting sexual stereotypes were not wholly successful. In the first season, "Angel One" attempted to portray a society in which

women dominated; they were physically larger and more powerful than the males of that culture and held the political power. An away team from the *Enterprise* sought to reclaim Federation citizens whose craft had apparently crashed on the alien planet. The episode showed women to be no more effective than men when attempting to dominate the other gender. Unfortunately, the show deteriorated rapidly as the leader of the society seduced the classic seducer, Commander Riker, and it was only when Riker stepped in to point out the virtues of mercy that the female leader relented in her intransigence toward some Starfleet prisoners. As one critic noted, "Ironically, this episode, which condemns sexism, is probably one of the worst perpetrators of it since the classic series' 'Turnabout Intruder.'"[104]

Later efforts, consistent with the effort to portray gender equality, went further toward attaining Roddenberry's goals. In the fourth season, *ST:TNG* broached the issue of sexual orientation in an episode titled "The Host." In this show, Dr. Beverly Crusher fell in love with an alien named Odan, a handsome man, apparently in his 30s, with little to distinguish him physically from a human male. Odan was aboard the *Enterprise* for a negotiation mission between two warring peoples. When Odan is injured in an attack upon a shuttle manned by Commander Riker, Crusher operates, only to discover that the being she knew as Odan was really only a host body. The essence of Odan's character, emotions and intellect were embodied in a parasitic, worm-like entity inhabiting the body of its symbiot, a being of the Trill species. For the remainder of the episode, Crusher is torn between her love for Odan and his altered physical state. When Riker becomes the temporary host for Odan, it is only after a great struggle of conscience that Crusher recognizes she can love Odan even in the body of her platonic friend, Riker. This development in Crusher's awareness is stopped short, however, when Odan's new permanent host-a beautiful young woman-arrives. Crusher realizes, lamentably, that she cannot love Odan in his new incarnation. "Someday, perhaps...," she rues, and the episode ends as Crusher is disconcerted by a passionate kiss on the hand by Odan's new host-body.

Regrettably, this episode was seen as a cop-out by many viewers.[105] "The fact that Crusher doesn't embrace Odan [in the female host's body] or continue the relationship was, to some fans, an effort to play it safe by a show which is often challenging."[106] Critics opined that the series wasted a perfect opportunity to confront bias toward sexual orientation. Had Crusher recognized that love is gender blind, she could have continued her affair with Odan and affirmed an important social principle. Other commentators suggest that, to the contrary, "The Host" was ground-breaking material. "As the world's tolerance of homosexuality increased in the 1980s, Roddenberry decided to explore beyond the male/female sexual relationship. He pushed sexuality to a new frontier" in shows like "The Host."[107]

It is our view that "The Host" was a significant first step in the series' efforts at promoting an end to sexual bias. Watching Beverly Crusher wrestle with her conflicting emotions and previously unexamined views about love allows us to undertake the same soul searching and, perhaps, begin to deal with our own prejudice. While a happy ending might be more satisfying, it is precisely this satisfaction that the show denies us. We are left uncomfortable, as perhaps we should be.

It would not be until the fifth season, however, that *ST:TNG* took the next step. In a controversial[108] but critically praised episode "The Outcast," the series finally confronted the issue of sexual orientation and societal bias toward certain sexual orientations. In that episode, the *Enterprise* is assisting the J'naii, a race of people who are, in the majority, gender neutral. While at one time the species had a male and female gender, now virtually everyone is neuter. In this show, Riker works closely with Soren, one of the J'naii, and eventually a warm affection between the two engenders romantic sparks. Soren confesses to Riker that there are a limited number of exceptions among her people-individuals who feel drawn to one gender over another. She is one such individual, who has always considered herself female. She has muted and masked such inclinations, since to reveal oneself as gender preferential is to risk psychotechtic treatment: treatment to erase the gender preference, to recognize it as unwise and antisocial and to inculcate the gender-neutral tendency. Riker returns Soren's feelings, but the romance is detected, or at least sufficiently suspected, and Soren is recalled/abducted by her people and "treated."[109] Riker, in direct contravention of the Prime Directive, but with the loyal assistance of Lieutenant Worf, attempts a rescue, but is too late. Soren apologizes that she no longer feels that way about him and indeed was wrong/sick to have felt that way before.

The point of the episode is clear. Social and legal pressures to conform to the majority view on sexual orientation are wrong (more than just unwise) and not just ineffective (indeed, Soren's "treatment" proved "successful"), but morally and ethically wrong. Moreover, such conformity is seen as unnatural, just as freedom of sexual orientation is natural. Soren's inclination to follow the female orientation was patently a fitting, natural choice for her. Different species may offer different choices, but freedom to choose sexual orientation is intrinsic and essential to the individual in any species.

Jonathan Frakes, the series' Commander Will Riker, said the show should have gone one step further. Soren was played by a female actor, Melinda Culea, thus making it easier for audiences to accept a romance between her and Riker. Frakes suggested that Soren should have been portrayed by a male actor.[110] In this way, audiences would have had to recognize and accept the implicit message: Even homosexual love, as we in our century and species know it, is natural. Said Frakes, "We've gotten a lot of mail on this episode, but I'm not sure it was as good as it could have been-if they were trying to do what they call a gay episode."[111]

Co-executive producer Jeri Taylor comments that she "really wanted to write this episode .... We had wanted to do a gay rights story and had not been able to figure out how to do it in an interesting science-fiction, *Star Trek*-ian way."[112] Producer Rick Berman acknowledged the difficulty faced in casting the role.

> We were either going to cast with non
> masculine men, no femine [sic] females or
> females who could play an androgynous char-
> acter. Obviously you wouldn't pick a 6'4"
> musclebound man nor a voluptuous woman
> .... It might have been interesting
> to go with men, but it was a choice that
> we made.[113]

Producer Michael Piller mentioned that *ST:TNG* had "been the target of a concerted organized movement by gay activists to put a gay character in the show."[114] Berman agreed, and adds: "[We] came up with a very obvious metaphor for the gay community and the intolerance they receive on this planet."[115] Returning to the theme of the "better" Federation person, above the fray and without conflict, Berman points out:

> I think we dealt with well meaning people
> and their intolerance and our people in the
> 24th century's absolute lack of acceptance of
> their intolerance and the frustration of fight-
> ing it .... I think it did deal with the issue of
> intolerance towards sexual orientation and it
> met that objective well.[116]

Nevertheless, reaction was mixed.

> We have people ... who salute us for doing it,
> then there are people that say we didn't go far
> enough-that it was too subtle, it was too oblique
> and wanted it to be more upfront, blunt and
> obvious. Other people were just freaked out that
> it was an assault on values .... [117]

One commentator noted the similarities to "The Host,"[118] but called the earlier show "the more effective-and certainly most subtle-of the two."[119] Another commentator noted that "[Jeri] Taylor's script is a stunning reminder of how effective the science fiction genre can be in providing allegorical explorations of political and social concerns."[120] Another stated, "[while] the episode doesn't provide any solutions to society's intolerance toward the homosexual community, [it] brings their argument to the forefront, and that's at least a step in the right direction."[121]

As can be seen, the episode and the reaction to it raise interesting issues. Given the comments of Frakes, Berman and Braga, did the show actually avoid the hard issues that it could have confronted more forthrightly? Did the show give in to the perceived contemporary intolerance of the audience, rather than simply depicting the intolerance of an alien race hundreds of years into the future? Given the controversial[122] reaction to the episode, it is our view that the episode went just about as far as it could go without being annoyingly heavy-handed. Unless an episode entertains, the attempt to broaden the viewer's mind will fail, as the message becomes more pervasive than the story.

It should be noted that, in a rather humorous vein, the episode admits that, even in the enlightened future of the 24th century, gender stereotyping has not disappeared. Soren asks Crusher for characterization of our two genders, and she notes that, while there used to be prescribed roles for the two sexes, this has faded over time. Then, in a conversation with Worf, she realizes the ancient prejudices remain. Thus, even given the weakness of ST:TNG's first blow at exploding the myths of gender bias, the series has succeeded in offering its condemnation of sexual stereotyping in an effective one-two punch. Both "The Host" and "The Outcast" will be remembered by viewers as dramatically striking and morally compelling.

Late 20th-century viewers are, in the main, trapped in a state of arrested development with regard to sexual orientation. Noteworthy advances in this area are marked by two strides forward, one step back. It is significant that viewer response to these two episodes was vociferous, yet mixed. Many fans applauded the courage of the latter episode, and many decried the risk-avoidance of the former, but there were still viewers who felt offended by the message in both. It is doubtful the series could have gone any further without alienating its audience and suffering critical disaffection for sacrificing the story for the message.

Thus, the message of tolerance is consistent throughout the *Star Trek* world, even while it recognizes and causes us to realize that it is difficult to break traditional stereotypes. If a message is to be drawn from the series, and from these individual episodes, it may be that the effort is not just worthwhile, but essential.

From a legal point of view, the only thing wrong with the treatment of the issue in "The Outcast" is that the Prime Directive effectively prevents the question from being considered in a legal way. The planetary government's laws, although repulsive, are internal matters the Federation may not address. Since it was one of their own citizens they were "treating," there was no legal issue raised that could be addressed directly.

The Meaning of Life/Defining the Person

In a succession of episodes, *ST:TNG* has expounded upon the question of what it means to be "human" or a "person," i.e., to be entitled to legal rights and autonomy. While this is a hotly debated issue in contemporary society in the context of abortion,[123] *ST:TNG* has asked the question more generally and in a wide variety of contexts. It is one of the most interesting continuing themes and one that often provides a setting for legal resolution.

ST:TNG has attempted to define what is life under the various labels of what is sentient life, what is intelligent life, and what life forms can be considered property. The issues ranged from whether an image Data encountered in the holodeck is entitled to existence ("Elementary, Dear Data") to whether Data himself ("The Measure of a Man") and, later, Data's daughter ("The Offspring") are. The problematic alien entities ranged from the crystalline entity ("Silicon Avatar") to a race known colloquially as "microbrain" ("Home Soil")[124] for their computer-like nature to a race of nanites ("Evolution"). In the entire *ST:TNG* oeuvre, however, one message is clear-the respect for all forms of intelligent life and the right of intelligent life to self-determination.

Holodeck creations were the subjects of this inquiry in two very different episodes that resolved the query in markedly different fashions. In the first season's "The Big Goodbye," Picard manages to convince the arch-villain, Cyrus Redblock, the Sydney Greenstreet-clone portrayed by Lawrence Tierney, of the

exis-
tence of a world outside the holodeck, yet allows him to follow Picard outside
the holodeck to his "death," or at least to the end of his existence. Apparently,
this was not a fitting end for another arch-villain, Professor Moriarty, in
"Elementary, Dear Data." There, the fate of the professor was seen as almost
tragic. Moriarty argues, comparing himself to Data, that both are alive because
they are both self-aware: "Cogito ergo sum." "Moriarty ... the captain promises,
you will not be extinguished. We will save this program and hopefully in time,
when we know enough, bring you back in a form which could leave the
holodeck."[125]

Producer Maurice Hurley notes there was some disagreement about
that ending.

> There was an ending cut off of that show by
> Gene. We had a large fight about it. In that
> ending, Picard knew how to defeat Moriarty.
> He tricked him. He knew all along that
> Moriarty could leave the holodeck whenever
> he wanted to, and he knew because when
> Data came out and showed him a drawing of
> the Enterprise, if that piece of paper could
> leave the holodeck, that means the fail-safe
> had broken down. In turn, this means that
> the matter-energy converter which creates
> the holodeck, now allowed the matter to
> leave the holodeck, which was, up to that
> point, impossible. When he knew that paper
> had left the holodeck, he knew that Moriarty
> could as well, so he lied to him. The doctor
> says, "How could you lie to Moriarty?"
> Picard basically says, "Well, after all, dear
> doctor, it is Moriarty, and until we know
> whether he is saying what he's saying because
> that's how he really feels or if it's more of his
> guile and deceit, it's best to be very safe with
> this." It was better than I'm saying, but that
> whole rationale was missing. Gene basically
> thought it made Picard look deceitful, dis-
> honest and it hurt the character. I thought it

> made him look clever, and since you are deal-
> ing with maybe the most profound criminal
> mind in literature, you've got to be careful.[126]

We are pleased the alternate ending was not used. Nor was it established that merely because an object could leave the holodeck, a computer-created sentient being could. We stress this because we believe the ending as actually aired was a much stronger message that sentient beings have rights than the alternate ending would have been.

The two episodes can be easily reconciled, however. Cyrus Redblock was merely a facsimile created by and limited to the holodeck. He had no self-awareness and was not, therefore, a being with rights. Professor Moriarty, however, had been given self-awareness and the ability to introspect due to the order given to the holodeck that it create an enemy that could defeat Data. Only a sentient being would have any chance to do so. *ST:TNG* has established its position, through a number of shows, that sentience is a key criterion for the right to life. Thus, Moriarty was a being with rights as entitled to life as Data or Picard. Merely to dissolve him was, therefore, no answer. Assuming he could not leave the holodeck and survive, as stated in the show, the option to save him in the computer had to be taken. To merely turn off the program would have killed him unjustly.

ST:TNG's inquiry into whether a being merits a right to life based on whether it is sentient resounds with the philosophical tenet, "I think, therefore I am." The question has ongoing legal implications in defining not just life but death. If I never think and never will think, perhaps I am not.

Recently in Florida, the Supreme Court heard and decided a case that directly tested this point. The so-called "Baby Theresa" case dealt with an infant born anencephalic, without a brain, possessing a brain stem only. Medically, such a child could live at most a few weeks. The higher thought processes associated with human beings were impossible due to the physical absence of the brain. The parents wanted to harvest Theresa's organs and donate them to needy children. If they waited until brain stem activity ceased, the organs would have deteriorated too much to be of use to others. The infant's parents sought to have her declared dead so that her organs could be harvested. Florida law, which "parallels the law of all 42 states that have faced this question," defines brain death as the cessation of all brain activity.[127]

The law that defines death was enacted in 1980 in response to dramatic advances in medical technology. Even if someone is breathing and physically functioning with artificial life support, the law allows a physician to declare the patient dead when the brain has ceased to function. The law allows no such declaration if there is a functioning brain stem controlling breathing and other functions ....[128]

Both the trial and intermediate appellate courts held that the baby was not dead. On November 12, 1992, the Florida Supreme Court upheld the lower courts' decisions.[129]

The question posed starkly was whether Theresa was dead even though her heartbeat and some automatic functions controlled by the brain stem continued. If sentience, or even the remote possibility of sentience, is the criterion for human life, then Theresa does not and cannot qualify. Thus, in thinking through this issue, *ST:TNG* is addressing an important issue of current law.

Similarly, in "Home Soil," a first season entry, a group of Federation terraformers on Velara III was discovered to be violating the rights of a preexisting race of beings. A planet to be terraformed "must be without life or the prospect of life developing naturally." The *Enterprise* crew discovers one of the indigenous entities and engages in an exploration of whether the entity-microscopic in size and non-carbon based-is life. Picard lists a set of criteria for organic life, including the ability to assimilate, respirate, reproduce, grow and develop, move and secrete and excrete, but notes no similar definition for inorganic life. The entity does in fact reproduce and even threatens the ship, but Picard refrains from destroying this race of beings, "intelligent life" as they have now been found to be. Indeed, the "microbrains" decline to enter into relations with humans, who they perceive to be "ugly bags of mostly water."

Similarly, in the third season's "Evolution," Dr. Paul Stubbs, played by Ken Jenkins, is an erstwhile child prodigy seeking to reestablish his noteworthiness with an experiment on a neutron star. This experiment, to be performed aboard the *Enterprise*, is possible only every 196 years. Unfortunately for Dr. Stubbs, Wesley Crusher accidentally releases a science project into the ship's computer: two nanites, described as "little tiny robots ... designed to enter living cells to conduct repairs."[130] Wesley's plan had been to "see how they would act in tandem," in effect, as Guinan puts it, "to make better nanites." The nanites do very well "in tandem," combining and reproducing to such an extent that the ship's main computer starts to malfunction, placing Dr. Stubbs' experiment in jeopardy. The nanites are said to have "evolved."[131]

"How can a machine evolve?" an angry Stubbs argues,[132] but Dr. Crusher maintains that the nanites have a new collective intelligence. For Stubbs, they may be life, but not the kind of life with rights. He challenges Crusher with the question, "How many disease germs have you destroyed?"[133] Picard insists they cannot destroy something that may be intelligent and orders Stubbs and Data to try removing the nanites safely from the computer core. If that does not work, stronger measures may be necessary. Stubbs is impatient and fires a high-level gamma radiation burst to try to destroy the nanites, which respond by attacking Stubbs. Picard is reluctantly poised to give up his attempts at communication, but just in time Data succeeds in establishing contact.[134] Data serves as conduit for the nanites, to whom Stubbs is ordered by Picard to apologize. The apology is accepted, and the nanites, for whom life is too confining aboard one starship, are awarded a planet of their own on which to exist.[135]

This regard for intelligent life reached an acme – or, perhaps, a nadir – in the fifth season's "Silicon Avatar." Although this episode is consistent with the other right-to-life episodes, it reached a level some viewers and critics found extremist and, as a result, almost amusing. In it, Picard quarrels with Riker regarding the fate of the extraordinarily destructive crystalline entity, which first appeared on the series in the first season's "Datalore." The entity has proven itself capable of destroying entire planets, yet Picard refuses to destroy it when the opportunity for communication remains.[136] The episode was seen by some as portraying Picard at his most intellectually ineffectual. Captain James T. Kirk would have blasted the crystalline entity into nothingness (at which point Bones would, no doubt, have noted, "He's dead, Jim").[137]

If "Silicon Avatar" was the low point, critically speaking, in the debate of what is life, "The Measure of a Man" is doubtless the zenith. It so well answered the question of what is life that a later episode, "The Offspring," in which the question is asked not about Data but about his creation, Lal, was seen by many as superfluous.[138] In "The Measure of a Man," Data is ordered to report to Commander Bruce Maddox for experimentation. Maddox is "a gung-ho cybernetics expert [who] wants to disassemble Data in order to learn more about his inner-workings,"[139] in an attempt to reproduce Data for a wide variety of usage in the Federation and Starfleet.[140]

Data believes Maddox's plans are ill-conceived and decides to fight the transfer. He is informed he has no such right. Dangerous assignments are not valid bases for fighting transfer. His next choice is to resien from Starfleet, and from there the battle is joined. Captain Phillipa Louvois of the Judge Advocate General's Office orders a hearing on whether Data is a sentient being at liberty to resign from Starfleet. Picard is designated to defend Data, and Riker is unwillingly drafted to prosecute.[141]

Riker attempts to show Data is not human, i.e., that he was built by a human (Dr. Noonien Soong), that he has superhuman strength and that he can be disassembled and even "shut down" by a human, which Riker proceeds to demonstrate. Picard tells Guinan of Riker's "devastating" prosecution, and it is only when the bartender suggests that a race of Datas would be nothing more than slave fodder for the Federation that Picard is inspired. Guinan says:

> In the history of many worlds there have always been dispos-
> able creatures. They do the dirty work. They do the work that
> no one else wants to do because it's too difficult or too haz-
> ardous. And an army of Datas, all disposable ... you don't have
> to think about their welfare, you don't think about how they
> feel. Whole generations of disposable people.[142]

In his opening speech, Captain Picard admits that Riker has proven Data to be a machine, but argues that humans too are machines. This concession, according to Picard, does not answer the larger question of whether Data is property. Picard questions Maddox about the qualifications for sentience: intelligence, self-awareness and consciousness. Maddox concedes Data has at least intelligence and self-awareness, while the third criterion remains in question. Picard then suggests that whatever decision is made in that hearing would have enormous consequences for the future. "Are we ready to consign an entire race of Datas to the status of disenfranchised property?" Picard asks rhetorically.[143]

Captain Louvois acknowledges that the question they are all "dancing around" is whether Data has a soul.[144] Louvois admits she does not know and does not, in fact, even know whether she herself possesses a soul. In the absence of proof to the contrary, she declares herself unwilling to find Data soulless, and therefore property. She finds in Data's favor, and the android formally rejects Maddox's request.[145]

Picard is again called upon to defend the right to life, as preliminary to an android's right to choose, in "The Offspring," another third-season episode, which has been alternately praised as well done[146] and panned as unnecessary.[147] In that case, it is Data's creation, his "daughter," Lal, played by Hallie Todd. The threat this time comes from Starfleet Admiral Haftel, portrayed by Nicholas Coster, who wants not to disassemble Lal, but to take Lal away from Data for study and a "proper" upbringing.[148]

Early in the episode, when Captain Picard discovers Data has created the android Lal and calls it his "child," Picard, upset at the discovery, tells Counselor Troi that it is "an invention," not a child. Troi replies, "Why should biology rather than technology determine whether it is a child?"[149] When Picard lectures Data that the latter's actions will have serious repercussions, Data asks whether the captain wishes to have Lal deactivated. "It's a life, Data," Picard says. "It can't be activated and deactivated ...."[150]

Following the test established in "The Measure of a Man," Data notes that Lal is becoming "sentient by developing the awareness to question and examine [her] perceptions."[151] Lal is again referred to as a "living, sentient being" by Picard, who tells Admiral Haftel that "[androids'] rights and privileges have been defined. I helped define them,"[152] in a clear reference to "The Measure of a Man." Yet it is by no means clear, in this later episode, that Lal has a right to choose.[153] It is only after Lal's rights have been discussed by the captain, crew and Haftel that Picard finally asks Lal for her wishes, as if this is a new and surprising avenue to pursue. Notwithstanding Lal's wishes to remain with Data, Haftel still asks, then orders, Data to deliver Lal to Starfleet for research and training.[154] Picard tells Data to "belay that order," telling Haftel that he, Picard, will take the issue to Starfleet. "I am Starfleet," Haftel storms. Picard says, "You acknowledge their sentience but you ignore their personal liberties and freedom."[155] The issue then becomes moot as Lal develops a terminal case of emotional awareness, leading to systems failure and "death."[156]

Perhaps the issue need not have been explored, even assuming for the sake of argument it need have been raised, because of the resolution in "The Measure of a Man."

While Lal was a well-defined character, and the show was excellently directed by cast member Jonathan Frakes, the point of the episode was so consistent with that of "The Measure of a Man" that it seemed superfluous. Questions resolved in "The Measure of a Man" arose again in "The Offspring," seemingly for no other purpose than to propel the story. Because it was a good story and because it adhered to the *ST:TNG* tenets regarding right to life, the episode was nonetheless a valuable entry in the series.

A recent episode considering the right to life was the fifth season's "I, Borg," which considered the question almost as if "The Measure of a Man" had never existed. In "I, Borg," an away team discovers the crash site of a Borg ship with one survivor, an individual Borg, which the crew realizes is something of a contradiction in terms. Aboard the *Enterprise*, there is a strong memory of the destruction and tragedy wreaked by the Borg in the past;[157] Picard is still so shaken by his past abduction that he refuses to see the prisoner.[158]

Soon, the prisoner becomes something of a guest, or even a pet, of the *Enterprise*.[159] LaForge names him "Hugh" and, along with Dr. Crusher, teaches him what it is to be an individual, separate and apart from the Borg collective. The *Enterprise* plan is to program Hugh with a destructive command to disable the Borg collective when Hugh is reassimilated by his "people." However, somehow this plan becomes untenable, as LaForge, then the reluctant Guinan (whose entire species had been devastated by the Borg) and finally even the recalcitrant Picard conclude that this would constitute murder, perhaps even the genocidal destruction of an entire race. It is not until Picard realizes that Hugh has developed knowledge of self, in effect, individuality, that he abandons the plan.[160] An argument could be made that exceptions for self-defense or war would support the action, yet there are flaws with both of these theories. The episode makes clear that there has been no formal declaration of war against the Borg by the Federation Council. Further, while the Borg as a group pose a terrible threat to the Federation, Hugh does not.

ST:TNG's view of the right to life closely follows the Roddenberry view of a utopian, egalitarian society. Even when we find that the show sometimes "re-litigates" an issue that should be understood to be decided, it does consistently come up with the same answer. All "born" sentient life is precious, and even the decision to kill such a being in self-defense is a decision fraught with moral ambiguity. It seems clear that so long as communication and discussion are possible, i.e., that a chance exists for reason to prevail, even self-defense is viewed as premature. In this, the 24th century appears to take a view of self-defense that is significantly more limited than that which the 20th century recognizes.

The Right to Privacy

For the most part, *ST:TNG* has consistently reflected the contemporary struggle with the privacy issue, while exhibiting a more advanced step along the road to complete protection of privacy rights. In the 20th-century perspective, the privacy rights may be said to be four-fold. The four separate bases for invasion of privacy are: "unreasonable intrusion upon the seclusion of another; appropriation of the other's name or likeness; ... unreasonable publicity given to the other's private life; ... [and] publicity that unreasonably places the other in a false light before the public...."[161] Several of these theories of liability have application to *ST:TNG*'s treatment of privacy issues.

The most striking, and certainly most didactic, of the right to privacy episodes is "Up the Long Ladder," a second season show written by attorney Melinda Snodgrass. In this episode, a race of clones attempts to steal the DNA of Riker and Doctor Pulaski in an effort to ensure their race's survival. Riker and Pulaski had already objected to a request for the DNA, and when they discover the deception, Riker destroys the clones with a phaser blast. "We certainly have a right to exercise control over our own bodies,"[162] Riker argues. Snodgrass speaks about the episode:

> It is ironic, because I got enormous flack
> from the right to life coalition because they
> destroyed the clones .... They thought I was
> condoning abortion. In fact, I did put a line
> in Riker's mouth that was very pro-choice
> and the right to life coalition went crazy. He
> says I told you that you can't clone me and
> you did it against my will, and I have the
> right to have control over my own body.
> That's my feeling and it was my soapbox, and
> it was one I got to get on.[163]

The show suggests a strong right to privacy in one's physical person, including, but not limited to, reproduction. *ST:TNG* also presents privacy in a broader context that considers whether a person can control his or her image, likeness and personality. In the 20th century, such issues are generally raised in the context of commercial appropriation of name or likeness, but in the 24th century, advanced technology makes other kinds of personal invasions possible.

Several episodes explore the appropriation of one's likeness through use of the holodeck, which has the ability to create corporeal three-dimensional people closely patterned on real individuals. These episodes raise important questions about privacy and freedom of thought. For example, in "Hollow Pursuits," the awkward, reclusive Lieutenant Reginald Barclay, nicknamed "Broccoli" by the amused crew, escapes from the uneasiness of social requirements and ship's duty by spending an inordinate amount of time on the holodeck, where he creates characters who look like and sometimes act like actual members of the crew.[164]

While some have seen this episode as a comment on "trekkies" who escape from reality into the fantasy of the *Star Trek* universe,[165] more fundamentally, it is a show about privacy. In numerous scenes, Barclay reproduces facsimiles of his crewmates, including Picard, Riker, Crusher, Troi and LaForge on the holodeck, putting them in embarrassing and often ludicrous roles and situations. When the crew finds out, they are outraged at the use to which Barclay is putting their likenesses without their consent.[166]

Yet, it can be asked, how it is that we feel we can control the mental fantasies others might have about us? To do this is to control their minds, which violates their own autonomy and privacy. The holodeck is, in one sense, just a 3-D corporeal computer enhancement of our thoughts. Surely one's thoughts are private even if they involve others.

It also should be noticed that the privacy issue is two-edged here. "When Geordi violates [Barclay's] privacy by walking into this holodeck fantasy, the issue of violation of privacy is never tackled by our holier-than-thou crew. Sure, just walk right in on the poor guy. Good thing he was only fencing with the Musketeers and not giving Pee-Wee a hand."[167] This would approximate a privacy invasion under the first ground: "intrusion, physical ... or otherwise, upon the solitude or seclusion of another or his private affairs or concerns ... if the intrusion would be highly offensive to a reasonable person."[168]

Another's holodeck fantasy may seem humorous rather than intrusive, yet *ST:TNG* also shows us that it may not be quite so humorous when we are the "borrowed" image. In "Hollow Pursuits," for example, Counselor Troi, envisioned as the Goddess of Empathy, is empathetic with Barclay's needs until she meets her own simulated alter ego. At another point, Riker asks whether there is some regulation forbidding such use of the holodeck. When told that there is not, he fumes "Well, there ought to be."[169]

A potentially more serious invasion of privacy involving the use of the images of crew members in the holodeck can be seen in "Booby Trap," in which LaForge is able to access the personnel file of Leah Brahms, the designer of the *Enterprise*'s engines, in order to create not just a visual image but one including detailed and complete information about the person replicated. His motive is good. Needing to work quickly in a crisis situation, he finds it convenient to have the holodeck create her image. Their interaction, however, becomes personal, intimate and romantic. LaForge is smitten.[170]

Interestingly, during a later episode, "Galaxy's Child," Leah Brahms visits the *Enterprise* and stumbles upon the program. She is outraged at the use of her computer-created self as a gross invasion of her privacy. "I have been invaded, violated. How dare you use me like this? ... How far did it go, anyway? Was it good for you?"[171] Eventually, Leah is won over by LaForge, and the charge of violation of privacy is not again considered. As with all of the holodeck episodes, there is an uneasy, unresolved feeling that technology has outrun a clear resolution of the issue. Perhaps this question will be explored again.

In the previously discussed "Up the Long Ladder," involving the theft of cells from *Enterprise* crew members for the creation of clones, Riker articulates his feeling that the cloning of his cells "diminished [him] in ways [he] can't even begin to imagine."[172] This echoed the point made in "The Measure of a Man" that reproducing a race of "Datas" vitiates the uniqueness of each person, in effect the ultimate privacy violation.

From our perspective, these episodes create and perpetuate a view of privacy that suggests every individual is entitled to live a life untrammeled by other people's interference. One's body, mind and image are one's own. Even when not protected in law, customary morality creates pressure to preserve the privacy of others. Those who violate this privacy appear to be confronted and generally acknowledge that they have done wrong.

Today, a cause of action exists for invasion of privacy by appropriation of name or likeness for the defendant's benefit.[173] Usually this is economic, but "injury caused by an appropriation ... may ... be mental and subjective'-in the nature of humiliation, embarrassment and outrage."[174] It may be that such an action would be needed in the 24th century, regardless of whether it is done for personal gratification or pecuniary benefit, in order to take account of the increased ability to violate privacy that the advanced holodeck technology creates.

In the episode titled "Violations," invasion of privacy is seen for the first time as an actionable offense. This fifth-season episode was one of the most powerful and effective of not just the fifth season, but of the series' entire run. In this story, the *Enterprise* is transporting a delegation of Ullians, "an alien race of telepathic historians who conduct research by probing their subjects' long forgotten memories."[175] Counselor Troi and then Commander Riker fall into inexplicable comas; initially, only the audience is privy to their thoughts before they lose consciousness.

Each of the two crew members experiences violent flashbacks, Troi to a romantic incident with Riker that then turned ugly, and Riker to a stressful ship disaster wherein lives were lost, implicitly because of a command decision he had made. When Troi regains consciousness, we learn one of the Ullians has invaded her thoughts and altered the memory for her.

> You have to make sure you don't misinterpret what this guy was doing.... He was basically going into your memories and playing in them for his own amusement, pleasure and fulfillment. He was not going in and exploring any character's greatest fear. He might go in and feel that today he wants to see Troi's sexual secrets and tomorrow he may want to see Riker's unhappiest memory and see him suffer.[176]

When the wrongdoing is discovered, the other apologetic Ullians explain that many years earlier this type of mind rape had been a particularly heinous crime among their people. It had been believed the species had evolved beyond the need to commit such a crime, but apparently this was not so. In the 20th century, the invasion "may ... be by the use of the defendant's senses ... to oversee or overhear the plaintiff's private affairs."[177] By extension, therefore, the use of extrasensory abilities-from the Ullians' ability to recreate memories to Counselor Troi's ability to sense emotion-could constitute an invasion of privacy.[178]

This episode represents what *ST:TNG* and, indeed, all of *Star Trek* does best: taking a meaningful social, legal, political or philosophical issue and elucidating it by giving it a science fiction twist. It is only when viewed through the prism of fiction, and especially science fiction, that people are sufficiently distanced from the problem to see the "moral" of the story. Thus, as "The Outcast" throws new light on gender discrimination, "Violations" offers a new perspective on crimes (and by implication, civil causes of action) impinging on a person's freedom-in this instance, freedom of thought.

Conclusion

ST:TNG presents an interesting example of a legal system that is both a logical extension of the 24th century portrayed in the show and significantly different from our own. In particular, the dual-track system demonstrates serious concern about human rights while attempting to move away from formalistic procedures. The system, as portrayed, relies heavily on the evolved goodness of the people involved and on informal mechanisms of dispute resolution. It does not appear that the informal part of the 24th-century system always functions as well as would be expected either to arrive at accurate factual findings or to protect individual rights. Further, the problem appears to be an aspect of the informality of the system, which continues to exist even when evolved people act in good faith.

Within the context of the show, accurate fact-finding and the correct resolution of disputes seem to be aided by some structure of formal procedural safeguards. Those who decry the formal nature of the 20th-century legal system may fail to fully recognize the positive aspects of such a system.

ST:TNG generally handles issues of legal procedure well. The system portrayed is inventive, challenging and largely consistent with the 24th century as portrayed on the show. Yet, some issues, such as jurisdiction and choice of law, require some additional development.

ST:TNG also examines substantive legal questions. Issues such as sexual orientation, gender equality, the right to life, the definition of "person" and privacy have all been considered. In general, there is strong support for the notion that a sentient creature has rights, including life, liberty and privacy. The control of one's person and persona is an important value. In general, we find the substantive law is consistent with the more general vision of the 24th century portrayed in the show. We also note, however, that just as these questions cause controversy in the 20th century, their resolution is not always clear in the 24th.

Finally, we want to acknowledge that the makers of *ST:TNG* are primarily concerned with creating and producing a high-quality television entertainment program. They did not set out to produce a treatise or documentary on government and law. It is their outstanding success in creating a believable and creative vision of the future that led us first to watch the show with such pleasure and then to think and write seriously about the legal issues discussed herein.

We have not, in every instance, agreed with the details of the future they present. For example, we think that procedural formalities can play a larger part in ensuring substantive justice than the *ST:TNG* legal system might suggest and that lawyers may not be such a bad idea, even in the future. This is not intended, however, to be a criticism of the show's overall believability and high quality. More fundamentally, nothing in our analysis challenges the core vision of the show. *ST:TNG* presents a provocative and emotionally compelling vision of a positive and hopeful future in which all kinds of people can learn to live together in harmony, to care for and respect each other and to allow each individual to pursue his or her hopes and dreams with dignity. It is a vision of the future to which we subscribe.

Endnotes

1. "After a quarter century, *Star Trek* has become a permanent fixture in America's cultural landscape." Charles Paikert, "After 25 Years, Still ... Cruising at Warp Speed," *Variety*, Dec. 2, 1991, at 49 [hereinafter "Warp Speed"]. In another article in the same issue, Paikert called *Star Trek* a "cultural icon." Charles Paikert, "Gene Roddenberry: American Mythmaker," *Variety*, Dec. 2, 1991, at 49, 62 [hereinafter "Mythmaker"].

2. Only massive letter-writing campaigns saved the show from earlier cancellation.

3. All but one of the films made money in theatrical release. A brisk video rental market exists. "We've sold about 10 million units, and our numbers have been remarkably steady over the years," says Alan Perper, senior VP of marketing for Paramount's video division. "Our core audience has grown. Each new film and the new TV show build a connection; they inspire people to go back." Stuart Miller, "No Skid on Homevid for First Four Flicks," *Variety*, Dec. 2, 1991, at 56.

4. In 25 years, the saga has spawned well over 100 titles and over 30 million copies in print. And interest in the books is peaking. In 1991 alone, Simon & Schuster's Pocket Books division, a unit of Paramount Communications and the sole publishers of *Star Trek* books since 1979, has sold about four million copies of old and new titles.

   When they first appeared in 1988, *The Next Generation* titles sold less well than books based on the original series. But now, with five million copies in print, the *Next* titles are just as popular.

   William Stevenson, "Fans Devour Books with Trek Hook," *Variety*, Dec. 2, 1991, at 52.

5. From chess sets to comic books, from T-shirts to computer programs, from recordings to disappearing-ink mugs, *Trek* merchandise is selling briskly-spurred by the fanaticism of Trekkers, the seemingly indestructible popularity of the show, and the hype and hoopla surrounding the 25th-anniversary promotions.

   According to Jim Arnold, administrator of corporate communications at Paramount Pictures, which issues official licenses to merchandise manufacturers, some $500 million has been spent to date on *Trek* goods. Paramount has licensed 35 companies to pump out *Trek* items, Arnold says, and additional firms may be signed up in the future.

   Jay Blickstein, "Trek Merchandise Sales Beaming Up," *Variety*, Dec. 2, 1991, at 54.

6. See "Warp Speed," supra note 1, at 49.

7. The first parody, featuring John Belushi as James T. Kirk and Chevy Chase as Mr. Spock, aired in 1976. The sketch takes place on the Star Trek set as an NBC network executive, played by Elliot Gould, comes to tell the cast the show has been canceled. The cast, completely caught up in their roles and not realizing they are actors in a television series, reacts as you might expect. A draft script for the sketch and a copy of a letter from Gene Roddenberry calling the sketch "delicious" appears in Saturday Night Live (Anne Beatts & John Head eds., 1977). The second parody featured guest William Shatner, playing himself, speaking at a Star Trek convention at which he tells Trekkies to "get a life."

8. A recent article noted that, while ratings for many syndicated shows are down, ratings for *ST:TNG* continue to be strong. Bill Carter, "Syndicated Shows Sagging? You Bet Your Life," *N.Y. Times*, Oct. 26, 1992, at C6.

9. The early publicity for the series outlines the premise, setting and characters, but does not detail any treatment of law or legal issues. See Mark Altman, "Star Trek: Deep Space Nine, Spin-Off Series Preview," Cinefantastique, Oct. 1992, at 80. The possible exception to this is a Bajoran constable who, in the words of Michael Pillar, will "take the law into his own hands[.]" Id. at 82.

10. *Star Trek*'s creator died on October 24, 1991. George Ramos, "Gene Roddenberry, Creator of *Star Trek*, Dies at 70," *L.A. Times*, Oct. 25, 1991, at A3.

11. Above all, the team works to Gene Roddenberry's plan. Dorothy Fontana, story editor on *Star Trek*, once said – and this is an important clue to why *Star Trek* worked – "when Gene wasn't available and we had a problem that had to be solved, we tried to ask ourselves, How would Gene do it?"'

   David Gerrold, *The World of Star Trek* 203 (1973).

12. "Mythmaker," supra note 1, at 49, 62.

13. Rick Berman may be to *Star Trek* what Michael Eisner is to Disney. Both have had to develop and diversify their properties in new directions while also keeping faith with the memory and vision of high-profile pioneers. "While many still associate late *Star Trek* creator Gene Roddenberry as the name behind *Next Generation*, it has actually been Berman who successfully molded the series into one of the highest-rated hour dramas on television." Mark Altman, "Rick Berman, *Trek*'s New Great Bird," *Cinefantastique*, Oct. 1992, at 36 [hereinafter "Great Bird"]. "Berman has taken on Roddenberry's vision and made it his own." Mark Altman, "*The Next Generation*: Rick Berman, Production Mogul," *Cinefantastique*, Oct. 1991, at 18. See also Mark Altman, "*The Next Generation*: The Power Behind the Throne," *Cinefantastique*, Sept. 1990, at 31.

14. "The key element for success for Berman is maintaining the show's philosophical bent." Mark Altman, "Science Fiction's First Franchise, *Star Trek: The Next Generation*," *Cinefantastique*, Oct. 1992, at 32, 59-60.

15. The goals for the show are set by Rick Berman, who outlined his mandate for the writing staff. "Foremost, *Star Trek* has got to be entertaining," said Berman. "Secondarily, it has to be true to Gene Roddenberry's vision of the 24th century. That's something we bend and twist a little bit but basically I'm obsessive about it. Then the show has to deal with character and it's got to deal with ideas that very often fall into the realm of contemporary issues. *Star Trek* at its best is good allegory."

   Id. at 59.

16. In 1991, *Star Trek: The Next Generation* was selected as one of the 25 best series by Viewers for Quality Television and as one of the 15 best shows in a poll of television critics. "Viewers' Group Poll Picks Its Top Dozen Quality Shows,"

Miami Herald, Nov. 27, 1991.

17. For a dissenting view, see Melinda Snodgrass, "Boldly Going Nowhere?," *Omni*, Dec. 1991, at 14, 52.

18. Over the last three years, Next has continuously averaged a powerhouse 10 rating, making it by far the most popular weekly series in first-run syndication. Its 11.6 season-to-date household rating so far this year is higher than at any other comparable period in the previous four years, allowing Paramount to charge $100,000 for a 30-second national spot.

   Ad-agency sources say no other syndicated series charges that much for a national spot, not even King World's high-rated game show strips *Wheel of Fortune* and *Jeopardy.*

   John Dempsey, "TV's Syndie Smash," *Variety*, Dec. 2, 1991, at 50.

19. "During its network run, I was always flirting too closely with saying things; I had to give up many points just to keep the small audience the show did have."' David McDonnell, *Star Trek 25th Anniversary Special* 8 (1991) (quoting Gene Roddenberry).

20. "The right kind of story is one that interests today's audience despite its 24th century setting." Gene Roddenberry, *ST:TNG Writers/Directors Guide* 2 (3d season, Aug. 1989) [hereafter *WDG*], 1989, Paramount Pictures Corporation, Inc. All rights reserved. Quotes used with permission. "Whatever the time frame of dramatic stories, in the end they are all about today!" Id. at 3.

21. Show a somewhat better kind of human than today's average. Our continuing characters are the kind of people that the *Star Trek* audience would like to be themselves. They are not perfect, but their flaws do not include falsehood, petty jealousies and the banal hypocrisies common in the Twentieth Century. Id.

22. "[*ST:TNG*] will hopefully create something that will live on in the future, which is a way to look at ourselves through these characters, to see our possible failings and strengths." Edward Gross, "Writer Richard Krzemien-Beyond 'The Last Outpost'," *ST:TNG Mag.*, Mar. 1988, at 18, 20 (quoting Richard Krzemien, who wrote the episode "The Last Outpost").

23. Gene has a pretty optimistic view about our progress, which I tend to agree with. I don't feel that the human race is crazy enough, foolish enough or ignorant enough to blow itself to pieces. We're going to be here for a long time to come. I know that Gene Roddenberry holds that point-of-view. He feels we're eventually going to evolve into something better, and that the phase we're going through-a phase that the human race has gone through before-will pass and we will again reach a more concerned outlook on life.

   Edward Gross, "Marina Sirtis-Counselor Deanna Troi," *ST:TNG Mag.*, Mar. 1988, at 50, 51 (quoting Marina Sirtis).

24. The most detailed presentation involves the space service Starfleet, but the structure and culture of Starfleet inevitably reflect more general facets of 24th-century life.

25. There is a mystery at the heart of *Star Trek* that touches people. It's composed of elements like hope, optimism, companionship, comradeship and courtesy, legitimacy and boldness. It lies in this assurance, which can only be a theoretical assurance, that we're going to survive – that some of us will make it.

   Patrick Stewart Interview, *Playboy*, Nov. 1992, at 139.

26. " Many people just watch a TV show for entertainment, but if you're so inclined, you'll see the message in [*ST:TNG*]."' Gross, supra note 23, at 51 (quoting Marina Sirtis).

27. It's an optimistic series. *Star Trek* not only says the human race is going to make it, but that we're going to make it in a very civilized way. Looking different and being different will be OK. We won't interfere with the evolvement of other peoples and civilizations. These are not warships going out, but spaceships exploring for new life, furthering the ideas of humanity.

   McDonnell, supra note 19, at 8 (quoting Gene Roddenberry).

28. "There has been no formal development of the issues of law in the 24th century; we have approached each legal incident on an individual basis, and have been guided largely by our interpretation of Gene Roddenberry's vision of the future." Letter from Jeri Taylor, Supervising (now Co-Executive) Producer, *ST:TNG* (Feb. 3, 1992) (on file with authors).

29.

While the exact way in which law and culture interact may be subject to debate, it seems to us that an extensive body of writing in legal philosophy, inclusive, at a minimum, of historical and sociological jurisprudence as well as legal realism and critical legal studies, combine to make the claim that some relation exists no longer controversial. See generally Roger B.M. Cotterrell, *The Politics of Jurisprudence: A Critical Introduction to Legal Philosophy* (1992).

30. It is not our claim that there is a one-to-one correspondence between every aspect of a present-day culture and its legal system. A legal system is not updated weekly in response to cultural change and the process by which law and culture interact is complex. Concerns about stability and continuity in law may impede rapid change.

The medieval writ system, for example, continued long after its usefulness was hard to justify. The separation of law and equity courts lingered on in at least one state until quite recently. Just as our legal system may continue to contain some doctrines or practices which seem to have no more justification than a long history, the 24th-century legal system can be expected to retain some outdated traditions from earlier times.

31. *WDG*, supra note 20.

32. All dialogue quotes from episodes of *ST:TNG* are from the televised version. We use the following citation format: *ST:TNG*, Episode Title, episode number (original airdate). The episode number and orieinal airdate information are taken from Edward Gross & Mark Altman, *New Voyages: The Next Generation Guidebook* (1991) [hereinafter *New Voyages*] and Mark Altman & Edward Gross, *New Voyages II: The Next Generation 5th Season Guidebook* (1992) [hereinafter *New Voyages II*].

33. The roots of this system can be traced to medieval trials by battle and the view that God would give victory to the righteous.

34. The complexity of the system that results makes it almost impossible to plead one's own cause. Only a trained lawyer knows enough about our complex formalistic system to adequately present a litigant's case.

35. In *ST:TNG* "Encounter at Farpoint Pt. I" (Sept. 26, 1987), the character of Q, a powerful being played by John deLancie, prosecutes all of humanity through its "class representatives," senior members of the Enterprise crew. Q replicates a trial from the year 2079 during the "post atomic horror." The system of law during this period is explained in an exchange between Q and Picard:

Q: "Legal trickery is not permitted. This is a court of fact."

Picard: "I recognize this court's system as the one that agreed with that line from Shakespeare, kill all the lawyers."'

Q: "Which was done."

Picard: "Leading to the rule guilty until proven innocent."'

Q: "Of course, bringing the innocent to trial would be unfair."

36. *WDG*, supra note 20, at 51.

37. "Money no longer exists. There are whole new standards of value. The transporter [sic] can make almost anything one needs." Id. at 41. For those interested in *Star Trek* technical consistency, it should be noted that the *Writers and Directors Guide* is in error here. *Star Trek* uses the transporter to move and reassemble but not to create matter. A replicator device based on the same technology would be used to create matter from energy and is used, for example, to create food and drink on command. See Letter from Jeri Taylor, Co-Executive Producer, *ST:TNG* (June 29, 1992) (on file with the authors) [hereinafter Taylor Letter].

38. "[Earth has] a literate and compassionate population that has learned to appreciate life as a grand adventure." *WDG*, supra note 20, at 51. "Our continuing characters are the kind of people that the *Star Trek* audience would like to be themselves. They are not perfect, but their flaws do not include falsehood, petty jealousies and the banal hypocrisies common in the Twentieth Century.... Regular characters all share a feeling of being part of a band of brothers and sisters." Id. at 3. "Most 24th Century humans believe that Life should be lived, not postponed." Id. at 41. "The crew members of the *Enterprise* are intelligent, witty, thoughtful, compassionate, caring human beings. They do have human faults and weaknesses, but not as many or as severe as in our time.... We should see in them the kind of people we aspire to be ourselves." Id. at 32.

"Today, Starfleet Command is puzzled that the concept of human engineering was not practiced centuries ago when giant business corporations began appearing." Id. at 18.

39. *ST:TNG*: "The Drumhead," No. 94 (Apr. 29, 1991).

40. "I won't treat a man as a criminal unless there is cause to do so." Id. (Picard).

41. "On the advice of my counsel, I refuse to answer that question in that the answer might serve to incriminate me." Id. (Tarses).

42. "The Seventh Guarantee is one of the most important rights granted by the Federation. We cannot take a fundamental principle of the Constitution and turn it against a citizen." Id. (Picard).

43. *ST:TNG*: "The Measure of a Man," No. 34 (Feb. 11, 1988) [hereinafter "Measure"]. In a striking speech from "The Drumhead," Picard reminds us of an earlier more barbaric time. "Five hundred years ago military officers would upend a drum on the battlefield. They'd sit at it and dispense summary justice. Decisions were quick, punishments severe, appeals denied. Those who came to a drumhead were doomed." *ST:TNG*: "The Drumhead," supra note 39 (Picard).

44. The original *Star Trek* series, while sharing these broad outlines, portrays a somewhat more formalistic legal structure than that seen on *ST:TNG*. For example, in "Court Martial," Captain Kirk is represented by a lawyer, Samuel T. Cogley, played by Elisha Cook Jr., who in some ways acts very much like a lawyer would in the 20th century. The trial scenes in that episode, as well as in "The Menagerie," have a more formal feel than similar scenes in *ST:TNG*. This would be consistent with the idea that the legal system is evolving from more to less reliance on formalism and procedural devices.

45. "Trust, fairness, harmony, mutual responsibility-inform much of the behavior of our characters, and it would follow that the legal procedures they employ would derive from those same precepts." Taylor Letter, supra note 37.

46. *ST:TNG*: "A Matter of Perspective," No. 61 (Feb. 10, 1990) (Krag) [hereinafter "Perspective"].

47. Id. (Picard).

48. Id.

49. Id.

50. It is likely that one invoking such procedures would be thought a little odd or something of a throwback unless the reason for doing so was apparent. In fact, it is likely that lawyers and judges, while useful at times, are also a bit suspect as relics of a less enlightened, less trusting and less humanistic time. Thus, in "The Measure of a Man," Picard's assessment of Phillipa Louvois, the head of the Judge Advocate General's office in sector 23, is that she has "always enjoyed the adversarial process more than getting at the truth." "Measure," supra note 43 (Picard).

51. It may be that an analogy can be drawn with the concept of "consensus" as practiced by the Society of Friends, sometimes known as Quakers. As we understand the concept, decisions require consensus, that is, unanimity. Even one dissenting voice can block the decision. At the same time, once the majority will is clear, each individual will feel morally responsible not to break consensus without a very serious reason. Thus, it could well be that a person would say, "I disagree, but will not block consensus." Such a system requires that the deeply held views of others be taken seriously just as it requires each individual to consider his responsibilities to the group process rather than just to himself. Professor Mike Sells, of Haverford College, generally confirms, from his own experience, our description of the working of a consensus-based system. Telephone interview with Professor Mike Sells (Nov. 24, 1992). Similarly, in the 24th-century legal system, any party can invoke formal procedure but would not be willing to do so merely because he or she did not like the outcome of more informal adjudicatory methods.

52. The formal hearing employed in "Measure," supra note 43, provides a model for such a formal hearing. A JAG officer presides, lawyers are used unless unavailable, in which case senior officers are substituted, formal objections and evidentiary rulings are made, cross examination is permitted, and a witness may be called as "hostile," allowing a more intensive type of questioning, and opening and closing statements are permitted.

53. It is likely that centuries of historical precedent, which are only slowly giving way to 24th-century sensibilities, mean that, by custom, certain very serious events still trigger the historical formal procedures. Thus, in "The Measure of a Man" we learn that "a court-martial is standard procedure when a ship is lost." "Measure," supra note 43. It may well be that by

the 25th or 26th centuries such a procedure will not be standard, but will be invoked only in extraordinary circumstances. Such is the process of social and cultural evolution.

54. "The Drumhead," supra note 39.

55. Id. (Picard). As will be seen shortly, however, when *ST:TNG* uses the term "counsel," this is not necessarily synonymous with "lawyer."

56. Id. (Picard).

57. Id. (Tarses).

58. Id. (Picard).

59. Id.

60. "Here are Starfleet's transfer orders separating Commander Data from the Enterprise, and reassigning it to Starbase 173 under my command." "Measure," supra note 43 (Maddox).

61. Id.

62. "Captain, I believe his basic research lacks the specifics necessary to support an experiment of this magnitude." Id. (Data).

63. Id. (Picard).

64. Id. In the 20th century, it would be unthinkable that this sort of dispute could proceed so far before anyone felt it necessary to look up the controlling law.

65. Id.

66. Id.

67. Id. (Picard & Louvois).

68. Id. (Louvois & Picard).

69. Melinda Snodgrass, who wrote the script for "The Measure of a Man," and who was, for a time, a member of the *ST:TNG* staff, says that it was Gene Roddenberry's view that lawyers would not exist in the 24th century. Telephone Interview with Melinda Snodgrass, scriptwriter, "The Measure of a Man" (Apr. 6, 1992) [hereinafter Interview].

70. This is so both because procedure is generally simple (the computer can be consulted for procedural guidance when necessary) and because the proceeding tends to be less adversarial than in the 20th century. Each side is interested in determining what is true and just, not merely in winning; thus, questioning tends to be more straightforward, generally any relevant information is admissible, parties and witnesses can make statements in addition to answering questions and the rhetorical devices of lawyers have a minimized role. It would also be likely that, as part of a good basic education, most people in the 24th century would have received training in logical argumentation sufficient to present their case in a competent manner.

71. Note, however, that it appears that the captain/senior officer is to apply local law and procedure in such cases unless there is good reason not to do so. Examples of the interplay between the captain's authority and responsibility include "A Matter of Perspective," "Devil's Due," and "Justice." We discuss the issues of jurisdiction and choice of law in III(C).

72. In "Perspective," supra note 46, Picard initially indicates that it would not be proper to talk with Riker about the charges against him. Krag has accused Riker of murder. Shortly thereafter Riker asks, "Captain, may I have a word with you?" and Picard answers, "Under the circumstances, Number One, I think that would be inappropriate." It must be remembered, however, that Krag has just challenged Picard's fairness and has with difficulty accepted Picard as the decision maker. Thus, it is likely that Picard is "bending over backward" to demonstrate fairness, rather than applying a rule of procedure. It should be recalled that Picard has just come from a meeting between himself and Krag at which Riker was excluded. If formal procedures had been invoked, that meeting would also have been improper.

73. The idea that fundamental change in the structure of society will alter the character of the human beings who comprise it is not new. For example, in the old Soviet Union, on the occasion of the implementation of the 1977 "Brezhnev Constitution,"

one commentator noted that the "expansion [of the scope of national planning] can be ideologically justified on the basis of the social engineering (i.e., the development of the new Soviet man and communist morality) necessary for the building of communism, the stated preoccupation of the mature, developed socialist society of the Soviet Union." Bernard A. Ramundo, "The Brezhnev Constitution: A New Approach to Constitutionalism?," 13 _J. Int'l L. & Econ._ 41, 46 (1978). Socialist doctrine held that, with the evolution of an ideal Soviet citizen, the state would be able to adapt and eventually wither away.

74. Such an image of our legal system is not new. The irony so effectively exploited by Dickens in Bleak House is that the court of conscience had become the nation's worst example of legal abuses. This made it the perfect target for a moralist who believed (very much in the spirit of the Romantic movement) that institutions pervert the inborn goodness of people. Richard Posner, _Law and Literature: A Misunderstood Relation_ 131 (1988).

75. One continuing theme of legal theory has been the question of judicial discretion. While legislators are expected to make rules based on their own best judgment of what is good for society generally (in a representative form of government, it might be argued that this is what we hire such folks to do), judges are not. Rather, judges are supposed to decide particular cases in conformity with pre-existing legal rules. Fear of the consequences of judicial discretion is embodied in Legal Formalism, the doctrine that judges do not make law, but merely "find" it in the pre-existing seamless web of the common law. See Joseph Horovitz, _Law and Logic_ 123-33 (1972) (discussing formalism and critiques thereof).

Much of modern legal theory has been dedicated to the task of demonstrating that Legal Formalism is wrong-that legal rules do not and cannot control legal decisions. From Legal Realism onward, the point has been made that judges have discretion whether we like it or not. They make new ex post facto laws in every case and are seldom if ever truly bound by prior precedents and rules. There is always a way around the rules, say the skeptics, because neither the rules nor the facts are ever really clear in their meaning. What appears to be the following of a clearly applicable legal rule is, in reality, merely the selection of one of two opposite but both logically applicable rules. It is the basis of the selection that we should examine.

This philosophical approach has been applied to argumentation about almost every modern controversy, including those involving fundamental constitutional rights. If, for example, the First Amendment has no real meaning (since no rule of law can have any objective meaning), it becomes possible to argue that "hate speech" has no protection under it. What had appeared to be a fundamental rule protecting rights becomes no more than a dominant political power imposing its perspective and subject to rejection should political power change. Thus, questions about the nature and importance of rules have relevance throughout the legal arena.

76. We know well that people's prejudices, training, and social position-the movements in which they are caught up and the ideologies linked with these-strongly influence their consciences and their speculations. Whether we consider this a merit or a demerit depends upon our judgment of the judges, and particularly upon comparative judgments we make between them, the legislators, and the holders of executive office. Which of these three, with their characteristic methods and the influences to which they are exposed or from which they are sheltered, are the more to be trusted with the opportunity for partly independent decision in the making and remaking of the law? Should we give up some certainty and determinacy about what the law is, and some freedom for legislators to decide what it shall be, in order to give greater weight to what judges will see as people's rights or just claims? I do not know what answer to give, but I want it to be clear that this is the choice.

John Mackie, "The Third Theory of Law," 7 _Phil. & Pub. Aff._ 3, 16 (1977), reprinted in Joel Feinberg & Hyman Gross, _Philosophy of Law_ 181, 187 (4th ed. 1991).

77. See supra notes 29-30 and accompanying text.

78. "Perspective", supra note 46.

79. For an article using this episode as a starting point from which to discuss the use of re-creations in court, see Robert D. Brain & Daniel J. Broderick, "Demonstrative Evidence: The Next Generation," 17 _Litig. Mag._ 21 (1991).

80. Id. In the absence of beings with empathic abilities, the holodeck procedure would have been even more uncertain since there was no attempt made to use it to decide who was telling the truth. That determination was left to Counselor Troi.

Yet, it is likely that the holodeck could have been used in a more proactive fashion. For example, the computer could have been asked to compare the various depositions, find whatever discrepancies exist and extrapolate its own best theoretical estimate of the actual truth.

81. "Captain, I have established motive, method and opportunity. In any court in the Federation, that is sufficient to warrant the extradition of the accused." "Perspective," supra note 46 (Krag to Picard).

82. Id.

83. In *ST:TNG*: "The First Duty," No. 119 (Mar. 30, 1992), a court martial-type inquiry of Wesley Crusher and others is held at Starfleet Academy after the crash of their squadron's ships kills a student. The procedure looks, on the face of it, like a formal hearing, but really it is not. The youths do not have counsel, and cross-examination does not take place. Although "depositions" are taken and the youths are questioned by the hearing officers, they are mostly permitted to present their stories through narratives supplemented with computer data. At the conclusion of the hearing there is suspicion but no proof that Wesley and the rest have lied. While the refusal to condemn on suspicion alone demonstrates a concern for the human rights of the accused, we would also suggest that more rigorous examination, in the style of a 20th-century proceeding, might have uncovered the increasingly thin tissue of lies. Of course, they could have refused to testify had they wished to invoke that right.

It should be noted that Wesley eventually comes forward and tells the truth through a combination of his growing guilty conscience and strong pressure from Picard, who has independently discovered the truth and threatens to come forward himself if Wesley does not. Thus, we again see that the truth is discovered through a means other than the normal working of the 24th-century legal system. An effective fact-finding process is clearly necessary since the show establishes that people of the 24th century can and do lie. Wesley's companions, for example, showed no sign that they were likely to tell the truth of their own accord, and Wesley does so only when exposure is certain.

Parenthetically, since we assume that the black mark on his record would foreclose Wesley from obtaining a plum assignment such as the Enterprise after graduation, we wonder if he might find himself instead assigned to the Starbase home of *Deep Space Nine*.

84. It may be a cliché that "the person acting as his own lawyer has a fool for a client," but clichés, by definition, develop because of the continual repeating (and eventual loss of emotional impact) of a statement containing a core of truth. We are often too emotionally involved in our own situation and our view of events to understand that others may see things differently. We may lack the emotional detachment and objectivity needed to convince neutral decision makers. This seems to be true in the 24th century as much as in the 20th.

85. Another episode, *ST:TNG*: "Devil's Due," No. 86 (Feb. 4, 1991), deals with a contract signed 1,000 years previously by the people of Ventax II. Under the terms of the contract, a metamorphing devil figure, Ardra, agreed to provide 1,000 years of peace and prosperity. In return, Ardra would become the absolute master of Ventax II when the 1,000 years expired. The episode considers whether the being presenting herself as Ardra is in fact Ardra and whether the terms of the contract were fulfilled by her.

To the extent that informal means of resolution can be said to have been tried, they were unsuccessful. When the law of Ventax is researched, however, it is discovered that, because the case involves a dispute with a non-Ventaxan, a formal arbitration procedure can be invoked. With Data acting as judge (selected by Ardra), Picard presents the case that the contract has not been fulfilled and that Ardra is a fraud. Eventually, evidence is introduced that unmasks Ardra as a fraud.

Note that in both "Devil's Due" and "A Matter of Perspective" the key evidence is discovered by the crew of the *Enterprise*. The difference is that, in "Devil's Due," the crew is mobilized by Picard to deal with the issue at stake in the arbitration. In "A Matter of Perspective," a shell-shocked Riker does not instigate the investigation. Rather, seemingly independent problems on the ship lead to investigations that are eventually found to also prove Riker's innocence.

86. A humorous comment on all of this, but one that demonstrates that formal procedure can be used to resolve disputes with intransigent adversaries, can be found in *ST:TNG*: "The Ensigns of Command," No. 49 (Sept. 30, 1989), in which Picard comes into conflict with the Sheliak, a race of beings so formalistic and unyielding that no resolution seems possible. The only prior contact between the Federation and the Sheliak took place during the negotiation of a 500,000-word treaty. The

Sheliak may be intended to portray our worst nightmare of the lawyer caught up in legal formalism. Yet, formalism also provides the answer when all else has failed. Picard tries every way he can imagine to resolve his problem with the Sheliak until, late in act five, he finally decides to read the treaty, in which he finds a clause that allows him to prevail.

Yes, the Sheliak are absurd, but they are also an example of the type of adversary with whom informal dispute resolution procedures are unlikely to work. They do not care about fairness or how nice you are. They are not interested in Picard at all. They have their own interests to pursue and will govern their behavior to further their own ends, limited only by whatever binding agreements they have made. "Interview," supra note 69. When confronted with such beings, formal procedure can provide the structure needed for dispute resolution.

87. "Measure," supra note 43 (Picard). "You see, sometimes it does work," Louvois says of the formal adjudicatory system after Data's rights are affirmed and he declines to submit to the procedure. Id. (Louvois).

88. In "The Measure of a Man," reference was made to a Federation Constitution including guarantees of civil liberties in many ways the same or similar to those in our own Bill of Rights. Id.

89. In this respect, the situation in the Federation appears to be similar to that in the United States before the passage of the Fourteenth Amendment. During this period, the Bill of Rights only limited actions of the federal government and not of the states. See *Barron v. Mayor & City Council of Baltimore*, 32 U.S. (7 Pet.) 243 (1833). It should be noted, however, that even before passage of the Fourteenth Amendment, the United States Constitution contained some specific limitations on states, including, inter alia, prohibitions on impairing the obligation of contracts and enacting bills of attainder or ex post facto laws. U.S. Const., art. I, 10. There is no indication that these limits exist in the Federation Constitution.

90. It should be noted, of course, that the nature of a planetary government might mean that it would not qualify for membership in the United Federation of Planets in the first place. In *ST:TNG*: "The Hunted," No. 58 (Jan. 6, 1990), revelations about the government's inhumane treatment of its genetically altered soldier class convince Picard that Angosia III is not ready for Federation membership. This would also suggest that a planet that radically changed its government in a negative manner might be thrown out of the Federation, but this issue has not yet arisen in *ST:TNG*.

91. Former *ST:TNG* staffer Melinda Snodgrass, who is also a lawyer, suggested that diplomatic immunity, a special court empowered to hear such cases or a clear conflict of laws rule would almost certainly exist to deal with such problems. "Interview," supra note 69.

92. See, e.g., 22 U.S.C. 254(d) (1988) (providing for dismissal of suit brought against anyone having diplomatic immunity "under the Vienna Convention on Diplomatic Relations, under section 254(b) or 254(c) of this title, or under any other laws extending diplomatic privileges and immunities ....").

93. "Perspective," supra note 46.

94. Id.

95. In "Perspective," the following exchange takes place between Chief Investigator Krag and Captain Picard:

Krag: "[Riker] will be given a chance to prove his innocence."

Picard: "Investigator, in our system of jurisprudence, a man is innocent until proved guilty."

Krag: "In ours, he is guilty until he is proved innocent. And you are under our jurisdiction. If I understand Federation regulations on this matter, and I just happened to look them up before .."

Picard: "I am aware of Federation regulations sir, and if you investigate further you will find the captain decides if extradition is warranted."

Id.

96. *ST:TNG*: "Justice," No. 7 (Nov. 7, 1987).

97. Id.

98. A very interesting legal question is skirted in "Devil's Due." The question is whether a contract to sell one's descendants into slavery, or for that matter to obligate them in other ways, can ever be binding. The question is avoided by the plot device

of having the population of the planet accept the binding nature of the contract, thus leaving the questions of whether its terms had been fulfilled and whether the claimant was actually Ardra, the contracting party.

We wish some consideration had been given to the more fundamental question, because the story presents a dark and uncomfortably personalized version of the "social contract" theory that is often offered as the philosophical basis for the legitimacy of the modern democratic state. "At least since Locke's impassioned defense of the natural freedom of men born into nonnatural states, the doctrine of personal consent has dominated both ordinary and philosophical thinking on the subject of our political bonds." A. John Simmons, *Moral Principles and Political Obligations* 57 (1979).

99. "Great Bird," supra note 13, at 36-37.

100. See, e.g., "Communications, Elegies," *Starlog: The Science Fiction Universe* Feb. 1992, at 12-16; "Letters," *T.V. Zone: The Monthly Mag. of Cult Television*, Sept. 1991, at 12-13.

101. See supra notes 73-98 and accompanying text.

102. *Star Trek: The Official Fan Club*, Mar./Apr. 1992, at 5-6 [hereafter Fan Club].

103. See Mark Altman, "Marina Sirtis Ship's Counselor," Cinefantastique, Oct. 1991, at 39.

The women on this show are very non-threatening .... I don't think it's realistic. It's not realistic for the 20th century so it's definitely not realistic for the 24th century. Ever since Denise [Crosby, as Security Chief Tasha Yar] left the show ... the two women that are left are both doctors in the caring professions. You do see female admirals, but ... the fans don't really care about our guest stars. They care about the regulars and what they want to see are the regular women having more power.

Id. (quoting Marina Sirtis).

104. *New Voyages*, supra note 32, at 29 (quoting Altman).

105. See, e.g., *Cinefantastique*, Oct. 1991, at 46.

106. Bill Florence, Marvin V. "Rush Guide to 'The Host'," *Star Trek: The Next Generation, The Official Mag.*, June 1992, at 56.

107. Fan Club, supra note 102, at 6.

108. Mark Altman, "The Next Generation Tackling Gay Rights," *Cinefantastique*, Oct. 1992, at 71 ("one of the most commented on shows they ever had").

109. In the 20th century, "the rehabilitation theory rests upon the belief that human behavior is the product of antecedent causes, that these causes can be identified, and that on this basis therapeutic measures can be employed to effect changes in the behavior of the person treated."

Wayne R. LaFave & Austin W. Scott, Jr., *Criminal Law* 1.5, at 24 (2d ed. 1986).

110. New Voyages II, supra note 32, at 72. Series writer Brannon Braga marveled that Frakes would have nonetheless been willing to kiss Soren in the episode's love scene.

111. Id.

112. Id.

113. Id.

114. Id.

115. Id.

116. Id. at 72-73.

117. Id. at 73.

118. Id.

119. Id.

120. Altman, supra note 108, at 71.

121. *New Voyages II*, supra note 32, at 72.

122. Staff writer Brannon Braga ... was mystified by the negative mail. Some people reacted to the show in a way that I didn't understand .... They thought we were advocating a particular sexual preference. I don't think that's true at all. We were advocating tolerance. What's so risky about making a statement that intolerance is bad?

    Altman, supra note 108, at 74 (quoting Brannon Braga).

123. *ST:TNG* appears to conclude that the 24th century is pro-choice. In one episode, for example, Troi becomes pregnant by a unique being that enters her body while she sleeps. It is made clear that she could terminate the pregnancy but chooses not to do so.

124. Funnily enough, this is the same sobriquet Q gave to Worf.

125. *ST:TNG*: "Elementary, Dear Data," No. 28 (Dec. 3, 1988). See also Brian Alan Lane, "'Elementary, Dear Data' Mission Report," *Star Trek: The Next Generation, The Official Mag.*, Apr. 1989, at 25.

126. *New Voyages*, supra note 32, at 59-60.

127. S.A. Terilli, "Case Adds New Urgency to Long-Running Debate," *Miami Herald*, Mar. 28, 1992, at A13. See Fla. Stat. Ann. 382.009 (West Supp. 1992).

128. S.A. Terilli, "Legislature Considered Changing Law Dilemma Depends On Definition of Death," *Miami Herald*, Mar. 27, 1992, at A17.

129. Charles E. Hecker, "Court: Baby Born Without Brain Was Alive," *Miami Herald*, Nov. 13, 1992, at A1.

130. *ST:TNG*: "Evolution," No. 48 (Sept. 23, 1988).

131. Id.

132. Id. (Stubbs).

133. Id. (Stubbs).

134. Id.

135. Id.

136. *ST:TNG*: "Silicon Avatar," No. 104 (Oct. 14, 1991).

137. It's difficult not to imagine how Captain James T. Kirk and his crew would have handled the same situation.

    Chekhov: "Approaching crystalline entity, Captain."

    Kirk: "Hold position, Mr. Chekhov. Mr. Sulu, lock phasers on target and await my order."

    Spock: "Jim, it's attempting to communicate with us."

    Kirk: "I realize that, Spock. I just don't like what it has to say.... Fire!"

    New Voyages II, supra note 32, at 35.

138. See, e.g., *Cinefantastique*, Sept. 1990, at 46 (citing Melinda Snodgrass, author of "The Measure of a Man").

139. *New Voyages*, supra note 32, at 66.

140. "Measure," supra note 43.

141. Id.

142. Id. (Guinan).

143. Id.

144. We were somewhat disappointed to hear the most lawyerly of all *ST:TNG* characters turning the issue in this direction, especially when neither Riker nor Picard showed any inclination to do so. Her curious characterization marks a shift away from the objective scientific tests of awareness and intellect to the more amorphous religious test of being, in essence, "touched by God." Assuming that the separation of church and state is embodied in the Federation Constitution, this particular formulation would not be the basis for decision. Contrast her religious approach with the narrowly focused branch of the United States Supreme Court's decision in *Roe v. Wade*, 410 U.S. 113, 158 (1973), holding that a fetus is not a "person" within the meaning of the Fourteenth Amendment.

145. "Measure," supra note 43.

146. *New Voyages*, supra note 32, at 106.

147. Id. at 106-07.

148. ST:TNG: "The Offspring," No. 63 (Mar. 10, 1990).

149. Id. (Troi).

150. Id. (Picard).

151. Id. (Data).

152. Id. (Picard)

153. We see this as further evidence that the lack of formal regularity in the 24th-century legal system has a downside to it. In a more formalistic system, the precedent established in "The Measure of a Man" would likely have been deemed to be controlling. Here, it seems that the prior decision has some persuasive value but does not clearly control te decision as to Lal.

154. "The Offspring," supra note 148.

155. Id. (Haftel, Picard).

156. A legal issue seemingly overlooked was the culpability of the admiral in the death of Lal. Knowing her to be a sentient being, he seemed to hound her into breakdown and death. We suggest that criminal charges would have been appropriate in this situation.

157. See *ST:TNG*: "The Best of Both Worlds Part I," No. 73 (Sept. 17, 1990); ST:TNG: "The Best of Both Worlds Part II," No. 74 (Sept. 24, 1990).

158. *ST:TNG:* "I, Borg," No. 123 (May 18, 1992).

159. This episode has been criticized as "totally emasculating the single greatest antagonist ever created for *Star Trek.*" *New Voyages II*, supra note 32, at 92 (quoting Altman).

160. "I, Borg," supra note 158.

161. Restatement (Second) of Torts 652A (1977).

162. *ST:TNG*: "Up the Long Ladder," No. 43 (May 20, 1989).

163. New Voyages, supra note 32, at 77-78 (quoting Melinda Snodgrass).

164. *ST:TNG*: "Hollow Pursuits," No. 68 (May 5, 1990).

165. Michael Piller says: "It really was not intended directly at *Star Trek* fans. It was certainly about fantasy life versus reality." Id. at 112. But see id. at 112 ("A wake-up call for Trekkies which, like William Shatner's *Saturday Night Live* admonition, 'It's only a TV show' should remind obsessed Trek fans to turn off the tube, take off the 'make it so' buttons and go outside and get a life."). See also Edward Gross, "Cliff Bole Of 'Redemption' & 'Unification'," *Star Trek: The Next Generation, The Official Mag.*, Feb. 1992, at 31.

166. "Hollow Pursuits," supra note 164.

167. *New Voyages*, supra note 32, at 112 (quoting Michael Altman).

168. "Restatement," supra note 161, 652B.

169. "Hollow Pursuits," supra note 164 (Riker).

170. *ST:TNG*: "Booby Trap," No. 53 (Oct. 28, 1989).

171. *ST:TNG*: "Galaxy's Child," No. 89 (Mar. 11, 1991). See also "Mission Report: 'Galaxy's Child'," *Star Trek: The Next Generation, The Official Mag.*, Sept. 1990, at 39.

172. *ST:TNG:* "Up the Long Ladder," supra note 162 (Riker).

173. "Restatement," supra note 161, 652C.

174. 2 Thomas D. Selz, et al., *Entertainment Law* 18.01, at 18-5 (2d ed. 1992) (quoting Motshenbacher v. RJ Reynolds Tobacco Co., 498 F.2d 821, 824 (9th Cir. 1974)).

175. *New Voyages II*, supra note 32, at 56.

176. Id. at 57 (quoting Michael Piller).

177. "Restatement," supra note 161, 652B cmt. b.

178. The use of telepathy or empathic abilities in the criminal context arise in "The Drumhead," where Admiral Satie's use of a telepathic inquisitor makes Picard think about the propriety of his use of Troi's abilities in his own investigations. "The Drumhead," supra note 39.

The Interstellar Relations of the Federation:
INTERNATIONAL LAW AND
"STAR TREK: THE NEXT GENERATION"

MICHAEL P. SCHARF, JD, LLM
AND
LAWRENCE D. ROBERT, J°D

THE AUTHORS WOULD LIKE TO THANK DEBBIE MIREK FOR HER
INVALUABLE ASSISTANCE IN PROVIDING SOURCE MATERIAL FOR THIS
ARTICLE AND EDITORIAL ADVICE TO CONFORM TO THE STYLE AND
SPELLING GUIDELINES ESTABLISHED BY PARAMOUNT PICTURES
CORPORATION. WE ALSO WISH TO ACKNOWLEDGE THE SPIRITED CON-
TRIBUTIONS OF THE MEMBERS OF COMPUSERVE'S SCIENCE FICTION
AND FANTASY FORUM. THEIR EFFORTS MADE WHAT WOULD OTHER-
WISE HAVE BEEN AN ARDUOUS PROCESS A TRUE PLEASURE. WE WOULD
ALSO LIKE TO THANK MICHAEL OKUDA OF PARAMOUNT PICTURES
AND PAUL JOSEPH OF THE NOVA SOUTHEASTERN UNIVERSITY LAW
CENTER FOR THEIR HELPFUL COMMENTS ON THIS ARTICLE. STAR TREK,
STAR TREK: THE NEXT GENERATION, STAR TREK: DEEP SPACE NINE,
STAR TREK: VOYAGER AND U.S.S. ENTERPRISE ARE REGISTERED TRADE-
MARKS OF PARAMOUNT PICTURES CORPORATION.

Introduction

A recent *University of Toledo Law Review* article concerning the legal issues dealt with in the television series *Star Trek: The Next Generation* (*ST:TNG*)[1] became an overnight, national sensation.[2] Given that during its seven seasons of first-run episodes,[3] *ST:TNG* had been the most popular syndicated series on American television,[4] it is perhaps not surprising the article should engender so much public attention. The article, written by law professors Paul Joseph and Sharon Carton of Nova Southeastern University Law School, was not intended as entertainment, however. Rather, it was a serious examination of the way *ST:TNG*'s United Federation of Planets dealt with such weighty legal issues as the right to privacy,[5] the right to life[6] and rights to sexual orientation[7] as an implicit commentary on the salient issues facing American courts in the 1990s.

Written from the perspective of professors who teach domestic law courses, the Joseph and Carton article limited its primary focus to law as applied within the Federation, rather than between members of the Federation and foreign worlds. The same rationales for examining the Federation's internal substantive and procedural law are applicable to an in-depth exploration of interstellar legal relations in *ST:TNG*. The purpose of this article is to re-examine the law of *ST:TNG* from an international legal perspective. Many of *ST:TNG*'s episodes raise issues of interstellar law analogous to fundamental tenets of today's international law. The series has, for example, dealt with rules of treaty interpretation, state succession, diplomatic relations and immunities, international dispute resolution, membership in international organizations, law of the sea concepts, international environmental law, terrorism, extradition, extraterritorial jurisdiction, extraterritorial apprehensions, asylum, human rights, war crimes, genocide, the principle of non-interference in domestic affairs, humanitarian intervention, the principle of "jus cogens" and rules governing use of force and violations of territorial sovereignty.[8]

In an effort to deal with interstellar legal questions consistently, *ST:TNG* has transported international law into the 24th century. While there are a score of television series today portraying domestic law in operation,[9] *ST:TNG* is the only example of episodic television that regularly deals with principles of international law, albeit in a futuristic interstellar context. Unique among television series in this respect, *ST:TNG* can be used as a pedagogical aid to international law teaching, just as the original *Star Trek* series has been used to teach ethics at the undergraduate level.[10]

Using ST:TNG *To Teach International Law*

Although a relatively recent phenomenon, the examination of law in literature has seen explosive growth in academic circles. The works of Shakespeare, for example, have proven to be an extremely popular subject for analysis,[11] as have those of Nietzsche[12] and Dickens.[13] It may seem odd at first to speak of *ST:TNG* in the same breath with such classics. Yet because of its immense popularity, *ST:TNG*'s starship, the *U.S.S. Enterprise* N.C.C. 1701-D (*Enterprise*), might in fact prove to be a better vehicle for exploration and discussion of important legal principles in the classroom than these more traditional works.

ST:TNG is watched by tens of millions of viewers in the United States and several foreign countries on a daily and weekly basis. The crew of *ST:TNG*'s *Enterprise* is soon to be featured in a major motion picture. One spin-off series, *Star Trek: Deep Space Nine*, is rapidly gaining popularity and a second, *Star Trek: Voyager*, is scheduled to begin airing next year.[14] Meanwhile, more than

130 books set in the *Star Trek* universe, both novelizations of series episodes and new fiction, have appeared in print, with more than 70 attaining best-seller status.[15] *Star Trek* video games, amusement park entertainment, models, posters, action figurines, T-shirts, Halloween costumes and even Christmas ornaments abound.[16] *ST:TNG* has become such an important part of popular culture that many of today's students are likely to be more familiar with Picard than Pol Pot, Klingons than Koreans, the United Federation of Planets than the United Nations, and are more likely to be able to identify the demilitarized zone that separates the Romulan or Cardassian Empires from the Federation than the DMZ between Iraq and Kuwait or between North Korea and South Korea.

Rather than decry the decline of cultural literacy among today's student population, teachers can take advantage of students' existing store of knowledge concerning *Star Trek* to illustrate points of international law.[17] While it may at first seem unorthodox, referring to episodes of *ST:TNG* during classroom discussion is really no more unconventional than the common tactics of using illustrative fictional hypotheticals crafted by the teacher or employing well-known fictional characters in final examinations.

ST:TNG's widespread appeal also offers an opportunity to increase the visibility of international law by exposing the principles to students at virtually all levels of development. While the authors have had success employing *ST:TNG* in a law school setting, the popularity of the series makes it possible to craft teaching exercises that would appeal to grade school, high school and undergraduate students as well.[18] In this way, *ST:TNG* can be used to implement one of the main goals of the "United Nations Decade of International Law,"[19] namely, exposing students to international law concepts at the earliest practicable point in their education.

To facilitate the use of *ST:TNG* in international law teaching, the remainder of this article surveys the international law issues raised in the series,[20] comparing application of interstellar law in the 24th century to late 20th-century international law. While the similarities are striking, the article also illustrates the ways in which *ST:TNG*'s conception of international law deviates from existing international law.

International Law in the 24th Century

The episodes of *ST:TNG* revolve around the adventures of the *U.S.S. Enterprise* and its captain and crew.[21] While the *Enterprise*'s mission is ostensibly "to explore strange new worlds, to seek out new life and civilizations, to boldly go where no one has gone before,"[22] its function is really more akin to that naval vessels in the early age of mercantilism. In describing the similarities, series creator Gene Roddenberry noted:

> In those days ships of the major powers were assigned to patrol specific areas of the world's oceans. They represented their governments in those areas and protected the national interests of their respective countries. Out of contact with the admiralty office back home for long periods of time, the captains of these ships had very broad discretionary powers. These included regulating trade, fighting bush wars, putting down slave traders, lending aid to scientific expeditions, conducting exploration on a broad scale, [and] engaging in diplomatic exchanges and affairs. . . .[23]

Perhaps not coincidentally, it was in response to the needs of international relations during the mercantile period that modern international law evolved.[24] It is therefore appropriate that the universe of *Star Trek* would develop an analogous system of interstellar law.

ST:TNG actually depicts two separate systems of law. The first, which is analogous to our domestic law, applies within the United Federation of Planets. The Federation, which *ST:TNG* tells us was formed in the year 2161,[25] is a sort of evolved United Nations. The Federation is governed by a Council similar to the U.N. Security Council, whose members are representatives of the planets making up the Federation.[26] To become a member of the Federation, the government of a planet[27] must apply for membership and convince the Council that the planet's people are ready and willing to fulfill the terms of the Federation constitution, much in the same way a state applies for membership in the United Nations today.[28] The Federation is headquartered in the city of San Francisco on Earth,[29] where Earth's United Nations was first established in 1945. Two notable distinctions between the Federation and today's United Nations are that the Federation's constitution guarantees individual rights[30] and that the Federation has a standing military force, in the form of Starfleet, which protects the Federation from external threats.[31] However, unlike U.N. peacekeeping forces, Starfleet cannot be used to impose order within the Federation or the planets with whom the Federation is in alliance.[32]

As Joseph and Carton explain in their article, within the Federation relations are governed by "a legal system in which formality has been replaced by informality and procedural safeguards have been replaced by trust."[33] In contrast, relations with those from the many worlds outside the Federation – especially the Cardassians, Romulans, Sheliak, Ferengi and to some extent the Klingons, with whom the Federation is in an uneasy alliance – are marked by mistrust and occasional hostility.[34] As illustrated below, this second system of law portrayed in *ST:TNG* is governed by rules analogous to today's international law.

Treaties in the 24th Century

Under today's principles of international law, binding international agreements are referred to generically as "treaties," although a particular agreement may be labeled a convention, pact, protocol, charter, covenant, declaration, exchange of notes, modus vivendi or communiqué. On 20th-century Earth, treaties are the principal, though not exclusive, source of obligation in international law. The other major source of obligation is international custom, as evidence of a general practice accepted as law.[35] While a number of *ST:TNG* episodes concern the application of treaties between foreign worlds and the Federation, no episode mentions a 24th-century counterpart to customary international law. The 24th-century preference for treaty over custom makes sense in the context of a universe in which most parties have had little past interaction with one another and therefore have not developed anything approaching a general practice. Moreover, given their likely divergent conceptions of law, the worlds of the 24th century would wisely choose to govern their relations through negotiation of written, concrete instruments, which clearly express their intentions. The disappearance of the concept of customary international law in the next 400 years might be the natural outcome of the contemporary effort to codify custom in texts that bring clarity and precision where there had been obscurity and doubt.

Many of the treaties at issue in *ST:TNG* are types that are common in today's international legal system. For instance, there are several episodes dealing with mutual defense treaties, treaties defining territorial boundaries[36] and peace treaties.[37] Notable examples include the treaties with the Klingons, Romulans and Cardassians. In "Redemption,"[38] viewers learn that the Federation-Klingon Treaty of Alliance includes a pledge of mutual defense. This treaty is similar to the North Atlantic Treaty,[39] which established the North

Atlantic Treaty Organization in 1949 and the Treaty of Friendship, Co-operation and Mutual Assistance,[40] which established the Warsaw Pact in 1955.
Several episodes deal with the Federation-Romulan Treaty of Algeron,[41] which
establishes the neutral zone, an area of space in which Federation and Romulan
ships are prohibited similar to the existing DMZ between North and South
Korea. In "The Wounded,"[42] viewers are told that in the year 2367, the
Federation signed a peace treaty with the planet Cardassia, concluding a long
and bloody conflict with its inhabitants.

   Today's international law makes a somewhat artificial distinction between
agreements that are governed by international law and agreements between
states that by their very nature do not constitute international treaties. An
often-cited example of the latter type of agreement is a contract between states
for the purchase of commodities.[43] Interestingly, interstellar law does not appear
to recognize such a distinction. In "Code of Honor,"[44] for example, the
Enterprise is on a "diplomatic mission" to establish a "treaty" with planet Ligon
II to acquire a rare vaccine needed to treat the outbreak of a virulent plague on
planet Stryris IV. The treaty is essentially a contract for a commodity.

   One episode in particular, "The Ensigns of Command,"[45] is especially useful in illustrating a range of 24th-century principles of treaty interpretation in
operation. In that episode, the *Enterprise* receives a message from a race known
as the Sheliak demanding the immediate removal from planet Tau Cygna V of
Federation colonists who have been on the planet for 93 years. The Sheliak
claim the settlement exists in contravention of the Treaty of Armens, in which
the Federation, inter alia, ceded the planet to the Sheliak. The Sheliak tell
Captain Picard that if the Federation colony is not immediately removed, the
Sheliak will exercise their right under the treaty to destroy the colony. Seizing
on the treaty's arbitration clause, providing that in the event of a dispute concerning the treaty's interpretation each side would be represented by an arbitrator of its choosing, Picard asserts his right by selecting as his arbitrator a member of a race that is in the midst of a six-month period of dormancy, thereby
buying time to evacuate the colonists.

   While Captain Picard spends hours studying the text of the treaty for a way
out of his dilemma, it is curious that he never turns to the treaty's travaux
preparatoires (negotiating record) for a possible answer. By confining himself to
the text of the treaty, Picard's action suggests that, in the 24th century, the text
is the primary, and possibly sole, source of treaty interpretation.[46] This also has
been the practice of the International Court of Justice, which has consistently
declined to "resort to preparatory work if the text of a convention is sufficiently
clear in itself."[47] Other courts, however, including the U.S. Supreme Court, are

quicker to resort to the negotiating record in interpreting an international treaty.[48] In addition to examining the record for clues regarding original intent, courts also frequently examine the subsequent conduct of the parties as evidence of such intent.[49] Had Picard done so in "The Ensigns of Command,"[50] he could have argued that the Sheliaks' failure to protest the establishment of the colony for 93 years was evidence the treaty should be interpreted as permitting the continued existence of the colony.

Finally, the Sheliaks' acquiescence in Picard's delay tactic of selecting an unavailable arbitrator indicates a propensity for stricter adherence to the treaty text than usually found in today's cases of treaty interpretation. In two recent cases before the International Court of Justice, for example, the World Court read an exception for futility into a treaty clause that provided for a six-month period of arbitration as a precondition before resort to the court.[51] In one case, the president of the World Court stated that "the Respondent's argument whereby the Court's jurisdiction is denied through the non-lapse of the six-month period would appear too legalistic."[52]

"The Ensigns of Command" also demonstrated *ST:TNG*'s recognition of the international law rule that a violation of a treaty by one party does not automatically render the treaty null. Rather, a material breach gives rise to a right in the other party to terminate the treaty or to suspend the performance of its own obligations under the treaty.[53] Thus, the Sheliak do not claim that the Federation's breach of the Treaty of Armens ipso facto puts an end to the treaty.

A similar point is made in "The Enemy,"[54] in which the *Enterprise* responds to a distress signal from the wreckage of a Romulan vessel at planet Galorndon Core, located a half-light-year within Federation space. When a Romulan warship arrives to take custody of the survivor of the wreck, the Romulan commander, Tomalak, denies that the incursion was a treaty violation, claiming it was the result of a navigational error. Although doubting the validity of the claim, Picard lets the incident pass with just a warning. This situation also illustrates the 24th-century analogue to the international law principle that states responsibility for a violation of an international obligation "is precluded if the act was due to an irresistible force or to an unforeseen external event beyond its control."[55] This episode is similar to the 1983 incident involving the Soviet downing of a Korean civilian airplane. In assessing whether the Soviet Union violated international law, commentators have noted that the question turns on whether the plane was in Soviet airspace as the result of a navigational error or other inadvertence.[56]

The seventh-season episode titled "The *Pegasus*"[57] indicates that in the 24th century, violations of some treaties result in individual criminal responsibility. In this episode, Rear Admiral Eric Pressman is beamed aboard the *Enterprise* with a secret mission: to beat the Romulans in locating the *U.S.S. Pegasus*, which disappeared years ago while experimenting with a phasing cloaking device that not only renders matter invisible, but also allows it to pass unimpeded through normal matter. Such devices were outlawed by the Federation-Romulan peace treaty known as the Treaty of Algeron. When, at Admiral Pressman's insistence, the *Enterprise* enters a hollow asteroid to retrieve the device from the *Pegasus*, the Romulans seal off the entrance, trapping the *Enterprise* inside. To save his ship, Picard orders the device installed aboard the *Enterprise*. The device works, and the ship escapes the asteroid. Picard then orders the *Enterprise* to decloak directly in front of the Romulan ship, thus revealing the illegal possession of the cloaking device. Picard assures the Romulans that their government will be contacted regarding the incident and places Admiral Pressman under arrest for violating the treaty, "a treaty by which we are sworn to abide."[58] Starfleet Command then orders an investigation, which Picard tells Riker will probably result in the general court-martial of Pressman and several others in Starfleet Intelligence behind the secret mission.

Individual criminal responsibility for the breach of a treaty is rare under today's international law. Under traditional principles of international law, violations of treaties are the responsibility of the state, not the government officials and military personnel involved.[59] The post-World War II Nuremberg Tribunal established there could be individual criminal responsibility for violations of treaties codifying the laws of war.[60] Since then, a handful of conventions have been adopted establishing individual liability for specified violations of international law,[61] but the vast majority of today's treaties do not contemplate individual criminal responsibility for their breach. It is not clear from "The *Pegasus*"[62] whether the Treaty of Algeron uniquely provides for individual responsibility, or whether in the 24th-century individuals are criminally liable for violations of any treaty. A subsequent episode, "Lower Decks,"[63] suggests the answer to this question. To find Ensign Sito, who disappeared while on a covert mission to return a Cardassian spy who was working for the Federation, Captain Picard orders a probe launched into Cardassian space. While Commander Riker warns Picard that such action would be a clear treaty violation, he does not raise the possibility of individual criminal responsibility, suggesting the Treaty of Algeron may be unique in this respect.

State Succession

Under today's international law, when territory passes from one state to another, issues arise relating to the extent the territory continues to be governed by the laws and treaties applicable to its former sovereign as opposed to those of its new sovereign.[64] Recently, the question of state succession has arisen in connection with the absorption of East Germany by West Germany to form a unified Germany, the merger of the Yemen Arab Republic (North Yemen) and the People's Democratic Republic of Yemen (South Yemen) to form the unified Republic of Yemen, and the dissolution of the former Soviet Union, Yugoslavia and Czechoslovakia. In *ST:TNG*, the 24th-century version of state succession is at issue in two seventh-season episodes, "Journey's End"[65] and "Preemptive Strike."[66]

Both episodes involve Federation colonies located on planets that have been ceded to the Cardassian Empire as part of the Federation-Cardassian peace treaty. In "Journey's End," the colonists, who are descendants of American Indians, choose to become Cardassian citizens, subject to Cardassian rule, rather than relocate to another planet in Federation space. In contrast, the colonists of the planets concerned in "Preemptive Strike" decide to launch a war of independence rather than agree either to evacuate their planet or come under Cardassian rule. These episodes demonstrate that in the 24th century, when a planet comes under the sovereignty of another, the inhabitants become citizens of the latter planet and subject to its laws. This is consistent with the contemporary rules of state succession, as codified in the Vienna Convention on Succession of States in Respect of Treaties.[67] Applying today's precedent to *ST:TNG*, the former Federation colonists would not only lose their Federation citizenship and the rights that accrue there from, but also the benefit of any treaties that had previously been applicable to their planet as part of the Federation.

If the colonists in "Preemptive Strike" succeeded in their quest for independence, 20th-century international law would suggest their planet should be given a clean slate, with neither rights nor obligations under the treaties of its predecessor.[68] There is a modern debate over whether human rights treaties should be exempt from the clean slate theory.[69] The question is particularly relevant to *ST:TNG* since viewers learn in another episode[70] that the Federation and the Cardassian Empire are both parties to the Seldonis IV convention, which governs the treatment of prisoners of war. If the clean slate theory applies even to this convention, then the newly independent worlds would be free to mistreat any Cardassian or Federation prisoners captured during the fight for independence.

Diplomatic Relations

In "Sarek,"[71] viewers find the *Enterprise* on a diplomatic mission to host a conference between Federation Ambassador Sarek of Vulcan and a delegation from Legara IV. After difficult negotiations, the Legarans agree to diplomatic relations with the Federation. Although the accomplishment is hailed as the final triumph of Sarek's distinguished career, the episode does not indicate the legal significance of establishing diplomatic relations in the 24th century.

Under today's international law, the establishment or maintenance of diplomatic relations between states does not necessarily constitute a seal of approval.[72] Technically, the establishment of diplomatic relations means only that a state will send diplomatic representatives to a country and agree to receive that country's diplomatic representatives in turn. As a consequence of establishing such relations, diplomatic premises and diplomatic agents (and members of their families) are entitled to certain privileges and immunities, such as immunity from arrest or criminal prosecution.[73] *ST:TNG* recognizes a similar concept of diplomatic immunity in "The Mind's Eye,"[74] in which Klingon Ambassador Kell, accused of being an accomplice in the attempted assassination of the Kriosian Governor, declares that as an emissary of the Klingon High Council, he cannot be searched without his consent.

Interstellar Dispute Resolution

There exists in *ST:TNG* no counterpart to today's International Court of Justice. Nor are domestic courts seen as having jurisdiction over interstellar disputes. This is perhaps due to a broader concept of foreign sovereign immunity than is currently applied under international law. Originally under international law, states were immune in all cases from suit in the courts of other states. This absolute immunity was based on the concept that all states are equal and that no state may exercise authority over any other.[75] As states became increasingly involved in commercial activities, the absolute immunity has been replaced by a restrictive doctrine of immunity. This restrictive doctrine provides that a state can be sued in the courts of another state on issues involving activity or property that is commercial rather than public in nature.[76] Apparently, immunity in *ST:TNG* follows the original absolute rule rather than the modern doctrine.

Rather than resort to interstellar adjudication, most disputes in *ST:TNG* are settled by non-adjudicatory procedures, referred to in today's lexicon as "alternative dispute resolution."[77] Two types of non-adjudicatory measures for dispute resolution frequently mentioned in *ST:TNG* are mediation and arbitration.

Under international law, mediation is the use of a third party to induce quarreling parties to resolve their dispute. The mediator takes an active role in defining areas of difference and agreement and making proposals for compromise. The mediator can be a state, an international organization, or a private party. Similarly, the mediators portrayed in *ST:TNG* include a private individual, a starship captain and a Federation ambassador. In "Loud as a Whisper,"[78] the *Enterprise* is assigned to transport famed mediator Riva to help resolve a bitter conflict on planet Solais V. Events in "The Outrageous Okona"[79] require Captain Picard to mediate a dispute between the twin planets Altec and Straleb, whose ruling families have filed claims against erstwhile Captain Thadiun Okona. Federation Ambassador Odan is assigned in "The Host"[80] to diplomatic duty aboard the *Enterprise* to help mediate a dispute between the two moons of the Peliar Zel system.

The second form of non-adjudicatory dispute resolution portrayed in *ST:TNG* is arbitration. Under today's international law, arbitration, in contrast to mediation, leads to a binding dispute settlement on the basis of law. Arbitration differs from adjudication in that the parties themselves pick the arbitrators,[81] determine the procedure and indicate the applicable law. As mentioned above, the dispute between the Sheliak and the Federation in "The Ensigns of Command"[82] is resolved by referring it to arbitration. The episode clearly demonstrates the right under arbitration for the parties to choose their arbitrator. In "Redemption,"[83] Picard presides over an arbitration to decide which of two Klingons[84] should succeed as Leader of the High Council of the Klingon Empire. This episode focused particularly on the choice of governing law. Though Picard is a Starfleet officer, this arbitration is governed by Klingon rather than Federation rules of procedure and substantive law.

Membership in Interstellar Organizations

Several episodes of *ST:TNG* concern application by alien worlds for membership in the United Federation of Planets.[85] These episodes indicate that the criteria for membership in the Federation are similar to the criteria for membership in the United Nations as laid down in Article 4 of the U.N. Charter.[86] Article 4 requires the applicant be a peace-loving state that is ready and willing to fulfill the obligations of the Charter.

In "The Hunted,"[87] revelations about the Angosia III government's inhumane treatment of its genetically altered soldier class convince Picard to recommend against Federation membership for Angosia III.[88] One of the obligations of the U.N. Charter, which applicants must demonstrate a willingness to fulfill, is the obligation to "promot[e] and encourage respect for human rights."[89] Just as Picard recommends that the Angosian application for membership in the Federation be rejected, the United Nations may deny membership to an applicant with a record of human rights abuses.[90]

Similarly, in "Lonely Among Us,"[91] the *Enterprise* is on a diplomatic mission to transport delegates from planets Antica and Selay in the Beta Renner system to an interstellar conference in hope of resolving conflicts between the two antagonistic planets, both of which have applied for membership in the Federation. This episode indicates that the Federation, like the United Nations, will not admit an applicant that has failed to demonstrate it is "peace-loving." The principle also is illustrated in the seventh-season episode "Attached,"[92] in which Commander Riker tells the Kes ambassador he will submit the following report on Kes admission to the Federation: "Kesprytt, a deeply troubled world – social, political, military problems that they have yet to solve. The Kes, while a friendly and democratic people, are driven by suspicion, deviousness and paranoia. It is the opinion of this officer that they are not ready for membership."[93]

After admission to either the Federation or the United Nations, members might commit acts incompatible with the principles of the organization. While *ST:TNG* has not yet tackled the issue of expelling a member, Article 6 of the U.N. Charter provides a model. It stipulates that a member of the United Nations "which has persistently violated the Principles contained in the present Charter may be expelled from the Organization by the General Assembly upon recommendation of the Security Council."[94] The United Nations, however, has never acted under this provision.[95]

Interstellar Law as an Analogy to Law of the Sea

In "The Price,"[96] the *Enterprise* serves as host for negotiations for use of the Barzan wormhole, a phenomenon that would allow almost instant travel to an unexplored corner of the galaxy. The Barzan government hopes the proceeds from the sale of rights to use the wormhole will bolster the economy of its poor planet. The assumption underlying the episode is that Barzan has the right to control the wormhole as it pleases since the entrance to the wormhole is in Barzan space. This would be consistent with international law if the wormhole were viewed as an international watercourse, which is usually a river that connects land-locked states to the high seas through coastal states. There is no customary international law right of freedom of navigation in an international watercourse. Any state controlling both banks of the river is free, in the absence of a controlling treaty, to regulate and even block shipping to and from upper and lower riparian states.[97]

On the other hand, the wormhole has many of the characteristics of an international strait, which is a route between two parts of the high seas. Under the law of the sea, international straits are treated as international highways through which merchant vessels have a right to free and unlimited passage.[98] By analogy, the parties in "The Price" could have argued that Barzan's authority to control use of the wormhole was limited to prescribing regulations for safety and prevention of pollution.[99] Barzan did not have authority to auction off rights to the wormhole's exclusive use. Interestingly, the central plot of *ST:TNG*'s spin-off series *Star Trek: Deep Space Nine* concerns a stable wormhole discovered in the Bajoran system. While the Federation station *Deep Space Nine* is moved to the mouth of the wormhole to help ensure the security of Bajor, neither Bajor nor the Federation seeks to control or even regulate use of the wormhole by alien races. *ST:TNG*'s concept of wormholes can be particularly useful when exploring the reasons for the distinctions between the international law of watercourses and international straits.

Interstellar Environmental Law

Recently, large-scale climatic changes, such as depletion of the stratospheric ozone layer protecting the Earth from radiation and the possible melting of polar ice, have become the focus of attention. Similar issues have been raised in *ST:TNG*. In "Force of Nature,"[100] the *Enterprise* discovers that persistent warp (faster than light) travel in certain regions of space is causing damage to the very fabric of space and, consequently, causing gravitational shifts that change the climates of nearby planets. The episode concludes with the following colloquy between the *Enterprise*'s officers:

> Picard: Ah, we've received new directives from the Federation Council on this matter. Until we can find a way to counteract the warp field effect, the Council feels the best course is to slow the damage as much as possible. Therefore, areas of space found susceptible to warp fields will be restricted to

essential travel only and, effective immediately, all Federation vehicles will be restricted to
a speed of Warp 5, except in cases of
extreme emergency.

Worf: The Klingons will observe these
restrictions, but the Romulans will not.

Troi: And what about the Ferengi, and the
Cardassians for that matter?

Picard: The Federation is sharing all our
data with warp capable species. We can only
hope that they realize it's in their own interest to take similar action.[101]

The above exchange tells us several things about the state of interstellar
environmental law in the 24th century. First, it indicates there is a "necessity"
limitation to the protection of the environment, i.e., notwithstanding the harm
to the environment, "essential" travel is still permitted and speeds over Warp 5
are allowed in "cases of emergency." This concept is similar to 20th-century
provisions of the law of war that permit destruction of the environment when
"justified by military necessity."[102] In contrast to interstellar law in the 24th century, however, the international law exception for environmental damage justified by necessity is limited to the context of armed conflict. During peacetime,
states are required without exception to "ensure that activities under their jurisdiction or control are so conducted as not to cause damage by pollution to
other States and their environment."[103] The question of which rule is better suited to the 24th-century environmental situation is likely to lead to a lively classroom discussion.[104]

Second, the episode indicates there is no 24th-century counterpart to
today's customary law concerning the environment.[105] While the Federation can
obtain the agreement of its allies to comply,[106] it must hope other worlds[107] will
voluntarily follow the Federation's practice out of self-interest. Despite the existence of customary international law with vague admonitions about damaging
the environment, today's international environmental law, too, has proceeded
largely through negotiation of treaties. Recent examples include the 1990
Protocol on Substances that Deplete the Ozone Layer[108] and the 1992
Convention on Climate Change.[109] Like the Federation, the international com-

munity must hope key countries will ratify and comply with these instruments.

Perhaps the closest analogy to the hazard described in "Force of Nature" is the contemporary problem of orbiting space debris.[110] Like the fictional hazard, orbiting debris is most hazardous in regions of space that are particularly suited to spacecraft operations.[111] In addition, regulation of space debris is extremely limited.[112] International control of debris, such as it is, is effected through market incentives derived from international accords such as The Outer Space Treaty and the Convention on International Liability for Damage Caused by Space Objects.[113]

Just as the Federation Council has unilaterally promulgated environmentally friendly administrative regulations for the operation of its vessels, the United States has produced its own standards and operating procedures for the control of space debris. As early as 1981, the National Aeronautics and Space Administration (NASA) vented propellants and other pressurized gases from the spent upper stages of Delta launch vehicles in order to reduce the likelihood of an explosion in orbit.[114] The first formal policy statement from the U.S. government on the subject of space debris appeared in 1987.[115] Unwilling to merely lead by example, the United States has undertaken the task of prompting other space-faring nations to follow suit.[116] It would seem, however, that the regulatory arm of the United Federation of Planets is less willing to exert its influence to encourage adherence to mutually beneficial environmental standards.

Terrorism

Several of *ST:TNG*'s episodes deal with terrorism, particularly the offense of hostage taking. For example, in "Samaritan Snare,"[117] a Pakled ship uses a fake distress call to capture *Enterprise* Chief Engineer Geordi LaForge in an unsuccessful attempt to gain access to Federation weapons technology. "Too Short a Season"[118] finds the *Enterprise* transporting Admiral Mark Jameson to planet Mordan IV to negotiate the release of Federation hostages. While at planet Rutia IV to deliver medical supplies following reports of local unrest on the planet in "The High Ground,"[119] *Enterprise* Chief Medical Officer Beverly Crusher and Captain Picard are taken hostage by Ansatan separatist movement members, who demand Federation intervention in their plight.

Hostage taking has likewise been a persistent problem for today's international community. Efforts by the international community to combat such acts have led to the conclusion of the International Hostage Taking Convention.[120]

The convention obligates states to cooperate to resolve hostage-taking incidents and to prosecute alleged offenders found within their territory or to extradite them to another state for prosecution. Moreover, in 1985 the U.N. Security Council adopted a resolution condemning all acts of hostage taking and abduction and declaring that all states are obligated to prevent such acts.[121] Although the problem is pervasive in the 24th century, there seems to be no interstellar parallel in _ST:TNG_ to today's international law against terrorism.

In the 24th century, bargaining with terrorists for the release of hostages seems to be the standard operating procedure. Admiral Jameson in "Too Short a Season" reveals that his celebrated negotiations, which led to the release of Federation hostages on Mordan IV some 45 years ago, was actually an arms-for-hostages deal with marked similarities to the events surrounding the Iran-Contra scandal. "The High Ground" shows the _Enterprise_ crew trying unsuccessfully to bargain with the leader of a group of IRA-like terrorists, Kyril Finn, for the release of Doctor Crusher and Captain Picard. In "Ensign Ro,"[122] Starfleet authorizes Picard to offer amnesty to Bajoran terrorists who have attacked a Federation settlement on planet Solarion IV in return for their promise to discontinue attacks on Federation outposts. Similarly, in "The Vengeance Factor,"[123] Picard negotiates a truce with the Acamarian outlaw group called the Gatherers, which was responsible for terrorist raids against Federation outposts near the Acamarian system. It is surprising that the worlds in _ST:TNG_ regularly bargain with terrorists and that the Federation would grant them amnesty for their crimes. This is perhaps an unwarranted departure from today's conventional wisdom that bargaining with terrorists only leads to more terrorism.[124]

Extradition

Extradition is the surrender by one state to another of an individual accused or convicted of a crime within the jurisdiction of the requesting state.[125] Until the 19th century, extradition of fugitives was rare and was a matter of sovereign discretion rather than obligation. Faced with the growing internationalization of crime, states began to conclude bilateral extradition treaties requiring the extradition of fugitives when the terms of the treaties were met. Under U.S. law, a fugitive cannot be surrendered except pursuant to such a treaty.[126] This is not the law of the Federation in _ST:TNG_.

Six of _ST:TNG_'s episodes involve questions of extradition. Not once, however, is the existence of a relevant extradition treaty mentioned. Nor does

ST:TNG concern itself with any of the grounds for denying extradition traditionally found in extradition treaties – e.g., that the act is not a crime under the
law of both states; that the act is considered a political offense; that the requesting state seeks to try or punish the fugitive for crimes in addition to the crimes
for which (s)he was extradited; that the requested state is not obligated to surrender its nationals; or that the requested state views the requesting state's proceedings as fundamentally unfair.[127] A survey of *ST:TNG*'s extradition practice
demonstrates it is foreign from the modern-day conception.

In "The Hunted,"[128] Captain Picard agrees to turn over to Angosian authorities a prisoner escaped from a high-security penal colony, despite evidence that
the prisoner's only crime is he had been an Angosian soldier, and after the war
the Angosian government perceived all its soldiers as a threat to society. In
today's practice, extradition of the fugitive would be denied on grounds that the
crime of being a former soldier is not a crime under Federation law (lack of double criminality) or that, under the circumstances, the act constitutes a political
offense.

An opposite result is reached in "Transfigurations."[129] In that episode, the
Enterprise discovers the wreckage of a small space vehicle and rescues a survivor, referred to as "John Doe," who suffers from memory loss and appears to
be undergoing a mysterious cellular mutation. A Zalkonian vessel arrives, and
the vessel's captain demands the surrender of Doe for crimes against his people.
Captain Picard refuses Doe's surrender when Doe is found to be metamorphos-
ing into an energy-based being and Picard learns that the Zalkonian captain's
mission is to prevent this evolution by hunting down all mutating Zalkonians.
Here, though Picard cites only broad humanitarian grounds for his refusal to
surrender Doe, the denial of the Zalkon request could have been justified under
the principle of double criminality or the political offense exception.

In "A Matter of Perspective,"[130] Commander Riker is accused of murdering
Dr. Nel Apgar, an intergallactically respected scientist. Local Tanugan authorities demand the *Enterprise* surrender Riker for prosecution. Under Tanugan
law, alleged offenders are presumed guilty. Although Captain Picard negotiates
a stay of extradition pending an investigation, he never questions his obligation
to turn Riker over to the Tanugans if the investigation does not prove Riker's
innocence. Following today's extradition practice, Picard could have denied
Riker's extradition on the ground that the Federation is not bound to surrender
its own nationals, that Riker has diplomatic immunity[131] or that the Federation
would view proceedings under the Tanugan presumption of guilt as incompatible with fundamental due process.[132]

The *Enterprise* transports a Vulcan ambassador to the Romulan Neutral

Zone for negotiations in "Data's Day."[133] When it is revealed the ambassador is really a Romulan spy who has been conducting covert operations in Federation territory, Picard does nothing to seek her return for prosecution. Although Picard is later chastised by his superiors in Starfleet for his inaction,[134] an extradition request in these circumstances may have been deemed futile for a variety of reasons. It is possible that no extradition relations existed between the Federation and the Romulans, since the two worlds had not communicated for the last 53 years, or that espionage is deemed a political offense for which extradition is regularly denied.

In "Heart of Glory,"[135] the *Enterprise* takes custody of three renegade Klingons who commandeered a Talarian ship and attacked and destroyed a Klingon cruiser. A Klingon ship approaches and demands Picard surrender the Klingon renegades as soon as the two ships are in range. Picard agrees to hand them over despite Lieutenant Worf's protestations that "they will be tried and executed."[136] This was a particularly surprising result given that an earlier episode established the Federation has outlawed the death penalty.[137] A year after "Heart of Glory" first aired, this issue was litigated before the European Court of Human Rights in the Soering case.[138] In that case, a German national named Jens Soering sought to prevent his extradition from the United Kingdom to the United States, where he would face the death penalty for his crimes. The court blocked Soering's extradition on the grounds it would expose him to a real risk of inhuman or degrading punishment in violation of the European Convention on Human Rights. After the court's decision, the prosecutor amended the charges to remove the offense of capital murder, and the United Kingdom then extradited Soering for trial in the United States. Similarly, Picard could have insisted on an assurance that the death penalty would not be imposed before surrendering the renegades. That he did not is further evidence of the underdevelopment of extradition law in the 24th century. As is apparent from these episodes, the absence of rules governing the surrender of fugitives can lead to international conflict.

Extraterritorial Jurisdiction

Several episodes involving extradition indicate *ST:TNG*'s expansive concept of what is known as "nationality-based jurisdiction." In "The Drumhead,"[139] Klingon exobiologist J'Ddan is found responsible for the transmission of technical schematics from the *Enterprise* to the Romulans and is arrested and referred to Klingon authorities on charges of espionage. Under today's international law, the Klingons' basis of jurisdiction over J'Ddan would be under the nationality principle, i.e., that the Klingon government has authority to prosecute Klingon citizens for certain crimes committed outside Klingon territory.[140]

The crime of treason (which would encompass J'Ddan's acts) is one of the few crimes for which the United States asserts criminal jurisdiction over its citizens for acts committed outside U.S. territory.[141] In contrast, civil law countries, such as France and Germany, exercise jurisdiction over any crime committed by their citizens abroad. At least one alien society portrayed in *ST:TNG*, the Ullians, was seen to exercise similarly expansive nationality-based jurisdiction over its citizens. In "Violations,"[142] an Ullian found to have committed a form of rape involving memory invasion aboard the *Enterprise* is returned to Ullian authorities for prosecution. In contrast, the United States' nationality-based jurisdiction does not extend to rape. Thus, unlike the Ullians, under existing law the United States could not prosecute one of its citizens for committing a rape abroad.

The Federation presumably had concurrent jurisdiction in these two episodes since the crimes occurred aboard a Federation-registered starship.[143] Under contemporary international law, the state of registry has jurisdiction over crimes committed aboard its vessels, aircraft and spacecraft.[144] The situations presented in "The Drumhead" and "Violations," therefore, can be used to explore international law issues of conflict of jurisdiction and choice of law – i.e., if both the Federation and the Klingons/Ullians had asserted jurisdiction, where would the case be tried and whose law would apply?[145]

Interestingly, the possibility of asserting concurrent jurisdiction was never raised in "Heart of Glory," discussed above in the context of extradition. The crimes for which the Klingon renegades in that episode were accused, seizing a space vessel and using it to attack another, could have been analogous to today's crimes of piracy and maritime terrorism, over which all nations have universal jurisdiction to prosecute offenders.[146] If the Federation could have asserted such jurisdiction, it could have conducted its own trial of the renegades, thereby ensuring that both the process and punishment comported with Federation notions of fairness.

Extraterritorial Apprehensions

In "Encounter at Farpoint,"[147] Picard asks Commander Riker if he would object to "a clearly illegal kidnapping"[148] of the leader of the Bandi, Groppler Zorn, who had refused to inform the *Enterprise* of the identity and nature of an attacking alien ship. Just as Picard orders that Groppler Zorn be "beamed aboard," a being claiming to be part of an all-knowing super race known as the Q, which has been monitoring the *Enterprise*'s mission in order to judge the human race, materializes on board the *Enterprise* and tells Picard he has condemned the human race by failing to follow even his own rules. This brief exchange touches upon one of the most controversial issues of modern international law: the right of authorities of one state to abduct a person from another state without the latter's consent. Picard's acknowledgment that the kidnapping would be "clearly illegal"[149] suggests the Federation recognizes a principle analogous to the international law rule that unconsented abductions abroad are considered a violation of the territorial state's sovereignty.[150]

There is growing debate over whether there should be an exception to the prohibition on unconsented extraterritorial law enforcement action for situations involving the right of self-defense. The right of self-defense might, for example, justify a hostage-rescue attempt by the authorities of one state in the territory of another.[151] It also might justify intervention to apprehend terrorists who constitute a continuing threat to the intervening state.[152] The expanding notion of self-defense is, however, extremely vulnerable to abuse, and it is noteworthy that Picard does not invoke the notion to excuse his actions, though the kidnapping of Groppler Zorn could be seen as necessary to repel an alien attack.

Asylum and Refugee Status

A number of *ST:TNG*'s episodes deal with requests by individuals for asylum aboard the *Enterprise*. For example, in "The Defector,"[153] Romulan Admiral Jarok flees across the Neutral Zone and requests asylum aboard the *Enterprise*. He is willing to trade military secrets for asylum and says he wishes to defect because of the blind aggression of the new Romulan command. In "The Mind's Eye,"[154] Klingon Special Emissary Kell, accused of being an accomplice to the Romulan plot to assassinate Kriosian Governor Vagh, requests asylum aboard the *Enterprise* rather than face "Klingon justice."[155] Picard says he will grant asylum only if Kell is cleared of the charges. In another episode,[156] Picard agrees to give asylum to 60-year-old Kaelon scientist Timicin so he does not have to face the Kaelon practice of "Resolution" (voluntary suicide at age 60). In "I, Borg,"[157] Picard offers asylum to a young Borg[158] who achieves individuality aboard the *Enterprise*. Picard grants asylum in "The Masterpiece Society"[159] to Hannah Bates and 22 other colonists of Moab IV who wish to leave their genetically engineered bubble-society after contact with the *Enterprise* crew. Picard tells the leader of the bubble-society, "If you force them to stay, you will be suppressing their human rights .... I cannot ignore the request of humans who wish to be transported away from here. If they choose to leave, the *Enterprise* will not turn them away."[160]

These situations suggest Picard, as captain of the *Enterprise*, has wide discretion and authority over the granting of asylum to aliens. No rules are mentioned that restrict or counsel his decision. In contrast, the current-day practice of granting asylum is the subject of a number of international conventions that permit giving asylum only for political refugees and in cases of humanitarian concern.[161] Moreover, according to the U.N. Universal Declaration of Human Rights, the right to asylum "may not be invoked in the case of prosecutions genuinely arising from non-political crimes."[162]

The term "asylum" is generally used only with regard to the granting of sanctuary within a foreign state's embassy of an individual wanted by the authorities of the territorial state. While in orbit around a planet, the *Enterprise* can be likened to a diplomatic embassy, capable of granting asylum. Alternatively, the *Enterprise* can be viewed as an extension of Federation territory, and, therefore, rules relating to refugee status rather than asylum should apply.[163] Under the Convention Relating to the Status of Refugees, states are prohibited from returning a refugee to a state where his or her life or freedom is threatened because of race, religion, nationality or political beliefs.[164] The convention provides an exception for persons who have committed serious nonpolitical offenses.[165]

Of those requesting asylum in *ST:TNG*, only Kaelon scientist Timicin and the young Borg Hugh would clearly qualify for asylum or refugee status under international law. Upon Timicin's return to Kaelon III, he would likely receive ill treatment because of his political opposition to the Kaelon tradition of "Resolution." The young Borg faced forcible assimilation through a form of brainwashing to suppress his yearnings for individual expression. In contrast, Romulan Admiral Jarok and Klingon Special Emissary Kell would be excluded from asylum or refugee status because they have committed serious, non-political offenses. Similarly, the 23 Moab IV colonists desire to leave not because they are facing persecution, but because they wish to travel throughout the galaxy. On the other hand, the Universal Declaration of Human Rights[166] states that "everyone has the right to leave any country, including his own, and to return to his country."[167] This provision might be read as suggesting that international law recognizes a right to asylum for persons whose right to travel abroad is being abridged.

War Crimes and Crimes Against Humanity

Several of *ST:TNG*'s episodes serve as a useful starting point for a discussion of international humanitarian law – the law of war. The issue is explored in "I, Borg,"[168] when the *Enterprise* crew captures an injured Borg, nurses him back to health and debates whether to return him to the Borg collective with a computer virus that would destroy the entire Borg race. Dr. Crusher makes the point that "even in war there are rules; you don't just kill civilians indiscriminately."[169]

Apparently, the Romulans do not feel bound by such rules. In "The Mind's Eye,"[170] the Romulans subject *Enterprise* Chief Engineer Geordi LaForge to "mental reprogramming" to induce him to assassinate the governor of the Klingon Kriosian colony. This "brainwashing" would constitute a grave breach of the Geneva Convention if it occurred on 20th-century Earth.[171] The Geneva Convention prohibits such acts during war or armed conflict, requires the state whose military authorities have committed such violations to bring the perpetrators to punishment and authorizes other states to try the perpetrators if they obtain custody over them. Surprisingly, the episode never references any 24th-century equivalent to the Geneva Convention that would prohibit mental reprogramming of captured enemy officers.

In contrast, such a treaty provision is mentioned in "Chain of Command, Part II,"[172] in which the Cardassians capture and torture Captain Picard. Picard warns his captors that "torture is expressly prohibited by the Seldonis IV Convention governing the treatment of prisoners of war."[173] Since Picard was captured during a covert mission that the Federation would not acknowledge, the Cardassians claimed he was not entitled to the convention's protection. The Geneva Convention would provide even less protection under the circumstances since it is applicable only during war or armed conflict[174] and applies only to persons wearing a distinctive uniform, not to spies.[175]

While the Geneva Convention applies to war crimes, crimes against humanity committed both during war or peace are prohibited by the Convention on the Prevention and Punishment of the Crime of Genocide.[176] The Genocide Convention defines "genocide" as murder, deportation and other acts committed with the intent to destroy a racial, national, ethnic or religious population in whole or in part.[177] Several episodes indicate that *ST:TNG* does not have any analogue to the Genocide Convention.

In "The Survivors,"[178] a powerful being known as a Douwd admits to Captain Picard that, in a fit of anger, he wiped out an entire race of beings who were responsible for the death of his human wife. Picard responds, "We're not qualified to judge you; we have no law to fit your crime."[179]

In "Haven,"[180] viewers learn the people of the planet Tarella, having fled their war-devastated world, have been hunted to virtual extinction because they are carriers of deadly biological warfare agents. While the crew of the *Enterprise* expresses regret at the Tarellian tragedy, there is no mention during the episode that the systematic extermination of the Tarellians constituted a crime against humanity or violation of interstellar law. Rather, Picard bases his refusal to destroy the last Tarellian ship solely on the ground that "Federation policy requires that we assist life forms in need, which must include the Tarellians."[181]

In "The Vengeance Factor,"[182] the Federation supports efforts by the leader of Acamar to offer amnesty to the Gatherers, ending nearly a century of inter-stellar piracy and terrorism. The leader of the Gatherers, Chorgan, is a member of the Lornack clan, which had been responsible for the massacre of the Tralesta clan 80 years earlier. There have been similar modern-day proposals to give amnesty to those responsible for atrocities in former Yugoslavia in return for their cooperation in the peace process. The United States has rejected such proposals as inconsistent with international law.[183] In particular, the granting of amnesty to those responsible for genocide would be incompatible with provi-sions of the Genocide Convention, which provides an absolute obligation to prosecute and punish the perpetrators of genocide.[184] Moreover, there is no statute of limitations for genocide.[185] "The Vengeance Factor"[186] avoids the issue by leaving it unclear whether Chorgan personally participated in the slaughter of the Tralesta clan or was merely a descendent of one of those responsible.

The Principle of "Jus Cogens"

Under contemporary international law, a treaty is void if it conflicts with certain peremptory norms recognized by the international community.[187] Slavery, which is criminal under international law, is one such norm.[188] Under this principle, known as "jus cogens" (or peremptory norms), an international agreement resulting in the enslavement of a population would not be valid.

In "Devil's Due,"[189] the *Enterprise* visits planet Ventax II, a world whose people are in the grip of widespread panic due to the anticipated arrival of Ardra, a legendary supernatural being. It seems the pollution-plagued, war-torn Ventaxians made a pact with Ardra generations ago: 1000 years of peace and health in return for their eternal slavery afterward. Picard tries to convince the Ventaxian leader, Jared, that his people are responsible for their own prosperity.

But when Ardra begins to demonstrate her powers, Jared agrees to submit to her will, pursuant to the contract, until the crew of the *Enterprise* locates Ardra's hidden ship and power source and reveals her as a con-artist. Surprisingly, in contesting the validity of the contract, Picard does not argue the principle of "jus cogens."

From "Devil's Due,"[190] viewers can deduce either that interstellar law does not have a concept comparable to "jus cogens"[191] or that slavery is not uniformly condemned by the interstellar community.

Self-Defense Justifications for Use of Force

Article 2(4) of the U.N. Charter provides that "[a]ll Members shall refrain in their international relations from the threat or use of force against the territorial integrity or political independence of any state."[192] Article 51 of the charter provides an exception for the use of force in collective or individual self-defense "if an armed attack occurs against a Member of the United Nations."[193] The interplay between the prohibition on the use of force and the exception for self-defense is at issue in several episodes of *ST:TNG*.

In "Redemption,"[194] Starfleet sends an armada of 23 starships, including the *Enterprise*, to blockade a Romulan convoy suspected of being the source of supplies to forces trying to overthrow the ruling Klingon regime in a civil war. The parallels between "Redemption" and the situation leading to the 1984 International Court of Justice (ICJ) case between Nicaragua and the United States are unmistakable. Nicaragua brought proceedings before the World Court charging the United States with unlawful use of force against Nicaragua and its vessels. The United States argued it was acting in collective self-defense (on behalf of El Salvador) in response to Nicaragua's support for Salvadorian rebels. The ICJ found that Nicaragua's financing and arming the rebels did not rise to the level of "an armed attack" against El Salvador and, thus, the United States did not have a right to use force against Nicaragua in self-defense on El Salvador's behalf.[195] If an analogue to the Nicaragua precedent were to apply in the 24th century, the Federation would not be justified in blockading Romulan ships since the provision of support to rebels does not constitute an armed attack that would justify the right to self-defense.

In "The Wounded,"[196] Starfleet orders the *Enterprise* to prevent a Federation starship commanded by Captain Ben Maxwell from attacking Cardassian vessels. Starfleet issues the order despite learning Captain Maxwell's actions were an attempt to prevent a suspected Cardassian military offensive

against the Federation. This episode raises the issue of the legitimacy of anticipatory self-defense under international law. The question of whether self-
defense requires an actual armed attack or whether it is permissible in anticipation of an attack has given rise to much controversy among international
lawyers. It has been argued that states faced with a perceived danger of immediate attack cannot be expected to await the attack like sitting ducks before
they can lawfully respond.[197] This justification was cited by Israel when it
bombed an Iraqi nuclear reactor in 1981. The action of Captain Maxwell seems
equally premised on this rationale. Like Starfleet in "The Wounded," however,
the U.N. Security Council rejected the Israeli position and condemned the
bombing as a violation of international law.[198] The official statements of the
Security Council members indicate that the right of anticipatory self-defense is
limited to situations in which an attack is imminent.[199]

ST:TNG's attitude toward anticipatory self-defense is not consistent, how-
ever. In "The Defector,"[200] the *Enterprise* picks up Romulan Admiral Alidar
Jarok, who claims to have defected to warn of a potentially destabilizing new
Romulan outpost at planet Nelvana III, inside the Neutral Zone. Because of the
potential threat to the Federation, Picard orders the *Enterprise* into the Neutral
Zone, in violation of the Treaty of Algeron,[201] to investigate Jarok's claim (which
turns out to be false), nearly provoking a renewal of hostilities with the
Romulans. Picard's preemptive actions in "The Defector" suggest a more
expansive concept of anticipatory self-defense than his actions in "The
Wounded," perhaps warranted by the greater and more imminent threat posed
by the existence of a Romulan outpost in the Neutral Zone.

Non-interference in Domestic Affairs

Article 2(7) of the U.N. Charter provides that "nothing contained in the
present Charter shall authorize the United Nations to intervene in matters
which are essentially within the domestic jurisdiction of any State."[202] The ICJ
has recognized the principle of non-intervention as part of customary international law.[203] Interstellar law, as portrayed in *ST:TNG*, recognizes a similar principle contained in Starfleet General Order Number One, known as the Prime
Directive.

No less than 13 episodes of *ST:TNG* deal with the Prime Directive.[204]
Captain Picard defines the Prime Directive in "First Contact"[205] as prohibiting
members of the Federation from interfering in a culture's natural development.[206] In "Half a Life,"[207] Picard says the Prime Directive "forbids us to inter-

fere with the social order of any planet."[208] He cites Prime Directive considerations in "The Hunted"[209] as justification for declining Starfleet intervention in an uprising of soldiers who had been imprisoned by the Angosian government for fear of having warriors loose in normal society. In "Symbiosis,"[210] the *Enterprise* discovers two planets – one is addicted to the drug Felissium, and the other produces and supplies the drug at a tremendous price. Deferring to the Prime Directive, Captain Picard prohibits his medical officer from informing the planet of addicts that the drug no longer has any medicinal value and is instead simply a narcotic. In "The Outcast,"[211] Picard, citing Prime Directive considerations, refuses to intervene with the J'naii, a race that has outlawed gender, to halt the prosecution of a J'naii who had engaged in an unlawful relationship with Commander Riker of the *Enterprise*. Evidently, the Prime Directive applies to worlds in alliance with the Federation as well as to foreign worlds. In "The Mind's Eye,"[212] Picard states that the "Federation would not interfere in the internal affairs of the Klingon Empire."[213]

Although the Prime Directive appears to have no exceptions, it is subject to frequent breach, apparently without penalty when accompanied by compelling justification. In "The Drumhead,"[214] a Starfleet admiral states that Captain Picard has violated the Prime Directive on nine occasions. In "A Matter of Time,"[215] Picard says to the time traveler Rasmussen: "You know of the Prime Directive, which forbids us from interfering in the natural evolution of a society. I've disregarded it on more than one occasion because I thought it was the right thing to do."[216] Such an occasion occurred in "Pen Pals,"[217] an episode in which Lieutenant Commander Data responds to a radio distress call from a life form on planet Drema IV, even though such a response violated Prime Directive protection. After hearing the plea for help from what sounds like a very young and frightened child, Captain Picard determines that assistance to reverse geologic instability on the planet is appropriate even though such intervention further violates the Prime Directive. In "Justice,"[218] a member of the *Enterprise* on shore leave on planet Rubicun III[219] accidentally commits a minor transgression of local laws (he steps on a flower bed), but authorities impose the death sentence in accordance with planetary law. Captain Picard violates the Prime Directive by securing the crew member's release in contravention of local law.

The debate over whether Picard was justified in ignoring the Prime Directive in these situations mirrors the contemporary international law debate over the right of "humanitarian intervention."[220] The rationale has been raised to justify intervention to prevent gross violations of human rights[221] or to protect nationals from imminent peril or injury in a foreign country,[222] although most governments believe the "scope for abusing such a right argues strongly against its creation."[223] If there is a humanitarian exception to the Prime Directive, it has been no more consistently applied than our own concept of humanitarian intervention. In "Ensign Ro,"[224] for example, viewers learn the Federation has refused for years to intervene in the Cardassian subjugation of Bajor and their gross violations of the Bajorans' human rights.

Conclusion

The preceding survey of international law issues appearing in *ST:TNG* has shown that, with just a handful of exceptions, 24th-century interstellar law as portrayed in the series is remarkably similar to today's international law. Because of these similarities, and the immense popularity of the series, *ST:TNG* can be an effective pedagogical aid to teaching the fundamental principles of international law.[225]

In drawing upon the interstellar law of *ST:TNG*, the teacher needs to be aware of the major differences between interstellar law and contemporary international law, namely: (1) interstellar law does not recognize the principle of customary international law; (2) there is no interstellar counterpart to the ICJ; (3) interstellar law adheres to an outdated doctrine of absolute sovereign immunity; (4) interstellar law does not recognize the traditional grounds for refusing to extradite a fugitive; (5) the Federation lacks universal jurisdiction to prosecute persons responsible for terrorism or piracy; and (6) a Federation captain's authority to grant asylum is apparently unrestricted.

These distinctions are not the result of sloppy research on the part of *ST:TNG*'s technical and production staff. Rather, most are the consequence of series creator Gene Roddenberry's particular conception of the future. Given Roddenberry's goal of a television series revolving around the adventures of a space-age Captain Horatio Hornblower,[226] it is not surprising that much of the international structure would be based upon the law as it existed during the heyday of the fighting sail. In contrast to our contemporary world, in which international telephone communications are instantaneous and where travel from any one point on the globe to any other can be accomplished in under a day's time, the planets on *ST:TNG* sometimes go for decades without communicating with one another, and the time to travel from one planet to another (even at warp speed) is measured in days, weeks or years – not hours.

In such a decentralized legal system, there would not be enough repetition of practice to develop customary law. Planets that rarely communicate with one another would be even less likely than today's states to submit disputes to uncertain, time-consuming and troublesome litigation before a panel of potentially hostile judges. Since disputes between planets would largely be about territory and other sovereignty issues rather than about commercial transactions, planets would insist on absolute immunity from liability in a foreign world's courts as a manifestation of the perfect equality and absolute independence of sovereigns. Given the difficulties and time-consuming nature of interstellar travel and the myriad of available destinations, the number of criminals fleeing to foreign worlds would be relatively small. Consequently, planets would be more likely to apply an analogue to pre-19th-century extradition law, which regarded surrender of fugitives a matter of sovereign discretion. Similarly, since concepts of fairness and justice vary widely throughout the interstellar system, it would not be appropriate to restrict the discretion of the captain of a starship over questions of asylum. Viewed within this context, even these deviations from contemporary international law can be used to encourage students' thinking about the historic origins, rationale and development of the law of nations.

Of the departures from international law portrayed in *ST:TNG*, only the absence of universal jurisdiction to try persons for piracy seems to defy any logical or historical explanation. Since the 14th century, pirates were regarded as international outlaws and the enemies of all mankind who could be arrested and taken in for trial by any state.[227] In modern times, universal jurisdiction has been extended to cover war criminals, hostage-takers, aircraft hijackers and saboteurs. In the 24th century, piracy seems to be similarly heinous, pirates appear to be equally difficult to apprehend and there seems to be a universal interest in their prompt arrest and punishment. It is therefore puzzling that in episode after episode, the Federation fails to assert its jurisdiction to try space-age pirates or terrorists who come within the custody of the *Enterprise*.

That this is the only instance in which *ST:TNG*'s portrayal of international law misses the mark is an extraordinary achievement considering the makers of the series set out to create a high-quality television entertainment program, not a treatise or documentary on international law. It is their outstanding success in creating a realistic vision of the future that has made *ST:TNG*, and the other series in the *Star Trek* family, "a permanent fixture in America's cultural landscape."

Appendix

EPISODE TITLE	EPISODE #	INTERNATIONAL LEGAL ISSUES
"Attached"	160	International Organizations (membership)
"Chain of Command, Part II"	137	Humanitarian Law (prisoners of war)
"Code of Honor"	3	Treaties (scope)
"Contagion"	36	Treaties (territorial boundaries)
"Data's Day"	84	Extradition; Treaties (territorial boundaries)
"The Defector"	57	Asylum; Self-Defense (anticipatory); Treaties (territorial boundaries)
"Devil's Due"	86	Jus Cogens
"The Drumhead"	94	Extradition; Extraterritorial Jurisdiction; Sovereignty (violation of non-intervention)
"Encounter at Farpoint"	1	Extraterritorial Apprehension
"The Enemy"	54	Treaties (territorial boundaries)
"Ensign Ro"	102	Sovereignty (non-intervention); Terrorism
"The Ensigns of Command"	49	Treaties (interpretation); Arbitration
"First Contact"	88	Sovereignty (non-intervention)
"Force of Nature"	158	International Environmental Law; Space Law
"Future Imperfect"	81	Treaties (territorial boundaries)
"Half a Life"	95	Asylum; Sovereignty (non-intervention)
"Haven"	10	Genocide, Space Law
"Heart of Glory"	19	Extradition
"The High Ground"	160	Terrorism
"The Host"	96	Mediation
"The Hunted"	58	Extradition; International Organizations (membership); Sovereignty (non-intervention)
"I, Borg"	122	Asylum; Humanitarian Law (conduct of hostilities)
"Journey's End"	172	State Succession
"Justice"	7	Sovereignty (exception to non-intervention)
"Lonely Among Us"	6	International Organizations (membership)
"Loud as a Whisper"	30	Mediation
"Lower Decks"	167	Treaties (enforceability)
"Manhunt"	44	International Organizations
"The Masterpiece Society"	112	Asylum
"A Matter of Perspective"	61	Extradition
"A Matter of Time"	108	Sovereignty (exception to non-intervention)
"The Mind's Eye"	97	Asylum; Diplomatic Relations (privileges and immunities); Humanitarian Law (prisoners of war); Sovereignty (non-intervention)
"The Outcast"	116	Sovereignty (non-intervention)
"The Outrageous Okona"	29	Mediation
"The *Pegasus*"	164	Treaties (individual responsibility for breach)
"Pen Pals"	40	Sovereignty (violation of non-intervention)
"Preemptive Strike"	176	State Succession
"The Price"	55	Law of the Sea
"Redemption II"	99	Arbitration (choice of law); Peacekeeping; Self-Defense; Treaties (collective security)
"Samaritan Snare"	42	Terrorism
"Sarek"	70	Diplomatic Relations
"Suddenly Human"	77	Peace Treaty
"Symbiosis"	21	Sovereignty (non-intervention)
"Too Short a Season"	15	Terrorism
"Transfigurations"	72	Extradition
"The Vengeance Factor"	56	Humanitarian Law (amnesty); Terrorism
"Violations"	111	Extraterritorial Jurisdiction
"The Wounded"	85	Self-Defense (anticipatory); Peace Treaty

Endnotes

1. Paul Joseph & Sharon Carton, "The Law of the Federation: Images of Law, Lawyers, and the Legal System in *Star Trek: The Next Generation*," *24 U. Tol. L. Rev.* 43 (1992).

2. The Nova Southeastern University clipping service has documented 175 newspaper articles and radio stories about the article. See, e.g., Richard Cole, "Lawyering at Warp Speed," *L.A. Times*, Mar. 28, 1993 (Sunday Home Edition TV Times Section), at 7; Richard Cole, "*Star Trek* Gives Lawyers Hope," *Toronto Star*, Mar. 23, 1993, at D4; "Enterprising Critique of the Law," *Chi. Daily L. Bull.*, Mar. 8, 1993, at 3; Kurt Greenbaum, "Law Professors Boldly Go Into *Star Trek* Research," *Orlando Sentinel Trib.*, Mar. 1, 1993, at D1; Pat Sims, "*Star Trek:* The Next Litigation," *Nat. L.J.*, Apr. 19, 1993, at 43. See also Mark A. Altman, "UFP Law: The Legal Quagmires of the Federation," *Star Trek: The Official Fan Club*, Sept./Oct. 1993, at 2.

3. The series ran from 1987 to 1994.

4. See Steve McClellan, "*Star Trek: The Next Generation* Bests *Wheel of Fortune* in Ratings," *Broadcasting*, Dec. 2, 1991, at 6.

5. Joseph & Carton, supra note 1, at 80-84.

6. Id. at 72-80.

7. Id. at 67-72.

8. Strictly speaking, virtually all of the interstellar legal issues raised in *ST:TNG* might properly be characterized as falling within the relatively nascent field of "space law." Many of the issues raised by the series have been recognized by space law commentators as worthy of future analysis. Nevertheless, the level of technological development and interspecies interaction in *ST:TNG* is so far beyond the scope of the existing aerospace literature that, with few exceptions, the issues raised by the series are more akin to terrestrial international law than contemporary space law.

9. E.g., *L.A. Law* (NBC television broadcast), *Law and Order* (NBC television broadcast), *Equal Justice* (ABC television broadcast), *The People's Court* (syndicated), and *Matlock* (NBC and ABC television broadcasts).

10. Ethics courses based on *Star Trek* have been offered at some of the nation's most prestigious colleges. See Jeffrey H. Mills, "Star Trek in the Classroom," in *The Best Of The Best Of Trek* 324 (Walter Irwin & G.B. Love eds., 1990) (describing the course entitled "The Cultural Relevance of *Star Trek*" taught at Oberlin College in Ohio).

11. See, e.g., Richard A. Posner, *Law And Literature: A Misunderstood Relation* (1988); Theodor Meron, "The Laws of War and *Henry V*," in *Interpreting Law And Literature: A Hermeneutic Reader* (Sanford Levinson & Steven Mailloux eds., 1988) [hereinafter *Hermeneutic Reader*]; Charles Fried, "'Sonnet LXV'" and the 'Black Ink' of the Framers' Intention," in *Hermeneutic Reader*, supra.

12. See Richard Weisberg, "On the Use and Abuse of Nietzsche for Modern Constitutional Theory," in *Hermeneutic Reader*, supra note 11, at 181.

13. See Larry M. Wertheim, "Law, Literature and Morality in the Novels of Charles Dickens," *20 Wm. Mitchell L. Rev. 111 (1994);* Allen Boyer, "The Antiquarian and the Utilitarian: Charles Dickens vs. James Fitzjames Stephen," *56 Tenn. L. Rev.* 595 (1989).

14. John Lippman, "*Star Trek* Has Been A Virtual Money Machine. Now A New Series, Film Are Due With Paramount Set "To Boldly Go," *L.A. Times*, May 21, 1994, at D1; "*Star Trek: The Next Generation* Logs Its Last Stardate On TV After Going Where But One TV Series Had Gone Before — And Beyond," *Newsday*, May 19, 1994, at B4; Daniel Cerone, "Trek On Into the 21st Century: In the Beginning, There Was *Star Trek*, Which Begat *Star Trek: The Next Generation*, Which Begat *Star Trek: Deep Space Nine*, Which is Begetting *Star Trek: Voyager*, Whose Stars Will No Doubt Get A Film Series of Their Own," *L.A. Times*, April 2, 1994, at F1.

15. "*Star Trek*: The Next Publication," U.P.I., May 31, 1994, available in Lexis Nexis Library, UPI File.

16. Official *Star Trek* merchandise can be ordered through the magazine *Star Trek: The Official Fan Club*, widely available at newsstands and bookstores or by writing P.O. Box 111000, Aurora, Colorado 80042.

17. Recognizing *Star Trek*'s impact in popular culture, a recent article in the *Journal Of Legal Education* suggested that the original *Star Trek*'s Captain Kirk reverberates more strongly than Magellan as a common reference

point in talking about sailing into new, uncharted territory. See Lawrence Frolik, "Cultural Literacy: Or Why is Magellan Better than Kirk," *43 J. Legal Educ. 283, 286 (1993).*

18. For the teacher who may not have watched the series as diligently as his/her students during the last seven years, or who desires a fuller description of relevant episodes than is provided in this article, a number of books containing plot summaries of *ST:TNG*'s 175 episodes are commercially available. For the most detailed collections of plot summaries, see Phil Farrand, *The Nitpicker's Guide For Next Generation Trekkers* (1993); Larry Nemecek, *The Star Trek: The Next Generation Companion* (1992). See Also Michael Okuda Et Al., *The Star Trek Encyclopedia: A Reference Guide To The Future* (1994); Michael Okuda & Denise Okuda, *Star Trek Chronology: The History Of The Future* (1993).

19. See Annex to G.A. Res. 47/32, Sec. IV, U.N. GAOR, 47th Sess., Supp. No. 49, at 285, U.N. Doc. A/RES/47/32 (1992) (Program for the activities to be commenced during the second term (1993-94) of the United Nations Decade of International Law). With the globalization of business and trade, knowledge of the basic concepts of international law is becoming a critical component of an educated citizenry. International law is no longer the prerogative of a small circle of lawyers and academics; it has become a feature of everyday life to be reckoned with throughout the nation. See *A.B.A. Section on International Law and Practice, Report on Testing International Law on the Bar Exam*, 1993. Unfortunately, the United States lags far behind most developed countries in finding ways to incorporate international law into the "national curriculum."

20. All dialogue quotes from episodes of *ST:TNG* are from the televised version. The following citation format is used: *ST:TNG* "Episode Title," episode number (original air date). The episode number and original airdate information for the first five seasons are taken from Nemecek, supra note 18, at 209-211. For sixth- and seventh-season episodes, the airdate is reported by year only. The authors express their gratitude to Debbie Mirek, a co-author of "Okuda" et al., supra note 18, for providing detailed information about seventh-season episodes via the Internet.

21. The captain of *ST:TNG*'s *U.S.S. Enterprise* is Jean Luc Picard. Other characters regularly appearing on *ST:TNG* include: the first officer, Commander William Riker; the science officer, an android, Lieutenant Commander Data; the chief engineer, Geordie LaForge; the medical officer, Beverly Crusher; the ship's counselor, Deanna Troi and the Klingon-born security officer, Lieutenant Worf.

22. *ST:TNG*: episode introduction narration (from the Starfleet Charter).

23. See Stephen Whitefield & Gene Roddenberry, *The Making Of Star Trek* 203 (1968).

24. See Hugo Grotius, *De Jure Belli Ac Pacis Libri Tres* (James B. Scott ed. & Francis W. Kelsey et al. trans., 1925) (1623). This text is generally regarded as the foundation of modern international law.

25. See Okuda & Okuda, supra note 18, at 24 (citing *ST:TNG*: "The First Duty," No. 118 (May 30, 1992); *ST:TNG*: "The Outcast," No. 116 (Mar. 16, 1992)).

26. Id.

27. It is established in the seventh-season episode "Attached" that a planet must have a unified planetary government to qualify for Federation membership.

28. See infra notes 85-95, and accompanying text.

29. See Okuda & Okuda, supra note 18, at 24.

30. See id. at 24. While the U.N. Charter states in Article 55 that the organization "shall promote. . . universal respect for, and observance of, human rights and fundamental freedoms for all without distinction as to race, sex, language, or religion," such rights are not enumerated or guaranteed by the Charter. *U.N. Charter* at 55. Many of the members of the United Nations, however, are party to the International Covenant on Political and Civil Rights, Dec. 16, 1966, 999 U.N.T.S. 171. This treaty, which was negotiated under U.N. auspices, guarantees the same sorts of specific individual rights as are guaranteed by the Federation constitution.

31. See Okuda & Okuda, supra note 18, at 24. The United Nations is currently debating proposals to establish a standing U.N. military force. Until such a force is established, the United Nations must rely on personnel and equipment loaned from its member countries. See generally U.N. Dep't Of Public Info., *The Blue Helmets: A Review Of United Nations Peacekeeping*, U.N. Sales No. E.90.I.18 (1990).

32. See *ST:TNG*: "Redemption II," No. 100 (Sept. 23, 1991) (including a scene where Picard tells the leader of the

Klingon High Council that Starfleet has no authority to prevent an anticipated coup by another Klingon faction).

33. Joseph & Carton, supra note 1, at 59.

34. For a text providing detailed descriptions of the worlds making up the Federation and the worlds outside the Federation, see Shane Johnson, *Star Trek: The Worlds Of The Federation* (1989).

35. Customary international law is similar to domestic common law in that it is legally binding though it is not contained in a treaty or statute.

36. See, e.g., *ST:TNG*: "The Ensigns of Command," No. 49 (Oct. 2, 1989) (demonstrating that through the Treaty of Armens, the Federation ceded planet Tau Cygna V to the Sheliak Corporate).

37. See, e.g., *ST:TNG*: "Suddenly Human," No. 77 (Oct. 15, 1990) (referring to a peace agreement between the Federation and the Talarians).

38. *ST:TNG*: "Redemption," No. 99 (June 17, 1991).

39. North Atlantic Treaty, Apr. 4, 1949, 63 Stat. 2241, 34 U.N.T.S. 243.

40. Treaty on Friendship, Co-operation and Mutual Assistance (Warsaw Pact), May 14, 1955, 219 U.N.T.S. 3.

41. See, e.g., *ST:TNG*: "Data's Day," No. 84 (Jan. 7, 1991); *ST:TNG*: "Future Imperfect," No. 81 (Nov. 12, 1990); *ST:TNG*: "The Defector," No. 57 (Jan. 1, 1990); *ST:TNG*: "The Enemy," No. 54 (Nov. 6, 1989); *ST:TNG*: "Contagion," No. 36 (Mar. 20, 1989); *ST:TNG*: "The Neutral Zone," No. 25 (May 16, 1988).

42. *ST:TNG*: "The Wounded," No. 85 (Jan. 28, 1991).

43. See Louiq Henkin et al., *International Law: Cases And Materials* 421 (3d ed. 1993).

44. *ST:TNG*: "Code of Honor," No. 3 (Oct. 12, 1987).

45. "The Ensigns of Command," supra note 36.

46. It is also possible that this approach is unique to the agreement with the Sheliak, a race of beings so formalistic that they required a 500,000-word treaty in order to eliminate any ambiguity. The question of whether the "words alone" approach can be generally applied to other races highlights the difficulty inherent in extrapolating broad legal principles from anecdotal material.

47. *Conditions of Admission of a State to Membership in the United Nations*, 1948 ICJ 57, 63 (Advisory Opinion May 28, 1948). See also Article 32 of the Vienna Convention on the Law of Treaties, U.N. Doc. A/Conf. 39/27 (May 23, 1969), reprinted in *63 AM. J. INT'L L. 875 (1969)*.

48. See *United States v. Stuart, 489 U.S. 353 (1989)* (looking to Senate Committee Report, the floor debates and the President's transmittal letter and proclamation in interpreting a treaty).

49. See *Sumitomo Shoji America, Inc. v. Avagliano, 457 U.S. 176,* (1982).

50. "The Ensigns of Command," supra note 36.

51. See "Case Concerning United States Diplomatic and Consular Staff in Tehran" (*U.S. v. Iran*), 1980 ICJ 3, 48 (Judgment of May 24, 1980); "Case Concerning Questions of Interpretation and Application of the 1971 Montreal Convention Arising from the Aerial Incident at Lockerbie" (*Libya v. U.S. s/b U.K.*), Provisional Measures, 1992 ICJ 3 (Order of Apr. 14, 1992).

52. "Case Concerning Questions of Interpretation and Application of the 1971 Montreal Convention Arising from the Aerial Incident at Lockerbie" (*Libya v. U.S. s/b U.K.*), Provisional Measures, 1992 ICJ 3, 130 (Order of Apr. 14, 1992).

53. *International Law Commission Report* (1966) 2 Y.B. *Int'l L. Comm'n* 169, 253-55.

54. "The Enemy," supra note 41.

55. Article 31 of the *Draft Articles on State Responsibility*, (1979) 2 Y.B. Int'l L. Comm'n 22, U.N. Doc. A/CN.4/SER.A/1979/Add.1 (Part 2).

56. See Note, "Legal Argumentation in International Crises: The Downing of Korean Air Lines Flight 007," *97 Harv. L. Rev. 1198 (1984)*.

57. *ST:TNG*: "The *Pegasus,*" No. 164 (1994).

58. Id. (Picard).

59. See *History Of The United Nations War Crimes Commission And The Development Of The Laws Of War*, Compiled By The United Nations War Crimes Commission 263-65 (1948).

60. See *Agreement for the Prosecution and Punishment of Major War Criminals of the European Axis*, Charter of the International Military Tribunal, Aug. 8, 1945, Art. 7, 82 Stat. 1544, 82 U.N.T.S. 279.

61. Such treaties include the Geneva Convention for the Amelioration of the Condition of the Wounded and Sick in Armed Forces in the Field, Aug. 12, 1949, *6 U.S.T. 3114,* 75 U.N.T.S. 31; Geneva Convention for the Amelioration of the Condition of the Wounded, Sick and Shipwrecked Members of Armed Forces at Sea, Aug. 12, 1949, *6 U.S.T. 3217,* 75 U.N.T.S. 85; Geneva Convention Relative to the Treatment of Prisoners of War, Aug. 12, 1949, *6 U.S.T. 3316,* 75 U.N.T.S. 135; Geneva Convention Relative to the Protection of Civilian Persons in Time of War, Aug. 12, 1949, *6 U.S.T. 3516,* 75 U.N.T.S. 287; Protocol Additional to the Geneva Convention of August 12, 1949, and Relating to the Protection of Victims of International Armed Conflicts, opened for signature Dec. 12, 1977, 1125 U.N.T.S. 3 [Protocol I]; Convention for the Suppression of the Unlawful Seizure of Aircraft (Hague Convention) Dec. 16, 1970, *22 U.S.T. 1641,* 860 U.N.T.S. 105; Convention for the Suppression of Unlawful Acts Against the Safety of Civil Aviation (Montreal Convention) Sept. 23, 1971, *24 U.S.T. 564,* T.I.A.S. No. 7570; International Convention on the Suppression and Punishment of the Crime of Apartheid, Nov. 30, 1973, G.A. Res. 3068, U.N. GAOR, 28th Sess., Supp. No. 30, U.N. Doc. A/9030 (1974); Convention on the Prevention and Punishment of Crimes Against Internationally Protected Persons including Diplomatic Agents (New York Convention) Dec. 14, 1973, *28 U.S.T. 1975,* 1035 U.N.T.S. 167; International Convention Against the Taking of Hostages, Dec. 17, 1979, reprinted in *18 I.L.M. 1456 (1979);* Convention Against Torture and Other Cruel, Inhuman or Degrading Treatment or Punishment, Dec. 10, 1984, G.A. Res. 39/46, reprinted in *23 I.L.M. 1027 (1984);* Convention for the Suppression of Unlawful Acts Against the Safety of Maritime Navigation (Rome Convention) March 10, 1988, reprinted in *27 I.L.M. 672 (1988);* Protocol for the Suppression of Unlawful Acts Against the Safety of Fixed Platforms Located on the Continental Shelf (Rome Convention) March 10, 1988, reprinted in *27 I.L.M. 685 (1988);* United Nations: Convention Against Illicit Traffic in Narcotic Drugs and Psychotropic Substances (Vienna Convention) Dec. 19, 1988, U.N. Doc. E/Conf. 82/15 (1988), reprinted in *28 I.L.M. 493 (1989).* See Report of the Working Group on a draft statute for an International Criminal Court, U.N. GAOR, 48th Sess., Supp. No. 10, at 255, U.N. Doc. A/48/10 (1993).

62. "The *Pegasus,*" supra note 57.

63. *ST:TNG*: "Lower Decks," No. 167 (1994).

64. See generally D.P. O'Connell, *State Succession In Municipal Law And International Law* (1967).

65. *ST:TNG*: "Journey's End," No. 172 (1994).

66. *ST:TNG*: "Preemptive Strike," No. 176 (1994).

67. Vienna Convention on Succession of States in Respect of Treaties, U.N. Doc. A/Conf. 80/31, reprinted in *72 Am. J. Int'l L. 971 (1978)* (not in force).

When part of the territory of a State, or when any territory for the international relations of which a State is responsible, not being part of the territory of that State, becomes part of the territory of another State:

(a) treaties of the predecessor State cease to be in force in respect of the territory to which the succession of States relates from the date of the succession of States; and

(b) treaties of the successor State are in force in respect of the territory to which the succession of States relates from the date of the succession of States, unless it appears from the treaty or is otherwise established that the application of the treaty to that territory would be incompatible with the object and purpose of the treaty or would radically change the conditions for its operation.

Id. at art. 15.

68. Vienna Convention on Succession of States in Respect of Treaties, U.N. Doc. A/Conf. 80/31, reprinted in *72 Am. J. Int'l L. 971 (1978)* (not in force).

A newly independent State is not bound to maintain in force, or to become a party to, any treaty by reason only of the fact that at the date of the succession of States the treaty was in force in respect of the territory to which the succession of States relates.

Id. at art. 16.

69. Compare U.N. Human Rights Comm'n Res. 1993/23 of Mar. 9, 1993, U.N. Doc. E/CN.4/1993/L.11/Add.5 (1993) (recognizing that successor states continue to be bound to international human rights treaties to which the predecessor states have been parties) with Restatement (Third) Of The Foreign Relations Law Of The United States § 210, cmt. f (asserting that the clean slate theory applies to new states unless the new state indicates a desire to adopt a particular agreement and the other party or parties agree).

70. *ST:TNG*: "Chain of Command, Part II," No. 137 (1993).

71 *ST:TNG*: "Sarek," No. 70 (May 14, 1990).

72. Then Deputy Secretary of State Warren Christopher stated as follows in a speech at Occidental College June 11, 1977:

> We maintain diplomatic relations with many governments of which we do not necessarily approve. The reality is that, in this day and age, coups and other unscheduled changes of government are not exceptional developments. Withholding diplomatic relations from these regimes, after they have obtained effective control, penalizes us. It means that we forsake much of the chance to influence the attitudes and conduct of a new regime. Without relations, we forfeit opportunities to transmit our values and communicate our policies. Isolation may well bring out the worst in the new government.

Henkin et al., supra note 43, at 263.

73. See Vienna Convention on Diplomatic Relations, Apr. 18, 1961, *23 U.S.T. 3227,* 500 U.N.T.S. 95; Restatement (Third) Of The Foreign Relations Law Of The United States, § § 464-466 (1987). Under international law, diplomatic envoys and their families are, inter alia, accorded absolute immunity from arrest or criminal prosecution, and their personal baggage is exempt from inspection.

74. *ST:TNG*: "The Mind's Eye," No. 97 (May 27, 1991).

75. See *The Schooner Exchange v. McFaddon, 11 U.S. (7 Cranch) 116 (1812).*

76. See Foreign Sovereign Immunities Act of 1976, 90 Stat. 2891 (codified at *28 U.S.C. § § 1602*-1606).

77. See Kathryn L. Hale, Note, "Nonbinding Arbitration: An Oxymoron?," *24 U. Tol. L. Rev. 1003, 1004 (1993);* Joseph B. Stulberg, "Training Interveners for ADR Processes," *81 Ky. L.J. 977, 977, 978 (1993).*

78. *ST:TNG*: "Loud as a Whisper," No. 30 (Jan. 9, 1989).

79. *ST:TNG*: "The Outrageous Okona," No. 29 (Dec. 12, 1988).

80. *ST:TNG*: "The Host," No. 96 (May 13, 1991).

81. Roger T. Patterson, "Dispute Resolution in a World of Alternatives," *37 Cath. U. L. Rev. 591, 593 (1988)* (stating that usually each party selects one arbitrator, and the two arbitrators select a third).

82. "The Ensigns of Command," supra note 36.

83. "Redemption," supra note 38.

84. Gowron or Duras. Id.

85. See, e.g., *ST:TNG*: "Manhunt," No. 44 (June 19, 1989). In this episode, the *Enterprise* is on a diplomatic mission to transport Antedian and Betazoid delegates to a conference on the planet Pacifica to consider the question of admitting planet Antede III to the Federation.

86. Charter of the United Nations, June 26, 1945, art. IV, para. 1, 59 Stat. 1031, 1038, T.S. No. 993, *3 Bevans 1153, 1155.*

87. *ST:TNG*: "The Hunted," No. 58 (Jan. 8, 1990).

88. See "The Hunted," supra note 87.

89. Charter of the United Nations, June 26, 1945, art. I, para. 3, 1031, T.S. No. 933, *3 Bevans 1153*.

90. The United States has recently taken such a position with respect to the admission of Serbia-Montenegro:

> [The United States] looks forward to the day when [it] can support Serbia-Montenegro's application for admission to the United Nations. Unfortunately that day appears to be far away. Earlier this week the Bosnian Serbs launched new attacks on Bosnian Government positions near Bihac. Gross violations of human rights continue. There are close to two million displaced persons. Many have been killed and physically and mentally abused. It appears that the Serbs are making a special effort to show their contempt for this institution. The Belgrade authorities must end their support for the Bosnian Serbs. They must end their support for aggression in Bosnia and Croatia. The international community and this organization have gone on record as demanding that the Bosnian Serbs sign and implement the peace plan that the other two parties have signed. Until that day they will remain international pariahs. The United States will support Serbia-Montenegro's membership in this organization when, and only when, Serbia-Montenegro meets the criteria in the United Nations Charter. That is, Serbia-Montenegro must show that it is a peace loving state and demonstrate its willingness to comply fully with Chapter Seven resolutions.

USUN Press Release 59-(93) (REV), April 29, 1993 (statement of Ambassador Madeleine K. Albright, U.S. Representative to the 47th Session of the U.N. General Assembly, in Resumed Session, on the Situation in the Former Yugoslavia).

91. *ST:TNG*: "Lonely Among Us," No. 6 (Nov. 2, 1987).

92. *ST:TNG*: "Attached," No. 160 (1994)

93. Id. (Riker).

94. Charter of the United Nations, June 26, 1945, art. VI, 59 Stat. 1031, 1038, T.S. No. 993, *3 Bevans 1153, 1156*.

95. However, the United Nations has acted on two occasions to exclude a member from participating in the work of the organization. South Africa was excluded on the basis of a credentials challenge. See *Report On U.S. Participation In The United Nations For The Year 1974* 112 (1975). The Federal Republic of Yugoslavia (Serbia and Montenegro) was excluded under the theory that after the break up of Yugoslavia, Serbia and Montenegro could not automatically assume the former Yugoslavia's membership in the organization. See U.N. Security Council Resolution 777 (Sept. 19, 1992).

96 *ST:TNG*: "The Price," No. 55 (Nov. 13, 1989).

97. See Richard Baxter, *The Law Of International Waterways* 149-59 (1964).

98. See Corfu Channel Case (*U.K. v. Alb.*), 1949 ICJ 4, 28 (April 9, 1949). See also *United Nations Convention On The Law Of The Sea* 14, art. 38, U.N. Doc. A/Conf. 62/122 (1982), reprinted in *21 I.L.M. 1261, 1277*.

99. See *United Nations Convention On The Law Of The Sea* 16-17, art. 42, U.N. Doc. A/Conf. 62/122 (1982), reprinted in *21 I.L.M. 1261, 1277-78*.

100. *ST:TNG*: "Force of Nature," No. 158 (1994).

101. "Force of Nature," supra note 100.

102. G.A. Res. 37, "Protection of the Environment in Times of Armed Conflict," U.N. EAOR, 47th Sess., Supp. No. 49, 73d plan. mtg. 290, U.N. Doc. A/47/49 (1992).

103. *United Nations Convention On The Law Of The Sea* 86, art. 194(2), U.N. Doc. A/Conf. 62/122 (1982), reprinted in *21 I.L.M. 1261, 1308*.

104. Given the importance of warp travel and the speculative nature of the damage to the fabric of space, the wartime rule is arguably more appropriate for the situation in *ST:TNG*. On the other hand, considering the

immense extent of possible damage, perhaps a stricter standard should be employed.

105. See Trail Smelter Arbitration (U.S. v. Can.), 3 R.I.A.A. 1911 (1941) (considered the landmark decision on customary law concerning the environment).

106. For example, the Klingons.

107. For example, the Ferengi, Cardassians and Romulans.

108. Reprinted in Barry E. Carter & Philip B. Trimble, *International Law: Selected Documents And New Developments* 690-705 (1994) (setting a timetable for the reduction of ozone-depleting CFCs). See Dale S. Bryk, Note, "The Montreal Protocol and Recent Developments to Protect the Ozone Layer," *15 Harv. Envtl. L. Rev. 275 (1991).*

109. Reprinted in Barry E. Carter & Philip B. Trimble, *International Law: Selected Documents And New Developments* 734-47 (1994) (signed June 1992 at the Earth Summit in Rio where parties pledged to reduce growth in emission of earth-warming gasses).

110. See Lawrence Roberts, "Addressing the Problem of Orbital Debris: Combining International Regulatory and Liability Regimes," *15 B.C. Int'l & Comp. L. Rev. 51 (1992)* (discussing more comprehensively the space debris problem).

111. The warp corridor might best be compared to Earth's geosynchronous Orbit, a region of space located along the equatorial plane, 22,300 miles above the Earth's surface.

112. See, e.g., Treaty on Principles Governing the Activities of States in the Exploration and Use of Outer Space, Including the Moon and Other Celestial Bodies, Jan. 27, 1967, *18 U.S.T. 2410,* 610 U.N.T.S. 205 [hereinafter Outer Space Treaty]. This treaty limits its protection of the space environment to the prevention of harmful contamination by those parties to the treaty conducting exploration or studies. Outer Space Treaty, supra at art. IX. Though more comprehensive in its prohibition than the Outer Space Treaty, the Agreement Governing the Activities of States on the Moon and Other Celestial Bodies, opened for signature Dec. 5, 1979, G.A. Res. 68, U.N. GAOR, 34th Sess., Supp. No. 46, U.N. Doc. A/68 (1979), *18 I.L.M. 1434* (entered into force July 11, 1984), having been ratified by a mere seven nations, is considered a dead letter.

113. Convention on International Liability for Damage Caused by Space Objects, opened for signature Mar. 29, 1972, *24 U.S.T. 2389* (entered into force Oct. 3, 1973), reprinted in 3 United States Space Law II.A.4 (Stephen Gorove ed., 1986).

114. U.S. Congress, Office Of Technology Assessment, *Orbiting Debris: A Space Environmental Problem — Background Paper* 5 (1990) [hereinafter *Orbiting Debris*].

115. "[The U.S. Department of Defense] will seek to minimize the impact of space debris on its military operations. Design and operations of [Department of Defense] space tests, experiments and systems will strive to minimize or reduce accumulation of space debris consistent with mission requirements." Office of the Secretary of Defense, "Department of Defense Space Policy Statement," Mar. 10, 1987, reprinted in *Orbiting Debris*, supra note 114, at 33.

116. "The United States Government will encourage other space-faring nations to adopt policies and practices aimed at debris minimization." White House, President Bush's Space Policy, November 1989, Fact Sheet n.34, reprinted in *Orbiting Debris*, supra note 114, at 33.

117. *ST:TNG*: "Samaritan Snare," No. 42 (May 15, 1989).

118 *ST:TNG*: "Too Short a Season," No. 15 (Feb. 8, 1988).

119. *ST:TNG*: "The High Ground," No. 59 (Jan. 29, 1990).

120. International Convention Against the Taking of Hostages, U.N. GAOR, 105th mtg., U.N. Doc. A/res/34/146 (1979).

121. S.C. Res 579, U.N. SCOR, 2637th mtg., U.N. Doc. S/Res/579 (1985).

122. *ST:TNG*: "Ensign Ro," No. 102 (Oct. 7, 1991).

123. *ST:TNG*: "The Vengeance Factor," No. 56 (Nov. 20, 1989).

124 See *Patterns Of Global Terrorism*: 1988, at iii (U.S. Department of State, March 1989) ("The first element of our counter terrorism policy is that we do not make concessions of any kind to terrorists. We do not pay ransom,

release convicted terrorists from prison, or change our policies to accommodate terrorist demands – such actions would only lead to more terrorism.").

125. Michael P. Scharf, "Foreign Courts on Trial: Why U.S. Courts Should Avoid Applying the Inquiry Provision of the Supplementary U.S. - U.K. Extradition Treaty," 25 Stan. J. Int'l L. 257, 257 n.2 (1988).

126. *Factor v. Laubenheimer, 290 U.S. 276, 287 (1933).*

127. *International Criminal Law* 413-17 (M. Sherif Bassiouni ed., 1986).

128. "The Hunted," supra note 87.

129. *ST:TNG*: "Transfigurations," No. 72 (June 4, 1990).

130. *ST:TNG*: "A Matter of Perspective," No. 61 (Feb. 12, 1990).

131. During the episode, Riker was on a diplomatic mission for the Federation. "A Matter of Perspective," supra note 130. As such, he should be accorded the immunities of diplomats, who are exempt from the municipal law of the host country. "The reason of the immunity of diplomatic agents is clear, namely: that Governments may not be hampered in their foreign relations by the arrest or forcible prevention of the exercise of a duty in the person of a governmental agent or representative. If such agent be offensive and his conduct is unacceptable to the accredited nation it is proper to request his recall; if the request be not honored he may be in extreme cases escorted to the boundary and thus removed from the country." "Exemption From Judicial Process," 4 *Hackworth Digest* § 400 (1942).

132. See Note, "Executive Discretion in Extradition," *62 Colum. L. Rev. 1313, 1325 (1962)*. See also *Ahmad v. Wigen, 910 F.2d 1063, 1067 (2d Cir. 1990)* ("So far as we know, the Secretary [of State] never has directed extradition in the face of proof that the extraditee would be subjected to procedures or punishment antipathetic to a federal court's sense of decency.").

133. "Data's Day," supra note 41.

134. *ST:TNG*: "The Drumhead," No. 94 (Apr. 29, 1991).

135. *ST:TNG*: "Heart of Glory," No. 20 (Mar. 21, 1988).

136. Id. (Worf).

137. See *ST:TNG*: "Justice," No. 7 (Nov. 9, 1987).

138. Soering Case, 161 Eur. Ct. H.R. (ser. A) at 11 (1989), 11 Eur. H.R. Rep. 439 (1989), *28 I.L.M. 1063 (1989)*.

139. "The Drumhead," supra note 134.

140. See generally Geoffrey R. Watson, "Offenders Abroad: The Case for Nationality-Based Criminal Jurisdiction," *17 Yale J. Int'l L. 41, 41-84 (1992)*.

141. *United States v. Zehe, 601 F. Supp. 196, 197 (D. Mass. 1985)*.

142. *ST:TNG*: "Violations," No. 111 (Feb. 3, 1992).

143. In *ST:TNG*, the *Enterprise*'s registration number is N.C.C. 1701-D. The Federation would not have jurisdiction if, unlike the Ullians, it did not have a statute criminalizing memory invasion. Given the peculiar nature of the offense, it is possible that the Federation would treat it only as a tortuous assault.

144. See United Nations Convention On The Law Of The Sea, art. 97, U.N. Doc. A/Conf. 62/122 (1982), reprinted in *21 I.L.M. 1261;* Convention on International Civil Aviation, opened for signature Dec. 7, 1944, art. 17, 61 Stat. 1180, 1185, T.I.A.S. No. 1590, 15 U.N.T.S. 295, 308; Treaty on Principles Governing the Activities of States in the Exploration and Use of Outer Space, Including the Moon and other Celestial Bodies, Jan. 27, 1967, art. 8, *18 U.S.T. 2410, 2416*, T.I.A.S. No. 6347, 610 U.N.T.S. 205, 209.

145. For an interesting comment on choice of law in space, see generally Helen Shin, Comment, "Oh I Have Slipped the Surly Bonds of Earth: Multinational Space Stations and Choice of Law," *78 Cal. L. Rev. 1375 (1990)*.

146. See United Nations Convention On The Law Of The Sea art. 100-107, U.N. Doc. A/Conf. 62/122 (1982), reprinted in *21 I.L.M. 1261, 1277-78*. See also Convention for the Suppression of Unlawful Acts Against the Safety of Maritime Navigation, Rome, Mar. 10, 1988.

147. *ST:TNG*: "Encounter at Farpoint, Part 1" (Sept. 28, 1987).

148. Id. (Picard).

149. Id. (Picard).

150. In 1992, the U.S. Supreme Court ruled that U.S. courts could try a person apprehended in Mexico by U.S. agents without Mexico's consent. See *United States v. Alvarez-Machain, 112 S. Ct. 2188, 2197 (1992).* In response to the contpoversial decision, 21 Latin American countries proposed that the U.N. General Assembly request from the International Court of Justice an advisory opinion clarifying that states may not exercise criminal jurisdiction over persons abducted from another state without the latter's consent. See HENKIN ET AL., supra note 43, at 177. The General Assembly decided to defer the question while the United States and Mexico continued negotiations for a revised extradition treaty that would prohibit such abductions.

151. Compare Louis Henkin, "Use of Force: Law and U.S. Policy," in *Right V. Might: International Law And The Use Of Force* 37, 41-42 (2d ed. 1991) with Ian Brownlie, *International Law And The Use Of Force By States* 301-08 (1963).

152. See Abraham Sofaer, "Terrorism, The Law, and National Defense," *26 Mil. L. Rev. 89, 90-122 (1989).* Acting under this theory of self defense, in 1985, U.S. military planes intercepted an Egyptian aircraft over the Mediterranean Sea, compelling it to land so that alleged terrorists aboard the aircraft could be prosecuted for seizing the Achille Lauro cruise ship, taking hostages and murdering a U.S. citizen. See Oscar Schachter, "In Defense of International Rules on the Use of Force," *53 U. Chi. L. Rev. 113, 139-40 (1986).*

153. "The Defector," supra note 41.

154. "The Mind's Eye," supra note 74.

155. Id. (Kell).

156. *ST:TNG*: "Half a Life," No. 95 (May 6, 1991).

157. *ST:TNG*: "I, Borg," No. 123 (May 11, 1992).

158. The Borg are a hostile race with one collective mind and are committed to the forcible assimilation of all other races. See *ST:TNG*: "Q Who," No. 41 (May 8, 1989).

159. *ST:TNG*: "The Masterpiece Society," No. 112 (Feb. 10, 1992).

160. Id. (Picard).

161. See Henkin et al., supra note 43, at 1203. In the Asylum Case (*Colombia v. Peru*), 1950 ICJ 266, the International Court of Justice observed:

> A decision to grant diplomatic asylum involves derogation from the sovereignty of that State. It withdraws the offender from the jurisdiction of the territorial State and constitutes an intervention in matters that are exclusively within the competence of that State. Such derogation from territorial sovereignty cannot be recognized unless its legal basis is established in each particular case.

Id.

162. Universal Declaration of Human Rights, 6 A. Res. 217, art. 14, U.N. Doc. A/III (1948).

163. But see *Sale v. Haitian Centers Council, Inc., 113 S. Ct. 3028 (1993)* (ruling that the Refugee Convention did not apply extraterritorially and therefore did not prevent the United States from returning Haitian refugees interdicted by U.S. vessels on the high seas).

164. Convention Relating to the Status of Refugees, 606 U.N.T.S. 267, *19 U.S.T. 6223,* T.I.A.S. No. 6577 (Nov. 1, 1968).

165. Id.

166. G.A. Res. 217, U.N. Doc. A/III (1948).

167. Id. at art. 13, para. 2.

168. "I, Borg," supra note 157.

169. Id. (Crusher). It is questionable, however, whether any members of the Borg society could be considered inno-celt civilians since the Borg share a single collective thought process. As a consequence, all members of the Borg Collective arguably share responsibility for that race's military conduct.

170. "The Mind's Eye," supra note 74.

171. See 1949 Geneva Convention Relative to the Treatment of Prisoners of War, supra note 61.

172. "Chain of Command, Part II," supra note 70.

173. Id. (Picard). *The Star Trek Encyclopedia* describes this convention as an "interstellar treaty governing the treat-ment of prisoners of war. Both the United Federation of Planets and the Cardassian Union were signatories to the accord." Okuda et al., supra note 18, at 295. Evidently, the Romulan Empire is not a party to the Convention and does not recognize it as the 24th-century equivalent of customary international law.

174. See supra note 61.

175. See *United States v. Yunis, 924 F.2d 1086, 1097-98 (D.C. Cir. 1991).*

176. 78 U.N.T.S. 277 (Dec. 9, 1948).

177. Id.

178. *ST:TNG*: "The Survivors," No. 50 (Oct. 9, 1989).

179. Id. (Picard).

180. *ST:TNG*: "Haven," No. 10 (Nov. 30, 1987).

181. Id. (Picard). In this respect, Federation policy is remarkably similar to the Outer Space Treaty, which provides: "In carrying on activities in outer space and on celestial bodies, the astronauts of one State Party shall render all possible assistance to the astronauts [in distress] of other State Parties." Outer Space Treaty, supra, at art. V. para. 2.

182. "The Vengeance Factor," supra note 123.

183. See Madeleine K. Albright, "War Crimes in Bosnia," *S.F. Chron*, Dec. 4, 1993, at A22 ("We have made it clear that we will not recognize – and do not believe the international community will recognize – any deal to immunize the accused from culpability.").

184. See Articles 4 and 5 of the Genocide Convention, supra note 61.

185. See Convention on the Non-Applicability of Statutory Limitations to War Crimes and Crimes , Res. 2391(XXIII) Nov. 26, 1968 (entered into force Nov. 11, 1970).

186. "The Vengeance Factor," supra note 123.

187. *Oppenheim's International Law* 7-8 (9th ed. 1992). See Vienna Convention on the Law of Treaties, U.N. Doc. A/Conf. 39/27, art. III (1969), reprinted in 63 *Am. J. Int'l I. & Pol'y* 875 (1969); Gordon Christie, "The World Court and Jus Cogens," 81 *Am. J. Int'l I. & Pol'y* 93 (1987).

188. *Oppenheim's International Law*, supra note 187, at 7-8.

189. *ST:TNG*: "Devil's Due," No. 86 (Feb. 4, 1991).

190. Id.

191. This would be consistent with the absence of customary international law, as discussed above.

192. Charter of the United Nations, June 26, 1945, art. II, 59 Stat. 1031, 1038, T.S. No. 993, *3 Bevans 1153, 1155*.

193. Id. at art. 51 ("Nothing in the present Charter shall impair the inherent right of individual or collective self-defense if an armed attack occurs against a Member of the United Nations, until the Security Council has taken measures necessary to maintain international peace and security.").

194. "Redemption II," supra note 32.

195. "Military and Paramilitary Activities in and Against Nicaragua" (*Nicaragua v. U.S.*), 1986 ICJ 14, 103-23.

196. "The Wounded," supra note 42.

197. See Oscar Schachter, "The Right of States to Use Armed Force," *82 Mich. L. Rev. 1620, 1633-35 (1983).*

198. Id.

199. Id.

200. "The Defector," supra note 41.

201. The Federation-Romulan Treaty prohibits ships of either side to enter the Neutral Zone.

202. See U.N. Charter, supra note 86.

203. See "Military and Paramilitary Activities in and Against Nicaragua" (*Nicaragua v. U.S.*), 1986 ICJ 14, 126.

204. "I, Borg," supra note 157; "The Masterpiece Society," supra note 159; *ST:TNG*: "A Matter of Time," No. 108 (Nov. 18, 1991); "Half a Life," supra note 156; "The Drumhead," supra note 134; "Devil's Due," supra note 189; *ST:TNG*: "First Contact," No. 88 (Feb. 18, 1991); "The Hunted," supra note 87; *ST:TNG*: "Who Watches the Watchers?," No. 51 (Oct. 16, 1989); *ST:TNG*: "Pen Pals," No. 40 (May 1, 1989); *ST:TNG*: "Symbiosis," No. 21 (Apr. 18, 1988); "Too Short a Season," supra note 118; "Justice," supra note 137.

205. "First Contact," supra note 204.

206. Id. (Picard). In this episode, the *Enterprise* crew is on a reconnaissance mission on the planet Malcoria III, which is on the verge of warp travel, in preparation for the Federation revealing itself to the inhabitants of the planet. When Commander Riker (in native disguise) is captured, Picard contacts Chancellor Durken, the leader of the world, to convince him of the Federation's good intentions. Picard tells Durken that, under the Prime Directive, the *Enterprise* is obliged to leave without further contact if that is the Chancellor's wish.

207. "Half a Life," supra note 156.

208. Id. (Picard). At issue in this episode is the practice on planet Kaelon II of voluntary suicide of all citizens who reach age 60 as a form of population control and to minimize welfare costs. While Picard refuses to press for a change in Kaelon's seemingly barbaric practice, he was willing to grant Timicin, a 60-year-old scientist, asylum aboard the *Enterprise*.

209. "The Hunted," supra note 87.

210. "Symbiosis," supra note 204.

211. "The Outcast," supra note 25.

212. "The Mind's Eye," supra note 74.

213. Id. (Picard).

214. "The Drumhead," supra note 134.

215. "A Matter of Time," supra note 204.

216. Id. (Picard).

217. "Pen Pals," supra note 204.

218. "Justice," supra note 137.

219. This crew member is Ensign Wesley Crusher, the son of the *Enterprise*'s chief medical officer.

220. See Ian Brownlie, "Humanitarian Intervention," in *Law And Civil War In The Modern World* 218-19 (Moore ed., 1974); Richard B. Lillich, "A Reply to Dr. Brownlie and a Plea for Constructive Alternatives," in id. at 247-48.

221. India relied on the rationale when it sent troops into East Pakistan to protect the Bengali population during the 1971 civil war with Pakistan. Similarly, Vietnam relied on the rationale in invading Cambodia in 1978, and Tanzania invoked the rationale to justify its 1979 invasion of Uganda. Despite considerable sympathy for the oppressed Bengalis, Cambodians and Ugandans, however, resolutions condemning these actions were passed by large majorities in the U.N. General Assembly. See Henkin et al., supra note 43, at 930, 933.

222. The right to intervene to protect nationals was one of the grounds invoked by the United States for its invasions

of Grenada in 1983 and Panama in 1989. See Christopher C. Joyner, "The United States Action in Grenada," *78 Am. J.I.L. 131 (1984);* "Use of Force, Protection of Nationals – Deployment of U.S. Forces in Panama" (U.S. Digest, Ch. 14, Section 1), reprinted in *84 Am. J.I.L. 545 (1990).* It was also invoked for the intervention by Israel in Uganda to release Israeli hostages from a hijacked plane at Entebbe. See U.N. Doc. S/PV. 1939, at 51-59 (July 1976), reprinted in *15 I.L.M. 1224 (1976).*

223. United Kingdom Foreign Office Policy Document No. 148, reprinted in 57 *Y.B. Brit. Int'l L.* 614 (1986). See generally Schachter, supra note 197 (discussing attitudes of other states toward humanitarian intervention).

224. "Ensign Ro," supra note 122.

225. See Appendix (referencing *ST:TNG* episodes to corresponding international legal issues).

226. Whitfield & Roddenberry, supra note 23, at 28.

227. Edwin D. Dickinson, "Is the Crime of Piracy Obsolete," *38 Harv. L. Rev. 334, 334-360 (1925).*

228. Charles Paikert, "After 25 Years, Still . . . Cruising at Warp Speed," *Variety,* Dec. 2, 1991, at 49.

Legal Development:
CAPTAIN JAMES T. KIRK AND THE ENTERPRISE OF CONSTITUTIONAL INTERPRETATION

MICHAEL STOKES PAULSEN, JD

The Omega Glory

In episode 54 of the original *Star Trek* TV series, titled "The Omega Glory," we find a stunning and prophetic parable about constitutional interpretation. Well, all right, maybe the producers didn't quite intend the episode as making a point about constitutional interpretation. But as a "trekkie" and a law professor, I can find stunning and prophetic constitutional insights in *Star Trek* reruns if I want.

For those cultural illiterates not familiar with the most important literary form of the last 30 years, *Star Trek* chronicles the voyages of the starship *Enterprise* of the United Federation of Planets, a coalition of humanoid life forms who have united for mutual defense and the peaceful exploration of the galaxy, carefully observing the Prime Directive of the Federation not to interfere with the normal development of the other humanoid cultures they encounter.[2] The *U.S.S. Enterprise* is commanded (in the original series) by James T. Kirk, the young swashbuckling captain portrayed by William Shatner (before he became old and fat and started doing margarine commercials).

For those who might not recall the details of episode 54,[3] our heroes, Captain Kirk, his half-human, half-Vulcan first officer, Mr. Spock, and the ship's surgeon, Dr. Leonard McCoy (generally useless friend of Jim's), have beamed down to planet Omega IV to find Captain Ronald Tracey, apparently the last survivor of the starship *U.S.S. Exeter*, found abandoned in orbit. It seems the entire crew of the *Exeter* contracted a deadly virus, which now infects the crew of the *Enterprise*. The planet's atmosphere, however, confers immunity. Kirk, Spock, and McCoy find Captain Tracey alive and well on Omega IV.

Captain Tracey explains that something in the planet's atmosphere or elements not only confers immunity from this disease, but stops all aging in humans. Tracey believes he has found the fountain of youth on Omega IV, where humanoid beings live to be more than 1,000 years old. While attempting to isolate exactly what it is that confers eternal youth, Tracey has allied himself with one side of a centuries-old war, the Kohms, an Asiatic-looking race whose mortal enemies are the Yangs, a tribe of hulking, barbarous Hun-like humanoids. Since Captain Tracey's actions are an inexplicable violation of the Prime Directive, there is quickly a falling out with the unfailingly honorable Captain James T. Kirk of the starship *Enterprise.*

Alas, it turns out Tracey has *not* found a fountain of youth. Rather, in yet another compelling illustration of Somebody-or-other's Law of Parallel Planet Development (a law that always seems to produce some apt social commentary for old Earth of the mid-1960s), what Captain Tracey has discovered are the mutated descendants produced by a devastating nuclear holocaust from the senseless war of the Yangs ("Bones—Yangs... Yankees!") and the Kohms ("Communists?!"), a war that has largely destroyed both civilizations.[4]

A strange byproduct of the holocaust is that descendants of the initial survivors, who carry on the war, have great longevity. But there is nothing "in the water" (so to speak) to take home and sell as youth-tonic. People on Omega IV live longer because, as Dr. McCoy eventually figures out, "it's natural for them, damnit."[5]

The Yangs were once an advanced civilization, but now they communicate largely through grunts and violence, as Captain James T. Kirk learns when Captain Tracey throws him into a prison cell with two captured Yang barbarians, on account of Kirk's refusal to abet Tracey's violations of the Prime Directive. After surviving a dreadfully acted hand-to-hand battle with the male Yang, Kirk, resting in a corner, urges Spock (who is locked in the adjoining cell), to keep trying to loosen the window bars of the cell "if we are to regain our freedom."

"Freedom?" queries the Yang, in his first speech other than grunts and growls. (Everybody on distant planets speaks English, of course.) "You speak one of our worship words."

"Well, well, well," Kirk replies. "It is our worship word, too." And Kirk begins to try to reach a detente with the Yang brute, who accommodates Kirk by knocking him senseless.

The episode comes to a climax when the Yangs, led by the brute whom Kirk has helped free (who turns out to be the Yangs' leader), overrun the Kohm defenses and take both Captain Tracey and Captain Kirk as prisoners. The victorious Yangs bring forth an American flag and start to recite more worship words, which Kirk immediately recognizes as the Preamble to the Constitution of the United States. To show that he is, in sooth, a friend of the Yangs, Kirk finishes the worship words of the Preamble for them, speaking the words far more clearly than did the Yang leader and causing much stir among the Yang people.

You see – and now we're finally getting to the point – it seems the words of the Yang Constitution, as spoken by their leaders, have been badly mangled by centuries of disuse and by the original document having been locked up as a sacred treasure in a chest, with only the high priests of the Yangs from generation to generation being allowed to recite its words and speak its commands. Unfortunately, in the years since the holocaust, the words themselves have been rendered unintelligible to the Yang people, and their content has been long forgotten, even by the Yang leaders.

The episode ends with a fierce hand-to-hand duel to the death between Captain Kirk and the renegade Captain Tracey, staged by the Yangs to decide which one is good and which one is evil. (You see, the Yangs are uncertain about Kirk. Although he knows their worship words – knows them better than they do, in fact – the renegade Captain Tracey, no fool he, has pointed out that the devil can quote scripture for his own purposes, and that Mr. Spock, Kirk's Vulcan sidekick, has pointed ears.).

Kirk wins his fight with Tracey, just as Lieutenant Sum beams down from the *Enterprise* with a rescue party. The Yangs think Kirk has summoned his angels, and he is a god. Kirk quickly disabuses them of that notion, even as he takes advantage of their awe to rip open the treasure chest and commit the heresy of heresies (and why this isn't a violation of the Prime Directive, too, I'm not really sure) of – gasp! – taking the Constitution out of hiding and actually *reading* it to the assembled people. Kirk notes with emphasis that the document was written for "*We the People*" and exhorts the Yang leaders, in classic William Shatner overacting: "Don't you see? These words are not meant for leaders only. They are meant for everybody, Yangs and Kohms alike. They are meant to be read. These words must belong to everybody or they mean nothing at all! *Do you understand?*"

Our Forgotten Constitution

The story of Omega IV and the Yangs and the Kohms contains some lessons about constitutional interpretation for "We the People" of 21st century America. We are, of course, the Yangs. True, our Constitution has not been forcibly buried away for hundreds of years by a nuclear holocaust. But it has been lost to the People, rendered nearly unintelligible by the high priests who have assumed (and whom we have *allowed* to assume) responsibility for inter-

preting it. The Supreme Court's present style of constitutional discourse is the
practical equivalent, so far as the mass of the People is concerned, of the Yangs'
inarticulate grunts. The Court speaks in terms of multi-part tests and tiers of
scrutiny, language that corrupts the plain spoken words of a document intended
to be accessible to all, and to belong to all, by adding a veneer of pseudo-
sophisticated legalese. This corruption serves to distance the People from their
Constitution by rendering it inaccessible to common understanding.
Simultaneously, it removes the Constitution from the People's view and from
their control. Thus corrupted, the words of the Constitution, our fundamental
charter of rights and of government, have become the exclusive province of an
elite cabal of high priests. The priests are careful to recite the formulae of their
predecessors, rather than the words of the document itself, and so keep up the
illusion their guardianship is necessary in order to translate an increasingly
incomprehensible document (which they have made so) into concrete commands they then issue to the (small "p") people as "law." The People are treated, rightly as it turns out, as constitutional illiterates who lack the understanding necessary to read the Constitution with their own eyes. That task must be
performed by a special class of intermediaries. That this is the operating conception of our constitutional high priests is illustrated by the shockingly candid
words of a recent Supreme Court majority opinion. Referring to the commitment of *We the People* to the rule of law under a written Constitution, the
Court said:

> Their belief in themselves as such a people [a
> revealing construction – whatever happened to
> "We the People"?] is not readily separable from
> their understanding of the Court invested with the
> authority to decide their constitutional cases and
> speak before all others for their constitutional
> ideals.[6]

The Constitution has become a relic to be worshiped, rather than a document *of* the People, intended to be read, understood, and applied *by* the
People, in order to produce government *for* the People. We don't bury the document in a treasure chest, but we do the next best thing: we place it under glass
at the National Archives so tourists can walk past and gaze at old parchment
for 20 seconds apiece. We don't read or study its words. Instead, we worship a
document we do not read and allow our constitutional high priests to speak
unintelligible words in the name of the document, issuing commands we blindly

obey. In the end, the danger becomes that we don't even worship the Constitution any more. We simply genuflect to the priests who control it, placing enormous importance on who the priests are. *We the People* becomes, in popular understanding, "They the Justices" (who, in turn, speak of *We the People* not as "us" but as "them")

Against the reality of our current constitutional practice, the words of Captain James T. Kirk ring out clearly from the 23rd century: The words of the Constitution must belong to everyone, or they mean nothing at all. The ultimate betrayal of a Constitution that begins with the three bold words *We the People* is for the People to be denied any effective role in the interpretation of that Constitution.

I submit to you that Captain James T. Kirk was right – righter than he knew and surely more on target than the producers of *Star Trek* could possibly have intended. The task of interpreting the Constitution is not the exclusive province of the Supreme Court or of any other government official or group of officials. No provision of the Constitution vests such interpretive supremacy in the Supreme Court or in any other organ of government. Rather, I submit, the words most important to the question of who has the power to interpret the Constitution are its first three: *We the People*. All questions of interpretive authority must be asked in the shadow of those three words. It is *We the People* who have ordained and established the Constitution. Consequently, in interpreting the Constitution, its words cannot be the exclusive province of any one branch of government or of government in general. Any reading of the Constitution that denies this premise, or any reading that vests interpretive supremacy over *We the People* in a body of high priests and denies interpretive access to the People is a contradiction of the very first principle of the Constitution. These words must belong to everyone, or they mean nothing at all!

Some Modest Proposals

We have no Captain Kirk to throw open the treasure chest, dust off the Constitution, and explain to our leaders their fundamental misunderstanding of that which they purport to uphold as worship words. How, then, do we recover the Constitution as a document to be understood, interpreted, and applied by *We the People*? I offer five modest proposals for returning the Constitution to the interpretive supremacy of the People. None of them is original. Most of them are truths well accepted in earlier eras, but long forgotten through disuse.

Many of them will sound controversial, perhaps even outlandish, to modern ears – much as Jim Kirk's radical reinterpretation upset centuries of settled constitutional practice among the Yangs in order to return them to the understanding they had lost. I offer them in the spirit of a provocateur, unsure of the soundness of some of them, but quite certain our present practice is one of constitutional atavism.

Modest Proposal Number One:

WRITE INTELLIGIBLE, STRAIGHTFORWARD JUDICIAL OPINIONS

This proposal is directed to the high priests of our courts and should be relatively uncontroversial. For many years, many commentators have noted and decried the descent of the Supreme Court into terminal jargon-itis in its written opinions.[7] No one, to my knowledge, disagrees. But while these commentators note that the opinions thus written are arid, technical, unhelpful, boring, and difficult to understand, they fail to emphasize the greatest constitutional problem with unintelligible opinions: They prevent *We the People* from effectively evaluating whether the Supreme Court is faithfully interpreting and applying our Constitution or has strayed from the proper understanding of our Constitution. This is because *We the People* often cannot make heads or tails out of the judicial opinion.

Why, it might be asked, should *We the People* be particularly concerned about whether the Supreme Court got it right or not? After all, it's not like we can do anything about it. I will take on that last premise in a moment. For now, it is sufficient to point out how Yang-like that attitude is: The Constitution is a document that can only be read, understood, and discussed by a small elite of judges, law professors, lawyers, and (maybe) second- and third-year law students. It is simply *too hard* for *We the People* to understand.

Notice how this attitude removes the Constitution from the view of the People. Surely, at the very least, *We the People* have the right to *know* what is going on with constitutional interpretation. The words spoken by the high priests in the name of the Constitution must therefore be intelligible to ordinary ears and persons of common understanding. The justices should at *least* write their opinions in the common language of plain English, not in the formulaic gobbledygook of tiers of scrutiny, multi-pronged tests, and needlessly complex doctrinal theories.[8]

Modest Proposal Number Two:
ABANDON THE IDEA OF "STARE DECISIS" FOR QUESTIONS OF CONSTITUTIONAL LAW

One of the reasons Supreme Court opinions are so unintell-igible these days is that all the justices seem to do is cite their own prior constitutional decisions and debate the meaning of the prolix majority opinions, plurality opinions, concurrences, partial concur-rences, dissents, and partial dissents. The debates are obscure (even to those familiar with the precedents and especially to those who are not). Worse, the debate is *derivative*, not primary. Often it seems the justices are arguing exclusively about the meaning of precedents interpreting the Constitution and have completely lost track of the idea that perhaps what they should be arguing about is the meaning of the Constitution, not their own prior opinions. It is, after all, a *constitution* we are expounding, not the most recent four-part, three-pronged, intermediate-lite scrutiny, balancing test propounded in the most recent plurality (or even minority) opinion.[9]

There are two points here. The first is just this discussion *ad nauseam* of precedent is, for *We the People*, not helpful or illuminating in the least and serves to further distance the People from our Constitution. In this respect, the Court's use of precedent is just like its use of doctrinal formulae or other legalese. It obscures rather than enlightens.

The second point is more fundamental. When precedent is relied on as *controlling* subsequent constitutional decisions – that is, where the doctrine of *stare decisis* is invoked to *foreclose* judges from interpreting the Constitution directly and to require instead that only the precedents be looked at – the Constitution has truly been buried away and a different form of words, increasingly refracted, mangled distortions of the originals, substituted in its place.

That, I submit, is what the doctrine of "*stare decisis*" (literally, "standing by what has been decided") implies. Taken seriously, *stare decisis* means a deliberate practice of adhering to precedents one knows to be incorrect interpretations of the Constitution, simply because that is what has been done before. Taken unseriously, stare decisis means that precedents are cited even though it doesn't really matter to the present decision what a prior case held. Discussion of the precedents is, in that event, merely so much more obfuscation. Thus, in the one case stare decisis is a doctrine of deliberately interpreting the Constitution in a way you know to be wrong; in the other, it is a doctrine seemingly designed to hide the ball.

Who in his or her right mind would defend such a destructive and/or dishonest doctrine? The justices of the Supreme Court would, and do, at least from time to time and depending on the issue. Consider the Court's stunning 1992 decision reaffirming the right to abortion, *Planned Parenthood v. Casey*.[10]

Casey reaffirmed *Roe v. Wade*[11] despite the evident hand-wringing of Justices O'Connor, Kennedy, and Souter on the issue of whether *Roe* was correctly or incorrectly decided as an original matter.[12] These three justices produced a "Joint Opinion" which became, in relevant part, the opinion of the Court. None of the authors of the Joint Opinion was prepared to say *Roe* was rightly decided. Rather, the Joint Opinion rested squarely on the ground of *stare decisis*. It was necessary for the Court to adhere to *Roe* simply because Roe had been decided before people had become accustomed to easy abortion, and it would be harmful to the Court's institutional prestige if it were to admit error with respect to such an important and audacious decision.[13] Moreover, it would look especially bad if the Court admitted error under pressure from pro-life advocates.[14] Now, say what you will about abortion and the Constitution. That's not my point. Some people think the Constitution can, and should, be read to embrace abortion rights. Others think quite the opposite, that the Constitution can and should be read as embracing a right to life that extends to the unborn. Still others think the Constitution cannot fairly be read in either manner. Each such position, however, is based on some sort of argument *about what the Constitution means. Casey* is not much concerned with that question at all. *Casey* is concerned with the question of how a decision overruling Roe might affect the public's perception of the Court's legitimacy and its claimed right to "speak before all others for their constitutional ideals."[15] *Casey* is, in other words, concerned not with what the Constitution says, but with what people might think of their high priests in black robes. For these reasons, and no other stated ones, the Court in *Casey* adhered to *Roe*, "whether or not mistaken."[16]

Thus understood, *stare decisis* is not just another bad idea. It is, I think, *unconstitutional.* Think about it for a moment. The Supreme Court has decided to give greater legal force to its own prior decisions than to the Constitution. In the event of a perceived conflict between the Constitution and judicial precedent, it is precedent that governs rather than the Constitution, so says the Supreme Court (again, at least from time to time or on some issues).[17] But whatever happened to the idea that acts contrary to the Constitution are void? Shouldn't this axiom apply to judicial decisions contrary to the Constitution, as well as acts of Congress and the Executive contrary to the Constitution? *Marbury v. Madison*[18] and *Federalist No.78*[19] say the Constitution always must be given preference over the faithless acts of mere government agents contrary to the Constitution. If this proposition is true, it follows that no court should ever deliberately adhere to what it is fully persuaded are the erroneous constitutional decisions of the past. To do so is to act in deliberate violation of the Constitution.[20]

My own impression is the justices very rarely do this. Rather, *stare decisis* is a hoax designed to provide cover for a particular outcome, not a genuine, principled ground of decision. Precedent is followed – except when it isn't. But if that is the case, then it is time to reveal the Grand Hoax of *Stare Decisis.* It is time to take the Constitution out from the storage chest and tell our Yang-like justices that what they have been doing simply is not consistent with the good stewardship of the Constitution they think they have been exercising these many years. If the Constitution is to belong to *We the People*, rather than hijacked by the high priests, the doctrine of *stare decisis* must be repudiated entirely in the area of constitutional law.[21]

Modest Proposal Number Three:
RECOGNIZE THE PROPRIETY OF EXECUTIVE AND CONGRESSIONAL "REVIEW" OF SUPREME COURT DECISIONS

My first two modest proposals for returning the Constitution to the People – cutting the jargon, repudiating *stare decisis* – are truly modest in that they work within the accepted modern framework of judicial supremacy and merely ask the Supreme Court to be somewhat less elitist, condescending, misguided, and self-absorbed in its exercise of that interpretive supremacy.

But who died and left it boss in the first place? Nowhere does the Constitution make the Supreme Court our master in matters of constitutional interpretation. Nowhere is it written in our holy words that the Supreme Court's interpretation binds the other branches of government. Indeed, to vest interpretive supremacy, the power to determine *the meaning of all other constitutional powers,* in just one branch of the national government is contrary to the founding generation's premises about separation-of-powers.[22] Rather, the framers intended that the power of constitutional interpretation, like many other important powers conferred on the federal government, be divided and shared among the three branches of government, with none literally bound by the decisions of any of the others. That way, the People would not lose control over their Constitution to *any* mere organ of government. Hear James Madison, writing in *The Federalist No. 49*:

> [T]he people are the only legitimate fountain of power, and it is from them that the constitutional charter, under which the several branches of government bold their power, is derived .... The sever-

> al departments being perfectly co-ordinate by the
> terms of their common commission, neither of
> them, it is evident, can pretend to an exclusive or
> superior right of settling the boundaries between
> their respective powers ....[23]

Somehow, we have lost sight of this most fundamental principle. Somehow, like the Yangs, we have acquiesced in letting a select body exercise exclusive control over the words of our most sacred (secular) text. Once we take the document out of hiding, however, we see its most basic structural principles reject any such exclusivity. Rather, to preserve the Constitution as one ordained by *We the People*, the regime established by the Constitution is one of *divided agency* with each set of agents checking and balancing the others in order to preserve the primacy of the principles. This constitutional axiom is no less true with regard to the power to interpret the Constitution's words than for any other power. In fact, I would say this axiom is *most* important when it comes to the question of who gets to control the Constitution's meaning.

Thus, my third modest proposal is that the other branches of the federal government should exercise independent constitutional review over the judgments and opinions of the Supreme Court. Where they believe the Supreme Court has erred in its interpretation of the Constitution, they should repudiate its decisions and oppose, with all the constitutional powers at their disposal, the Court's attempted imposition of such decisions on the People. Just as we have judicial review over acts of Congress, we have executive review over decisions of courts and congressional review over conduct of the Executive.

Thus, if the President believes a Supreme Court decision is wrong, he is not bound by it for purposes of exercising his constitutional powers. He may grant pardons and veto bills on constitutional grounds rejected by the Court; he may refuse to follow the decision as precedent for other cases; and he may even refuse to enforce the judgment in the specific case where rendered.

Yes, you heard that right. The President may decline to execute a Supreme Court judgment that he is persuaded is not consistent with the Constitution.[24] The proof of this proposition is remarkably straightforward and exactly parallels John Marshall's argument for judicial review in *Marbury v. Madison*: The Constitution is the supreme law. Acts of ordinary government agents contrary to the supreme law are not valid and, therefore, are not binding on other branches of government. Thus, *Marbury* concludes, an Act of Congress contrary to the Constitution should not be given effect by courts when exercising their power to decide lawsuits.[25] Similarly, a judicial decree contrary to the

Constitution should not be given effect by the Executive when exercising his power to take care that the laws be faithfully executed. Indeed, to do so is arguably a violation of his oath to uphold the Constitution as the supreme law. Thus, just as the Supreme Court in *Marbury* held that it must refuse to exercise a statutory grant of jurisdiction conferred in violation of Article III of the Constitution, the President would be duty-bound to refuse to enforce or obey any decree issued by the Court in such circumstances. If John Marshall had held that William Marbury was entitled to his commission as a justice of the peace and ordered President Jefferson's officers to deliver it, Jefferson could rightly have refused on the ground that the Court's exercise of jurisdiction was not consistent with the Constitution, invoking the very same reasoning as in the *Marbury* decision.[26]

Consider another not too far-fetched hypothetical. The year is 1861. Abraham Lincoln has been inaugurated as President and southern states are seceding in droves. Suppose the same southern-dominated Taney Court that decided *Dred Scott*[27] ruled the South could lawfully secede, and President Lincoln's prosecution of the Civil War was therefore unconstitutional. If Lincoln is persuaded that the decision is wrong, lawless, and immoral, is he nonetheless bound to recall Union troops, vacate the White House, and move the capital of the remaining states in the United States of America somewhere north of the Maryland border? Or suppose instead – quite plausibly, in light of *Dred Scott* – the Supreme Court declared the Emancipation Proclamation unconstitutional as a taking of property. Should Lincoln acquiesce in a judgment returning freed blacks to slavery?

I say, and Lincoln (by then) certainly would have said, absolutely not.[28] To Abraham Lincoln, that would be a Yang-like corruption of the Constitution of *We the People*. Rather, Lincoln's view presages Captain James T. Kirk's. (Interestingly, Abe Lincoln appears in another *Star Trek* episode as one of Captain Kirk's all-time historic heroes, but that's another story.) Indeed, Captain Kirk's impassioned speech strikes me as a variation on a theme sounded by Lincoln in his first inaugural address:

> [T]he candid citizen must confess that if the policy of the government, upon vital questions, affecting the whole people, is to be irrevocably fixed by decision of the Supreme Court, ... the people will have ceased, to be their own rulers, having, to that extent, practically resigned their government into the hands of that eminent tribunal.[29]

Those of us who have attended law school have been conditioned to be judge-lovers and politician-despisers (forgetting the extent to which the two sets of officeholders are drawn from the same pool and frequently resemble one another's behavior). We have exorbitant fears of what presidents might do in the name of the Constitution and extraordinary faith in what judges do do (doo-doo?) in the name of the Constitution. The historical record, however, does not support this confidence. Moreover, in principle, the point should be the same with respect to the judiciary and the executive. It is dangerous, unconstitutional, and simply wrong in principle to vest final, unreviewable, interpretive supremacy over the Constitution in any one branch of government, unchecked by an equal interpretive authority in the other branches.

Accordingly, as a modest step toward recapturing the Constitution from adverse possession by the judiciary, I seriously propose the President of the United States – President Bush or one of his successors – should seek an appropriate opportunity for the exercise of executive review of a Supreme Court decision that is contrary to the Constitution and publicly refuse to lend executive enforcement to the Court's judgment on the ground that doing so would violate *his* oath and *his* stewardship of the Constitution.

The same principle holds true for Congress. If Congress is persuaded that a Supreme Court decision is contrary to the Constitution, it may rightly refuse to honor it within the sphere of its legislative powers. The situation of the legislature in regard to exercising effective "review" of judicial decrees is less strategic than that of the executive, but there are opportunities nonetheless. For example, suppose a Supreme Court decision required an appropriation of funds to be effective, but Congress believed the Court's decision to be lawless. Must Congress appropriate the money? Absolutely not. Congress is not bound by the courts' judgments concerning the meaning of the Constitution any more than the courts are bound by congressional judgment. To deny this would be to deny the Constitution's separation of powers and to affirm, instead, that the judges own the Constitution.

A predictable objection to this is if Supreme Court decisions don't bind the other branches, we will have chaos. Hardly. We will have checks and balances, competing interpretations, tension, ongoing disagreement, struggle, compromise, interaction and (eventually) dynamic *equilibrium.* But tension and competition are not chaos. It is the same thing we experience every day as a consequence of separation of powers. Where disagreement persists, the debate must continue. This is not anarchy, but a more *democratic, decentralized,* and *desacrilized* approach to constitutional interpretation.

Modest Proposal Number Four:

REEVALUATE THE HERETOFORE DISCREDITED DOCTRINE OF "INTERPOSITION"
AND CONSIDER THE APPROPRIATE ROLE THAT STATE GOVERNMENT OFFICIALS
MAY HAVE IN GUARDING AGAINST DEPARTURES FROM THE CONSTITUTION BY
THE NATIONAL GOVERNMENT

My third modest proposal took separation-of-powers as its premise. My
fourth modest proposal takes as its premise the other key structural feature of
the Constitution: Federalism. If the several co-ordinate branches of the federal
government may "check" the Supreme Court's legal interpretations, because of
their structural parity and because of the Constitution's Oath Clause, can the
instrumentalities of state government make the same (or an analogous) claim?

"Interposition" and "nullification" are dirty words these days because they
have been invoked on the wrong sides of the great constitutional crises of our
nation's history – southern secessionists resisting the Union and southern segre-
gationists resisting *Brown v. Board of Education.*[30] But it is not too hard to imagine the shoe being on the other foot.

As a way of trying to consider this issue afresh, and counteracting our
instinctive biases, I ask you to consider the real-life case of *Lemmon v. The
People*[31] decided by the highest court of the Empire State, the New York Court
of Appeals, in 1860 on the eve of the Civil War. *Lemmon* is, in many ways, the
companion piece to *Dred Scott.*[32]

A Virginia family was traveling to Texas by way of New York City.[33] (That
was the most efficient route in those days, because of the efficiency of steam-
boat travel from New York City to New Orleans.) The Virginians brought their
eight slaves into New York state, where they were freed on a writ of habeas corpus.[34] New York was, of course, free soil. Under New York law, Negro slaves
voluntarily brought by their owners into New York immediately became free.
(Runaways were governed by the Fugitive Slave Clause and the Fugitive Slave
Act of 1850.[35]) The New York courts chose to apply their own state's law, rather
than the law of Virginia, to this choice-of-law situation.[36] The Court of Appeals
affirmed the lower courts' holding that these were free men and women.[37]

Suppose now that history had played out slightly differently in 1860 and
1861: Either Vice President John Breckenridge or Senator Stephen Douglas is
elected President in 1860 rather than Lincoln, and the South stays in the Union.
Lemmon goes up to the U.S. Supreme Court on appeal. The Taney Court
reverses the New York Court of Appeals on the authority of *Dred Scott's* recognition of the right to hold slaves as property and a determination that the
Privileges and Immunities Clause of Article IV protects a slaveholder's right to
keep that property when he travels to another state.[38]

This was a foreseeable, even an expected result, noted by Lincoln and a good many others in the aftermath of *Dred Scott. Lemmon* would be simply the next logical step from *Scott*. And, as a consequence, it would require that slavery be tolerated in the North, confirming Lincoln's prophecy that the nation could not survive half slave and half free. *Lemmon* would make slavery the law of the land. There could be no such thing as a "free" state.[39]

Suppose now that you are the governor of New York. The pro-slavery Taney Court has held that former slaves freed under the laws of New York must be returned to their Virginia masters. Indeed, anyone may move to New York from the South and keep their slaves. Moreover, it follows that native New Yorkers can start holding slaves, too. Under the Supreme Court's ruling, which you firmly believe is both wrong under the Constitution and wrong as a matter of morality, New York harbor is about to become the largest slave-trading port in the world. What do you do? Can you refuse to obey the Supreme Court's decision, refuse to return the freed slaves, and resist the Douglas or Breckenridge administration's attempted enforcement of the *Lemmon* decree?

I am inclined to say yes, yes, and yes. State government officials – governors, legislators, and judges – also swear an oath to support the federal Constitution.[40] Fidelity to that oath, I should think, requires resisting violations of the Constitution by the federal government with all the powers at your disposal as a state, including, perhaps, calling forth the militia. I have to tell you that, under this scenario, I would expect (or hope) that Governor Paulsen would be leading the Yankees into armed rebellion against the lawful government of the Union rather than acquiescing in the extension of slavery to free soil and the sending of freed men back to bondage.

Now this should be disturbing. For, in a sense, this *is* Governor George Wallace blocking the schoolhouse doors to resist integration. My point here is simply that interposition can be used for good or for ill, and its *legitimacy* should not turn on the historical accident that it has been most regularly invoked for ill.

There are other problems with interposition. Such a theory must rest on the Oath Clause alone, for the states, unlike the President and the Congress, do not *stand* in *a position* of "co-ordinance" to and, thus, interpretive parity with the Supreme Court. No one to date has given a convincing defense of the doctrine. So far as I am aware, all previous such attempts rest on a theory of state-federal sovereignty (namely, state supremacy) that is a manifestly unsound construction of the Constitution. But the fact that the theories that have been put forward in support of interposition have been flawed and the applications of those theories evil does not mean that no sound theory and just applications are possible. In principle, it seems to me that if the Constitution belongs to *We the People*, *all* government officials have a duty to guard against its usurpation or violation by others, and that this duty extends to government officials at the state, as well as national, levels. The idea of interposition thus strikes me as one that is not so absurd as to be excluded from the discussion, though I am not prepared to proclaim it sound. My modest proposal here is therefore only for serious rethinking of this issue.

Modest Proposal Number Five:
JURY REVIEW

I have no such reticence about my fifth, and final, modest proposal, jury review. Of any of my proposals, *this* is the one that most closely accomplishes the idea that the Constitution must belong to all the People. It is also the one that has the strongest support in the early history of our republic. For the jury was historically understood as the virtual embodiment of *We the People*, the representatives of the people, when called upon to apply the law to a particular case. And the jury was understood both as *the* single most important check on overweening government power and, relatedly, as a vital institution for putting the People in charge of the administration of government. Absence of adequate provision for jury trial was the issue that provoked the movement for a Bill of Rights, beginning at the federal convention in 1787.[41]

My proposition can be stated simply: *We the People*, acting through juries, may independently interpret the Constitution in the course of exercising our responsibilities as jurors to apply the law to a specific case. We have the absolute, unreviewable right to disregard judges' instructions concerning the meaning of the Constitution, and, instead, to decide for ourselves questions of constitutional interpretation that may arise in particular cases.

Note that this is not jury nullification – deliberate disregard for the law because one thinks it unjust. It is a case-specific power to refuse to accede to judicial *interpretations* of the Constitution that a jury thinks are wrong in any case where a jury determination is necessary in order to carry out the state's exercise of authority against persons. Lawyers should always be permitted to argue questions of constitutionality to a jury, and the jury should always be free to judge the meaning of the Constitution for itself. I therefore support the movement in some western states for passage of a Fully Informed Jury Act that would apprise juries of their right to act as judges of constitutionality and would require judges to so inform the jury.[42]

The idea of jury review has been advanced and defended by others, including most recently and prominently Professor Akbil Amar of Yale Law School.[43] The historical case is quite compelling. Juries had the power to judge the law at the time the Constitution was adopted, serving as the "lower house" of the judicial branch of government. The case seems at its most compelling concerning matters of constitutional interpretation. The jury was understood to be the very bulwark of constitutional liberty precisely because the jury puts the People in charge of the administration of their government and in charge of their Constitution. As Thomas Jefferson declared in 1789, "[w]ere I called upon to decide whether the people had best be omitted in the Legislative or Judicial department, I would say it is better to leave them out of the Legislative."[44]

Again, this strikes most people today as a bit strang, *Judges* decide the law; juries decide facts and facts only. Or so we all think. Professor Amar's response is the same as Captain Kirk's: We have forgotten what the Constitution is all about. In Amar's words:

> [P]erhaps the reason is we have lost the powerful and prevailing sense of 200 years ago that the Constitution was the people's law. Even if juries generally lacked competence to adjudicate intricate and technical "lawyer's law," the Constitution was not supposed to be a prolix code. It had been made, and could be unmade at will, by We the People of the United States.[45]

Jury review is popular interpretation of the Constitution. It proceeds on the same assumption as my other modest proposals: that judicial supremacy is a myth that has corrupted our constitutional discourse.

Conclusion

It is time to explode the myth of judicial supremacy and judicial exclusivity in constitutional interpretation – a myth that has lived long but ought not be allowed to prosper. I have offered a modest agenda for restoring the People's role in constitutional interpretation: (1) eliminate doctrinal jargon in judicial opinions, (2) eliminate the pernicious doctrine of *stare decisis*, (3) decentralize and desacrilize constitutional decision making by recognizing the propriety of independent constitutional judgment by the other branches of the federal government, (4) examine whether the same reasoning might not well support independent constitutional judgment by state government officers, and (5) reinvigorate the jury as an instrument of popular interpretation of the Constitution.

I am not certain that each of these proposals is perfect, but I am certain they are more in line with the spirit of the Constitution than is the prevailing orthodoxy of unthinking judicial supremacy, which strips the words *We the People* from the document of the People. But those words, written larger than all the others that follow it, cannot be ignored. As Captain James T. Kirk tells us, the words of the Constitution must belong to everyone or they mean nothing at all.

End Notes

1. This essay is a slight revision of the Albany Law School Enrichment Series Lecture presented at Albany Law School, November 14, 1994. I would like to thank the students and faculty of Albany Law School for their questions, comments and hospitality. In addition, I would like to thank William Riker and Katherine Janeway for their comments, Wesley Crusher for his excellent research assistance, and Deanna Troi for her wise counsel.

2. Apparently, the Prime Directive of noninterference with the peaceful development of other peoples on other worlds is a pure principle of convenience, honored when its constraints are necessary to make a challenging plot and dispensed with (often without mention) whenever its strictures would interfere with the tidy resolution of a plot in a way that the writers found desirable. This is sort of like the Supreme Court's treatment of the First Amendment's freedom of speech. Compare *Texas v. Johnson*, 491 U.S. 897, 420 (1989) (strict adherence to the prime directive of the First Amendment) with *Madsen v. Women's Health Center*, 1145. S. Ct. 2816, 2523-25 (1994) (violating the prime. directive where deemed inconvenient, by manipulating the "level of scrutiny" of direct, content-based prohibition of political speech in a public forum).

3. *Star Trek*: "The Omega Glory" (NBC television broadcast. Mar. 1, 1968). The details that follow are drawn from my personal memory of having viewed this episode some half-dozen times in my misbegotten youth and from *Star Trek-TOS Episode Guide Stackware* created by David Landis, Oak Mountain Software (and retrieved off the Internet for me by Mr. Chu Moy [Minnesota Law School '96]). Quotations are not warranted to be accurate, just close enough.

4. Kirk to Spock and McCoy, about halfway through the episode.

5. I don't remember if McCoy said "damnit" here, but he was always saying "damnit." I think it was a word the censors had just recently permitted.

6. *Planned Parenthood v. Casey*, 112 S. Ct. 2791. 2818 (1992) (emphasis added).

7. See, *e.g.*, Joe Goldstein, *The Intelligible Constitution* 3-7 (1992); Daniel K Ferber, "Missing the 'Play of Intelligence'." 36 *Wm. & Mary L. Rev.*147, 149-58 (1994); Morton J. Horowitz. "The Supreme Court, 1992 Term – Foreword: The Constitution of Change: Legal Fundamentality Without Fundamentalism," 107 *Harv. L. Rev.* 30, 44-51 (1993); Robert F. Nagel, "The Formulaic Constitution," 84 *Mich. L. Rev.* 165, 165-49 (1955).

8. Of course, law professors are even worse than judges on this score. If you want to read incomprehensible, preten-
tious, pompous, turgid, revolting, jargonistic gibberish, read the law reviews (the *Albany Law Review* excepted,
of course). It has often been noted by others that law reviews tend to place a premium on length, jargon, and
unintelligibility in selecting which articles to publish. Kenneth J, Lasson, "Scholarship Amok: Excesses in the
Pursuit of Truth and Tenure," 103 *Harv. L. Rev.* 926, 926-28 (1990). My colleague Dan Farber has made the same
point in a recent article, but is too nice a guy to give examples. Farber, *supra* note 6. at 158. I am not too nice a
guy, just too lazy.

9. Let me give just one example from my own area of specialty: First Amendment religion clause jurisprudence.
Hundreds more can be given from every nook and cranny of the law. *County of Allegheny v. ACLU*, 492 U.S. 573
(1989) involved an establishment clause challenge to the constitutionality of publicly sponsored displays of (1) a
nativity scene on the stairwell of a public courthouse and (2) a large menorah and a Christmas tree in front of a
government office building. Four justices thought the applicable test was a variation on the principle of "non-
coercion," and voted to allow both displays. Id. at 665-63, 679. Five justices thought the applicable test was
whether the display, in context, "endorsed" religion. Id. at 589-94. But of these five, three justices thought both
displays endorsed religion and two justices thought that the Christian nativity scene did, but the Jewish menorah did not. Id. at 578. The two-justice position thus became the holding of the Court, even though seven justices thought that different constitutional treatment of the two different religious symbols was unacceptable.
Id. at 598-602; see Michael Stokes Paulsen, "Lemon is Dead," 43 *Case W. Res. L. Rev.* 795, 813-17 (1993).

What's a lower court to do? In *Harris v. City of Zion*, 927 F.2d 1401 (7th Clr. 1991), *cert denied* 112 S. Ct. 3025
(1992), Judge Easterbrook (dissenting) noted the mild absurdity of attempting faithfully to follow the Supreme
Court's two-justice rule even though the rule was impossible to apply and contrary to the view of a majority of
the justices. Id. at 1423 (Easterbrook, J., dissenting). Easterbrook's dissent urges what should be obvious to any
constitutionalist who hasn't been corrupted by years of training in a Yang legal culture, Why not go back and
interpret the Establishment Clause directly, rather than waste one's effort interpreting the interpretations?

10. 112 S. Ct. 2791 (1992) (O'Connor, J.).

11. 410 U.S. 113 (1973).

12. *Casey*, 112 S. Ct. at 2809-21

13. *Id.* at 2814-16.

14. Id. at 2815-16 ("[W]hatever the premise of opposition may be, only the most convincing justification under accepted standards of precedent could suffice to demonstrate that a later decision overruling the first was anything
but a surrender to political pressure ... so to overrule under fire ... would subvert the Court's legitimacy ...")
Apparently, however, the Court thought it would not look bad if it adhered to *Roe* under pressure from pro-
choice advocates.

15. Id. at 2816.

16. Id. at 2810

17. Contrast, for example, the Supreme Court's quite different approach to precedent in *Adarand Constructors, Inc. v.
Pena*, 115 8. Ct. 2097 (1995) and the cases that Justice O'Connor collects in the portion of her opinion (joined
only by Justice Kennedy) attempting to justify this result and attempting (unpersuasively) to distinguish *Casey's*
stare decisis analysis. Id. at 2115-16.

18. 5 U.S. (1 Cranch) 137 (1802).

19. *The Federalist* No. 78 (Alexander Hamilton) (Clinton Rossiter ed., 1961).

20. I owe the argument of this paragraph in substantial part to Gary Lawson. Gary S. Lawson, "The Constitutional
Case Against Precedent," 17 *Harv. J.L. & Pub. Pol'y* 23 (1994). In earlier work, I have argued that lower court
judges are not literally "bound" to adhere to higher court precedents where they are fully persuaded that the
precedent is a fundamentally wrong interpretation of the law. Michael Stokes Paulsen, "Accusing Justice:

Some Variations On The Theme Of Robert M. Cover's *Justice Accused*," *7 J.L. & Religion* 33, 77-88 (1989). I hope to develop these ideas at greater length in a future article. Michael Stokes Paulsen, *The Pernicious Doctrine of Stare Decisis* (unpublished manuscript on file with the author).

21. That is not to say that precedent has no role. Precedent may persuade, enlighten, collate the judgments of past interpreters, and avoid the need to reinvent the wheel. All of these aid future interpreters. But it is an entirely different thing to argue that a past decision should control a future one, even when, after full and careful consideration of the past decision, the present interpreter is fully persuaded that the precedent was erroneous.

22. See Michael Stokes Paulsen, "The Most Dangerous Branch: Executive Power To Say *What* The Law Is," 88 *GEO. L.J.* 217, 228-61 (1994).

23. *The Federalist* No. 49, 313. -4 (James Madison) (Clinton Rossiter ed., 1961).

24. I have developed this idea at length in another article. See Paulsen, *supra* note 21, at 262-84.

25. *Marbury v. Madison*, 5 U.S. (1 Cranch) 137, 180 (1803).

26. Jefferson probably would have refused to comply with the Court's judgment ordering him (or his subordinates) to deliver Marbury's commission on the ground that separation of powers prevents the courts from ordering the President around at all. See Paulsen, *supra* note 21, at 306-308.

27. *Dred Scott v. Sanford*, 60 U.S. (19 How.) 393 (1856).

28. As a Senate candidate in 1858, Lincoln clearly affirmed the finality of Supreme Court judgments as law for the particular case where rendered. See Paulsen, *supra* note 28, at 275 (discussing Lincoln's position of "nonacquiescence" in *Dred Scott* as precedent binding on future congressional action). As I have argued elsewhere, it is difficult to sustain the distinction between nonacquiescence in the precedential force of a decision and nonacquiescence in the decision itself. Id. at 276-84. What happens when the Court asserts (as it has, at least since Cooper v. Aaron. 358 U.S. 1, 18 (1958)) that its holdings are binding "law"? Lincoln, spurred by wartime exigency (and perhaps by nonacquiescence in *his* authority as President, as well), eventually followed this slippery slope to its logical conclusion. By the time Chief Justice Taney was issuing orders freeing suspected rebel saboteurs on writs of habeas corpus, Lincoln was no longer enforcing judicial decrees. I have told the story of the evolution (or radicalization) of Lincoln's views on judicial authority elsewhere. Paulsen, *supra* note 21, 272-84; see also Michael Stokes Paulsen, "The Merryman Power and the Dilemma of Autonomous Executive Branch Interpretation." 15 *Cardozo L. Rev.* 81, 88-99 (1993).

29. Abraham Lincoln, "First Inaugural Address – Final Text" (Max. 4, 1861), in *4 The Collected Works Of Abraham Lincoln* 282, 268 (Roy P. Basler, ed .1953).

30. *Brown v. Board of Education*, 347 U.S. 483 (1954).

31. *Lemmon v. The People.* 20 N.Y. 562 (1860).

32. *Scott v. Sanford*, 60 U.S. 895 (1857).

33. *Lemmon*, 20 N.Y. at 599.

34. Id.

36. Fugitive Slave Act of 1850, ch. 60. 9 Stat. 462 (1850).

36. *Lemmon*, 20 N.Y. at 628.

37. Id. at 582

38. See *Dred Scott*, 60 U.S. at 451-52.

39. For an excellent overview of the historical significance of *Lemmon* and the legitimate fears of many northerners that it would become the next *Dred Scott* and mandate northern tolerance of slavery, see James M. McPherson, *Battle Cry Of Freedom: The Civil War Era* 179-81 (1988). For a detailed account, see Paul Finkleman,

An Imperfect Union: Slavery, Federalism And Comity 293-338 (1981); see also Don E. Fehrenbacher, *The Dred Scott Case: Its Significance* In *American Law And Politics* 444-45 (1978).

40. See U.S. Const. art. VII; N.Y. CON. art. XIII, sec. 1

41. For a powerful and illuminating treatment of the centrality of the jury to early American notions of constitutionalism, see Akhil R. Amar, "The Bill of Rights as a Constitution," 100 *Yale L.J.* 1131, 1182-91 (1991).

42. See Gail D. Cox, "Jurors Rise Up Over Principles and Their Perks," *Nat'l L.J.* May 29, 1995, at A1.

43. Amar, *supra* note 40; see also *Akhil R.* Amar, "Reinventing Juries Ten Suggested Reforms," 28 *U.C. Davis L. Rev.* 1169 (1995).

44. Letter from Thomas Jefferson to L'Abbe Arnoux (July 19, 1789) in *15 The Papers Of Thomas Jefferson*, 282, 283 (Julian P. Boyd, ed., 1958).

45. Amar, *supra* note 40, at 1195.

SECTION TWO
STAR TREK AND JUSTICE

If law is a complex dance of balancing the power of government with the needs, or wants, of particular members and groups within society, then social movements, demands for a specific dance of social justice, are akin to choreographers trying to represent ideas via movement. Within each person, each group, is an idea, a vision, of how the audience will see and appreciate the presentation. Choreographers know they are subject to a kind of law: what the director wants and the producer will pay for. Law and justice ideas are choreographies to the extent that proponents of a particular vision believe that if it reaches enough people, and sways them, law and justice will be changed.

It is axiomatic that law seldom equals justice for all. It cannot when there is little agreement on the meaning or practice of either term. The previous section, "*Star Trek* and Law," was largely about this point. People disagree about what is important, and they are often able to sway, even make law, to compel a certain vision of it. This is so in other arenas; in education, for example, there is substantial disagreement, perhaps too tame a phrase, about what the curriculum should be. In point, many argue that curriculum, what is taught, more reflects ideology about what should be truth than concerns about what is true. Within this line of thought, formal education can be seen as an attempt to instill the values of a society.

This attempt cannot be deemed good or bad; societies are defined by the beliefs and values they hold – and by their tolerance of that which differs from the mainstream. To the extent that formal education is congruent with the many other institutions that develop and inculcate beliefs and values, for example family and community, there will be stability. However, there is a negative side to stability. Too often, stability is defined as maintaining the status quo, a hierarchal status quo in which some must always be at the bottom and some will always be at the top.

Again, this may not be a bad thing. Competition, particularly the competition of ideas, is healthy. All things considered, we would rather have things be designed by a top flight engineer or be treated by the best physician. Few would argue that minimal intelligence and competence should not be a require-

ment for entering such professions. Starfleet Academy, for example, is portrayed as an exceptionally competitive place. However, the concept and practice of competition become unhealthy when "place" in society is assigned not
on merit, but on preconceptions about individual or group characteristics,
stereotypes if you will. Hence, much of human history has been the story of
excluding people from various enterprises and endeavors based on preconceptions about race, ethnicity, and gender. Similarly, much of the history of knowledge, including science, can be viewed as that of resisting every new idea.

   Viewed this way, history, including the future history of *Star Trek*, is the
story of the struggle for justice. It is the story of individuals and movements
that have changed, or at least ameliorated, the more negative aspects of status
quo. In this sense, *Star Trek* has always been visionary in its attempts to show
that 'better place,' and the struggle inherent in getting there. *Star Trek* is mas-
terful choreography. Professor Lentz explores the depictions of women and
gender issues throughout the *Star Trek* media, with a feminist critique of the
"vision" as all too similar to existing realities. Further, Professor Leone
overviews depictions of corrections institutions and practices in *Star Trek* and
suggests that *Star Trek* may simply ignore or naïvely present issues of social justice as a result of the limited background and knowledge of its writers and producers. Similarly, Professor Vivona finds the "Repentence" episode of *Star
Trek: Voyager* to be a wealth of depictions of criminology theories and ideas on
capital punishment, but the episode presents "nothing new under the sun."
Professor Stitt, whose chapter does not directly reference *Star Trek*, nevertheless addresses a common theme in *Star Trek*: that godlike beings often may act
"all too human." He argues that the examination of human nature, and the
study of evil, is a joint enterprise for both theology and the science of criminology. Finally, Professors Lentz and Chaires overview depictions of diversity
throughout the *Star Trek* media, finding that *Star Trek* sometimes projects and
reinforces, perhaps unconsciously, the negative stereotypes of American society.

'Where No Woman Has Gone Before':
FEMINIST PERSPECTIVES ON STAR TREK

SUSAN A. LENTZ JD, PHD

Introduction

The *Star Trek* journey to explore worlds where "no man" had gone before began in 1966. The original television series has generated four spin-offs, a series of feature films, and a cult industry. The first *Star Trek* was largely rooted in the social upheavals and movements of the '60s, with the exception perhaps of the women's movement and feminism. As the series evolved in its "science fiction" vision of our world and the universe in the not too distant future, the epigram became gender neutral. The crew of *Star Trek: The Next Generation* in the '80s journeyed to where "no one," or at least no human of planet Earth, had gone before. Thus, as the last decades of the 20th century reflected dramatic change in the lives of women, and men, in this country and many other countries around the world, the series began to reflect new visions and address issues of gender.

In interpreting that change and projecting it forward to succeeding centuries, the *Star Trek* series provides a unique opportunity to critically consider the evolving role of gender in this world. It is critical to keep in mind, however, that the voyages of *Star Trek* are limited by the knowledge, experiences, and outlook of the writers and producers of each episode. Consequently, unintended, even unconscious "images" may appear. In addition, as the audience, individual viewers bring their own backgrounds and viewpoints to the "messages" of *Star Trek* to the good, and bad, of our present world, shaping our visions of the future. For feminists, the question remains whether *Star Trek*'s "other worldly" vision of the universe remains essentially masculine. Much of planet Earth's history is perhaps unidimensional because its societies have been, for the most part, patriarchal. Patriarchy, or the rule of men, has, thus, defined what is feminine as well as masculine. Has *Star Trek*, in the context of gender, journeyed to where no woman, or man for that matter, has gone before? Modern feminist theories provide alternative world views in looking at our past and also at our future. Most important, these perspectives on gender relations and justice are critical to the evolution of our society and future world. It is a question not only of whether the Federation of *Star Trek* has escaped the male-dominated world of the 20th century, but of how it can do so.

This writing will set the stage by introducing gender and various feminist world views. From this foundation, it proceeds to examine the evolution of the *Star Trek* crew. From the mini-skirted nurse in the first series to the captain of the Federation starship *Voyager*, the roles of women in Starfleet dramatically change. Additionally, in many episodes, there is an opportunity to consider the society of *Star Trek*. Through its portrayal of other worlds within the *Star Trek* universe, the series also have explored issues of justice and gender in our past and potential future. Is that future gender-neutral, gender-dominated, or perhaps gender-free? The voyage to that future world has just begun.

Feminist Perspectives On Gendered Society

In addressing issues of gender, it must first be acknowledged that sex and sexuality are not synonymous with gender. While biological functions and physiological makeup have helped define what is masculine and feminine in our universe, gender itself is the socio-cultural construction that defines our values, institutions, environment, and lives as women and men. Thus, it is not a new concept; nor has it only recently been discovered. Today, however, gender is seen in a new light as feminist perspectives offer different world views of our past and present and of what our future may become. These worldviews have much to offer to the *Star Trek* universe.

Although distrustful critics often group feminists together under derogatory labels such as "male bashers" or even "man haters," there is no one, unified feminist theory. Like other moral and political theories, or ideologies, feminist perspectives are value laden. Several owe much to "masculine" political and economic theories such as liberalism and Marxism. Cultural feminism is more likely to stress natural differences between masculine and feminine. On the other hand, eco-feminism focuses on human efforts to control nature and the implications of such efforts for oppression in its many forms (see, e.g., Kourany, Sterba, and Tong, 1999). Significantly, certain feminist viewpoints have been criticized as presenting white, middle class views as though they represent the experiences of all women, yet women of color often do not identify with such perceptions or perspectives (e.g., Lugones and Spelman, 1999). Beyond the backlash rhetoric and divisions among feminists, feminist theories add critical gender analysis that has been missing from androcentric world views and, as such, they suggest a variety of alternate, future universes.

Two central feminist theories that have contributed significantly to discourse and change are liberal and radical feminism. They also have influenced other feminist perspectives and been influenced by this dialogue. Arguments and policies that are seen as "feminist" by the public often involve aspects of these two theories, yet they differ in their major assumptions about the role of gender in our society, the problems and the solutions.

LIBERAL FEMINISM

In the '60s and '70s, liberal feminist theory dominated legal reform aimed at gender inequality, such as employment discrimination and sexual harassment law. According to liberal feminists, women were historically denied equal opportunity and participation in the public world of politics, economics, religion, science, and education because of institutionalized sexism. Breaking down barriers will, thus, open doors to women. And, if given the chance, women can "do the job" as well as men, perhaps even better. Liberals, thus, seek to be "true equals" with men (Alleman, 1993).

To a degree, such equality emphasizes "sameness:" women and men are not so different. In fact, they are perhaps more alike than different. If, for example, men and women are treated the same on the job, they will essentially behave in similar ways. A further example of this emphasis on sameness can be seen in two early feminist theories of female crime that suggested that as women gained greater equality, female crime would rise to the much higher rates of male crime. According to Rita Adler, greater equality would bring an increase in violent crime as women adopted more masculine behaviors. Rita Simon, on the other hand, suggested that women's "liberation" would increase opportunities for women to commit economic crimes in the workplace (Alleman, 1993). The reality of women's offenses, however, remains very different from male crime today. The weakness, or incompleteness, of the sameness approach is that there are real differences between men and women. It is just difficult to distinguish these from longstanding stereotypes – like women are emotional and men are rational (often with the not- so subtle implication that so-called feminine traits are negative and are valued less).

In bringing about change, liberal feminists largely advocate working within the existing system. In the tradition of political liberalism, they also emphasize the individual and the values of free expression and individual autonomy. Historically, women, however, largely have not been socialized in these values, and their roles in society have been defined primarily by biology and by sex. On the one hand, women have been wives and mothers, the virtuous madonna. Society has long expected, and honored, the "good wife." Among the historic traits of this "good wife" has been obedience to her husband. On the other hand, women out in the public world, particularly single women, have been viewed as sexually accessible. Liberal feminists have acknowledged that as long as women are treated as sex objects, as subservient to men, they cannot be equal. In addition, women's work also has been undervalued in the public workplace and in the private world of the family as well. Liberal feminists (Okin, 1999), like radicals (Firestone, 1999), acknowledge that true equality requires "equality" in the home. The gender structure of the family, thus, has been a "major obstacle to equality of opportunity" (Okin, 1999: 316).

Although liberal feminists in many ways have no one world vision, most espouse, at the very least, a gender neutral theory of justice. This is exemplified in laws that prohibit employers taking into account a person's gender. Sexual harassment law has gone further to require that employers free the work place of "hostile environments" where women are viewed and treated as "sex objects" first and professionals a distant second. Yet gender neutrality is not necessarily the same as gender equality. Sterba (1999: 332) suggests that genuine equal opportunity requires a gender-free or androgynous society where roles are assigned based on desirable traits that are "equally available to both women and men, or in the case of virtues, equally expected of both women and men." Of course, traits that have been traditionally associated with subordination or discrimination must be rejected. This ideal of an androgynous society would require that roles in society be based on "(natural) ability, rational expectation, and choice" (Sterba, 1999).

The challenge for such a society is to get beyond sexual stereotyping that defines what is masculine and feminine. Rather than debate what this just society would look like, Sterba (1999) considers how to get there, suggesting, for example, that economic inequality can only be overcome by policies supporting affirmative action and comparable worth. Like radical feminists, he adds that overt violence directed at women, such as rape and domestic violence, must be eradicated. It is through such gender violence that men control women.

In sum, perhaps the ideal woman of a liberal feminist society would be an autonomous individual who has self-consciously and freely chosen her own path in life, and no paths have been denied to her. Most critically, her choice must not put her at a disadvantage in the regard to career or family.

RADICAL FEMINISM

While liberal feminism often is considered as mainstream, radical feminism is more likely to be seen as the "outer limits." Both, however, have been important forces in the last decades of the 20th century. For radical feminists, attacking inequality is insufficient because patriarchy is the root of women's subordination and oppression. Without eliminating patriarchy, equality is an illusion. Radical feminists are also more likely to celebrate difference. Yet, in doing so, they acknowledge that biological differences contributed to the enslavement of women and patriarchy itself (Brownmiller, 1975). Among feminists, radicals are most likely to address sexuality and sexual oppression in terms of patriarchy. At its core are the institutions of "heterosexuality, marriage, and motherhood"

(Frye, 1999). As Brownmiller (1975) posits, female subjection to men perhaps began because women feared an "open season of rape" (16). While the first rape may have been accidental, a woman resisted the advances of a man, the second was planned. Man learned he could achieve sexual penetration by force. According to Brownmiller (1975), 'protective mating' led to males taking "title" to particular females. And this burden of protection became formalized in society and law, reducing women to the status of chattel, of property. Other explanations for women's subordination may emphasize that such subjugation has been particularly associated with warrior cultures, societies that have grown out of inter-group competition for often scarce resources. In such societies, not only did notions of property develop, but men held a monopoly over weapons and the specialized skills to use them – skills that also could be used to control women.

SUBORDINATION AND DOUBLE STANDARDS

While physical, or biological, differences may have led to women's subordination, justifications for such subordination have included notions of women's intellectual inferiority. Thus, philosopher Benedict de Spinoza in the 17th century could ask the question whether women were under the rule of men by nature or institution and answer it simply by asserting that if women were equal to men in ability, there would certainly be examples of men and women ruling together or of men ruled by women. Since he could find none, Spinoza concluded women were under the authority of men because of their natural weakness (from *A Political Treatise*, cited in Spielvogel, 1991). Two centuries later, Charles Darwin also would assert, in a similar circular argument, that differences in men's and women's intellectual abilities could be shown by the evidence that man had attained a "higher eminence in whatever he takes up, than can woman – whether requiring deep thought, reason, or imagination, or merely the use of senses and hands" (from *The Descent of Man*, in Agnito, 1977:260). Other philosophers have explained the rule of men more particularly as a matter of paternal necessity – a man can only ensure he is the father of "his children" by controlling his wife's conduct (for example, Jean Jacques Rousseau in *A Discourse on Political Economy* and David Hume in *A Treatise of Human Nature*).

According to Firestone (1999: 355), the "biological family is an inherently unequal power distribution." It has been men's control of women's bodies, of procreation, that is the core of female subordination. Socialist feminists also acknowledge that male dominance, or power relationships, grew from the demands of biology and of human reproduction. In regard to inequality and oppression, for socialists, sex class is as fundamental as economic class is to Marxists (Alleman, 1993). While women's biology undoubtedly contributed to their subordination, men's biological urges, or needs, became an "excuse" for sexual oppression and violence. Those women who fell outside male protection became deviant (Alleman, 1995). Thus, prostitution has not only traditionally served men, but also has defined women as deviant, as whores.

Feminists generally acknowledge that women's sexuality has long been a "problem" for men. In their sexuality, women have been perceived as having power over men; they are seducers who can enslave men. By controlling women, men have less to fear from them. But while men want their wives to be chaste madonnas, they also will seek out those women seen to be sexually accessible. This even has been perceived as their biological imperative. Patriarchy has, thus, created the whores in sanctioning a double standard of sexual behavior. Even today, young men are not labeled as deviant for "sowing their wild oats," for being promiscuous. To many, they are to be emulated. Young women, on the other hand, who are promiscuous, or simply seen to be sexually provocative, are labeled sluts or "hos." And through the different media of pornography – visual and spoken images intended to sexually arouse (primarily males) - society continues to define all women as sex objects. Radical feminists, such as Andrea Dworkin (1993) and Catharine MacKinnon (1987), have been most vocal in calling for the eradication of all pornography as essential to the elimination of male domination and patriarchy.

Radical Solutions to the Problems of Patriarchy

Although radical feminists are more likely than liberals to stress "real" differences between men and women, and to value such difference, they also recognize that emphasizing perceived and imposed differences was used historically to deny women opportunities and equality. Perhaps most significantly, radical feminists stress that biological differences have been translated into gender roles that perpetuate subordination, such as dividing social interaction into both public and domestic spheres. Humanity has evolved far beyond the "demands of nature," yet sex class persists (Firestone, 1999). Patriarchy, or its remnants, continues to define what is masculine and feminine. According to MacKinnon (1987), what is feminine is difficult to determine because of such male domination. Are women naturally relationship-oriented, or have men imposed that attribute on women to their own advantage? MacKinnon concludes (39), "Women think in relational terms because our existence is defined in relation to men." Are women naturally more devious, as some stereotypes suggest, or have they learned to be evasive in order to survive in a male world where they have long existed as the personal property of fathers and husbands? Is such a stereotype imposed on women the better to justify controlling them?

Radical feminists, like liberals, are not of one voice. They, perhaps, most often differ among themselves and other feminists in regard to the solution to the "problem" of patriarchy. Radicals are most likely to criticize notions of equality as inadequate to address gender subordination. MacKinnon's domination theory suggests we cannot truly know what it is to be female or male until patriarchy is eliminated. Thus, autonomy for women in a gender-neutral society is most probably an illusion (see, e.g., Lentz and Stitt, 1996, in regard to the debate over legalization of prostitution). Socialist feminists would agree that economic "self-determination" for women and children in a capitalist society is illusionary. For socialist as well as radical feminists, fundamental change in society's economic and social structure is essential (Firestone, 1999). Radical feminists are more likely to seek a gender-free world. Because of male domination, such a world is only possible if women are "separated" or "free" from men. This may be expressed in a variety of ways.

Since control over women's bodies and procreation is at the core of male domination, some radicals have advocated artificial reproduction. Firestone (1999: 337), for example, suggests the "option" of artificial reproduction would permit children to be "born to both sexes equally, or independently of either." To be truly free of the "tyranny" of the biological family, the role of childbearing and child rearing must be diffused throughout society. According to Firestone (1999), the cultural significance of genital differences must be eliminated.

Although sexual intercourse may be unnecessary for reproduction, the human species does not have sex just to mate. Thus, access to contraception is a critical factor to equality for both liberal and radical feminists. To be free of male domination, women also must be free to reject sex, to choose celibacy, for example. According to Brownmiller (1975), however, rape has been a weapon by which men keep women in fear and subjugation. Radical feminists would argue that freedom to choose is an impossibility as long as rape remains a probability.

For many radical feminists, such as Brownmiller (1975), the freedom of a genderless society requires separation from men. Although there are many forms and acts of separation (Frye, 1999), a separate society itself is one that is not imposed but is freely chosen without patriarchal influence. For some, this may even mean a lesbian society, a rejection of heterosexuality itself. Yet, according to Kourany, Sterba, and Tong (1999), these radical visions are not necessarily of a unisex or sexless world but of societies where women can find their own sexuality. The vision of a unisex or androgynous world without sex or passion remains largely a masculine vision. After all, it is patriarchy that has defined violence as well as passion and creative powers. Love and sex in a gender-free society may be many different things.

Radical and liberal feminist visions of a just society are in many ways only a means to a future world of "science fiction." By addressing ways to achieve a gender neutral or gender free society, the course of the voyage has been plotted, but by no means is its destination clear. The *Star Trek* explorations, although rooted in the 20th century, provide an opportunity to examine alternate universes, or destinations, in regard to issues of gender.

The Women of the Federation

If we were to peer 200 to 300 years into the future, what will the "employees" of Earth commerce, of interstellar federations, or the crew of a starship look like? In more than 30 years of history, the crews of the *Star Trek* series have varied greatly in both their human and alien composition. The most dramatic changes have, however, probably occurred in the portrayal of the female crew members. Although the first starship *Enterprise* would go where "no man" had gone before, it did take along a few women. A couple of female crew members were part of the "background" (Bernardi, 1998) rather than central characters. The first *Star Trek* women most certainly were not the "bra burners" of the '60s women's movement. They wore mini skirts that set them apart as women and sex objects. In context, this was likely a conscious action on the part of the producers, undoubtedly designed to attract certain viewers.

Although in occasional guest shots, women could be Federation Commissioners (Episode 37, "Metamorphosis") or doctors (Episode 59, "Is There in Truth No Beauty?"), the women of the first series were largely the "girl Fridays" of the '60s. Of the regular cast members, only two were women. Nurse Chapel, who assisted Dr. Leonard McCoy, in "sick bay" served a role traditionally permitted for women. Chapel, in fact, gave up a promising career in bioresearch to sign onto a starship in the hope of finding her missing fiancé (Okuda and Okuda, 1996). Interestingly, in the pilot for the series, "The Cage," the Captain's Number One was a woman, actress Majel Barrett, who returned as Nurse Chapel. According to creator Gene Roddenberry, "Women in those days were just set dressing" (cited in Gross and Altman, 1995:13). Not only did Paramount feel it was inappropriate to have a woman as second in command, but the women in test audiences agreed, reportedly asking, "Who does she think she is?"(13).

As a role model, the most critical crew member of the first series was Lieutenant Uhura, a Black or African American communications officer.

Although a woman being a communications officer (reminiscent perhaps of the early 20th century switchboard operator) was not a radical departure, having a black woman on the command bridge, at a critical time in the Civil Rights Movement, is significant. Uhura was also the only African American serving on the bridge. Such a role proved perhaps a "mixed blessing." As actress Nichelle Nichols has noted, "My problem is being a black woman on top of being a woman" (Bernardi, 1998: 42). A token in regard to both race and gender, Bernardi (1998) also suggests Uhura is eroticized as a woman of color. Other than the Vulcan Spock and the Asian Sulu, the main characters were white males, of admittedly different nationalities or ethnic backgrounds. Although women's liberation was not consciously part of the first *Star Trek*, the 1960s' series did set the tone for an integrated and more diverse crew.

THE NEXT GENERATION

With *Star Trek: The Next Generation* in the 24th century, the liberal feminist vision of equality began to appear in the mid-'80s. Several central characters were female. Significantly, Beverly Crusher not only took on the traditionally male-dominated profession of medical doctor, she also was a single parent. Her character was not restricted to "sick bay," and she frequently participated in often dangerous "away missions." Of course, this was perhaps more a matter of plot development than of gender equality. Nevertheless, Dr. Crusher served as a role model for young women into the '90s. It is the character of Tasha Yar, however, that perhaps most challenged traditional gender roles. She was the security chief responsible for the *Enterprise*'s "police force" and military presence. Her role added physical demands. Lieutenant Yar was a tactician, soldier, and leader. Her loss was, to a degree, a set back for the portrayal of gender equality in the series. Her intriguing replacement was not only male but a Klingon, a warrior species that scorns "weak women" and thrives on battle.

The third central female character of *The Next Generation* was Counselor Deanna Troi. Her role can be seen as more traditionally "feminine," an empathetic listener. In this, she is also perhaps the ideal "perfect mate" (Roberts, 1999). Yet, Troi is truly an empath because she is half Betazoid. Perhaps women of the planet Betazed consciously have cultivated this trait. Troi exemplifies the portrayal of the alien as a cipher for humanity (Roberts, 1999); thus, through alien cultures, science fiction examines often controversial aspects of Earth-bound society. Her character was originally supposed to be simply telepathic (Nemecek, 1992). Significantly, Troi has special and valued skills the male crew members do not have. They are valued to the degree that she has a place on the bridge. Troi's place next to the captain is significant in the sense of her being a central character. It is less significant, perhaps, for the advancement of equality, as Roberts (1999: 67) suggests that Deanna Troi "represents a version of traditional femininity" and her job "reflects the perfect mate's desire and ability to become one with her partner." While she is a translator for the captain analyzing the emotions of aliens, she "in this way becomes a part of the captain" (67). Greenwald (1998) adds that the character of Troi dates *The Next Generation* in that having a therapist on the bridge is a reflection of the importance of therapy in the 1980s.

In the series, Troi advances to become Commander Troi. Nevertheless, the roles of both Troi and Crusher are nurturing; they "rarely give orders and almost always serve men" (Bernardi, 1998: 116). In addition, Troi is sexualized in her uniform, which, unlike other women of Starfleet, is cut in a deep V to emphasize her bust (Bernardi, 1998). The occasional female character has, however, also become a judge advocate general ("The Measure of a Man"), a starship captain ("Yesterday's *Enterprise*"), and even an admiral ("Conspiracy"). A more enigmatic character is the alien Guinan, a semi-regular on the series. Also a listener, she is a bartender (an occupation from which women were excluded, even by law, into the second half of the 20th century), and much more. Played by Whoopi Goldberg, Guinan is an "old one," quite literally. She is wisdom and experience and seemingly beyond gender.

The female crew members of *The Next Generation* represent a new woman. As Worf tells Jono, in "Suddenly Human," "You are human, and among humans, females can achieve anything males can" (cited in Sherwin, 1999: 128). While it is uncertain whether this woman is that of a liberal or radical feminist ideal, *The Next Generation* females are not dependent on men economically, socially, and, perhaps, even emotionally. Doctor Crusher's relationship with Captain Picard remains professional. Her life revolves around her career and her son. Of course, many women today might ask whether she has the time for an emotional, or sexual, relationship. The possibility of a deeper relationship, or perhaps simply an affair, acknowledged by occasional glances or comments, no doubt keeps the viewers guessing.

Although romance occasionally enters the lives of Crusher and Troi, sexual relations of the crew members are never central to the series. In one episode (Episode 27, "The Child"), Counselor Troi does have a child, but her pregnancy is in a sense an "immaculate," nonhuman conception; from another perspective, however, the alien impregnation of Troi is clearly a physical rape. In a later episode ("Violations"), she suffers a mental rape. Significantly, the episode emphasizes that rape is "an exercise of control and dominance, rather than a crime of passion" (Roberts, 1999:169). Troi never marries; she "chooses" her career. Again, while this is probably a matter of story line convenience, it also reflects the real dilemma of career women today. As the central characters sit around a table playing poker, a common motif of the series, one may speculate – have the crewwomen of the starship _Enterprise_ become "one of the boys" or has the _Enterprise_ become a gender-neutral even gender-free society?

SPACE NINE

The evolution of gender roles continued in the '90s with _Deep Space Nine_ (_DS9_), set in the same time period as _The Next Generation_. Significantly, the world of _Deep Space Nine_ is not a Federation starship exploring the universe; it is a space station and, thus, a more varied and complex society of human, humanoid, and alien species. The gender of _Deep Space Nine_ is not earthbound.

The only semi-regular human female of _Deep Space Nine_ is Keiko (Ishikawa), Chief O'Brien's wife, who also appeared in _The Next Generation_. They are an inter-cultural family: she is Japanese, and he is Irish. Although Keiko is a scientist in her own right, a botanist, her career appears to have come second to that of her husband. When Chief O'Brien is offered the post of chief operations officer on _Deep Space Nine_, they move. Such choices arise in all two-career families; her time will, perhaps, come. They must also both adapt to being parents. O'Brien is the family man of the _Star Trek_ series. Keiko adapts to her new world by first becoming a teacher. Since they have a young daughter and there appear to be no teachers on _DS9_, this seems a natural decision. It is, however, apparent from the beginning that there are few children, human or alien, on the space outpost. It is a crossroads of the galaxy, and the population is largely transient. Although _Star Trek_ episodes periodically have family issues or children as characters central to the plot, it is not a "family show," at least in the sense of a nuclear family. Eventually, Keiko leaves _Deep Space Nine_ to pursue her career as a botanist. Although she returns, this was likely an easy way to largely "write her out" of the series, but it also in many ways reflects the problems dual-career families continue to face in the 21st century. The remaining central female characters are humanoid from other worlds.

Major Kira Nerys is the Bajoran second in command of _Deep Space Nine_, a former resistance fighter/terrorist whose childhood was lost in war. Like Tasha Yar, she perhaps did not choose her role. Yar also faced a violent childhood that apparently groomed her for command. In addition, Kira's military role appears to be unique in her own society. When she learns that her mother "gave herself" to the enemy, and even fell in love with Kira's archenemy Gul Dukat, she wants to kill her as a traitor. Even after she hears her father's message that the family has survived because of her mother's actions, she cannot forgive her. As a warrior, and child abandoned by her mother, she cannot understand her mother's sacrifice or pain. Yet she is able to love and comes to deeply love Odo, a shapeshifter who chooses to be "human."

The most intriguing "female" character of *Deep Space Nine* is Jadzia Dax. Like Crusher in *The Next Generation*, she is also a scientist, but her role places her at the command center as science officer. Yet Jadzia Dax is only partly female; Jadzia is a woman but her symbiont is apparently without gender or combines the genders of all its hosts. Dax has lived as man and woman. Rather than eliminate gender, Jadzia Dax has a greater understanding of gender differences because she has "lived" them. While male earthling television viewers, no doubt, may find her physically attractive, Commander Worf is attracted to her perhaps because she can fight like a Klingon. She is more than Jadzia. After Jadzia is killed, the new, very reluctant host is also female, yet very different physically and emotionally. Ezri Dax is physically petite. She is less assured, insecure, and uncertain who she is. Of course, Jadzia may have herself once been such a host. The growth and evolution of Ezri unfold as she acknowledges her "past lives." In an early 1999 episode, in order to solve a murder, she calls on her dark past, a male host who in his lifetime murdered three people. Until she brought him to the surface of her consciousness, she had denied his existence, as had Jadzia. As Joran appears, Ezri becomes aggressive, cunning, and violent. He was, however, not simply a man but a murderer. He teaches her about what humans would call instincts, the primal. Ezri Dax is strong enough to face him. As Joran returns to her unconscious, he suggests that she must learn to live with him. Such characters perhaps in combining genders in their many lives may ultimately transcend gender.

Of the female characters who are semi-regulars of *Star Trek: Deep Space Nine*, Quark's mother, Ishka, is one of the most interesting. Ferengi society is the antithesis of a genderless society. It is an extreme that generally amuses rather than offends. On the Ferengi home world, women are not only subordinate but naked. They are only permitted to wear clothing on the rare occasions when they are in public. Such nakedness can be seen as a metaphor for women's subordination; at its most basic, a woman's purpose is to breed. And, Ishka is first and foremost a mother. As she tells Quark, "I'm your mother. I can't leave you alone" ("Profit and Lace," cited in Sherwin, 1999: 104). Ferengi society is a parody of all patriarchal societies. Quark tells Commander Sisko, "Women are the enemy. And we treat them accordingly. The key is never to let them get the upper hand" ("Indiscretion," cited in Sherwin, 1999: 129). To the Ferengi, like other patriarchal cultures, "It's all about control" (129). Ferengi society is also a caricature of an ultra-capitalist society, with it hundreds of

Rules of Acquisition. Quark and his family are mere shadows of the typical acquisitive and commercial Ferengi. Quark has no doubt been influenced by his mother, and he is "humanized" by the world of *Deep Space Nine*. He is attracted to independent and accomplished women, and he is secretly proud of his mother, a "mere female," who is a skilled trader and entrepreneur. Quark's mother, however, must hide her commercial acuity. In "Family Business," Quark is served with a Writ of Accountability by the Ferengi Commerce Authority charging him with the improper supervision of his mother. He and his brother Rom convince her to plead guilty to having earned profit and to divest her business activities. Ishka has, however, been able to live such a secret life for many years and in the end outwits them all. Unbeknown to Quark and the Commerce Authority, she retains control of most of her business assets. She continues to be a woman in a patriarchal society who must work "behind the scenes" and manipulate those around her in order to control her own destiny. A radical feminist might add that to overcome the restraints and restrictions of Ferengi society, she has had to deceive. In turn, patriarchal Ferengi society would condemn female deception and use it as a "justification" for the further control of women by husbands and sons.

Ferengi society sharply contrasts that of Betazed, although nudity is apparently significant in both cultures. First introduced in *The Next Generation*, Counselor Deanna Troi's mother, Lwaxana Troi, occasionally visits *Deep Space Nine*. Ambassador Lwaxana Troi is free of male domination. A radical feminist would add that such freedom is not the same as women dominating men. Betazed itself may be gender free. The custom of Betazed is to marry in the nude, a celebration of freedom and sexuality. In "Cost of Living" (Episode 120), when Lwaxana is to marry in a very public ceremony, she unabashedly defies her non-Betazoid groom and appears naked. The wedding is called off, and her point is made. Betazed women are perhaps akin to radical feminists who define their own sexuality.

STAR TREK VOYAGER

Sex and sexuality remain largely peripheral to much of the *Star Trek* series. The original series, *The Next Generation*, and the most recent *Star Trek: Voyager* all take place on Federation starships. They are workplaces where the crew coincidentally lives. Relationships, however, are critical to the series. Yet it is the collective of the crew more than the coupling of individuals that binds the crew members together. This is perhaps most evident in *Star Trek: Voyager* where Federation officers and rebel Maquis are bound together in adversity in a universe distant from their home worlds. In *Voyager*, all crew members have lost families, broken with the past, yet are on a journey "home," a voyage led by a female commander.

Significantly, the major female characters of the series are scientists and engineers who are also of different ethnic, racial, or biological groups. As in the earlier series, *Voyager* tackles issues of both race and gender most often through its part human or nonhuman crew members. B'Elanna Torres, for example, is half Latina or Hispanic human, half alien Klingon; however, she apparently experiences her ethnic or racial identity solely though her Klingon half. Klingon society is not gender free, but could be gender neutral. Klingon men and women are warriors who fight side by side. As Worf tells Dax, "We consider Klingon women our partners in battle" ("To the Death," cited in Sherwin, 1999: 129). Klingon women are strong and assertive in making war and love. Nevertheless, in every episode addressing Klingons, the males always seem to outnumber the females—in command and in battle—perhaps an unintended oversight of the producers. As a consequence, Klingon women do not appear to be equal warriors. Both male and female Klingons as a species are also "victims" of their biology. Like Vulcans, they face biological "rights of passage." Unlike Vulcans, however, Klingons have not denied, or overcome, their emotions. Torres shows both her human and Klingon side when she is captured by Vidiians and genetically altered in their search for a cure to the Phage disease ("Faces").

Torres later tells Chakotay she came to admire much in her Klingon self, her strength and bravery. Perhaps significantly, her passion appears to be seen as part of her Klingon "nature" rather than a representation of the 20th century stereotype of the "volatile Latin." The "complete" Torres can perhaps relate to the inner battles of Lieutenant's Worf's first love in *The Next Generation*, K'Ehleyr, who rejects her Klingon "nature" in favor of her human half. She, nevertheless, becomes a diplomat representing the Klingon Empire. She and Worf also have a son. Yet Worf only learns he is a father several years later when they meet again, and she is killed (Episode 46, "The Emissary," and Episode 81, "The Reunion"). Klingon society may be gender-equal in the liberal feminist sense that men and women are more alike than different. Yet it appears to value most that which in current earthly society is more often defined as masculine–the creative energy of aggression and passion. Dax idealizes these traits to a degree in her explanation of what she sees in Worf: "He has the courage of a berserker cat and he has the heart of a poet" ("Let He Who is Without Sin," cited in Sherwin, 1999: 289).

For Torres, the human and Klingon continue to clash, as she concludes, "I guess I just have to accept the fact … that I'll spend the rest of my life fighting her" ("Faces," cited in Sherwin, 1999: 293). Like K'Ehleyr, Torres has chosen her humanity. Yet Torres ultimately admits her decision is based largely on her childhood experiences of rejection and loss of love, on being abandoned by her father, a human who could not deal with two female Klingons ("Lineage," Episode 258). Must the Klingon and the human, or the masculine and the feminine, always be at war? As B'Elanna Torres during her pregnancy ultimately comes to terms with her daughter's Klingon appearance, she perhaps is also able to accept herself. Ultimately, the "biraciality" of B'Elanna is, thus, presented as "a positive attribute" (Roberts, 2000: 207). B'Elanna's discovery of herself also is shaped by her life experiences. She is a former Maquis resistance fighter who disdains the Federation's treaties with imperialistic races. She is defiant and undisciplined. Yet, as the series progresses, she becomes part of the *Voyager* collective. Perhaps of greatest significance for the development of gender roles, B'Elanna Torres, also a scientist, achieves the status of chief engineer.

The most provocative member of the *Voyager* crew is Seven of Nine. Originally human, she becomes Borg, the ultimate communistic society, a collective where there is no privacy or individuality. As a sexless society that also appears gender free – without masculine or feminine – it is not attractive to humans of any generation. Rather than being inspired by some communitarian utopia, the Borg collective is akin to the insect world of ants or bees, a society of drones led by an earth-mother, an unpleasant queen. This earth mother may be a goddess, the origin of the Borg, but she is portrayed decidedly as the "evil witch."

The *Voyager* crew teaches Seven of Nine what it means to be human, including the expression of emotions. Significantly, Seven does not "identify" as being female. She doesn't realize she is a beautiful, sexually attractive woman and, also significantly, the crew largely does not treat her as such. The fact, however, is that the audience does see. While Seven may not qualify to wear the unisex Starfleet uniform, her monotone body suit leaves no doubt of her latent sexuality to prepubescent boys and perennially adolescent men. According to Cranny-Francis (2000:158), Seven is "a cross between Barbie and Tomb Raider Games heroine Lara Croft." Flowers adds (1999: 44) that Jeri Lynn Ryan did for *Voyager* much as Heather Locklear did for *Melrose Place;* she raised the ratings with her "bombshell looks and connection to the overwhelmingly popular Borg."

Seven of Nine becomes a contradiction. In this, the 21st century audience is drawn ultimately toward wanting her to find out that she is a woman, first and foremost. Perhaps sexuality need not be denied in a gender-neutral, if not gender-free, society of the 24th century. Yet, Cranny-Francis (2000) argues that

Seven's "humanization" is not gender neutral. When Captain Picard had to rediscover his humanity apart from the Borg Locutus in *The Next Generation*, it was a matter of "reestablishing authority" of his mind, but Seven must instead reconfigure herself in the "production" of her decidedly female body (158). In addition, to become an acceptable female, Seven must "retune" her voice and make her body seem "soft and (com)pliant" (159). Moreover, Seven's rationality is questioned and her resistance to humanization is often treated as "childish dependency and fear" (159). This infantilization of Seven of Nine may, however, be related in part to her being different biologically—in a technological sense, that is, "racially" different. In Euro-centric culture, "inferior" races often have been portrayed as weak, as "feminine." (For the treatment of race in *Star Trek*, see Lentz and Chaires, "What Color is an Android" in this volume).

While the character of Seven clouds the status of gender in the 24th century, *Voyager* is significantly worlds away from the original series in its captain, a woman from Earth, albeit a white Euro-American woman. Captain Katherine Janeway chose her career as a Starfleet officer. She remains single, although this is not necessarily by choice, since her fiancé is in another quadrant of the universe. To a large degree, the eligibility of most of *Star Trek*'s lead characters from the original series forward is a matter of maintaining a storyline rather than a conscious gender decision. Captain Kirk, Scotty, and Doctor McCoy apparently remained single, and available, throughout their Starfleet careers. Significantly, as a male, even Captain Kirk was permitted to have sexual relations. Janeway, as the captain and a professional, rejects sexual relations with any members of her crew. The only sex she appears to have during the entire series is when her memory is taken away and she is transported with other crew members to an alien mining planet. While some might argue that her "no nonsense" style of command (read – even cold or frigid), particularly in the first years, suggests that she "needs to get laid," radical feminists, and many working women today, would recognize ongoing gender issues in continuing male-dominated workplaces. Women in the early 21st century public world of work are still often seen as women first and professionals second. To be feminine may, thus, be viewed as being "sexy" and sexually accessible. In point, would it be suggested that a male with Janeway's style of command "needs to be laid"? (For various views on Janeway, see Greenwald, 1998: 138-143; 220-230).

Evolution in the *Star Trek* series reflects the possibility of change in our own humankind. Women are now surgeons, engineers, police chiefs, military generals, Supreme Court justices, and governors. These are all roles once reserved to men. Yet, even in our society, the door is not open all the way, and women are often not fully accepted in such roles and occupations. A stark example is policing, where women today still often face a very masculine culture and organization. As such, they remain tokens, outsiders (Martin and Jurik, 1997). Women entering such roles will often adapt by adopting traits seen as necessary to the occupation. In male-dominated jobs, these may be traits traditionally defined as masculine. For example, police officers are still often expected to be "big and strong" in order to employ necessary force and to command respect even though policing today is recognized as requiring, above all, strong verbal communication skills. Policewomen face a quandary—must they be physically aggressive, even macho, to perform the job, to find respect and acceptance? The legal profession, on the other hand, involves verbal rather than physical aggression. Law, also traditionally a masculine enterprise, is adversarial. The female lawyer who is non-confrontational may be labeled incompetent because she is too "feminine" while a female attorney who is very assertive may still not be accepted because she is a "bitch." The policewoman who adopts a "masculine" persona may even be identified as a bull dyke, neither male nor female (Martin and Jurik, 1997).

Gender neutrality, thus, remains problematic in the 21st century. Moreover, to the extent that institutions as they exist today represent the vestiges of patriarchy, the fact that women may be attorneys, for example, does not mean there is gender equality. Law, legal education, the legal system, the employment structure, and legal culture remain to a degree masculine. Janeway is the most critical human role model for gender development in the _Star Trek_ series as a captain who is respected, and accepted, by her crew and by her audience. As she evolves, Janeway does not adopt a masculine persona to fit into a mold, to become "one of the boys." Ultimately, Janeway is comfortable being different, being a woman. Although her world may be gender-neutral in the sense of equality, it is, however, probably not gender-free – there remain the masculine and the feminine. Perhaps this becomes a question that must be directed to the _Voyager_ men. According to Sterba (1999), a gender-free society is one where desirable traits appear in both men and women.

These issues of what are desirable traits juxtaposed in a gendered society are also critical in other ways in _Voyager_. Janeway is a scientist, and so are B'Elanna Torres and Seven of Nine. These central characters are women in one "of the last bastions of male dominance, and perhaps most resistant to change" (Roberts, 2000:278). In addition, perhaps the most central relationships of the series are those among these female crew members, Janeway with Seven of Nine (and before her Kes) and with B'Elanna Torres. On the one hand, these could be seen, stereotypically, as mother-daughter relationships (note, a male captain probably would not be stereotyped as a "father" in these circumstances). For

feminists who stress difference, and believe that women are relationship-oriented by nature rather than the dictates of a patriarchal society, Janeway's relationships with these women would reflect what women can bring to command and
science. According to Roberts (2000), Janeway and Torres, in particular, represent different perspectives on science itself and scientific ethics. Roberts
(2000:277) asserts that the series "presents a version of science that embraces
feminist ideas about how women can alter the practice of science." This is so in
regard to both scientific research and technology. Janeway represents abstract,
presumably objective science. Torres represents science as feeling, as valuing
sympathy for the object being studied. Janeway comes to understand, and
accept, B'Elanna's scientific method probably, in part, because *Voyager* is 75
light years away from Federation space, and the still, perhaps, masculine influence of Starfleet. Working together they reflect a "holistic view of science"
(Roberts, 2000: 278; see also Roberts, 2000, for discussion of particular
episodes).

Star Trek *Justice and Gender*

In regard to, at least, the roles of women and men, *Star Trek* appears to
have evolved to a gender neutral society envisioned by many liberal feminists.
Equal opportunity is the norm. However, it must be kept in mind that the society of the *Enterprise* or *Voyager* is partly a product of its setting, a Starfleet ship.
It is uncertain whether the crew represents a microcosm of Earth society. A
society where women are more likely than men to give up family for a career
would not be equal or gender neutral.

The roles of reproduction and family, so critical to the history of the subordination of women, are only hinted at in much of the series. We do see male and
female couples, and sex is implied. Women appear to have control of their own
bodies. The world of *Star Trek* is not a sexless or androgynous society. Artificial
reproduction does not appear to be the norm. We do see glimpses of childbirth,
but no pregnant crew members, with the exception of B'Elanna Torres during
the last season of *Voyager*. There are children, but they are usually on another
deck, unseen. Someone is raising them. To liberal feminists such as Okin (1999),
perhaps equality in the worlds of work and family has been achieved. To others,
perhaps what is most significant is the redefinition of what have been traditionally "female" virtues, such as compassion and nurturance, as positive for men and
women (Sterba, 1999). And the feminine is perhaps no longer undervalued.
Most significantly, female officers do not have to act "like men."

Much can be learned about gender and justice in the *Star Trek* future from the many alien and humanoid species encountered by the crew. These alien societies represent various gender possibilities. The crew members' interaction with such species also can be revealing. A central tenet of *Star Trek* justice is the Prime Directive, i.e., that the Federation will not interfere with the internal affairs of other worlds. Another core principle, however, is recognition of the autonomy of the individual, a right acknowledged for all sentient beings. A tension clearly exists between these principles. In several episodes gender issues provide the setting for their interplay.

GENDER AND INDIVIDUAL AUTONOMY

In the episode "Angel One" of *The Next Generation*, the *Enterprise* crew encounters a matriarchal, as opposed to a patriarchal, society. Women are the rulers and men the subordinates. Troi and Yar are sent as diplomats. Yet, the Odein society appears patriarchal in most respects; women play out the roles of men. Those who do not conform to the status quo of female rule are outcasts. It becomes a matter of whether the away team should rescue the outcasts, now sentenced to death for being renegades. Although Troi and Yar fail, Riker uses his sex and sleeps "his way to the top" to save the day, a role reversal of sexual stereotypes (Gross and Altman, 1995: 162). Although it might be expected that men would be rebels against such a system, the Odein outcasts are women (Nemecek, 1992). Perhaps it is not so much a matter of wanting to be submissive subordinates to men, but of rejecting dominant masculine roles in an intolerant society. It is a lesson in role reversal that misses the significance of gender. It is a masculine lesson.

In the *Star Trek, The Next Generation* episode "The Outcast" (No. 117), Captain Picard and the *Enterprise* crew encounter an androgynous society. Physical reproduction is rejected by this gray, unisex society. To make matters worse, they all dress alike and look alike (yet, significantly all the actors are women). The focus of the plot, however, puts heterosexuals "in the shoes" of homosexuals; in the J'naii society, the heterosexuals are deviant, sick and must be cured. Although the episode purports to be about gender, it comes down to sex. Riker and a J'naii shuttle pilot, Soren, discuss sexual differences. Soren explains that at one time the J'naii had two sexes, but now they find "gender" primitive. She/it, however, indicates there are occasional "throwbacks" who feel sexual urges to be male or female. Since she was very young, she has known she is different. Now, she is attracted to Riker.

When their illicit attractions are discovered, Soren is put on trial. Captain Picard indicates that he cannot intervene, but he only mildly attempts to discourage Riker from a rescue mission that in the end comes too late. Soren has already been "reeducated" and is puzzled to think she could ever have had sexual feelings. Although this is a very interesting episode, it is not about a gender-free society in any feminist sense. The only comment that perhaps comes close to gender as an issue is Dr. Crusher's statement to Soren that on the *Enterprise* neither men nor women are superior. Yet sexuality continues to exist; women still paint their nails, eyes, and lips primarily to attract males. "The Outcast" addresses sexuality; the episode "Angel One" is about gender roles. Both societies clash with the *Enterprise* over the issue of individual autonomy. Neither society tolerates diversity. The Prime Directive is perhaps acknowledged as much in its violation as in its compliance. Radical feminists, at least, would add, however, that in both instances the Prime Directive is ignored when women are "behaving badly," that is, acting "like men" or denying their sexuality, their bodies, to men.

Clearly, a gender-free society is not the same as a homosexual society. As noted previously, sex and gender are two different aspects of being human. Yet the *Star Trek* series perhaps comes closest to addressing what that issue of gender may mean in confronting sexuality. In the fourth year of *The Next Generation*, Crusher is attracted to the Federation ambassador Odan, who is a joined being. Her attraction goes beyond the physical. Yet when the male host dies and is replaced with a female host, Crusher is unable to continue the relationship, which in this century would certainly be seen as having homosexual implications. The internal Odan, the intelligence and personality, cannot be separated from the exterior Odan, the male body. In the last scene, Crusher suggests that maybe someday love will not be so limited (Gross and Altman, 1995). The female Odan kisses Beverly's hand and leaves.

The scenario is essentially reversed in a *Deep Space Nine* episode, "Rejoined," where Jadzia Dax meets another Trill scientist, Lenara Kahn, and learns that both in previous hosts had been married. The bodies are wholly different and now both are female; the symbionts remain. Although Trill society prohibits rejoining, significantly, the symbionts briefly resume their relationship through Jadzia and Lenara. This is as close to crossing sexual barriers as *Star Trek* comes. Homosexuality is never acknowledged among the various starship crews. This does not mean that homosexuality no longer exists in the 24th century. Viewers and fans, however, are largely left to their own fantasies (e.g., the Gaylaxians, an international organization of gay, lesbian, and bisexual fans). Although certain television networks in the late 20th century have addressed sexual orientation openly, in the supposedly more tolerant universe of the 24th century, homosexuality has apparently returned to a world of secrecy.

GENDER AND THE PRIME DIRECTIVE

Several episodes after "The Outcast," *The Next Generation* series revisited an issue that had been addressed in the first series episode "Elaan of Troyius," a thinly veiled reference to Helen of Troy and the power of women to bring disaster upon men. In the original series, the *Enterprise* is escorting Elaan of Elas to her marriage ceremony. The unwilling bride has been offered in marriage to bring peace among warring planets. Captain Kirk falls in love with her because he comes in contact with her tears. He is powerless. In the end, the marriage proceeds. In *The Next Generation* episode "The Perfect Mate," (No. 121) the empathic, metamorph Kamala is also a peace offering. She has the ability to be what any man wants her to be, but she can bond with only one man. When Picard sees the effect she has on the male crew members, he assigns Data to be her guide and escort. She also is not permitted to interact with females. According to Hegarty (1995), Kamala threatens the bonding of the male crew members; her sexuality undermines male relationships.

Kamala is both the ultimate male fantasy and a faithless woman; she is a victim of her own biology (Hegarty, 1995). She has been preparing all her life for her role as peacemaker. Although Captain Picard at first warns the Kriosan ambassador that slavery is illegal in the Federation, he later cites the Prime Directive in response to Doctor Crusher's complaint that Kamala is being prostituted (Hegarty, 1995). Kamala herself admits she has known no alternative and has never been asked what she wanted. She dutifully fulfills her role as a peace offering even though she has "bonded" with Picard. She will be able to fool her mate by sensing and responding to his desires. Unlike the "rebels" of "Angel One" and "The Outcast" who live in societies overtly suppressing diverse sexual or gender roles, Kamala's autonomy comes second to the Prime Directive. Picard does not discourage Kamala from fulfilling her "duty" because ultimately she would distract him from his duties as captain. Nor does he step in to stop the ceremony. The captain simply notes that arranged marriages have been recognized by the Federation, and Kamala is a "willing" peace offering. As the radical feminist would add, free will in a patriarchal society is an illusion. Only Dr. Beverly Crusher seems to have recognized this (for additional discussion of the "perfect mate," see Roberts, 1999: 66-87).

THE COLLECTIVE AND DIVERSITY

In the *Star Trek* series, the tension between the value of individual autonomy and the importance of the collective often is apparent. In reaching a balance, however, the *Star Trek* world is not without gender bias, as "The Perfect Mate" exemplifies. The community of the series is the collective of the *Star Trek* crews. Individuals will sacrifice themselves for the greater good, yet risks also will be taken to rescue the few. This collective even may have overshadowed the role of the biological family, although this is a matter of the setting and storyline rather than of gender. *Star Trek* is not a nuclear family "lost in space."

The *Star Trek* collective also has been international and intergalactic since the first series. In this, it sets an important example for Earth at the beginning of the 21st century. Yet examples of cultural diversity largely have been exhibited in the alien or part alien crew members, visitors, and worlds. And sexuality in *Star Trek* remains heterosexuality. Some feminists would speculate: has the multicultural, humanoid crew "melted" into an Anglo male, middle-class version of a just society in the 24th century?

Conclusion

To radical feminists, the worlds of *The Next Generation*, *Deep Space Nine*, and *Voyager* are unlikely to be gender-free, unless patriarchy is wholly extirpated in the next few centuries. Women are not "free" of men or of being labeled female. The question remains whether society can be gender-free or even neutral if sexuality continues to drive human interaction. But there have been significant acts of separation from men. Most appear, however, to be "accidental" consequences of the setting and storyline. Thus, marriage, children, and the nuclear family are not central to any *Star Trek* series.

Most significantly, the women of *Star Trek* have been positive role models for women of the last decades of the 20th century and into the 21st. The glass ceiling of prior centuries appears to have been shattered. The men of *Star Trek* also appear to value the legal or liberal feminist concept of gender equality. Although different feminist perspectives are still largely absent from the series, different images of women from other parts of the universe enable 21st century humans to examine their own issues of sexuality and gender. The future world of Earth and the Federation remains tentative. Although the production of the *Star Trek* TV series of the distant future has come to an end, they will continue to be viewed, and, no doubt, compared to the new "prequel" series *Enterprise*. In regard to gender development, *Voyager* will be a very hard act to follow. The fact the new series occurs closer in time to the present should not be seen as "an excuse" to revert to old gender roles and stereotypes. After all, our knowledge and understanding of gender issues in this new millennium have gone where "no man" had expected to journey in the 1960s. It will be up to humans residing on the real Earth to determine the role of gender in that future. There remain yet a few voyages to places where "no woman or man has gone before."

References

Agnito, Rosemary (ed.) (1977). *History of Ideas on Women: A Source Book.* New York, NY; Perigee Books.

Alleman, Ted (1993). "Varieties of Feminist Thought and Their Application to Crime and Criminal Justice" in Roslyn Muraskin and Ted Alleman (eds.), *It's A Crime: Women and Justice.* Englewood Cliffs, NJ: Regents/Prentice Hall: 3-42.

Bernardi, Daniel Leonard (1998). *Star Trek and History: Race-ing Toward A White Future,* New Brunswick, NJ: Rutgers University Press.

Brownmiller, Susan (1975). *Against Our Will: Men, Women and Rape.* New York; The Free Press.

Cranny-Francis, Anne (2000). "The Erotics of the (cy)Borg: Authority and Gender in the Sociocultural Imagery" in Marleen S. Barr (ed.), *Future Females, The Next Generation: New Voices and Velocities in Feminist Science Fiction Criticism.* Lanham, Maryland: Rowan & Littlefield Publishers: 145-163.

Dworkin, Andrea (1993). "Against the Male Flood: Censorship, Pornography and Equality" in Catherine Itzin (ed.), *Pornography: Women, Violence and Civil Liberties,* reprint. Oxford; Oxford University Press: 515-536.

Firestone, Shulamith (1999). "The Dialectic of Sex" in Janet A. Kourany, James P. Sterba, and Rosemarie Tong (eds.), *Feminist Philosophies: Problems, Theories, and Applications,* 2nd ed. Upper Saddle River, NJ; Prentice Hall: 353-359.

Flowers, James R., Jr. (1999). *The Incredible Internet Guide for Trekkers.* Tempe, AZ: Facts on Demand Press.

Frye, Marilyn (1999). "Some Reflections on Separation and Power" in Janet A. Kourany, James P. Sterba, and Rosemarie Tong (eds.), *Feminist Philosophies: Problems, Theories, and Applications,* 2nd ed. Upper Saddle River, NJ; Prentice Hall: 359-366.

Greenwald, Jeff (1998). *Future Perfect: How Star Trek Conquered Planet Earth.* New York, NY; Viking.

Gross, Edward and Mark A. Altman (1995). *Captains' Logs: The Unauthorized Complete Trek Voyages.* Boston; Little, Brown and Company.

Hegarty, Emily (1995). "Some Suspect of Ill: Shakespeare's Sonnets and 'The Perfect Mate.'" *Extrapolation,* Vol. 36, No. 1 (Spring): 55-64.

Kourany, Janet A., James P. Sterba, and Rosemarie Tong (eds.) (1999). *Feminist Philosophies: Problems, Theories, and Applications,* 2nd ed. Upper Saddle River, NJ; Prentice Hall.

Lentz, Susan and B. Grant Stitt (1996). "Women as Victims of 'Victimless Crimes:' The Case of Prostitution. *Journal of Contemporary Criminal Justice,* Vol. 12, No. 2: 173-186.

Lugones, Maria and Elizabeth Spelman (1999). "Have We Got a Theory for You! Feminist Theory, Cultural Imperialism, and the Demand for 'The Woman's Voice'" in Janet A. Kourany, James P. Sterba, and Rosemarie Tong (eds.), *Feminist Philosophies: Problems, Theories, and Applications,* 2nd ed. Upper Saddle River, NJ; Prentice Hall: 474-486.

MacKinnon, Catharine A. (1987). *Feminism Unmodified: Discourses on Life and Law.* Cambridge, MA; Harvard University Press.

Martin, Susan Erlich and Nancy Jurik (1996). *Doing Justice, Doing Gender: Women in Law and Criminal Justice Occupations.* Thousand Oaks, CA; Sage Publications.

Nemecek, Larry (1992). *The Star Trek: The Next Generation Companion.* New York, NY; Pocket Books.

Okin, Susan Moller (1999). "Justice, Gender, and Family" in Janet A. Kourany, James P. Sterba, and Rosemarie Tong (eds.), *Feminist Philosophies: Problems, Theories, and Applications,* 2nd ed. Upper Saddle River, NJ; Prentice Hall: 313-331.

Okuda, Michael and Denise Okuda (1996). *Star Trek Chronology: The History of the Future*. New York, NY: Pocket Books.

Roberts, Robin (1999). *Sexual Generations: "Star Trek: The Next Generation" and Gender*. Urbana and Chicago; University of Illinois Press.

Roberts, Robin (2000). "The Woman Scientist in *Star Trek: Voyager*" in Marleen S. Barr (ed.), *Future Females, The Next Generation: New Voices and Velocities in Feminist Science Fiction Criticism*. Lanham, Maryland: Rowan & Littlefield Publishers:277-290.

Sherwin, Jill (1999). *Quotable Star Trek*. New York, NY: Pocket Books.

Spielvogel, Jackson J. (1991). *Western Civilization: Since 1550*, Vol. 2. St. Paul, MN; West Publishing Company.

Sterba, James P. (1999). "Feminist Justice and Sexual Harassment" in Janet A. Kourany, James P. Sterba, and Rosemarie Tong (eds.) *Feminist Philosophies: Problems, Theories, and Applications*, 2nd ed. Upper Saddle River, NJ; Prentice Hall: 331-345.

Visions of Corrections in Star Trek:
Something Old, Nothing New

Matthew C. Leone, PhD

Introduction

The *Star Trek* saga began at a time when the United States was grappling with serious social problems and rapid social change. Technology had advanced dramatically in the 1950s, but the ethical and moral attitudes necessary to effectively deal with such change had not advanced at the same rate nor advanced the same distance. The nation "had a dream" and *Star Trek* made it seem possible that the problems the nation was facing could and would be overcome through technology, and a new, better society would result. Science, particularly chemistry and theoretical physics, had given society some ideas of what was possible and had even followed through on some of those promises, such as creating electricity from nuclear power and nuclear weaponry.

Technology, it turned out, was not unlimited in its ability to overcome social and physical limitations. Albert Einstein, in his theory of general relativity, indicated speeds beyond that of light were fundamentally impossible because of the infinite amount of energy required to accelerate a mass to those speeds. Science fiction, however, has never learned to take "no" for an answer, and later "warp" theories, which melded the mechanics of time, space, and energy, showed how ships would theoretically be able to travel in a time bubble. In this bubble, time would be distorted, or space would be expanded behind the ship and destroyed in front of it, essentially allowing it to ride a "wave" of space and exceed the speed of light (Krause, 1995).

In theory this would allow ships to travel great distances and do so in seemingly short periods of time, exactly the element of travel that made the *Star Trek* series unique and interesting to a generation who had grown up with technological advances and unending possibilities.

The irony here, as it applies to the field of corrections, is that in the *Star Trek* series the ships traveled through space to visit places that did little more than display different times in Earth's correctional history. Rather than traveling through time to a different place, they traveled through space and discovered little more than other examples of our own times. In essence, the *Star Trek* interpretation of corrections was more historical than visionary. In order, however, to appreciate the nostalgic visions of corrections offered in the series, it is necessary to first explain what is meant by corrections and why corrections exists in its current structure.

A Brief Primer On Corrections

The field of corrections is as old as organized society. Corrections has many goals, but the three considered primary to the field are: 1) to take the person whose behavior is outside the accepted norms of a given group and to do something to him that causes him to change his behavior and return to an accepted range of behaviors; 2) to show others in the same society and situation what will happen to them if they choose to behave in a similar manner; 3) to symbolically repair the damage done to the society by the actions of the person who acted outside the range of acceptable behaviors (Allen and Simonsen, 2001).

These goals have been accomplished using many social and practical methods, but the five primary methods that have been used repeatedly throughout western history are retribution, deterrence, incapacitation, rehabilitation, and restitution.

Retribution is based on the idea that the offender, as well as the offense, affects society in a negative way. The act has ramifications beyond just the victim. In essence, offenses make society less sound and integral. Punishment of the offender restores the society in a symbolic way, reinforcing the norms and rules of the society.

Deterrence is when the goal of the punishment is two-fold: to keep the offender from committing the act again and to inform the general society of what it can expect to happen should any one of them decide to commit the same act. Deterrence requires the punishment be swift, certain, and severe enough to overcome any benefits the offender associated with the crime. It also requires that the offender be made aware of the potential for punishment and the degree of the punishment that will be received.

Incapacitation is often utilized when the society recognizes the offender is unlikely to change his or her behaviors, and the only solution is to simply remove the person from the society he has victimized and offended. In pure incapacitation there is no reform offered to the offender while in prison, just a simple, set sentence that, when completed, allows the offender to re-enter the society.

Rehabilitation is based on the idea that crime is a symptom, rather than a problem. There is an underlying condition that drives the offender to commit crimes. This underlying cause, if addressed properly, will make the person law-abiding and remove any further risk of criminal conduct.

Restitution as a response to crime gained popularity when the victims of crime realized society was meting out punishments that did little to address the damage done at the personal level. Putting someone in prison who caused an accident and destroyed your car while drunk might make society safer, but it does little to repair your car. Restitution sought to rebuild the link between the offender and the victim, and to make sure the society considered the needs and losses of the victim when they were deciding the sentence the offender would receive (Allen and Simonsen, 2001).

Recently, a new adaptation of these ideas has resulted from improvements in technology. Electronic monitoring, the latest "technological fix" offered to the justice system, attempts to incapacitate the offender in his or her own home and allows him or her to leave home at specified times to attend work or reform-oriented programs. In essence, it is a low-cost method that attempts to mix the goals of deterrence, rehabilitation, and incapacitation. This change has resulted in increased faith in the ability of society to monitor and control the behaviors of its most dangerous element. But, as Meadows (1972:159) noted,

> Technology can relieve the symptoms of a problem without affecting the underlying causes. Faith in technology as the ultimate solution to all problems can thus divert our attention from the most fundamental problem – and prevent us from taking action to solve it.

Examples of the technological fix can be seen in *Star Trek* as it applies to social as well as justice system level corrections.

Corrections, however, is rooted in the philosophical beliefs of the time and the society. If the society, or at least the policymakers in that society, believes human behavior is the result of environment and that humans are, by their nature, neutral, the response will be to change the environment and thereby change the behavior. Conversely, if the policymakers in the society believe there are certain persons who are intrinsically evil or deviant, the response will be removal for the sake of the society.

This relationship between the nature of the individual and the response of the society has been exhibited many times in history. When crime was believed to be the result of biologically inferior persons who had not evolved as far as the remainder of society, science sought to identify these persons prior to their committing of criminal acts and separate them from society in a pro-active manner. Cesare Lombroso sought to identify these persons through the use of physical measurements in order to place them in more humane institutions prior to their committing of crimes.

The corrections system also indicates its beliefs regarding the causes of crime by its choice of sentences. Two types of sentences are typically given, with some mixture of the two occurring in times when the criminal justice system seems unclear as to its goals. At one end of the sentencing scale is determinate sentencing. In this case the person receives a set number of months or years and serves the entire sentence prior to release. The opposite sentence to this type is the indeterminate sentence. These sentences are given as a range, along the lines of one year to life. These persons are released only after they have proven to some releasing agency (such as a parole board) that they have indeed reformed and are ready to re-enter society.

To achieve maximum deterrence, sentences must be long and unalterable so the potential offender will see the punishment outweighs the crime, and behavior within the facility will have no bearing on release. In contrast, to achieve maximum rehabilitative value, sentences must be indeterminate. This is to motivate the offender to reform in order to be released and to make the offender aware that if reform is not completed, the facility is willing and able to hold him for the remainder of his natural life.

Causal Belief System Goal Sentence Type

Casual Belief	System Goal	Sentence Type
Biology (nature)	Deterrence	Determinate
Environment (nurture)	Reform	Indeterminate

Types of Corrections, Crime, and Their Interactions Within The Justice System

The corrections system has many challenges and limitations offered to it, most of which are driven by the ethical limitations of the time. In the United States, we have a Constitution that limits the use of "cruel and unusual" punishments and requires that persons accused of a crime be considered for bail in order to guarantee the technically innocent don't experience punishment. This allows, if it is necessary, the public to be protected from dangerous individuals prior to trial and the determination of guilt. For those detained prior to a trial, undergoing trial, or awaiting sentencing, the American system of justice utilizes jails for their detention. Jails also are used for those convicted of less serious crimes for which prison would be seen as inappropriate.

The legal system makes distinctions among crimes based on their impact on society. Misdemeanors are typically considered crimes of a low nature, where society at large has not been affected or endangered. These crimes usually carry a sentence that does not involve incarceration, unless the crime is a high-level (or gross) misdemeanor. Felonies, in comparison, are crimes that have an impact on the entire society and diminish the feelings of solidarity and security shared by the members of that society. Most felonies require a sentence of more than a year in a prison, rather than short-term confinement in a jail-type facility.

Jails, because of the level of the offender housed there, are not intended to be long-term detention facilities (although in many counties, they are used for longer periods than they were originally intended). Typically, modern jails are constructed with maximum visual control, somewhat smaller cells (because of the inmate's short-term status), and a near total absence of rehabilitative programs (Kerle, 1998). These factors are mirrored in the *Star Trek* version of the jail as well.

In *Star Trek*, the structure used in the justice system is similar to both military courts and the courts used for the general public. While the Federation is not considered a purely military organization, its rank structure, academy training, and use of vessels for exploration, protection, and colonization make it seem military to those with even a passing knowledge of military operations. As such, the use of the "brig" as a short-term detention facility is not unusual, but in many of the *Star Trek* episodes, the brig becomes more (or perhaps less) than a jail. Consider the visual aspect of the brig. It is a small cubicle, designed for a single detainee with a force field at the front to keep the detainee from escaping or getting to the person at the control panel. The control panel faces the cell, so the detainee is under constant visual surveillance and receives no privacy. The detainee typically has nothing in the cell except a bunk, molded into the back wall. There are no reading materials, personal effects, or toilet facilities (that one always puzzled me!). One could reasonably hope, given the advances in jail design over the past few decades, that decades or centuries in the future jails would be more humane, more effective, and designed with more personal dignity than we currently offer, but certainly not less.

In contrast to the jail, western society uses prisons for their long-term convicted offenders. These range in custody level from minimum-security camps, to maximum-security prisons. In spite of its futuristic visions and technological advances, it is obvious prisons still exist in each of the *Star Trek* series. Ensign Ro is "rescued" from a prison to participate in a covert operation orchestrated by Admiral Kennelly (*ST:TNG*: "Ensign Ro"); Thomas Riker is sent to a Cardassian prison following the theft of the *Defiant* and attacks on Cardassians in the Orias system (*ST:DS9*: "*Defiant*"), and Captain Janeway speaks of Telsian prisons (*ST:V*: "Live Fast and Prosper"). Clearly the prison still exists, in spite of technological advances and the apparent diminution of poverty, inequality, and social discontent.

Eras of Corrections and Star Trek *Examples*

The history of prisons in western society is marked with key points, which serve as examples of the beliefs, practices, and values of the time. It is important to remember, however, that prisons have not existed for the entirety of recorded history. While corrections, the use of practices or procedures to bring the person back into the "normal" range of society, have been around since society began, imprisonment to achieve that goal is a relatively recent development.

Prior to the use of imprisonment, the population was controlled and corrected using corporal punishments. Flogging, breaking on the wheel, the stocks and pillory were all common societal responses to deviant behavior (Allen and Simonsen, 2001). With few exceptions, these practices remained in power until the church developed political power and encouraged the use of more humane methods of punishment, such as prisons. It is no coincidence that the models for the first prisons were drawn from monasteries and convents. Thus, it also is no coincidence that the naming of the rooms "cells" was taken from the traditional religious term for a monk's or nun's room in a monastery or convent. What follows is a description of how art imitated life and created *Star Trek* representations of some critical times in correctional history.

THE BLOODY CODES

In the 16th century, England experienced a period of serious criminality, caused by economic problems and a changing social structure. The government's response to this increase in lawlessness was to increase correspondingly the levels of punishment offered in order to attempt to deter those who were committing these acts. The punishments offered were mostly corporal in nature, in that imprisonment was reserved for the nobility and members of the clergy. The most common punishment in this brief period was death. Many crimes carried this punishment, crimes which, by today's standards, would be considered relatively minimal. The goal was to encourage rule-following behavior by the threat of punishment and to thereby create a more perfect society, one where everyone followed the rules and no one had to fear the behaviors of others.

This situation is similar to the philosophy demonstrated by the Edo on Rubicun III (*ST:TNG: "*Justice"). In this episode, Wesley Crusher unknowingly violates a law that carries the sentence of death. The Edo, like the English, created these severe sanctions in response to their own history of lawlessness. Similar to English practice, the specifics of their laws were unknown by the population, which motivated the population never to break even the most minimal law because of the severity of the punishment and the unknown nature of enforcement.

FACTORIES WITH FENCES

During the 1920s, the United States experienced great prosperity and incredible industrial growth. Employment was generally good, and immigrants flocked to the U.S. to find jobs and start over (Allen and Simonsen, 2001). At the same time there was a movement in government to get as much for their tax-dollar investment as was possible. Since prisons were growing and prison costs were high, the idea of using prisons as factories gained popularity, and the industrial prison was born. The idea was to produce a product that was energy intensive, not too difficult to construct, and used by a large segment of the population to ensure sales. Later, due to the impact of the Depression of the 1930s, prisons began to produce products used only by the state in order to avoid unfair competition with outside manufacturers.

Again, we see similar elements in the *Star Trek* series. In "*Defiant*" (*ST:DS9*) Thomas Riker steals the *Defiant* from *Deep Space 9* and proceeds to attack Cardassian colonies in the Orias system. He agrees to return the ship and is sentenced to life imprisonment (rather than death) in the Lazon II labor camp. Labor camps also are mentioned in connection with Ro Laren, Tuvok, and others. It seems if the Cardassians, in particular, did not execute you, they enslaved you to perform labor to benefit Cardassia.

This is not historically unusual, but the times in question for the *Star Trek* series make it less understandable. It seems that they have controlled the transition of energy into matter, so what labor could these inmates be performing that technology could not provide more efficiently? There seem to be three primary reasons that these societies would use convict labor. First, there is an opportunity for labor to reform the offender through hard work and penitence. This seems unlikely given that Thomas Riker was sentenced to a term of life in the labor camp, and reform of an individual who is never going to be released seems illogical as well as inefficient. A life sentence does little to encourage reform. Second, those performing labor might be providing the means necessary for the conversion of energy to matter. Mining the various elements necessary to fuel the various warp cores would make sense. It would be difficult work, likely dangerous, and it would be to produce something that would benefit the society, not unlike inmates producing uniforms, blankets, and boots for the efforts in WWII. Lastly, it is possible they were again mining materials, but were mining materials that were too difficult or energy intensive to produce through replication, or possibly materials that were needed in such great quantities they had to be mined rather than replicated. Materials that come to mind would be those necessary to build a starship or perhaps a space station. The sheer enormity of starships and space stations would indicate that huge amounts of materials were necessary to create them. These vast quantities of materials would have to be mined and likely from metal-rich asteroids, which would be a convenient location for a prison labor colony.

These, however, would be the practical reasons to press into service those convicted of crimes against the state. From a less practical perspective, it is possible they were used as labor for punishment, and the utility of the labor was less important than the simple fact that they were being forced to work as their punishment. While such labor seems a waste of energy, it fosters compliance and rule-following, and tired inmates are less likely to riot or protest.

THE DEATH PENALTY

"We're a promising species, as predators go." (Captain Kirk, *ST*: "Arena"). With that quote Kirk summed up the struggle that has existed both in current society and those depicted in the series. The moral and ethical state that the persons have created is better than those of past generations, but not as perfect as they would like to be in the future. In "Arena," in his battle with the Gorn commanding officer, Kirk shows mercy at the end and in doing so saves rather than dooms his ship. The crew of the *Enterprise* learns the Federation not the Gorn was possibly the perpetrator of the attacks, and the Gorn response may have been understandable. Herein lies the problem with the death penalty in western societies. It is irrevocable, and it is possible it may be based on false or suspect information. Because of that, and the moral and ethical impacts of executions, we see execution as a response to crime in only a few episodes. We also see examples of persons who perpetrated crimes that would demand execution in most western societies today receive the standard "life in a labor camp" sentence.

In the case of *Furman v. Georgia* (408 U.S. 238, 33 L.Ed 2d 346, 92 S.Ct 2726, 1972), the United States Supreme Court (in a 5-4 decision) determined that the death penalty, as it was being handed out at the time, represented "random and capricious" behavior, and consequently was deemed unconstitutional. This moratorium lasted only a few years, and in 1976, in the case of *Gregg v. Georgia* (428 U.S. 153, 49L.Ed 2d 859, 96, S.Ct 2909), the courts determined the death penalty was constitutional, providing special protections were put into place that protected the accused (Champion, 2001). This was an attempt to make certain that society's most severe sanction was reserved for its most serious offenders, and guilt was beyond any doubt.

In "Power Struggle", (*ST:TNG*) we saw we were not the only society that had lost its appetite for revenge through the use of executions. Judges, in the time of the "Bloody Codes" would find a guilty person innocent because the specified sanction was seen as unjust. Similarly, the political dissidents from "Power Struggle," who in other times and places would have been simply executed, were disembodied and placed on the moon with intense electrical storms that kept their "spirits" alive but never allowed them to rest. Clearly, their society did not believe in execution, but perhaps because it was not punishing enough. These prisoners seemed to prefer the "rest" of death to the eternal torture of their souls on the planet.

A totally different approach to execution is taken in *ST:TNG*: "Justice." While it is an example of the injustices that can occur in a society that has severe sanctions that are not made apparent to those new to their world, it represents some fundamental inconsistencies in the relationship between punishment and ethics. As Georg Rusche and Otto Kirchheimer (1964) noted, punishments tend to increase in societies that have a large pool of surplus labor and are experiencing rapid economic changes. This finding is consistent with the times when the "Bloody Codes" were in place. Labor was plentiful, and the value of the individual laborer was low. With such low value, and a ready supply of others to fill his place, the execution of a single individual was of little consequence to the society. This does not seem to be the case in "Justice". The Edo seem to be a hedonistic and life-affirming society. While a desire to reinforce group norms using extreme punishments is not unusual, it is inconsistent for a society such as this. They argue that the threat of severe punishments is what makes their society so idyllic, but the underlying tone of the society is one of shallowness born of hedonism. In the past, when simple, severe punishments were offered, the result was either revolution or revoking of the laws by the lawmakers. But, as Beccaria noted in 1790, societies that punish to excess can cause their citizenry to lose faith in the justice of the society, and they will seek to install a new government that will operate with more care and concern for the people. It seems that, had Picard and the crew not come along, eventually the Edo would have rebelled against their own laws because they were random and, therefore, unjust.

THE CONVICT CODE

In the 1940s, social science researchers began to notice the striking behavioral similarities among inmates. This similarity was unrelated to location, crime, or, even to a limited degree, age. In 1958, Gresham Sykes wrote *A Society of Captives*, which outlined the social structure and inmate mentality in a prison in the eastern United States. Later, in 1960, Sykes and Messinger outlined the components of the inmate belief system. First termed the Convict Code, these beliefs serve to empower inmates in a powerless situation and create some order and stability in an environment where behaviors and circumstances are largely beyond the control of those who are most affected by them, namely the inmates. As Rush (2000:76) paraphrased, the Convict Code is:

> A value system among inmates that is heavily influenced by the Thieves Code, which includes these precepts: do your own time, never snitch on another prisoner, maintain dignity and respect, help other convicts, leave the majority of the other prisoners alone, and show no weakness.

In "Power Struggle" (ST:TNG), we witnessed a great example of the Convict Code in practice. The disembodied inmates whose "energies" were imprisoned on a small planet with constant, fierce electrical storms acted as a group, using fabricated signals and communications to deceive the *Enterprise* into sending down a shuttlecraft. A few of these disembodied "inmates" seized control of the crew's bodies and returned to the ship, intending to take control of the ship and use it to rescue their fellow convicts remaining on the planet. At the point when they seized the bodies of the crew and re-boarded the *Enterprise*, they easily could have taken a shuttle or simply escaped from the ship once it reached the next port. Instead, in keeping with the Convict Code, they chose to take a greater risk and attempt to help their fellow inmates, even though it may have doomed their own personal escapes. This behavior is strangely parallel to prison riots that seek to improve prison conditions through the use of conflict and resistance, but often create worse conditions due to the damage done to the facility in the course of the riot. The riot ultimately leaves those who sought to improve conditions in worse conditions than they experienced prior to the riot.

Corrections as a Zero-Sum Game

Prisons, because of their extremely limited resources, often are asked to decide which of their inmates will be receiving programs, and which will not. These decisions, which are often based on the prison counselor's beliefs regarding the likelihood of reform, affect the quality of life the individual endures, as well as the potential for parole release. This amounts to a zero-sum game for the inmates because one inmate's good is based on another inmate receiving nothing or perhaps getting less.

A similar phenomenon is noted in the *Star Trek* series, which is analogous to the thermodynamic law that states matter cannot be created or destroyed; its form can only be changed. In *Star Trek*, changes to individuals, structures, or societies always carried with them an aspect of negativity. This aspect might be minimal, or it might make the change in question less desirable, but there has been that element in most of the changes that occurred in the series.

Consider synthehol and warp drives as examples. Synthehol was designed to produce the euphoric effect of alcohol, but to be immediately reversible and less organically damaging. It achieved these goals, but at the expense of taste (some of Scotty's comments about synthehol are classic). Warp drives allowed ships to travel at speeds beyond that of light, but they created effects and a form of "pollution" that harmed the environments and well being of some of the species encountered. Both were intended to be technological fixes to problems, but both produced undesirable effects or fell short of the complete goal of the technological innovation.

As mentioned previously, corrections as a field seeks to return the individual to a range of behaviors considered normal by the group. In doing so, it is expected that there will be some changes in the individual wrought by the corrections process. From a *Star Trek* standpoint, these positive changes must be balanced by some negative aspects, and in examples drawn from the series we see that they are. In "The Outcast" (*ST:TNG*), the *Enterprise* encounters the J'naii, and Riker begins to work closely with a fellow pilot named Soren. The J'naii are a genderless society, and those in the society who exhibit traits of either gender are "rehabilitated" back to a gender-neutral state. Soren exhibits female traits, to the pleasure of Riker, but to the dismay of her society. Prior to the rehabilitation, Soren had passion and personality. Following her return to a gender-neutral state, however, she was impassive, detached, and a lesser being (especially in the eyes of Riker) than prior to her rehabilitation.

The Prison and the Borg

The Borg are one of the best examples of prison-based societies in the series. They simultaneously represent both the administration and the population of a "total institution" (Goffman, 1961). In the *Star Trek* series, the Borg are characterized as an individuality-free society, whose sole interests are the good of the collective and the expansion of the Borg collective. From a critical perspective, it could be argued that prisons operate in much the same manner. The individuals are assigned numbers, which become more important than their names to the operations of the prison. They are told when to work, where to work, what to wear, and when to sleep (or regenerate). They are not concerned with wages or saving; everything necessary for life is provided by the prison administration or the collective. Critical theorists would argue that the similarity even goes to the expansion of the prison, which would occur if the offender committed further crimes once released and returned to the prison, possibly creating new criminals at the same time and increasing the number under the control of the prison system. If that were not the case, prisons would have more and better programming to encourage and allow the inmate, once released, to be successful and survive on the outside. Absent that programming, the appearance is that the offender is expected to return to the prison, like the drones who are unable to survive outside the collective and must return in order to survive.

Conclusion

The experiences of *Star Trek* fly in the face of theories that have argued that crime is the result of biological predisposition, social disorganization, psychological problems, mental illness, and so on. These societies have advanced medical systems that can, supposedly, detect genetic problems and correct them. These societies also have, at least in theory, eliminated poverty, inequality, and injustice and corrected poor environmental conditions. In theory, with the supposed causes of crime eliminated crime as a social problem should have disappeared as well. Yet we still see crime and criminals in small places within the series. Consequently we see visions of corrections as well, but these visions offer the viewer little to hope for or to aspire toward. The practice of corrections seems to have changed little in the intervening 400 years. The series authors had a vision of what life could be like for normal (free) society. The viewer is left to ask the question if these more difficult problems could be addressed through technological methods, why not crime? It would not be unreasonable to expect that crime had all but disappeared, and that those few who engaged in crime received treatments that removed their need to commit crime while retaining their humanity and individuality.

The problem, which seems central to this lack of progress, lies not in the series, but rather in the experiences of those who created the series. In truth, few people know much about the corrections system and its peculiar relationship between history, philosophy, and practice. The news media and popular press drive our knowledge and our beliefs regarding the effectiveness of the corrections system. Unfortunately, what is most often seen is the unsuccessful case, the offender who, upon being released, commits a more serious and offensive act and is returned to the prison. Successes are rarely newsworthy. Consequently, most think all imprisonment is a failure and all offenders re-offend upon release. *Star Trek* is a reflection of the history and failures of the correctional system, but it did not have to be. After all, if the series is comfortable traveling at speeds in excess of the speed of light, then how hard can it be to keep someone from committing crime?

References

Allen, H and Simonsen, C. 2001. *Corrections in America*, 9th ed. New Jersey: Prentice Hall.

Beccaria, C. 1790. *An Essay on Crimes and Punishments*. Indianapolis, Indiana: Bobbs-Merrill.

Champion, D. 2001. *Corrections in the United States*, 3rd ed. New Jersey: Prentice Hall.

Goffman, E. 1961. *Asylums: Essays on the Social Situations of Mental Patients and Other Inmates*. Garden City NY: Anchor Press.

Kerle, K. 1998. *American Jails*. New York: Butterworth-Heinmann.

Krause, L. 1995 *The Physics of Star Trek*. New York: Basic Books.

Meadows, D., Meadows, D., Randers, J., and Behrens III, W. 1972. *The Limits to Growth*. NY: Universe Books.

Rusche, G. and Kirchheimer, O. 1964. *Punishment and Social Structure*. NY: Columbia University Press.

Rush, G. 2000. *The Dictionary of Criminal Justice*, 5th ed. Sluice Dock, Guilford, CT: Dushkin/McGraw Hill.

Sykes, G. 1958. *The Society of Captives: A Study of a Maximum Security Prison*. Princeton NJ: Princeton University Press.

Sykes, G. and Messinger, S. 1960. "The Inmate Social System". In R. Cloward, D. Cressy, R. McCleery, L. Ohlin, G. Sykes, and S. Messinger (Eds). *Theoretical Studies in Social Organization of the Prison*. NY: Social Science Research Council.

QUESTIONS FOR THOUGHT

- How could the various technologies we have seen in the *Star Trek* series be used to address criminality, and what advances in the justice system would you expect in the next 400 years?
- What types of crime would we expect to see in a society without deprivation?
- How would law enforcement improve with the technologies seen in the *Star Trek* series? How might their practices change?

REVIEW QUESTIONS

- What are the five responses to crime, and what do they imply about the offender?
- What were the "Bloody Codes" and what do they imply about the value of the individual in 16th century England?
- What social conditions could lead to the use of inmate labor, and what conditions could lead to the cessation of its use?
- Why is there so much controversy surrounding the death penalty? How might its use harm the integrity of our justice system?
- What caused the Convict Code to develop? What other places have similar codes, and why do their members follow them?

Crime and "Repentance":
*JUSTICE ADMINISTRATION AND THE
MORAL SELF IN A NEW AGE*

CHARLES M. VIVONA, PhD

The *Star Trek* episode "Repentance" has theatrical roots in 15th and 16th century morality plays.[1] Morality plays were allegorical dramas depicting good and evil in a struggle for man's soul, used for moral instruction.

This space-bound episode is considerably more complex and dynamic than the traditional morality play. It is more sophisticated and is placed in a futuristic setting. Yet this television show also functions as a vehicle for moral illumination. Lessons of right and wrong co-mingle with the show's entertainment value. The audience is pulled into dramatic conflicts that question the nature of good and evil and examine appropriate social responses to evil when it is criminal.

"Repentance" [*Voyager* series: aired January 31, 2001] deals with a wealth of criminological matters. At first blush, the plot appears to have been written by a consortium of criminologists and legal scholars. The dramatic events involved bear significance to the administration of criminal justice both in *Star Trek* and in our own world. The issues that absorb us in this television episode are ones that perplex criminologists, sociologists, social psychologists, and policy makers.

Capital Punishment and the Cultural Relativity Imperative

For example, in "Repentance" prisoners are brought aboard the *U.S.S. Voyager* to wait their transport to their Nygean homeworld in order to be executed for capital crimes. Those onboard the spacecraft debate the practice of capital punishment, a subject of heated contemporary debate.

Many involved in the earthly debate of capital punishment believe the execution of murderers and other heinous criminals is a valid and necessary exercise of state authority. The Old Testament teaches that God instituted capital punishment in the Jewish law code, and the principle of capital punishment precedes the Old Testament (Genesis 9:6: "Whoever sheds man's blood by man his blood shall be shed, for in the image of God, He made man.").[2] The Mosaic Law in the Old Testament specifies capital punishment for offenses including idolatry, blasphemy, magic, murder, adultery, bestiality, and incest. This position continues in Christian thought. In the New Testament the right of the state to execute seems taken for granted. In *The City Of God*, St. Augustine writes:

> The same divine law which forbids the killing of a
> human being allows certain exceptions, as when
> God authorizes killing by a general law ..... Since the
> agent of authority is but a sword in the hand, and is
> not responsible for the killing, it is in no way con-
> trary to the commandment, 'Thou shalt not kill', for
> the representatives of the State's authority to put
> criminals to death, according to law or the rule of
> rational justice.[3]

In the Middle Ages, religious scholars taught that the ecclesiastic courts should refrain from the death penalty and that the civil courts should impose it only for major crimes. The Catholic Church held positions sympathetic to the death penalty well into the 20th century, and until 1969 the Church had a penal code that included the death penalty for attempts to assassinate the pope. Pope Pius XII argued that when the State uses the death penalty, it does not exercise dominion over human life but only recognizes that the criminal, by a kind of moral suicide, has deprived himself of the right to life.

Capital punishment is an ultimate punishment in the United States. The federal government, U.S. military, and 38 of the states authorize it.[4] Many countries in Africa, the Middle East, and Asia retain the death penalty. Customary international law continues to permit the death penalty.

The Nygean guards onboard *Voyager* contend that their prisoners are abhorrent beings who deserve to die. The guards, taking a position similar to those just described, argue that execution is both a valid method of retribution and that it is a means of self-defense for society. Capital punishment prevents those executed from engaging in future crime.

The threat of death also is intended to discourage would-be offenders.

On the other side of this debate, many argue that both homicide and societal-authorized legal execution are killing. Whether by criminals or by the state, both takings of human life are immoral, unethical, and wrong. Opponents of capital punishment believe state-sanctioned executions are inhumane and unnecessary denials of human dignity. They conceive capital punishment as a relic of earlier eras, of societies with cultures of violence and absolutist theories of political power. One of the founding fathers of criminology, Cesare Beccaria, thought punishment by death was absolutely without justification.[5] Many contemporary Catholic scholars and many libertarian associations argue against the death penalty. They believe a New Testament ethic of love replaces Old Testament law. The Franciscan Gino Concetti views all human life as sacred and untouchable. He says that no matter how heinous the crime, the criminal does not lose his fundamental right to life, for that right is primordial, inviolable, and inalienable. No one has power over life.

Many of these opponents to the death penalty point to sociological data that suggest that ethnic and other social discriminations are at work in selection of those put to death. In 1980, the majority of Catholic bishops in the United States declared the death penalty as currently practiced in the United State is not justifiable. This was a contentious decision; some dissidents argued the proclamation vacated the traditional scriptural biblical bases of earlier Church doctrine on the subject. The bishops' statement did not rule out capital punishment altogether, but rather focused on its contemporary application in the U.S.

European countries, in reflection of these concerns, have outlawed capital punishment. There are a number of international conventions prohibiting the death penalty, including the European Convention On Human Rights. The European Union and Council of Europe have made the abolition of or a moratorium on the death penalty a condition of membership.[6]

The European perspective probably reflects its 20th century historical experience, where the potential for abuse of the state's right to decide issues of life and death was so horrifically apparent in the mass killings of the Third Reich.

> The deterrent effect of capital punishment has been strenuously debated. Many believe that the sociological evidence does not support the position that the threat reduces future crime.

Aboard the *Voyager*, the Doctor and most of his colleagues fall into the camp that rejects the use of capital punishment. They share the view that the Nygean criminal justice system's use of the death penalty is barbaric. They see the impending executions of the Benkaran prisoners as revenge – an eye for an eye – and not justice.

Nevertheless, the *Voyager* crew is restrained in the application of its ethical views. They do not thwart the Nygeans in their efforts to convey the prisoners to their death. The Starfleet abhorrence of capital punishment is held in check in deference to an overriding ethical constraint. The Starfleet to which *Voyager* belongs has a rule of such magnitude that it is called the "Prime Directive." This directive requires that Starfleet personnel not interfere with the normal and sacred cultural evolution of alien lives and cultures. It prohibits Starfleet from introducing superior knowledge, strength, or technologies into alien societies. Alien activities must be judged within the framework of the respective alien society, by its cultural terms, within its social frameworks. This Prime Directive is supposed to take precedence over any and all other considerations and carries with it the highest obligation.

In "Repentance," alien Benkaran prisoners and their Nygean prison guards have been taken aboard *Voyager* when their damaged Nygean vessel faces imminent destruction. The prisoners have been found guilty of murder and face execution by the Nygean criminal justice system on return to the Nygean homeworld. Respective to this episode, the Prime Directive requires that personnel aboard the *U.S.S. Voyager* avoid intruding into the Nygean administration of justice and avoid making decisions impacting the fate of the Benkaran prisoners removed from the crippled ship. *Voyager*'s crew feels obliged to facilitate the transport of the prisoners despite their strongly held belief that capital punishment is an evil, uncivilized practice.

The audience watching this television episode is apt to find the *Voyager*'s handling of the ethical quandary understandable, if discomforting. The audience is of a modern mind and cognizant of the multiplicity of empirical and moral frameworks. It is familiar with the sociological and anthropological tenets of cultural relativism. The concept of cultural relativism has popular acceptance: it is the product of everyday inter-societal contact in the contemporary globe and of increasing divisions of labor within modern industrial societies. Our daily experience reminds us that there are many ways of living and that other peoples have normative and value systems that are different than our own but legitimate on their own terms. Social scientists frequently cite an imperative that they understand human affairs from the cultural perspective of the people they observe; they judge human activities by the functioning of those activities within the social systems of which they are a part. Social scientists often hold forth as a "prime directive" that they be culturally or value-neutral and refrain from moral judgments regarding the activities of people in other cultures and societies. The *Star Trek* Prime Directive has intellectual roots in the now commonplace anthropological concepts of cultural diversity and cultural relativity.

Those who work – on Earth and in space – in organizations dealing with the modern administration of criminal justice are particularly apt to find the invocation of the Prime Directive a familiar phenomenon. They are used to dealing with multiple legal and social frameworks. They are used to dealing with people with quite different points of view. They are used to extraordinary mandates that transcend more common, day-to-day rules and obligations.

Professionals in all major justice organizations realize the need to step back from and reflect on their initial empirical and moral inclinations. Justice system participants in both worlds accept there are moral perspectives different from their own that may necessitate the suspension of certain often strongly held personal and moral views.

At the least, criminal justice professionals in modern legal systems recognize they are supposed to set aside their own views to meet the needs of their justice institution. Participants are bureaucrats who are supposed to subordinate their personal views to the views mandated by their roles in the justice system. This social psychological maneuvering is essential to organizational actions in all worlds. The competition between process demands such as the Prime Directive and substantive interests permeates all justice systems. The tasks of juxtaposing and relating diverse frameworks can be seen in the frequent conflicts between procedural criminal law and substantive criminal law in modern legal studies and popular entertainment.

Nevertheless, a growing body of social scientific studies shows the extrasystemic moral and social views of legal/justice system participants' impact on their official decisions. There is considerable research demonstrating that those engaged in official legal action routinely bring their extra-official views and values into play. There also is evidence that legal participants use legal frameworks to cloak their personal or (extra-legal) social views.

Skeptical viewers of the *Star Trek* series have similarly noted that the Prime Directive that prohibits Fleet members from interfering with the processes of alien life and culture is breached when it interferes with particularly strategic Starfleet objectives and *Star Trek* dramatic needs. They argue the Prime Directive is a theatrical tool that can be employed to neatly resolve entanglements in the plot that otherwise would be problematic and time-consuming. It does bear resemblance to the time honored theatrical *deus ex machina*, the gods in Greek drama who resolved the interminable complexities of plays by their supernatural intervention, often in forced and improbable ways.[7] All groups – *Star Trek*kers in their dealings with the Prime Directive, social scientists in social science research and policy-making, and justice system actors faced with conflicts between the law and their extra-legal views – may honor the imperatives of their legal and justice-system cultural ideals by their breach.

The Identity of the Moral Self and the Mind/Body Dilemma

As we watch the show, we ponder the nature of human (humanoid) morality and the circumstances of moral actions. The self is mental; its actions and experiences are heartfelt, the stuff of poets. The self equally is physiological: a question of body and brain matter that is subject to medical and surgical treatment. Where, we ask, is the locus of moral action? What should we make of free will, guilt and criminal responsibility? How do we reconcile these human attributes with the equally apparent forces of social, psychological and physiological determinism? What is the nature of a criminal's self and social identities and what are the possibilities of their transformation? How should we define that human identity? How should we appraise the moral self?

"Repentance" gives considerable attention to the workings of the mind and body of Iko, one of the Benkaran prisoners brought aboard the *U.S.S. Voyager*. Both subjective and objective facets of Iko's self-identity are implicated in his criminality and subsequent moral reformation. The *Voyager* crew attends to Iko's mental state – his conscience and to his corollary physical state – his brain. Both facets of Iko's self intermingle in participants' attempts to define his moral identity.

The main plot of "Repentance" revolves around the fate of Iko, who has been found guilty of murder by the Nygean criminal justice system. On coming aboard *Voyager*, Iko is jailed in a makeshift cell. During a physical thrashing by the Nygean guards, Iko is struck a blow on the head and suffers severe brain damage. The Doctor brings the prisoner to sick bay where he applies space age medicine. He inserts atomic and molecular-scale nanoprobes in Iko's brain to repair neurological damage resulting from the violent confrontation.

On regaining consciousness, Iko is calm but in pain. The Doctor soon observes radical changes in Iko's attitudes and behavior. There are several kinds of evidence intimating that Iko has experienced a moral transformation. The Doctor, his *Voyager* colleagues, and we, the television audience, begin to reassess and redefine Iko's moral identity.

We reconstruct the subjective, inner-life aspects of Iko's existence from his own verbal reports about his state of consciousness. Iko expresses remorse. He complains to the Doctor that he is suffering nausea and can't stop thinking about the man he killed.

We infer Iko's mental state from his actions. He regards his hands with disgust, envisioning them as tools of violence. We infer his mental state from his verbal statements. Iko remarks, "I hurt people. I deserve to die." Some evidence is in minutia: a little nod and a humble downward glance he gives Egrid, the prisoner whose food he used to steal, when he gives his prison meal to him.

Some of the behaviors we take into account seemingly are distant from the issue of Iko's criminality; the prisoner engages Seven of Nine in a poetic discussion regarding astronomy and the relations of stars. But such more distant evidence helps validate our emerging view that the physical pain the prisoner experiences has psychic origins and is rooted in his newfound sense of guilt.

Finally, evidence regarding Iko's moral persona derives from observations of aspects of Iko's physical being that are not under his immediate control. A scan of Iko's brain patterns finds that consequent to the insertion of the nanoprobes, his brain has new patterns of neural activity. The neurotransmitters in his brain have established new pathways about his cortex.

The Doctor's research determines that the prisoner was born with a congenital brain defect that made him prone to violent and sociopathic behavior. The surgical operation by which nanoprobes were inserted into his brain has repaired this condition. The nanoprobes have altered the brain organ that controls behavioral impulses and regulates decision-making. The Doctor explains that this organ, the pineal gland, is the physiological equivalent of what we mentally experience as a moral conscience. As a result of the operation, Iko is now able to control nascent violent impulses.

The subjective and objective, mental and physical evidence confirm one another. They mutually reinforce the diagnosis that Iko's overall moral pattern, his moral personality, has changed.

The *Voyager* crew discusses the patient's condition and concludes that Iko appears truly remorseful. He looks compassionate.

The Doctor conceives Iko as having been the victim of his biology, which now has been fundamentally altered by surgery. Seven of Nine states, "By some definitions … he is not the same man who committed the murder." He is a different person now and doesn't deserve to be executed.

The interest in the biology of crime and the criminal onboard *Voyager* mirrors recent developments in criminological discourse.

Predominating American criminological thought has its historical roots in sociology and related behavioral (psychological, social psychological) disciplines. Throughout the 20th century, the social sciences significantly increased our understanding of crime phenomena. The development of rational choice, social structure, social process, social ecology, conflict, and social interaction theories, and the integrated models combining these theories, has been sufficient to keep the social sciences in the forefront of American efforts to understand crime and juvenile delinquency.[8]

Students of social action, including criminological action, have articulated the need to understand such action from the standpoints of those who commit those actions. Many social scientists argue that in order to explain crime and juvenile delinquency we need to understand the subjective meanings of criminal actions to those involved. Subsequent research on the social meanings of crime has proven engaging and enlightening. This article has already reflected this widespread interest.

For decades, the dominant voices in criminological debates have disregarded medical models of crime causation and medical panaceas for crime treatment. Their disenchantment with the medical paradigm had several roots.

First, there has been a fragmentation of human knowledge. The tendency toward disciplinary focuses is self-reinforcing. Many social scientists reject medical and physiological theories of crime and methods of treatment of crime simply because such thinking is foreign to them and their discipline's scientific perspective. Practitioners gain a proprietary interest in their own discipline's approach to a field of study. It is difficult to remain current with developments in one's intellectual discipline, particularly when the growth of one's field is as dynamic as has been social science-based criminology. Remaining current with developments in parallel fields that share basic paradigms is even more challenging. The tendency toward intellectual myopia is further enhanced when the issues and developments are in disparate intellectual disciplines, having quite distinct premises, theories, and methods. Organizational priorities supercede intellectual needs.

Beyond these disciplinary forces that work to facilitate intellectual provincialism, there have been social policy issues and concerns detrimental to the acceptance of physiologically oriented models. Criminologists, civil libertarians, and social welfare practitioners usually have an aversion to medical and psychiatric explanations of crime.

Some in this group are recoiling over the plight of psychiatric patients, who they see as victims of modern scientific institutions. These critics are horrified by the shortcomings of lobotomies and other surgical and drug-based psychiatric remedies used for the "treatment" of criminality and mental illness. They are distraught by the social circumstances of people subjected to psychiatric institutionalization: they see conditions such as loss of freedom and social humiliation as dehumanizing, root sources of inmates' psychiatric problems (Goffman, Kittrie).[9] This group also includes social scientists who believe a focus on genetics and inherited causes of crime would foster incipient racism. If we find genetic links to crime, can't we then argue that there are ethnic and racial predispositions to crime? The temper of the times, inherited from 1960s and 1970s social rebelliousness and social activism, also has led to an emphasis on the sociological causes of crime rather than causes of crime internal to the person that would be the focus of biological explanations.

These diverse forces have fed on one another. Their combined weight led to the disparaging of – or outright politically-inspired taboo on – efforts that focus on the body as the source or motivating force in crime action.

The interest in organismic or physiological causes of crime action, while running counter to dominant American thinking regarding crime, is gaining ground. The quite successful social scientific paradigm is increasingly being confronted by newly successful physiological, biologically-based, psychiatric developments.

The concern for biological dimensions of criminal motivation and criminal identity on board the *U.S.S. Voyager* is apt to be less provocative in many European criminological schools, whose traditions are rooted in the biological sciences. Indeed, the criminological enterprise has among its earliest roots biological thinking. Lavater's 18th century concern with the facial features of criminals; Gall and Spurzheim's early 19th century concern with phrenology (the structure of skull and brain and its impact on criminal activity); and Lombroso's later 19th century concern with atavistic anomalies (inherited traits that, he thought, could be traced back to more primitive stages of human evolutionary development but whose contemporary recurrence now causes criminal behavior) are but a few examples of biologically-oriented thinking that we find early in the history of criminology.

Incredulous advances in a wide array of medical fields are heartening the return of the biology of crime from the periphery to the center of criminological debate. In addition to work in psychiatry, researchers are exploring the organic dynamics of crime in genetics, pharmacology, biochemistry, endocrinology, neurology and toxicology, to name but a few disciplines. Psychologists with a physiological focus also are facilitating the return to an organismic approach.

Some of the newest findings may echo ancient wisdoms. The pineal gland, the brain organ in humans analogous to that in Prisoner Iko altered by the operation aboard the *U.S.S. Voyager*, was the home of the "third eye" of Eastern religion and Western magical tradition. Psychiatry only now is beginning to understand its functions and functioning. It is known to control mental stability and mental and sexual growth. The approach to moral behavior taken by the Doctor aboard the *U.S.S. Voyager* parallels current medical interests in brain functioning and the impact of that functioning on human conduct.

The case of Iko mirrors other debates in modern criminal law, whose premises are being contested by findings in the physically oriented human sciences. The classic paradigm of substantive criminal law – and most other moral codes – is founded on such notions as free will, personal responsibility, and individual

volition. The legal paradigm rests on the premise that the criminal actor voluntarily chooses his criminal action, that the criminal is self-determining.

This classic model of criminal action recognizes criminals may be propelled
by forces beyond their control. The forces that limit individual responsibility
are incorporated in certain qualifications to the basic premises of free will and
individual responsibility. In the substantive criminal law, immaturity, mental
abnormality and mental illness are among classic mitigating circumstances that
reduce the criminal's responsibility for his actions. Iko's initial brain defect
might readily be included in current lively discourses over insanity and mental
illness. The Iko case highlights, nevertheless, an increased sensitivity to factors
within the individual that impede the human ability to be self-determining.
There is heated debate regarding the range of phenomena inside and outside
the person that limit human responsibility for criminal behavior and the appropriate legal classification of such phenomena. Recent cases have presented bat-
tered woman syndrome, adopted child syndrome, child abuse syndrome, pre-
menstrual syndrome, and excessive testosterone as conditions that limit a person's ability to control his or her actions and that ought be taken into consideration in diminishing a person's responsibility for his/her criminal actions.

The possibility of physiological and psychological states precluding free will
and, consequently, moral behavior certainly causes us to question the primary
premise of responsibility found in substantive criminal law. They remind us that
criminal law is a set of conventions and stereotypes. The idea of self-determination is one of those primary conventions. The law – as an intellectual framework, a system of symbols, and a social institution – necessarily rests, in a primordial way, on a system of conventions and stereotypes. It cannot avoid doing
so. The law is a bureaucratization of the imagination regarding moral behavior.[10]

Despite challenges such as those presented by the case of Iko, the paradigm of free will and personal responsibility can be expected to continue. This
paradigm will continue to dominate in the law for no other reason than it provides organized society an argument by which to impose crucial control functions on its members. But even more importantly, the concept of the human self
this paradigm provides accurately reflects much of our experience of humans in
action in normal, everyday life. The paradigm is born of our experience of the
human condition. The case of Iko and his brain might simply remind us of the
need for elasticity in that primary paradigm.

In his book *Becoming Deviant*, David Matza has argued the need for a
resilient interpretation of human responsibility. Matza finds much of deviant
behavior and criminal behavior is self-determined. People deliberate over using
drugs, joining a nudist colony, becoming members of a gang. They engage in

considerable dialogue with themselves as to whether they should do the unconventional. The actions of people engaging in deviant activities are wrought with
qualities of intentionality, willfulness, deliberativeness, consciousness and reflec-
tivity. Such qualities also characterize socially conventional action. They are
integral to human life. Human beings have selves because they are reflective.
They act impulsively and with consideration (malice aforethought, in the criminal sphere). They are subject beings who experience the world and think and
experience themselves as objects in that world.

Matza enticingly locates the forces of human action in a multi-leveled,
multi-faceted being:

> The subjective capacities develop within an organ-
> ism, and thus arises the possibility of a tyranny
> exerted by a lower order of being. Freud referred
> to the effects of such a tyranny as 'overdetermina-
> tion,' a curious, most revealing, and remarkable
> well-chosen term.... The meaning of overdetermi-
> nation should be apparent: literally being deter-
> mined. One's behavior can not be more than
> determined; but the idea of being determined can
> be weakened through sloppy or metaphoric usage,
> and Freud himself followed in that tradition.[11]

To talk of overdetermination, the lack of free will and responsibility is to
focus on the tyrannical captivity of the subject by the hegemony of the organ-
ism over the subject. In such a situation, the self cannot transcend its organismic being because it was caused simply by its physical attributes. This is what
we find has been happening to prisoner Iko.

Criminology and criminal law, by their very nature cross-disciplinary fields,
have intellectual battlegrounds between innumerable fields of knowledge,
including the social, physical, and medical sciences. When we discuss crime, we
often raise issues appropriate for epistemological discourse. We discuss the limits and validity of human knowledge. We can expect the physiological corre-
lates of human conscience and guilt spotlighted by the case of prisoner Iko to
be recurrent considerations of crime talk.

"Repentance" brings to popular culture ideas and concerns that are surfac-
ing with greater and greater frequency in the human sciences. The interest in
mind/body relations and their impact on moral and criminal actions that is presented dramatically onboard *Voyager* is indicative of an emerging state of intel-

lectual affairs. Even now there is a changing relationship among the academic disciplines. There is greater discourse among those disciplines. The physiological dimensions of criminal action and their implications for our understanding of crime are gaining increased attention in popular avenues of discourse, such as television, as well. The episode accurately highlights this subject area as among the more provocative in the field of crime.

The Social Construction of The Moral Self

The nature of Iko and his fellow prisoners' moral identities are at the core of "Repentance". The episode draws attention to a variety of processes by which moral identities are defined. This article already has taken up mind/body problems of defining Iko's moral identity. It now focuses on the social processes by which the Benkarans come to be conceived as prisoners and criminals.

The drama's focus on the moral identities of Iko and his fellow prisoners is to be expected. By their very nature, criminal and other deviant activities challenge conventional beliefs regarding the self. Sociologists studying crime and other forms of social deviance regularly seek to understand the social processes by which people's moral identities are constructed – by themselves and by others. Questions regarding the relations between a person's identity, actions, and motives are commonplace to the administration of criminal justice on earth as well as in space. The sociology of deviance, for instance, regularly alerts its students to the puzzling conventional social practice of labeling a person a criminal and seeing that criminality as the overriding feature (the essence) of that person's identity even when the person is found guilty of a criminal act that was just seconds long and when that criminal act was not typical behavior for or reflective of the person's usual personality

Here we look at the sequential changes in prisoners' moral identities. Howard S. Becker has alerted us to a useful conception for understanding such changes: the notion of "career."[12] The notion of career focuses our attention on the sequence of movements by which an individual moves from one position to another in an organized social setting. A person's social career has both internal/subjective and external/objective elements: how a person defines his life history and how his life story is defined by others. The person may have a subjectively-defined sense of his or her career – how the person involved conceives his or her past, present and future as a continuum through social space and time. There also are objective career patterns: how people typically move through an organized social setting. Prisoners have a view of what is happening to them and an ongoing notion of their lives. There is a typical pattern of social action that happens to them: what is done to those charged with crimes as part of the normal, institutionalized processes that are involved in the administration of criminal justice.

THE MORAL CAREER OF PRISONER IKO

When the episode begins and the *Voyager* crew and we, the television audience, meet Iko and his fellow prisoners, we are told by their Nygean guards that the Nygean criminal justice system already has judged them criminals. They now are prisoners being transported back for execution by the Nygeans. The guards initially attest to these prisoner and criminal identities. The *Voyager* crew and we accept these socially designated identities despite their being attributed to them by an alien society. Why are we so willing to accept Nygean perspective?

We have the Nygean verbal assertions as to what is taking place. But all the refugees from the damaged spacecraft seem to accept their respective definitions as prisoners or guards. They act and relate to one another correspondingly. No challenges are made. The *Voyager* crew thus buys into the Benkarans' prisoner identifications. They imprison the Benkarans aboard the spacecraft, where they initially are held under the surveillance of the Nygean guards. The television audience similarly goes along with the story and takes for granted that Iko and the others are prisoners. The prima facie evidence is sufficient: they are under guard and their actions restricted. They are confined to a cell and not at liberty. These are the defining conditions involved when we identify people as prisoners. These conditions are the meaning of the word.

The Nygeans also define Iko as a criminal – a murderer, no less. Yediq, the Nygean warden, relates that Iko has a history of dozens of violent crimes. He informs the *Voyager*'s officers that Iko has formally been judged a criminal by the Nygean criminal justice system. Thus, the whole Nygean criminal justice institution – which acts as the agent of the Nygean state and society – stands behind this social definition. We accept its institutional processes and judicial determination as legitimate. Iko has a criminal identity.

Norms of societal reciprocity – that political states accept other states' decisions regarding their internal affairs – encourage us to accept the Nygean decision. Like modern nations that reciprocally accept prima facie other nations' judicial determinations, we all – space folk and Earth folk – accept the legitimacy of the Nygean justice institution and its judgments, in general and in this particular case. The social trappings we expect to surround a society's formal determinations of criminal guilt seem to be there. The judgment of Iko was placed in the hands of the Nygean social institution that handles questions of justice and crime. We assume that the criminal justice institution has followed its own rules for the adjudication of criminal justice and we have no reason to question its procedures, either in general or in the specific. At the least, this is not the appropriate forum for the more general debate. The plot has its own momentum.

The *Voyager* crew and we (with perhaps the exception of a few particularly skeptical viewers) accept that he is a criminal. We can infer the crew's view from their actions; they willingly imprison him in a contrived jail when he boards their ship. We trust they would not do so if they felt it inappropriate. They and we trust that the Nygean determination of criminality is accurate and justified.

The *Voyager* crew and television audience have no philosophical urge to question the criminality of actions of the sort for which Iko has been charged. We also believe that murder is illegal, immoral, and properly subject to state sanction. We accept Iko acted criminally; we accept his actions were criminal.

Iko himself does not question the Nygean judicial process or its decision. Iko accepts he is a criminal. The label applied to him is sticking because all adhere to it.

Then we witness firsthand Iko's demeanor and behaviors. These corroborate our initial judgments. Seeking to escape, Iko holds Seven of Nine at knife-point. He threatens to kill Captain Janeway and the *Voyager* crew if his demands for release are not met. He is belligerent and violent in his cell. He intimates he will have the children of his Nygean warden harmed. We hear that he routinely steals a co-prisoner's meals. These actions and attitudes fulfill our stereotypic notions of criminals and murderers. Some of these acts are in themselves criminal. Others, in the current context, corroborate Iko's criminality.

The immediate evidence upholds the historical. His criminal behavior is not just a singular act. It reflects a general way of being in the world. All who encounter him believe the allocation of a criminal identity to Iko is on solid ground. While it takes but one act in one's lifetime to be labeled a criminal, we see evidence that Iko's criminal identity defines the essence of the man. He is a criminal being.

It is not surprising that we focus on Iko's prisoner and criminal identities and don't feel pressed to attend to other facets of his life. Howard S. Becker, a pioneer in the sociological study of social deviance, remarks in *Outsiders: Studies In The Sociology Of Deviance* that deviant identities are master identities.[13] Such identities override other ways of defining a person's character or social status. Deviant attributes tend to be the focus of our relations with those labeled as deviant. We are inclined to think that the negative moral attributes of those labeled deviant provide particularly significant insights into their souls.

(The general sociological tendency for people to focus on deviant identities well serves the theater; it reinforces the dramatic spotlight pointed at the Benkarans' criminal identities. It is theatrically revealing that the very moment when we begin to question Iko's existent moral identity and begin to consider redefining him as other than a criminal, the play's dramatic focus also expands to other aspects of Iko's identity: his fascination with the stars and the poetry of the universe.)

With his brain operation, Iko undergoes the remarkable transformation of organismic structure and social personality described in the earlier section of this paper. One by one, crew members begin to see Iko anew. The Doctor determines Iko was born with a congenital brain defect that made him prone to violence and sociopathic behavior. This neurological defect left him unable to control his own behavior. The medical operation has inadvertently repaired that defect. Iko's brain functioning has metamorphosed. The Doctor notes a corresponding change in Iko's attitudes and behavior. Iko's conscience has been activated. We all witness regret, sorrow, remorse, penitence, shame, and contrition.

The *Voyager* crew and we, the television audience, look at Iko from a number of perspectives. We look at him as a conscious (subject) being; we look at him as an acting being; we look at him as a physical (object) being. The television audience can watch him when he is interacting with others and when he is alone. We all look at the variety of ways he now behaves and the various ways he exhibits change. What is happening here may be conceived of as an unconscious and informal multivariate, multifactor assessment of Iko, all of which reinforces an emerging hypothesis that the man now has a different persona.

Voyager personnel come to a common recognition that Iko's personality no longer has a criminal essence. He is in control of his violent impulses; even the thought of violence leaves him ill and in pain. Let free now, he would not long be a threat. Seven of Nine says that by some definitions Iko is not the same man who committed the murder. He is a different person now, she avers, and does not deserve to be executed.

We all are socially influenced in our re-identification of Iko; we reaffirm to each other our personally held initial beliefs that something new is going on here. The television audience is constrained by its passive role in the proceedings. It can choose to opt out of this redefining, but then how is it to relate to the ongoing story line? (It must construct an alternative, dissident line of action that constantly is at odds with the story as conventionally defined.) However, important direct experiences and clear, intellectual thinking lie at the heart of both *Start Trek* group processes and television viewers' changes in view.

The plot next takes up *Voyager*'s attempts to reclassify Iko, to alter his moral identity in the world outside their own community. The ship's crew begins to think perhaps Iko should not be defined as a criminal by the world at large; perhaps he should not be formally treated as one. The repugnance they feel toward the death penalty becomes an even more formidable force when it is coupled with their emergent sense of injustice.

Their first steps toward the redefinition of Iko's moral identity are in their immediate locale. They present their views to the Nygean warden, Yediq.

Yediq reasserts his belief that Iko remains a dangerous man and a criminal. The transformations in his brain and personality do not alter the fact he did commit a murder. He continues to identify Iko as a criminal. Perhaps he maintains this view out of sheer habit. Or he has not yet seen what the *Voyager* crew and we have seen. We also can assume he feels pressured to maintain his existent definition of Iko and the criminal justice mission. He and his guards are agents of the Nygean criminal justice system and conceive themselves and their situation within its institutional perspective. They have their social roles to play. Their organizational mandate is to convey Iko to their homeworld. It is not their institutional prerogative to redefine his moral identity and initiate a new way of dealing with him. The consequences of their acting in unplanned and unknown ways outside of Nygean frames of reference are unfathomable to them. They are not the authors of their own story line.

The *Voyager* crew recognizes the limited authority of the local Nygean criminal justice personnel. The Nygeans must appeal to higher legal authorities. They channel this appeal through the warden, as the chief representative and agent of the alien legal institution.

While *Voyager* deals with a criminal justice system that is foreign to it and whose terms and specific features are different from the crew's own, they and we still feel we are on familiar terrain. With some filling in of particulars and details, they seem easily oriented. We all seem to understand what is going on. The appeal is directed to a social institution that has facets common to governmental institutions in general and criminal justice institutions in specific. The *Voyager* officers are dealing with an organization that appears much like their own. It is much like our own. The Nygean criminal justice system is bureaucratic.

We know little about it but can therefore surmise the Nygean justice system is hierarchical and has preset lines of authority. It consists of offices with specific duties and responsibilities, defined and limited powers, standardized procedures and rules of conduct. Witness the activities of the warden and the guards he supervises. They appear impersonal and to have a specialized division of labor. The organizational structure operates on the basis of certain governing principles, oriented around the attainment of organizational goals. These over-arching principles and goals legitimize specific organizational projects. They guide participants' actions, and they justify those actions. Max Weber describes these bureaucratic features as necessary for the large-scale planning and coordi-nation of the mass organizations of the modern state.

We are not surprised the guards decline to act independently of their organization. They are office holders and define themselves within their roles, their organization's contexts and frameworks. They seem tacitly to agree when Captain Janeway says, in an argument regarding the reexamination of Iko's case, "We could debate this all day, but the fact is that our personal opinions are irrelevant. All that matters is Nygean law." We also are not surprised when, despite personal reluctance and distaste for the prisoner and the petition, war-den Yediq feels required to provide information as to how Iko could appeal and then forwards the appeal to the appropriate Nygean authorities.

The criminal justice systems involved have similar societal functions. All are social control agencies that deal with people accused of violating the law. All have social mechanisms for formally charging people with criminal acts. All have institutionalized processes for determining whether a criminal act did indeed occur and if the accused were in fact the offenders who committed the crime. All have processes for determining the fate of those found guilty.

A parallel may be drawn between the American system of criminal justice and its system of juvenile justice. Both systems for the administration of justice are organizations that process people. Certain operations must take place in both instances because they have common systemic functions. In each case there is a staff that comprises the (more or less) permanent membership of the justice system. There are defendants who are charged with perpetrating the legal offense who are processed by that system, and there are victims who have been harmed by defendants' actions. (In the juvenile justice system, the offend-er may concurrently be conceived of as a perpetrator and a victim). The varia-tions in terminologies and procedures between adult criminal and juvenile jus-tice systems roles reflect differences in their philosophical purposes and goals. The similarities in processes reflect correspondences in their organizational functions.

They do the same thing to people who enter (as defendants) into them, but they relate to those people with different operating philosophies. In adult cases, a person is arrested and indicted (a formal written accusation of the crime is presented to a court). In juvenile cases, the youth is taken into custody and a petition of particular is presented to a court. The adult criminal may be able to plea bargain for lesser charges; the youthful offender may negotiate an adjustment of his or her charges. The adult case may go to trial before a judge and possible a jury who determine what event precipitated the criminal charges; the youth's case may go to a fact-finding hearing that makes an assessment of the youth and his or her situation. If the adult (youth) is convicted (adjudicated), a sentence hearing (dispositional hearing) will follow, and the person involved will be sentenced (disposed). The adult may be incarcerated in a prison. The youth may be committed to a youth development center or other program.

Voyager's concept of the administration of justice seems to have great resemblances to the American system of justice. An impartial third party (the judge or a sentencing commission) decides the fate of the convicted offender on the grounds that society as a whole – and not just the aggrieved victim – is offended and harmed by criminal action. It is assumed that victims are not able to come up with impartial verdicts that balance the reality of the offense with the diverse purposes of criminal sanctions. During sentencing, the criminal justice system deals with issues such as justice, incapacitation, punishment, deterrence, and rehabilitation, as well as retribution and restitution. We expect criminal justice personnel to balance these concerns. We not think it fair or possible for the victims of crimes to do so.

The *Voyager* officers are advised that the Nygean legal system has a different system of ends and, therefore, a different set of standards. It is based on a principle called "Vekto Valek K'Vadim" – ancient Nygean for "favor the victims." This principle determines the actions available when the Nygean institution administers justice. The assumption here is the victim and his or her family are the most harmed by the criminal action and therefore justice must center on their needs. Thus, the victim's family determines the sentence of a person convicted of murder. The family may choose the grounds of the sentence: they may opt for restitution or revenge. An impartial, third party such as a judge or sentencing commission does not decide the fate of the convict. Power is given to those most visibly harmed and not ceded to the state.

Defendants in Nygean capital cases have the right to appeal their sentences to the families of their victims. Iko's request is sent to the family of the man he murdered for their consideration.

The family, however, refuses to even consider the appeal and review the medical evidence (they find the request insulting). *Voyager*'s crew remains adamant that Iko's sentence of death should be vacated on account of his revolutionary and profound change in moral identity. Seven, who seems emotionally involved in Iko's case, argues that the Nygean government should insist the case be reviewed. Warden Yediq asserts the value and internal validity of the Nygean criminal justice process. He responds, "We have laws that protect victims from emotional distress." This law determines what legal actions are available.

Warden Yediq then points out the *Voyager* officers have agreed to work within the confines of the Nygean legal system. When Seven says the laws are flawed, Captain Janeway asserts the priority of the agreement regarding relations between the two societies' justice activities. While the *Voyager* crew might define Iko's identity by the substance of his actions and attitudes, his official history will be defined within the context of pre-established, overarching procedural frameworks. There are procedural laws in effect for resolving conflicts between Starfleet and Nygean legal affairs. These procedural mechanisms will determine the rules of the game by which Iko's moral identity is defined.

The Prime Directive (even if its validity is subject to question), which calls for non-interference in alien society's activities, has precedence over other normative frameworks. Its rules for constituting social reality and systems of morality trump *Voyager*'s empirical determination that Iko has morally transformed and atoned for actions (even if the Nygean prison staff concurs in the assessment). It trumps metaphysically based frameworks of justice that envision Iko's execution as inequitable and unwarranted. The Nygean process for the administration of justice places the sentencing decision in victims' hands. The Starfleet Prime Directive provides a process for *Voyager*'s dealing with alien cultures. It places the sentencing decision squarely in the hands of the Nygean institution for the administration of justice – and in the hands of the convicted murderer's victims. Social process rules will define Iko's societal identity and instruct Iko's fate.

THE MORAL CAREER OF PRISONER JOLEG

A second part of the story in "Repentance" revolves around the fate of the prisoner Joleg, who also has been found guilty of murder. We again deal with matters of justice administration that are central to contemporary criminological debates.

Through the conversations between Joleg and Neelix, a crew member who serves food to the prisoners, we develop a simple model of the Nygean social structure with regard to criminality and criminal justice.

Joleg tells Neelix that his arrest and subsequent conviction for murder were based on circumstantial evidence. He was found in the vicinity of the crime. He tells the sympathetic Neelix he initially became a suspect because of social discrimination. He is Benkaran, a minority group "known" by the dominant Nygeans to be criminally inclined. His proximity to the crime coupled with his species identity was sufficient to produce a guilty verdict.

In recounting his dealings with the criminal justice system, Joleg intimates that, in fact, he is innocent. At another point, Joleg contrasts himself to the other prisoners. He asserts he is not like them, again suggesting he is an innocent man.

We see in Neelix, the food server, a compassionate man with a strong sense of justice. Moved by Joleg's story, he determines to get more information about the Nygean criminal justice system. Communicating with the Nygean government seeking a "cultural exchange," he acquires statistics showing that Benkarans indeed are arrested at a rate disproportionate to their population in Nygean society. And they receive harsher sentences. They, for example, are ten times more likely than Nygeans to be executed for their crimes. Neelix accepts Joleg's claim that Nygean social discrimination – and not the prisoner's own actions – was the key factor that led to his conviction. Neelix is appalled that the man standing before him will be executed because of discrimination.

The television audience and students of crime are apt to find this a familiar story. Joleg's account of his run-in with the Nygean criminal justice system and the statistical summary of Nygean criminal affairs both paint pictures of the administration of justice akin to the pictures often presented to us regarding ethnic minorities and the administration of criminal justice on Earth.

In both settings, minority groups have official crime rates higher than average. Minority group members fill jails and court dockets well out of proportion to their percentage of the overall population. Many – including dominant group members, officials in the criminal justice system, and even minority members themselves – are apt to perceive minority group members as more criminally predisposed.

The belief that they are more criminally disposed leads police and other law enforcement agents to heighten their surveillance of minority members. In a self-fulfilling prophecy, their closer watch on minorities increases the likelihood minority group members will be observed committing crimes and be arrested, which in turn feeds the original perception that they are more apt to be criminals. From this perspective, official actions create official crime statistics that distort the true prevalence of crime. The system ignores the discriminatory processes that skew its enforcement of the law and sustain its beliefs regarding the causes of crime.

Some of the discriminatory results are caused not by prejudicial attitudes but by indirect biases in the justice system. As noted, the Benkaran justice system is based on the notion "favor the victims," in which the satisfaction of the injured party is the main mechanism of justice. Benkarans are less likely to be able to provide economic restitution for their crimes. When they cannot use monetary compensation to settle with their victims, Benkarans are more likely to receive harsher prison sentences or to be executed.

Prisoner Joleg's actions and demeanor seem to comport with his verbal claims of innocence. His behavior is not characteristic of criminals, or, more accurately stated, our stereotypic notions of criminals. For example, when Neelix first serves food, based on a homemade recipe, to the prisoners, Warden Yediq cuts him short. Yediq says prisoners do not deserve such an elaborate meal. The food server stands up to the warden: he retorts that Federation protocol requires prisoners be properly treated. Joleg thanks Neelix for standing up for the prisoners and that the food server's actions were kind. In general, Joleg is polite, articulate, deferential, even-tempered, and soft-spoken. We might contrast these personality attributes with current criminological theories that explain criminal behavior as resulting from lack of self-control or the inability to empathize with others.

We ordinarily consider behavioral and attitudinal manifestations of a person as less self-conscious, less under self-control, and less apt to be aimed at influencing others' perceptions than are verbal statements. We therefore are inclined to give Joleg's behavior considerable weight when we try to assess the man's moral identity. In this instance, his actions appear to reinforce the verbal picture of a decent man.

When Neelix offers to help Joleg appeal his case, the prisoner declares he would not do so if the appeal implies he is guilty. Our view of Joleg is further enhanced. We even entertain the idea that he really is a man above the average. He is a person of principle who welcomes punishment, even death, over the loss of honor.

Neelix and we, the television audience, thus have a number of reasons to sympathize with the prisoner. The story he offers, the external sociological facts of social discrimination, and our immediate observations onboard *Voyager* – all are suggestive of good, sound character and support a benevolent attitude toward the man. When all of Joleg's expressions of self – verbal, demeanor and behavioral – are taken as a whole, we, like Neelix, can entertain the possibility that he is not a criminal and murderer. Sympathetic viewers could justifiably be concerned with his plight and fashion an argument for his case and cause. At this point, some viewers probably believe, as apparently does Neelix, the convict is innocent.

As in the Iko case, we find ourselves reexamining and reconstituting Joleg's moral identity.

A fellow crew member discounts this view of prisoner Joleg. He counsels

Neelix that in prisons everyone has a tale to tell. Everyone champions his or her innocence and cause. Joleg's statements should be interpreted within a darker context. The crew member warns Neelix that he is a "soft touch," susceptible to the appeals of an underdog.

We are reminded that statements of innocence such as proffered by the convict often have limited credibility. People often say things that are not true and stage their actions in order to influence others' attitudes toward them and to gain support.

Criminologists and other students of social deviance recognize that systematic biases and official statistics distort our views of social reality and crime. But the Nygeans' perception of incidences of crime might be accurate. The Benkarans may actually be more inclined toward criminality (or more specifically, "street crime" such as robbery, assault and murder), whatever the cause (including their anger and sense of injustice resulting from their experience of a historically biased administration of criminal justice). Their statistically high rates of crime may result from Benkarans actually engaging in higher rates of crime. Nygean officials might be acting judiciously when they focus on "those" most apt to break the law. Employing a practical jurisprudence, they might conceive of themselves as wise administrators who use their limited resources efficiently and look where crime is most apt to happen. To them, Joleg might be a legitimate surveillance target because he is in a social (ethnic) class that empirical evidence proves is more likely to be associated with street crime.

The competing views of Prisoner Joleg are resolved as the plot line continues.

When Joleg states he does not want to appeal his case because it would imply guilt, he asks instead that Neelix communicate with his brother, to let his brother know what has happened to him. Neelix fulfills this request.

Shortly thereafter, the U.S.S. Voyager comes under attack by another spacecraft. It quickly becomes clear this hostile craft is trying to free the prisoners. The attack puts the power system onboard Voyager into disarray. The force fields that hold prisoners in their jail cells are temporarily disabled and all the prisoners – with the exception of the transformed Iko – attempt to escape. Iko looks out at the commotion and then returns to lie down in his cell. The rest of the prisoners attack their guards, at first hand-to-hand. When they overpower the guards, they take the guards' weapons. They then attack the guards using the weapons.

From the first, Joleg actively participates in the escape efforts. He, too, progresses through the sequence of hand-to-hand combat, acquisition of a weapon, and use of the weapon. Finally he holds Warden Yediq at gunpoint.

Joleg is at the point of shooting the warden when Iko emerges from his cell. Iko asks for the weapon, telling Joleg, "You saw how they beat me." He claims the privilege of shooting the warden for himself. He looks as if to have reversed to old form, allying himself with the group of prisoners who are attempting to escape. Joleg hands the gun over to Iko and laughs sardonically in anticipation of what he next expects to happen; the prisoner, having reversed roles and now raised to power, will execute his captor. Prisoner Iko turns, gun in hand, toward the warden, But Iko indeed has been transformed. Iko now commits himself to the institutionalized forces of justice. He hands the weapon to Warden Yediq, who moves quickly to shoot down the escapees. Iko stands silently and watches as the warden now points the weapon at him. But then Warden Yediq realizes that Iko's actions have just demonstrated his new socially-defined moral identity is a valid one. The warden's face warms and softens; he lowers the gun.

Voyager's conception of Iko as a good man has been validated in dramatic fashion. In a scene of life-and-death, Warden Yediq – the dramatic character who has till now been Iko's antithesis – corroborates the prisoner's new identity.

At the same time, nascent sympathies for Joleg have been quashed. We confirm he is "truly" a criminal and our emotion mechanism shuts off. Our consideration of his plight becomes reluctant and cerebral. Neither Joleg's fellow travelers nor the television audience care much about his fate.

One senses that all involved now share a common view, that Joleg is a criminal. His social identity and existential identity mirror one another. His claim not to be the murderer as charged could be true. It is logically possible, but much less plausible. Even if he has not actually murdered someone, he certainly is a potential murderer. He certainly would have killed the warden if fate had not intervened. He is violent and vicious; he has no respect for life or law. He is deceitful, manipulative, dishonest, and untrustworthy. We question the validity of all his past actions: verbal and behavioral. Neelix and we, the television audience, wonder if all was an act, that he has given us a "con job."

This negative view of Joleg's moral identity gains further support when we learn that it was Joleg's brother who led the attack on _Voyager_ in an attempt to abduct the prisoners. The brother had traced the transmission sent to him by Neelix back to _Voyager_.

Neelix's innate sense of justice is offended and he is hurt by his having been used. He now refuses to relate to the prisoner beyond the functional requirements of his food-serving role. He turns down Joleg's request for Kadis-Kot, a game the two had previously enjoyed. Joleg tries to turn Neelix by pleading innocence of the attack on the spacecraft and the attempted escape. He tells Neelix, "I had no idea he would do that. You have to believe me." None of us know if Joleg sent the message to facilitate an escape. But Neelix does know that prisoner Joleg nevertheless did threaten to kill the warden, and he points that out in retort. Saddened and wizened, he ignores the convict's plea and leaves.

Howard S. Becker, in *Outsiders*, suggests the moral definitions and rules of society change through the efforts of moral entrepreneurs, people who actively work for the change of those definitions. Social groups create deviance, he says, by making the rules whose infraction constitutes deviance and by applying those rules to particular people and labeling them as outsiders.[14]

From this point of view, deviance is not a quality of the act the person commits, but rather a consequence of the application by others of rules and sanctions to an offender. We see here the reverse situation. The removal of the deviant or outsider label also requires a moral entrepreneur who presses for change in the existent social fabric. Joleg will not find his moral identity changed because he has lost the support of his key sponsor.

The official Nygean views of Joleg have been vindicated. Our personal senses of justice radically violated, we find no desire to further challenge his conviction. For all practical purposes, Joleg's moral identity as prisoner-criminal-murderer stands. Our social realities confirm the formally-defined legal reality; time to put the matter to sleep.

"Repentance" as Morality Play

"Repentance" is theater that entertains. It also is theater that enhances our ethical sensibilities. It offers lessons on the complexities of morality and justice – and our social dealings with them – in the modern era.

"Repentance" underscores the social origins and social contexts of moral life. It seeks to delineate the social structure of justice and morality. But its insights into the nature of morality and justice go beyond the purely social and the mere conventional. In so doing, the drama deals with issues that permeate contemporary discussions regarding crime and justice.

"Repentance" portrays participants' understandings of morality as profoundly linked to their cultures. The people who meet aboard *Voyager* bring with them diverse cultural baggage. This baggage includes terms, concepts, frameworks, and perspectives for administering justice and conceiving moral identities. We watch as participants constitute their moral existence and moral identities using socially provided systems of meaning.

> Foremost among these are the institutional-
> ized frameworks provided by participants'
> diverse state systems for the administration
> of justice. Two state systems interface in
> "Repentance" as participants deal with the
> Benkaran prisoners: that of the Nygeans and
> that of their Starfleet hosts.

Warden Yediq and his guards perceive themselves as agents of the Nygean administrative system. They operate in terms of their institutionalized roles in that system. *Voyager*'s crew (despite some disagreements on how they should handle the specific case of prisoner Iko with which they are confronted) refer-ences their social system of law and justice when figuring out how they should act. They conceive themselves bound by the Starfleet's rules of process – its Prime Directive that defines their relations to alien cultures – and consequently decide they must facilitate the Nygean transport of the prisoners to their execu-tion.

Each system is holistic; each provides both guidelines for specific actions and value frameworks that explain and validate those guidelines and actions. *Voyager* and the Nygeans disagree as to the relative merits of their institutional-ly defined forms for the administration of justice. The two groups use the dif-fering philosophical frameworks provided by their respective institutions for administering justice in assessing those merits.

Thus, capital punishment is not an option in the Starfleet system of justice. *Voyager* views the death penalty as a relic of an earlier, less developed age, and the crew believes that objectivity and detachment are key qualities of state-administered systems of justice. To establish a fair system they place impartial parties at key decision-making points in the justice process. People not immedi-ately affected by the particular criminal case judge the case and sentence con-victed defendants.

In contrast, the Nygeans perceive the death penalty as an equitable resolu-tion for heinous crimes. They believe capital punishment functions as a means of retribution and as a deterrent. Nygeans believe that justice means making victims whole. Consequently, victimized parties stand at central points of the justice process. The Nygean justice system empowers victims and authorizes them to determine the sentences of convicted criminals.

The Benkaran prisoners' realization of law, justice and morality is quite dif-ferent. They are encapsulated by the Nygean system of justice. They recognize they are subject, albeit unwillingly, to the Nygean state's scheme of things. They must come to practical terms with its frameworks in order to manage their lives. But the prisoners deal with the Nygean justice as an object element – as a social reality that, having labeled them as prisoners and criminals, will determine their fate. They need to comprehend the Nygean system of justice for tactical purposes: to manage it for their own ends. It does not envelope them; they do not orient their lives by its principles. They may not even comprehend its concept of the criminal.

The prisoners' sense of ethics and justice is qualitatively different from those of the other travelers. Measured against both *Voyager* crew and Nygeans, the Benkaran prisoners' concepts of justice and morality are limited and undeveloped. The prisoners are moral agnostics. We may attribute a "moral perspective" to them within a sociological (cultural relativistic) context, but considerable irony is involved when we otherwise conceive of them as moral beings.

The moral perspective of the transformed prisoner Iko requires a description that is separate from that of his pre-transformed self. Before his metamorphosis, his held the amoral "moral view" of the other convicted criminals.

Transformed, prisoner Iko exhibits a "natural" sense of justice. He no longer is a criminogenic being and no longer is criminally motivated. His moral essence has changed and there has been a major transformation in his self-identity. Iko is now a transcendent being characterized by consciousness and freedom. This Iko – by virtue of his nanoprobe brain operation – defines his own essence and gives meaning to his own existence through the choices he makes. And he defines those existence choices positively and ethically.

Since his newfound sense of justice results from a metamorphosis of his brain functions, which leave them more biologically normal, it might be appropriate to consider this "natural" sense of justice natural in a true sense. The sentiments are innate and instinctive to the humanoid condition – not socially contrived.

As *Voyager* crew members and Nygeans deal with Iko, they contend with visions of morality and justice that extend beyond those provided by institutionalized society. *Voyager*, Nygeans, and transformed prisoner Iko act on a sense of justice and morality not bound by social definition, not distinguished by its having institutionalized social origins. Rather, their views and activities are permeated by a sense of justice that seems to have extra-social origins and are not constricted to socially defined realms.

Not only do participants recognize there are differences in their institutionalized views of justice, they also grasp there are culturally transcendent, intuitively derived visions of justice. Their intuited senses of justice, developed when confronted by the new Iko, draw them together despite differences in their cultural perspectives. They recognize there are visions of justice that lie outside of those provided by the various states and their bureaucratic orders – indeed, outside any socially formulated provisions for justice. *Voyager* crew, Nygeans and prisoner Iko accept there also is a "natural" sense of justice manifesting itself aboard *Voyager*. All participants (except the prisoners) intuit this vision of justice regardless of their cultural origin.

Their non-institutionalized sensibilities collide with participants' institutionalized attitudes toward the administration of justice. The *Voyager* crew recognizes Iko is a prisoner and convicted murder who has committed heinous crimes. But they come quickly to redefine his moral identity. Less anticipatable, even the cynical Warden Yediq comes to recognize Iko is a new and better person. So much so that he actively seeks to vacate Iko's death sentence via institutionalized Nygean appeal processes.

The dramatist Kenneth Burke considers these two ways of seeing as alternative rhythms of social life. One sense of justice, he would say, is the imagined and intuited. The other is the bureaucratized: "An imaginative possibility … is bureaucratized when it is embodied in the realities of a social texture, in all the complexity of language and habits … the methods of government … and in the development of rituals that re-enforce the same emphasis."[15] We intuit possibilities of justice in our imagination and then we carry out one of those possibilities. As we capture our initial insight of justice and transform it into a crystallized social action, we bureaucratize the imaginative element.

The saga of prisoner Iko impels the Starfleet officers and Nygeans to transcend their bureaucratic notions of justice that constitute him as prisoner and criminal. They return to their raw experience of the man so as to comprehend him on his own terms, as being-for-himself.

Participants embrace this "natural" vision of morality and justice to varying degrees.

Some embrace this natural vision tentatively and fleetingly. Some return to their socially prescribed lines of action, the institutionalized ways of seeing to which they are committed. Yediq stands behind Iko when the convict appeals for the commutation of his sentence. But when the family of the man he murdered denies Iko's request, Warden Yediq advises prisoner Iko that he must be returned to his cell. Warden Yediq's bureaucratically defined existence is reinstituted. He regrets what he must do, but the warden will carry on with his bureaucratic mission. Yediq relocates himself back in his organization. His identity is the property of his state's institution for the administration of justice. He is a social functionary; he is and will continue to be a (the) warden. For him to reject bureaucratized justice would be for him to reject his own identity.

Once he reattaches himself to his bureaucratic identity, he must do what he "must" do. Yediq will carry forward a conception of Iko's moral identity that deviates from that prescribed by his justice organization only at a personal level.

The possibility of a societal redefinition of Iko ends. The institutionalized concept will determine prisoner Iko's fate and define his history in larger social circles.

Others find themselves consumed by the natural sense of justice and morality they experience. Seven of Nine in particular has been moved by tensions between the two manifestations of justice. Her sentiments are informed by a quite different – and uniquely personal – set of issues. Iko's plight forces her to confront questions regarding her own moral identity. As she has witnessed Iko's fate over the course of the episode, she has been comparing their fortunes.

In Starfleet and onboard *Voyager*, Seven of Nine has a positive moral identity. She is considered "a good person." Yet, she agonizes, she has killed thousands of people earlier in her life, when she was a Borg. And she never has been held socially accountable for doing so. She has never been punished. She has never been asked to publicly atone for those killings the Borg Collective, of which she was part, considered justified.

Iko has personally repented for his killing. His grief over having committed criminal acts is heartfelt and it is comprehensive. His guilt and sorrow for having murdered a man have been expressed privately, publicly, passionately, and formally. In his current transformation, he is not a person who would kill again. Yet he still must atone for his past sinning by being put to death by the Nygean state.

Captain Janeway consoles Seven of Nine. She does not bear individual responsibility for her actions, as she was part of the Borg Collective's group mind. Despite this lack of responsibility, she regrets her past actions. She spent nearly 20 years of her life in the Borg Collective, removed from human society. Seven of Nine only recently has begun to rediscover her sense of individuality and humanity. She only recently has begun to reclaim her human soul. That, the captain says, has been punishment enough.

Endnotes

1. Marybeth Esposito's valuable comments significantly upgraded previous drafts

2. Kerby Anderson, "Capital Punishment," *Probe Ministries* (1992), http:www.leaderu.com/orgs/probe.

3. Avery Cardinal Dulles, "Catholicism & Capital Punishment," *First Things* 112 (April 2001) 30-35.

4. "The Death Penalty," *The Clark Country Prosecuting Attorney* (IN), http://www/clarkprosecutor.org, 11/12/2001.

5. John Willey Willis, "Capital Punishment," *The Catholic Encyclopedia* Online Edition, Volume XII (1999).

6. "Capital Punishment," *Wikipedia* (October 12, 2001), www.wikipeedia.com.

7. Chris Gregory describes the Directive as an invention of the original *Star Trek* series that reflected a certain political naïveté that the series later challenged. http://ww.digital-generation.co.uk/chrisgregory/books/star-trej/top20-20.htm

8. Larry J. Siegel provides a clear textbook analysis of the criminological field in *Criminology: Theories, Patterns, And Typologies*, Seventh Edition, Wadsworth: Thomson Learning, Inc. (2001).

9. Erving Goffman, *Asylums: Essays On The Social Situation Of Mental Patients And Other Inmates*, Anchor Books, 1961; Nicholas N. Kittrie, *The Right To Be Different: Deviance And Enforced Therapy*. Johns Hopkins University Press, 1972

10. Kenneth Burke, "Bureaucratization of the Imaginative," in *Attitudes Toward History*, Beacon Press (1961).

11. David Matza, *Becoming Deviant*, Prentice-Hall. Inc. (1969), p. 114.

12. Howard S. Becker, *Outsiders: Studies In The Sociology Of Deviance*, The Free Press (1963), pp. 24-26.

13. Becker, *Outsiders*.

14. Becker, *Outsiders*.

15. Kenneth Burke, *Attitudes Toward History*, Beacon Press (1961), p. 225.

The Understanding of Evil:
A JOINT QUEST FOR CRIMINOLOGY AND THEOLOGY

B. GRANT STITT, PhD

Introduction

It is generally agreed that shortly after the time of Galileo, the domains of science and religion were separated into that of the natural and supernatural respectively. When the phenomenon to be explained is human behavior, science, which is theoretically value-free, attempts to isolate causes in a deterministic sense in order to account for behavior as it would any other phenomenon of nature. Religious or theological explanations of human behavior invoke spiritual notions that suggest various types of supernatural factors have a resultant effect on behavior. Both scientific and theological explanations have been employed in an attempt to understand why people commit various antisocial behaviors. These antisocial behaviors are labeled either deviant or criminal by social scientists, while theologians refer to the same behaviors as sin or evil.

The concepts of sin or evil are not as widely used in our modern, highly technological society as they once were. The emergence of the social sciences in the mid-1800s resulted in these terms being accorded considerable disfavor. Further, as a result of the advocacy of determinism rather than free will as the force that shapes human behavior, the concept of individual responsibility has come into serious question as well. As Stanford Lyman points out:

> Once man was relieved of full responsibility
> for his deeds, once dark forces of the mind,
> of history, of heredity, or of culture were
> found to shape his thoughts and shackle his
> reason, sin with its insistence on the free-
> dom of will to choose between good and
> evil had to retreat into the recesses of a sus-
> pect theology; at the same time dire punish-
> ment as a deserved retribution for the will-
> ful commission of wrongful deeds had to
> give way to remediation and rehabilitation.
> (1978, p. 119)

Similarly, the notion of evil that bespeaks a grossness, an omnipresence, a transcendence and a grotesqueness seems to be a concept beyond our comprehension. In his discussion of the sociology of evil, Lyman notes that "Evil seems to be too great, too impersonal, too absurd to be a serious topic for sociological concern" (1978, p. 1).1 The fact of the matter is that to study evil seems to require one to make a value statement that is implicit in one's definition of evil. Many sociologists, and social scientists in general, insist on a stance of ethical and value neutrality, regardless of whether they consistently adhere to such a position. This seems to be a convenient cop-out. It is the thesis of this paper that what is needed is a re-examination of the concept of evil. Further, it seems that the re-examination of evil should be done in light of modern criminological and theological thought. Such an analysis will reveal how far apart these ideas really are and at the same time may shed light on an area of common ground: the understanding of human evil.

The first step that will be undertaken will be to provide a definitional discussion of evil. Next, it will be necessary to examine the basic nature of human behavior from both theological and criminological perspectives. Where do both perspectives stand on the issue of free will versus determinism as forces that shape human behavior? Inherent in this discussion is a consideration of the nature and existence of God, the essence of which may be ultimately unknowable.

What Is Evil

An issue that must be dealt with is whether evil is a quality of actions or actors or both. Clearly an evil deed is one resulting in harm to another being or beings. But can one commit an evil act without being an evil person? It should be pointed out that one evil act doth not an evil person make. The attribution of evil to a person seems a very serious matter that requires documentation of many evil acts over a substantial period of time. Before these points can be addressed, the concept of evil must be defined.

In many respects, evil is a concept that seems to defy precise definition. Evil is not a concrete concept. It is an abstract evaluative one that denotes an undesirable characteristic attributed to either an action or an actor. An action is labeled evil if its perceived consequences are harmful to a human or other animal. For the purpose of the present discussion harm shall have occurred to a human being if any of the following conditions are met:

- An individual is physically harmed (e.g., murder, assault or rape);
- An individual's property is harmed (e.g., theft or vandalism);

- An individual is psychologically harmed (e.g., threat of physical injury, trauma or fright);
- An individual is socially harmed (e.g., exploitation, debasement, slander or libel);
- An individual's freedom is taken away (e.g., invasion of privacy, kidnapping or false imprisonment). (Stitt, 1982, p.4)

Harm to non-human animals will be assumed to be either physical or psychological in nature. Thus, actions that meet any of these conditions may be labeled evil. Situational considerations, however, may confound the imputation of evil to human actions. For example, taking of lives during a time of war, such as the use of atomic bombs on Hiroshima and Nagasaki, may not be viewed by some as evil, but how are these instances of mass killing different from the My Lai massacre or Hitler's extermination of Jews (both popular examples of "collective evil")?

The concept of evil presented previously is not all that dissimilar from the Augustinian notion that evil is the transformation of that which is good or desirable into that which is bad or wrong and thus undesirable. In this sense, Hick notes that:

> ... everything which has being is good in its own way and degree, except in so far as it may have become spoiled or corrupted. Evil - whether it be an evil will, an instance of pain, or some disorder or decay in nature - has not been set there by God, but represents the distortion of something that is inherently valuable. (1980, p. 550)

This more general and clearly theological conception obviously subsumes the previous more concrete definition.

What, or who, then is the evil person? An evil person is one who has both committed many evil acts in the past and who, due to the lack of guilt or remorse and concern for others, possesses a great potential for the commission of additional evil acts in the future. Thus, this person has achieved the status of being evil. An evil person is one who has habitually committed evil acts and will likely pursue this same destructive course in the future.

The notion of destructiveness often is employed in discussions of evil. Scott Peck suggests killing and destroying as attributes of evil. He says evil is that which kills spirit and other essential attributes of human life such as "sentience, mobility, awareness, growth, autonomy, [and] will" (1983, p. 42). He further says:

> Evil ... is the force residing either inside or
> outside of human beings that seeks to kill life
> or liveliness. And goodness is its opposite.
> Goodness is that which promotes life and
> liveliness. (1983, p. 43)

Thus, an evil person is one whose essence is the harm continually wreaked upon others.

The Theological View

The issue of whether human behavior is the function of free will or determinism is most clearly focused, from a theological perspective, when the issue of the nature of God in relation to the existence of evil is examined. The conception of an omnipotent and benevolent God and the presence of evil represent a major dilemma for the theologian. The 18th century philosopher David Hume recognized this apparent contradiction when his character Philo remarks:

> Is he willing to prevent evil, but not able? Then
> he is impotent. Is he able, but not willing?
> Then is he malevolent. Is he both able and will-
> ing? Whence then is evil? (1965, p. 442)

These three propositions, that God is omnipotent, that God is totally good, and that evil nonetheless exists, are, though contradictory, essential parts of most theological positions. There would be, as McCloskey (1974, p. 2) points out, no contradiction if any one of the propositions were false. For the theologian the most problematic issue is the existence of any evil given the assumption of divine perfection. Beyond this, certainly the amount and quality of existing evil, both human and natural, seem incomprehensible given the supposed nature of God. Aside from the logical incompatibility, the moral incompatibility of such a supreme being allowing evil to exist is impossible to ignore.

That the existence of evil is the intentional will of God would be incompatible with the assumption of benevolence. An alternative is that evil is unintended on God's part. Natural evils (earthquakes, tornadoes, etc.) are a function of natural processes of change and in a sense the human suffering that accompanies such events is accidental. The traditional Christian response to such calamities is "to accept the adversities, pains, and afflictions which life brings, in order that they can be turned to a positive spiritual use" (Hick, 1980, p. 553). Moral evil, however, seems to be a different issue. Moral evil is the suffering inflicted upon animals and other human beings by human beings.

By virtue of our existence as human beings, we possess free will. John Hick points out that the "idea of a person who can be infallibly guaranteed always to act rightly is self-contradictory" (1980 p. 551). By act rightly, he means in a moral (non-evil) manner. Further, there can be no guarantee that a genuinely free moral agent will always choose the morally correct alternative. If such a guarantee existed, the individual's behavior would thus be determined, negating the possibility of choice. As Hick concludes, "the possibility of wrongdoing or sin is logically inseparable from the creation of finite persons, and to say that God should not have created beings who might sin amounts to saying that he should not have created people" (1980, p. 551). Thus, if human beings in fact possess free will, they must have the ability to commit evil acts. Therefore, it can be argued that God did not create evil, but he did create beings who, by their very nature, have the capacity to do evil.

Taken perhaps a step further, it can be argued that evil is necessary. As is the case regarding any evaluative dimension, the very existence of the particular characteristic logically requires that the opposite or bipolar characteristic exist or can be conceived to exist. What, for example, would wealth be without poverty, beauty without ugliness, justice without injustice, or love without hate? Would that which is morally good be meaningful, appreciable, or understandable without the existence or possibility of that which is morally evil? Such an argument further illustrates Hick's point, that without evil as part of the human condition the reality that we know would not exist. In short, the existence of, or possibility for, evil is a prerequisite for the existence of human kind.

Next, if God is also free, why does he not prevent us from doing evil? Further, since he does not, should he not share some of the responsibility for human evil? Given the existence of such evil, is it possible that evil is in some way part of God's plan? Or as Davies asks, "Is God not free after all to prevent us from acting against him?" (1983, p. 143).

The key to the present dilemma may be in the answer to this last question. It is a basic tenet of Christian doctrine that God is omniscient and eternal; he is all-knowing and transcends time. The notion of the freedom to choose is, however, a temporal one. If this infinite God knows what is happening everywhere and for all time, his intervention in the present may not be possible. This is because the concept of the "present," due to the theory of relativity, has a subjective reality that is unique to the being possessing it. The notions of past, present and future have been rendered meaningless as a result of the theory of relativity. Time is simply there, extending in either direction through space from any given moment. The essence of God is intertwined throughout time and space, and he does not have the ability to change himself. According to Davies:

> A God who is in time is subject to change.
> But what causes that change? If God is the
> cause of all existing things, then does it make
> sense to talk about that ultimate cause itself
> changing? (1983, p. 133).

Therefore, it is meaningless to suppose that the eternal God has the freedom of choice. Further, if we can assume that God in some way existed before time as we conceive it began (when the physical universe came into existence), then when he began the process of creating the physical universe as we know it, he gave up his ability to intervene in its processes. Further, as Davies points out:

> We seem forced to the paradoxical conclu-
> sion that freedom of choice is actually a
> restriction that we suffer – namely, our inabil-
> ity to know the future. God, released from
> his prison of the present, has no need of free
> will. (1983, p. 143)

The conclusion we have reached is that God, having chosen to create human beings as free moral agents, has allowed evil to exist. He could have chosen otherwise, but that choice would have precluded the existence of humanity as we know it. Having given up his freedom that we could be created in his image, one can only assume that the pain caused by human evil also must be felt by the God who gave it the possibility to exist. As human beings suffer, so God also must suffer.

Thus, from the theological point of view, the freedom of man to choose between good and evil is rarely argued. According to traditional Christian theology, the first choice was made by Adam in the Garden of Eden, and since then man has been burdened with an inclination to sin or do evil rather than good. A few theologians, such as St. Augustine, the Bishop of Hippo, who lived during the 4th century A.D., believed that all men were evil by nature as a result of original sin. Carried to its logical extreme, this position raises serious questions about man's free will and his ability to choose that which is good (Fox, 1985, p. 11). Such a theologically deterministic position is rarely taken in an extreme sense. The prevailing view is that man has the inclination to sin or do evil, but is not compelled to do either.

Most people most of the time do not do evil things. However, some people, it will be argued, do no evil not out of choice, but out of circumstance. Others, it could be argued, do great amounts of evil also not out of choice, but due to factors beyond their control. Still others have sufficient freedom to be able to choose between good and evil. These individuals, it will be argued from the scientific criminological view, are, relatively speaking, rare.

THE CRIMINOLOGICAL VIEW

Next let us examine the free-will versus determinism debate from the scientific point of view. After examining the logically possible positions for criminologists as scientists to take in this debate, a brief appraisal of the most popular position is made. Then attention will be turned to the position of "evil" in criminology.

First of all, there seem to be three possible positions that scientists can take regarding free will and determinism as factors influencing human behavior. One could believe that human behavior is totally determined, totally a product of choice or some combination of choice and determinism.

A totally deterministic situation would be one in which whatever one does is totally beyond one's control. In this instance behavior would be a direct result of environmental influences and in no way effected by the individual's will. Ultimately the scientist in such a situation could, if he/she knew all of the influences operating in that situation and all the laws governing human behavior, completely predict and, were it in his/her power to manipulate all influences, completely control the individual's behavior.

If, however, one's behavior were totally a function of free choice, the ability to choose say between alternatives A and B would be undetermined. That is, if in a situation an individual chooses alternative A and that same exact situation somehow could be duplicated (allowing no effect of the first choice), the individual could choose alternative B the second time around. This possibility is incompatible with determinism and the acceptance of such a conception of freedom would be a matter of pure faith (Davies, 1983, p. 139).

The third possibility is the compromise position in which all effects have a cause, but in some instances the causal factors are willed human actions. These notions of dualist philosophy suggest that in this scenario our minds are separate from the physical world, but are able to influence the physical properties in various ways. If, however, the causes of our decisions exist in the deterministically governed physical world, then our choices are determined and we are back where we started. If this is not the case, then what determines how we make choices? If we are left with the concept of self-causation, then does the idea of causeless causes make sense (Davies, 1983, p. 139)?

Truly deterministic criminologists, who are most definitely in the minority, would look upon criminology as a science in much the same way that Einstein conceived of physics. Einstein wrote, "The scientist is possessed by the sense of universal causation." This same idea was captured superbly by Robert Jastrow when he said, "There is a kind of religion in science; it is the religion of a person who believes there is order and harmony in the Universe, and every event can be explained in a rational way as the product of some previous event; every effect must have a cause; there is no First Cause" (1978, p. 113).[2]

A common response from the truly deterministic criminologist to the notion of free will as the cause of human behavior is that free will is unfalsifiable and, therefore, cannot be the subject of scientific attempts to understand human behavior. By unfalsifiable here the scientist is concerned with the tautological nature of the doctrine of free will, exemplified in the following fashion. When asked why one does a particular act the answer is, "Because I wanted to." At the same time, it can be argued that with the exception of truly accidental actions (e.g., while in a china store, one turns around and the result is that a vase placed too close to the edge of the shelf is knocked to the floor and shatters), one *never* does anything one does not choose to do. While we can all imagine actions that we would not like to engage in (e.g., perform indecent sexual acts), when confronted with threats to our lives should we choose to do otherwise, we choose to submit. If we did not submit and were, in fact, killed, it could be reasoned that we preferred death to the commission of those acts. Ergo, we never do anything that we do not choose to do.

At the same time, by virtue of their position as "scientists," having observed empirical regularities in human behavior and having accurately predicted and successfully controlled some behavior, virtually all criminologists seem most comfortable with the position that we should approach human choice (the possibility of which they refuse to deny) as if it were any other scientific phenomenon and attempt to devise theory to predict and understand such choices. In this vein, John Hick states that "If by free action we mean an action which is not externally compelled but which flows from the nature of the agent as he reacts to the circumstances in which he finds himself, there is, indeed, no contradiction between our being free and our actions being 'caused' (by our own nature) and therefore being in principle predictable" (1980, p. 551). The catch here is that we could never be able to totally explain these semi-free actions. The reason is if we could provide a complete causal explanation, then the act would not be free in any sense. It would be totally determined.

At this point is seems appropriate to examine some of the thoughts of criminologists, Daniel Glaser and Stephen Schafer with regard to the free-will/determinism controversy.

Daniel Glaser takes a stand on the free-will/determinism issue that is consistent with that of the majority of criminologists. He refers to free will and determinism as linguistic frames of reference, saying that persons imply "free will to ascribe conscious motives," but assume "determinism to explain behavior as the product of genetics or of live experiences" (1977, p. 486). Noting Hume's observation that causal determinism is never directly observable, Glaser says we infer the cause-effect connections because of the regular succession of events under study. Glaser takes a "soft" or "moderate" determinism position when he indicates that all human conduct is not completely determined since an unknown amount of originality and creativity may be involved. The question remains, what is this unknown amount? In his conclusion, Glaser recognizes that "the assumption that human actions can be shaped by rewards and punishments paradoxically implies both free will to choose that which is gratifying over that which is unpleasant in its consequences, and the determination of behavior by those who can affect its rewards and penalties" (1977, p. 489). Though he acknowledges the possibility of free choice in human behavior, Glaser seems to minimize its possible influence when he notes that "much determination of conduct and thought by our prior experiences is evident in the correlation of behavior with cultural contacts, yet some creativity is indicated by the view of thought and action as emergent from covert role-taking" (1977, p. 490).

Glaser's position is not greatly different from that of Stephen Schafer, to whom he was responding. Schafer is concerned with why, after more than a century of intense study of crime, we are not much nearer to an understanding of this phenomenon than we were when we started. After chastising criminologists for ignoring the free-will/determinism issue, Schafer undertakes his own analysis. He recalls that even Jonathan Edwards, the staunch indeterminist, recognized that a fully undetermined choice ought to be beyond the reach of all influences, but that choices are in fact influenced and thus never totally free.

Examining the human condition, Schafer concludes that if the individual is thoroughly socialized "the will has no freedom whatsoever" (1977, p. 485). This socialization process results in "man's bias and prejudice, likes and dislikes, beliefs and disbeliefs, affirmations and negations regarding the basic and guiding question of the world in which he is expected to live, to choose, to decide and to function" (1977, p. 485).

Schafer decides the essence of the free-will/determinism debate is not whether man can physically do otherwise, but "whether he can will to do otherwise" (1977, p. 485). Regarding the role of socialization in the free-will/determinism debate Schafer states:

> If the role of the socialization processes is posed here correctly, he cannot will to do otherwise. Consequently, it might be safe to say that man does have a freedom of will, yet it is a will that has been influenced, limited, and arrested even before it has evolved to the stage where man could will to will freely. (1977, p. 485)

Thus, the ability to choose is dependent upon the extent to which the individual is socialized. This notion is consistent with social control theory (Hirschi, 1969; Matza, 1964) where the socialized individual is bound to the social and moral order. Where the socialization process is incomplete, the individual is free to exercise the will and commit criminal or deviant acts; a likely outcome since it is assumed that man is born amoral and hedonistic in nature. Conversely, the successfully socialized individual is restrained from exercising his/her will in ways that society prohibits. Thus, this individual's behavior is determined. Schafer concludes by saying that "it appears man does have a freedom of will, but one's indeterminism, at least in its range, is determined by other indeterminants" (1977, p. 485).

In summary, it would seem the two perspectives can agree at least partially with regard to the free-will/determinism issue. Theological positions generally require the individual to have free will, while criminological positions allow some unspecified amount of choice to enter the behavioral calculus. Schafer's position, that one is free to choose to the extent that he/she is not socialized and, therefore, constrained to do otherwise, is generally representative of criminological thinking from a social science perspective. This position is not incompatible with the theological one.

Next it is necessary to examine the concept of evil as used by criminologists and behavioral scientists in general. The study of the origins of human evil may be the area where criminology and theology might find common ground. First of all, in what contexts and in what ways do criminologists use the term evil?

Evil: The Criminological View

The term "evil," which is rarely employed by criminologists in recent years, seems to be used in two contexts. The first has to do with references to that which is supernatural or metaphysical. Examples include:

> All misfortunes – whether crime, war,
> famine, flood, or infertility of women and of
> soil – were traced to mankind's evil nature,
> to Satan or to Divine Wrath. (Glaser, 1978,
> p. 105)

> The felon, it was thought, had yielded to the
> Devil's temptations, which played on our evil
> passions. (Glaser, 1978, p. 106)

According to Bartol, this same supernatural connection was made in years past with regard to psychopathic criminals:

> There were implications, which in some
> respect continue today, that psychopaths
> were evil, human vessels of the devil,
> designed to destroy the moral fabric of socie-
> ty – 'the devil made them do it.' (1980, p. 52)

The other use is not related to the supernatural or metaphysical but rather seems to connote the undesirability of crime in an evaluative sense. An example is Tannenbaum's statement that appeared in the foreword to the well-known Barnes and Teeters text first published in 1943:

> Crime is eternal – as eternal as society ...
> The more complex society becomes, the

> more difficult it is for the individual and the
> more frequent the human failures.
> Multiplication of laws and of sanctions for
> their observance merely increases the evil.

There is, however, one area of criminological study where one is more likely to encounter the term "evil" than any other. This is in the discussion of psychopathology and most recently the phenomena of serial and mass murders. In a discussion of the " ... capacity for evil," Kittrie quotes Seymore Halleck as saying, "Even within psychiatry there is widespread disagreement as to whether psychopathy is a form of mental illness, a form of *evil* or a form of fiction" (1971, p. 170). At any rate, it is readily apparent upon examining a profile of the psychopath that such an individual has a substantial capacity for evil. Hervey Cleckley lists the following 16 common characteristics of the psychopath.

1. Superficial charm and intelligence.
2. Absence of delusions and other signs of irrational thinking.
3. Absence of nervousness or neurotic manifestations.
4. Unreliability.
5. Untruthfulness and insincerity.
6. Lack of remorse or shame.
7. Antisocial behavior without apparent compunction.
8. Poor judgment and failure to learn from experience.
9. Pathologic egocentricity and incapacity for love.
10. General poverty in major affective relations.
11. Specific loss of insight.
12. Unresponsiveness in general interpersonal relations.
13. Fantastic and uninviting behavior with drink and sometimes without.
14. Suicide threats rarely carried out.
15. Sex life impersonal, trivial and poorly integrated.
16. Failure to follow any life plan (1970, p. 355-356).

The psychopath, because of such traits as unusual charm and absence of irrational delusions, displays a "mask of sanity," but the pursuit of narcissistic interests in a totally amoral manner often results in the production of evil. Is it any wonder that, as Bartol points out in his discussion of psychopathology: "In 1835 the British Psychiatrist J. C. Pritchard renamed the clinically strange group of disorders 'Moral Insanity,' since he felt the behaviors manifested a 'derangement' and a failure to abide by society's expectations of religious, ethical, and cultural conduct" (1980, p. 51-52)?

Recently, in their comprehensive treatment of mass and serial murders, Levin and Fox contend that the characteristics of the antisocial, psychopathic personality can be attributed to the perpetrators of a vast majority of such acts. Of these individuals they say, "They are often evil, but not crazy; they recognize the wrongfulness of their behavior but don't care" (1985, p. 210). Their acts often involve sex and sadism, with the killers having fun at the expense of their victims. The act of murder is not in these cases expressive, but instrumental in the sense that it is "an end in itself," the culmination of their attempt to totally control their victim. Levin and Fox are quick to note that the act is not that of a psychotic and does not conform itself to legal notions of insanity delineated in the statutes that spell out the various insanity defenses. They conclude:

> [T]he sociopath who commits a heinous and grotesque crime fits neither the psychiatric nor legal standards of insanity: he knows he's doing something wrong, can stop himself from doing it, but simply chooses not to. Crazy minds and crazy acts do not always go hand in hand. (1985, p. 210)

Though the ability of the sociopath-psychopath to "control" the behavior may not be empirically verifiable, the profile of the serial or mass murderer presented by Levin and Fox is certainly consistent with the psychiatric definition of the psychopath.

A characterization of the evil as narcissistic is indeed in line with the prototypical psychopath. Scott Peck indicates that "it is assumed that narcissism is something we generally 'grow out of' in the course of normal development, through a stable childhood, under the care of loving and understanding parents" (1983, p. 80-81). This immature, child-like nature of narcissism is not inconsistent with other immature characteristics of psychopaths. Those who are evil are those who, in significant ways, remain unsocialized and amoral. In the sense of normal moral development, they have not grown-up.

Peck discusses people who are evil and views them as being victims of "malignant narcissism," a form of pathology first popularized by Erich Fromm. Noting the extraordinary willfulness of evil people, Peck states, "They are men and women of obviously strong will, determined to have their own way. There is a remarkable power in the manner in which they attempt to control others" (1983, p. 78). These evil persons have retained their will and directed it in a narcissistic manner to defend their exceedingly vulnerable self-image. Mentally healthy individuals, Peck notes, "submit themselves one way or another to something higher than themselves, be it God or truth or love or some other ideal" (1983, p. 78). Peck says that this is a submission to the demands of conscience.[3] The evil, however, due to an insufficiently developed conscience, submit to no such ideals. Unbound by conscience or guilt, they are free to pursue their own selfish egoistic desires and in so doing harm others. Their narcissism renders the evil insensitive to others and allows them to ignore the humanity of the victims they sacrifice to their own narcissism (Peck, 1983, p. 136). Though not discussing the evil as specifically criminal, Peck notes that:

> As it gives them the motive for murder, so it also renders them insensitive to the act of killing. The blindness of the narcissist to others can extend even beyond a lack of empathy: narcissists may not see others at all.
> (1983, p. 136-37)

When this characteristic of malignant narcissism is coupled with sadism the potential for human evil is even greater. Such a person may be a full-blown psychopath.

In his discussion of different forms of human violence, Fromm depicts sadism as what seems to be the ultimate in human evil. He says the essence of sadism is "the drive for complete and absolute control over a living being, animal or man" (1964, p. 31-32). Fromm goes on to state that this drive is not the desire to inflict pain on others, but rather to have complete mastery over them. Fromm's description of the sadist seems to be synonymous with the typical portrait of the violent rapist. Fromm says that the sadist wishes to make the other person "a helpless object" of his will, "to become his god, to do with him as one pleases"(1964, p. 32). The sadist wishes to humiliate and enslave the other individual. In this sense the victim is a means to an end. Says Fromm, " … the most radical aim is to make him suffer, since there is no greater power over another person than that of forcing him to undergo suffering without his being able to defend himself" (1964, p. 32).

Peck refers to those he defines as evil as "people of the lie." This conception indeed fits those who are diagnosed as psychopaths or sociopaths as well as others, though not all of those we would label "habitual felons." They either deny that they victimize, lack a sense of guilt or remorse, are unable to differentiate truth from fiction or some combination of these things. To cure human evil, Peck suggests two things: the development of a psychology of evil (which certainly could be expanded to a general criminological status) and a methodology of love as a possible healing mechanism. To the traditional criminologist, such a message is indeed foreign, but, as Schafer seems to point out, what we have been doing has not worked.

Conclusion

It has been pointed out that what the theologian refers to as evil, the criminologist refers to as criminal behavior. In this context it seems clear that at least the dependent variable is the same regardless of the perspective. As Schafer pointed out, "Crime has been intensively studied for more than a century, but it is doubtful whether we are now much nearer to an understanding of man's criminal conduct" (1977, p. 481). Theologians have been contemplating the problematic behaviors that they label sin or evil for a considerably longer time and yet seem to offer nothing more specific than the tautological prescription that if people are "God-like" or "Christ-like" they will do good, not evil.

It seems that what might be needed is a fair and comprehensive evaluation by each perspective to determine what the other has to offer. Religion has traditionally been the major institution in society concerned with systematic moral teaching.

Whether any particular religion is more right or the extent to which religious associations have idiosyncratic beliefs that may not be totally moral and just in their content and application cannot be examined here. The fact remains that most religions, Christianity in particular, emphasize love, brotherhood, charity and the like. Setting aside the hypocrisy and overall failings of these groups, they do, generally speaking, advocate lofty moral principles as the model that adherents should follow.

At the same time, the knowledge that has been acquired by social scientists studying crime and other behavioral phenomena (especially social psychology) has revealed a great deal about human behavior. We have learned the importance of family and peer groups, as well as other social control mechanisms, in molding moral behavior. Phenomena such as the "norm of reciprocity," the dynamics of operant and social learning, and the effects of group pressure (especially in small primary group situations) have a great potential as a means of shaping attitudes and behavior.

The fact that neither theology nor criminology seems to take the other into account seems almost criminal in itself. Albert Einstein pointed out years ago that "Religion without science is blind. Science without religion is lame." In a world plagued with crime of all conceivable proportions and where fear of victimization seems to grow daily, the appeal "deliver us from evil" must be heard and addressed by theology and criminology jointly.

Endnotes

1. Sociology seems to be adopting philosophy as its model. As there is a philosophy of everything, there will soon be a sociology of everything as well.

2. This notion of universal causality has been eroded by Heisenberg's Uncertainty Principle, a product of quantum physics. However, most scientists still insist there must be causes for effects. Einstein said of such apparently random events, "God does not play dice".

3. This is not unlike sociological notions of social control theory (Hirschi, 1969).

References

Barnes, Harry E. and J. Negley K. Teeters (1943). *New Horizons In Criminology*, 1st ed. Englewood Cliffs, Prentice-Hall.

Bartol, Curt R. (1980), *Criminal Behavior: A Psychcosocial Approach*. Englewood Cliffs, Prentice-Hall.

Cleckley, Hervey (1970). *The Mask Of Sanity*. St. Louis, The C. V. Mosby.

Davies, Paul (1963). *God And The New Physics*. New York: Simon and Schuster.

Fox, Vernon (1985*). Introduction To Criminology*. Englewood Cliffs, Prentice-Hall.

Fromm, Erich (1964). *The Heart Of Man: Its Genius For Good And Evil*. New York, Harper & Row.

Glaser, Daniel (1977). "The Compatibility of Free Will And Determinism in Criminology: Comments on an Alleged Problem," *Journal Of Criminal Law and Criminology*, Vol. 67, No. 4, pp. 486-490. (1978*). Crime in Our Changing Society*. New York, Holt, Rinehart & Winston.

Hick, John (1980). "The Problem of Evil," in *Philosophy and the Human Condition*, Tom L. Beachamp, William T Blackstone, and Joel Feinberg (eds.), pp. 550-555. Englewood Cliffs, Prentice-Hall.

Hirschi, Travis (1969). *Causes of Delinquency*. Berkeley, University of California.

Hume, Davis (1965). "Evil and the Argument from Design," in *A Modern Introduction to Philosophy*, Paul Edwards and Arthur Pap (eds.) pp. 439-452. New York: The Free Press.

Jastrow, Robert (I 978). *God and the Astronomers*. New York: W. W. Norton.

Kilitie, Nicholas (1971). *The Right to Be Different*. Baltimore: The Johns Hopkins.

Levin, Jack and James Alan Fox (1985). *Mass Murder: America's Growing Menace*. New York, Plenum.

Lyman, Stanford M. (1973*). The Seven Deadly Sins: Society and Evil*. New York: St. Martin's.

Matza, David (1964). *Delinquency and Drift*. New York: John Wiley & Sons.

McCloskey, H.J. (1974). *God and Evil*. The Hague: Martinus Nijhoff.

Peck, Scott (1983). *People of the Lie: The Hope for Healing Human Evil*. New York: Simon & Schuster.

Schafer, Stephen (1977). "The Problem of Free Will in Criminology," *Journal of Criminal Law and Criminology*, Vol. 67, No. 4, pp. 481-485.

Stitt, B. Grant (1982). "Victimless Crimes: A Dilemma For a Free Democratic Society," presented at the 1982 Annual Meeting of the American Society of Criminology.

What Color is an Android?:
Some Reflections on Race and Intelligence in Star Trek

Susan A. Lentz, JD, PhD

AND

Robert H. Chaires, JD, PhD

Introduction

In *Star Trek*: *The Next Generation*'s (*ST:TNG*) episode "The Measure of a Man," Data is on trial for his life. More specifically, the issue is: is he alive and sentient or just a machine and, as such, the property of Starfleet. In the latter status, he would have no legally enforceable right to resist being used in a series of experiments to test his (its) "positronic" brain – experiments that might damage his brain and "kill" him as a thinking being. If he is the former, a sentient being, then he is alive and, as such, has enforceable rights. At the very least, he would have "standing," a legal term meaning the right to claim the protection of law and review by the courts as to the legality of a particular action.

It is important to note that even a finding that Data is sentient and alive does not necessarily mean he may not be used in an experiment. As a Starfleet officer, Data is subject to orders. It could be determined by Starfleet Command that the importance of the information to be gained by the study outweighs the risk to Data. After all, as has been pointed out in many *Star Trek* episodes, being a member of Starfleet is inherently risky and sometimes command decisions require ordering people to their death. Counselor Deanna Troi, for example, learns this lesson, albeit in a holographic simulation, when she was required to order Chief Engineer LaForge to his death in order to pass her "exams" for promotion to the rank of Starfleet commander (*ST:TNG*: "Thine Own Self").

Significantly, in *Star Trek* issues of sentience, of life, of discrimination and equality are most often addressed through a wide variety of alien species. Arguably, this would seem appropriate because the Federation community itself has supposedly evolved beyond intolerance and bigotry. The Federation symbolizes a society that is intercultural, international, and intergalactic. On the other hand, it may be more palatable for _Star Trek_ audiences to confront 20th and 21st century issues of "color" through aliens who are but ciphers for continuing human dilemmas and conflicts. Thus, it is important to examine the "color" of justice in _Star Trek_. Has _Star Trek_ escaped the stereotypes of the present or does it largely reflect a white, American vision of the Federation and future worlds, thus, perpetuating the bias of white superiority and "domination"?

In "The Measure of a Man" Data as a sentient being would have "rights" and choices: take part in the experiments voluntarily; be ordered to take part in the experiments and comply after noting his objections; refuse to take part and suffer the consequences. As an officer in Starfleet, there would be consequences for disobeying an order, ranging from oral reprimand to court martial and confinement. Yet Bernardi (1998:178-82) significantly notes that beyond all the rhetoric of freedom and slavery in Data's trial, there is a simple and obvious fact; Data has no real power, for it is a white human who defends him, it is a white human, albeit female, who judges him, and it is a white human, albeit under protest, who prosecutes him.

Few are going to hold that _Star Trek_ is intentionally racist. Virtually everything written about the visions of Gene Roddenberry and the various producers and directors of all the manifestations of _Star Trek_ speak the opposite. _Star Trek_ has been and remains one of the greatest visions of tolerance, of understanding, in mass media. Still, a real question is if _Star Trek_ is culturally biased to an extent that serves to perpetuate the mythology of cultural, even white racial superiority, and the idea that intelligence equates with accepting western values.

Precisely because _Star Trek_ is so often a vehicle of critical social commentary, fleeting visions into the darker sides of human experience, it is important to examine how the "real" past shapes the "undiscovered land" of the future. _Star Trek_ has always been somewhat comfortable as a means of reflecting on where we have been and are going because it shaped a future in which we survived the worst of our follies and became something better. It was "then" and we are "now"; there was time to change. The new series _Star Trek: Enterprise_, though, is coming uncomfortably close in time. In Okuda and Okuda's (1996:28) history of _Star Trek_, Zefram Cochrane "pilots Earth's first faster-than-light spaceflight" in 2063. He flies from a devastated Earth. It is now already the early years of the 21st century.

We are in a 21st century that ends its first real year with horrendous acts of terrorism, with the specter of a new cabinet post in America: The Office of Homeland Security. The rhetoric of WAR! slams into us from mass print, television and radio at the same time *The Effective Death Penalty and Antiterrorism Act of 1996*, already a frightening document, is expanded and strengthened. In too many ways we have forgotten the past.

It was only a decade ago in *Florida v. Bostick* (1991) that, ignoring the warnings of the Florida Supreme Court of images of people with swastika arm-bands taking citizens off of busses, the U.S. Supreme Court authorized suspicionless searches. After all, they said, it is a drug war. It was only a few decades ago when television overwhelmingly portrayed a social history that largely never was. Fathers knew best, mothers stayed at home in dresses, and "The Beaver" knew Indians were brutes who spoke in broken English and savaged the peaceful white settlers who were just following their "Manifest Destiny." It was only 60 years ago that a small man with a funny mustache screamed about the Father Land and the freedom and destiny of his people and set the world aflame. It was only a century ago that the U.S. entered the 20th century "more racially divided than when it entered the 19th" (Foner, 1998:135).

Star Trek is both vision and message. But all might not see and hear what the series creators, the numerous writers, intended.

The *Star Trek* Vision

The motives of the *Star Trek* producers and writers are difficult to question. As Greenwald (1998:4) points out in *Future Perfect*: "Captains James T. Kirk, Jean- Luc Picard, Benjamin Sisko, and Kathryn Janeway are neither superhuman nor godlike. They're our great-grandchildren, with far better health-care plans." *Star Trek,* through its many incarnations remains a formula, Gene Roddenberry's vision of a better future. Yet the *Star Trek* universe of the 24th century is far from perfect, and humans, while "socially evolved," still have their dark side, particularly after Rick Berman took over following the death of Roddenberry in 1991. As Berman himself has stated, "Gene's ghost is my greatest inspiration and my greatest limitation" (Greenwald, 1998: 64).

A central rule of Roddenberry was that there would be no petty conflict or squabbling among the officers and crew. According to Greenwald (1998: 13, 64), Roddenberry, often referred to as "The Great Bird of the Galaxy," kept this and other iron rules regarding continuity in his humanist vision of *Star Trek*. This vision has been described as a "blend of Ben Cartwright morality and Flash Gordon physics" and has turned out to be the most successful formula in popular media, or at least in television history (Greenwald, 1998: 13). It is a positive, idealistic vision of Earth's future. As Jeri Taylor, co-executive producer of *Voyager,* explains (cited in Greenwald, 1998:195), "We've left behind the bickering, jealousy, and materialism of the 20th century." Barad (2000iv) relates: "While our *Star Trek* heroes are far from perfect, they are nonetheless essentially decent beings whose interaction with new 'new life and new civilizations' is always guided by nobility and morality."

> [T]he show and its spin-offs cling to a wildly optimistic view of humanity's future. Poverty has been eradicated, racism is dead, and nobody breathes secondhand smoke. Money no longer exists, and Earthlings don't squabble or bicker; even organized religion is a thing of the past (Greenwald (1998:13)).

With these points, several questions are raised. Is *Star Trek* true to this vision or view? Has it truly evolved beyond, even escaped, this present and its past? And how did humanity reach such a future? Okuda and Okuda (1996) have fascinatingly "filled in" a *Star Trek* history dating back 15 billion years, and perhaps as the new series *Enterprise* evolves, some of these questions will be answered. Until then, and realizing that *Star Trek* is still entertainment to most, it seems appropriate to ask how much *Star Trek* unconsciously reflects the darker sides of its 20th century, and now 21st century, context.

A 20th Century Context

As Foner (1998:236-247) points out, post-WWII liberalism, especially in the arena of race, was fueled by horrors about Fascist extremes and a certain guilt about American racial conduct. After all, Jim Crow, the formal and informal segregation of races, had largely been the policy and practice of America since early post-Civil War days. Further, America, too, had engaged in is its own eugenics experiments during the 1930s and had a centuries long history of deeming non-white races to be "inferior." Indeed, in the latter part of the 19th century, Social Darwinists preached a politically powerful, pseudo-scientific message, in Herbert Spencer's words, of "survival of the fittest." The poor, regardless of race, were so because they had failed the test of competition; they were inferior and, so, deserved their fate, an idea suggested in *ST*: "The Cloud Minders".

"The Cloud Minders" also brought to mind the labor upheavals in the 19th and 20th centuries when attempts to unionize were characterized in the U.S. as "communist" attempts to undermine American freedom. It took the Great Depression of the 1930s to bring about a federally protected right to unionize (*National Labor Relations Act*), a pension plan for the elderly and disabled (*Social Security Act),* a guarantee of a minimum wage and protection from abusive work hours (*Fair Labor Standards Act*), and some minimal medical care for the elderly and poor children (*Medicare* and *Medicaid*). However, many of these benefits had not been extended to people of color even by the '60s. For example, one might have the right to unionize, but little compelled the unions to accept blacks, or any non Anglo-Saxons. Similarly, there might be a minimum wage but little to compel equal treatment in hiring.

The *Civil Rights Act of 1964* was still in birthing pains when the original *Star Trek* came into being. People of color and women in visible positions of authority, let alone on television, were still a relative rarity. At the same time, the U.S. Supreme Court under Chief Justice Warren generated a due process revolution in criminal justice in cases such as *Mapp v. Ohio* (367 U.S. 643, [1961], 4th Amendment exclusionary rule applies to states), *Gideon v. Wainright* (372 U.S. 335 [1963], 6th Amendment right to counsel applies to states) and *Griswold v. Connecticut* (381 U.S. 479 [1965], the totality of the Bill of Rights creates a fundamental right of privacy that limits state power to criminalize behavior).

Of course, the '60s did not end with humanity joining together, holding hands, and walking off into the glorious sunrise of the perfect day. With the '70s and '80s came reverse discrimination suits and complaints of discrimination against whites in employment. With the '90s came a retreat from federal involvement and a return to "states' rights." The cusp of the 21st century brought cases like *Kimmel v. Florida Board of Regents* (120 S.Ct. 631 [2000]) and *University of Alabama v. Garrett* (99-1240, decided Feb. 21, 2001), which respectively found the federal *Age Discrimination Act* and the *Americans With Disabilities Act* unconstitutional when applied to state employees. Thus, it again became legitimate to discriminate against at least some individuals based on physical characteristics.

One must wonder what the face of Starfleet would be like if current and emerging American public employment trends and law applied. Captain Picard would be too old, replaced by a younger, cheaper captain. The visually impaired Geordi LaForge would not be allowed to take a job from a fully sighted man. But, of course, Starfleet is not that way. That was the point all along – or is it?

The Dark Side of Star Trek

Within this line of thought, questioning Data's sentience because he is a machine, a machine constructed by a man, becomes a metaphor for the dark side of *Star Trek*. Yes, *Star Trek* is about tolerance, about compassion, about respecting individual and racial dignity and autonomy. But too often those terms are defined, interpreted, and applied in narrow human terms, more specifically sheltered American 20th century visions of what is right and wrong.

"Let That be Your Last Battlefield" in the first *Star Trek* series was perhaps the most symbolic – and obvious – of all *Star Trek* episodes in the matter of racial conflict. Bernardi (1998:26-29) uses the episode as a classic example of what he calls the *liberal-humanist* perspective that dominated the *Star Trek* of the '60s. In the midst of the 1960s and the many struggles for justice, of which race was only one, *Star Trek* portrayed the absurdity of intolerance and prejudice toward difference, as evidenced in the following dialogue.

> Commissioner Bele: It is obvious to the most simple-minded that Lokai is of an inferior breed.
>
> Spock: The obvious visual evidence, Commissioner, is that he is of the same "breed" as yourself.
>
> Commissioner Bele: Are you blind, Commander Spock? Well, look at me. Look at me.
>
> Spock: You're black on one side and white on the other.
>
> Commissioner Bele: I am black on the right side.
>
> Spock: I fail to see the difference . . .
>
> Commissioner Bele: Lokai is white on the right side. All his people are white on the right side.
>
> (Cited by Sherwin, 1999:224, her italics)

That "Last Battlefield" was simplistic and obvious does not mean it lacked visionary power. It portrayed the utter futility of such conflict by reducing differences to the absurd. Yet differences had evolved into inferiority that was "obvious" in the commissioner's world. Few can forget the scene in "Let This Be the Last Battlefield" where the commissioner chases Lokai through time and space superimposed against a background of burning cities. It was an eerie and compelling scene juxtaposed, as it was, in time against real American cities burning.

The '60s, like *Star Trek*, were a promise. We enacted the law; we built the programs. But as always in the history of federalism, many felt it was not the role of government, particularly a federal government, to engage itself in social justice. The '70s would begin a decline in the ascent "of justice for all." For too many, the law, the promises, would become hollow whispers. Whispers of *not you, not now, not ever …* While we might recognize the absurdity of Lokai's world, perhaps, also simplistically, many Americans have believed that obvious injustices rooted in the past could be undone in a matter of decades with advances in the law. That the law says we live in a colorblind society, however, does not make it so. Notions of inferiority and prejudice toward differences do not have to be intentional or even conscious. Thus, differences between what the law says and what is actually done, between what are the overt cues about "color" and "others" and what subtle images are actually portrayed, generate questions about the messages of *Star Trek*.

So, What Color Is An Android?

Beyond the obvious issues of sentience and individual rights, "The Measure of a Man" exhibits more subtle images. Pounds (1999) describes Data as being white-gold, while Bernardi (1998:178) sees the android as "silver-white." At times, Data has even seemed to exude a greenish hue. Whether Data's color in various versions of *Star Trek* is a make-up inconsistency or one of transition from small screen to big is largely irrelevant. The point of both Pounds and Bernardi is that a human-like Data who was say black or with non-Anglo features would have been harder to accept by the audience. To be an "intelligent" machine, Data had to appear within the most popular convention of what an intelligent being looks like. Was Data's "color" a conscious decision? Does it even matter?

Both Pounds (1999) and Bernardi (1998) focus on race and ethnicity in *Star Trek*. Both come to a similar conclusion. While on its face *Star Trek* is about tolerance, there are far too many subtle, and not so subtle, stereotypes and archetypes that reflect an American version of racial consciousness. In

"The Measure of a Man," one need only consider the symbolism of the trial. With Picard's ethical argument against a "race" of "intelligent" android slaves being produced, it would have seemed a natural to have the judge be a black, with all the historical imagery that would invoke. Perhaps at the time, it seemed enlightened just to have the judge be a woman. If, as Pounds might suggest, the decision not to have a Black play the role of judge was a conscious one based on production considerations of market demographics, one line of thought emerges about *Star Trek* and race. If, as Bernardi does suggest, *ST:TNG* really reflects a late '80s and '90s "neo-conservative" view of the future, a kind of "white man's burden" for the 24th century, neither view is complimentary since the former suggests a pragmatic and conscious awareness of prejudice and the latter a perhaps more dangerous unconscious bias, more dangerous perhaps, because one can "fix" what one is aware of. What one is unaware of presents substantially different problems.

Perhaps the most difficult to "fix" are the conscious or unconscious associations of race, intelligence, and criminal behavior. Foner (1998:131-132) relates that in the 1890s:

> The retreat from the ideals of Reconstruction
> went hand in hand with the resurgence of an
> Anglo-Saxonism that united patriotism, xeno-
> phobia, and an ethnocultural definition of
> nationhood in a renewed rhetoric of racial
> exclusiveness. Derogatory iconography
> depicting blacks and other 'lesser' groups as
> little more than savages and criminals filled
> the pages of popular periodicals ...

In 1994, well into the tolerant visions of *ST:TNG*, Herrnstein and Murray would write *The Bell Curve*, an argument that blacks were genetically inferior. Thus, Blacks' failure to succeed and their vastly disproportionate incarceration rate is a result of poor genes leading to low intellect, not social discrimination. While hotly debated, the book would become a best seller and a rallying point for political conservatives (see, Fraser, 1995). In 1996, while a Black male commanded *Deep Space Nine*, Bennett, the former Health, Education and Welfare Secretary under Reagan and Drug Czar under Bush Senior, wrote *Body Count* with Dilulio, the short lived director of Bush Junior's Office of Faith Based Initiatives, and Walters, director of a conservative anticrime group, and argue that the cause of American crime and economic distress was "moral poverty"

on
the part of the poor, especially minority poor. Some things never change. These
images, and the policies and practices that go with them, remain a constant
backdrop to *Star Trek*. Some things never change – except perhaps in *Star Trek*.

Images of Race, Intelligence and Morality

The "bad guys" in *Star Trek* are usually identifiable. While the '60s *Star
Trek*, with its bare-bones budget and limited special effects technology, largely
stayed with human-like bad guys, consciously or unconsciously, American, or at
least Western, stereotypical or archetypical images of non-white, non-middle-
class values often crept in. This is not, however, surprising. Pounds (1999:15-
30) describes the enormous effort invested during the '60s by groups like the
NAACP to change the negative stereotypes of nonwhite people in the movies
and on television. In this sense, *Star Trek* was a success – relatively. With an
Asian helmsman and a Black communications officer, let alone a Russian in
Starfleet in the midst of the Cold War, all series regulars, the bridge of the
Enterprise was an equal opportunity marvel for the time.

Mr. Spock, of course, added that alien element while not being too alien in
appearance. It also is noteworthy, though, that a female version of Spock did
not survive the initial screening. It is noteworthy that the Romulans, who look
just like Spock, were the deadly enemies of the Federation. There could be
"good" Indians and "bad" Indians, even in *Star Trek*, and the good Indians
always knew their place. As Pounds (1999:149) points out, "... as an alien
Other, Spock cannot call attention to himself, for fear of drawing unwanted
attention and raising reprisal for intruding into an area reserved for Terrans. In
addition, he must deny even to himself that he has earned command of a starship and would excel at it." Even with his superior intellect, Spock is always
beaten by Kirk at chess! Spock's use of "logic" to command is, in fact, most
often portrayed as a weakness.

A CONTEXT FOR "INTELLIGENCE"
McCrone (1993:1) relates in The Myth of Irrationality:

> It's the oldest cliché in science fiction. How
> often do you reach the last page of a book or
> the final moments of a film to find that the
> spaceman beat the aliens with a spark of irra-

tional genius? The aliens may be clever and
ruthless but the humans win through
because they have feelings and intuition —
qualities no bug-eyed monster could understand.

Thus, according to McCrone, the "super-rational" Spock of the 1960s *Star Trek* was a character who was inherently flawed. The half-human Spock person-ified the flawed duality of the "bad irrationality" of the body and the limited utility of pure reason. "It was some wordless, indefinable, irrational extra that was responsible for making the human race unique." Spock simply could not have that extra spark (1993:11).

That aliens can never beat humans is more than a plot convenience. In a series, the good guys have to "whup" the bad guys whether they are smarter (more technologically rational) or tougher (physiologically stronger or just plain meaner) if there is to be a next episode. Humans can even whup super-beings, including super-machines, by the device of irrational cleverness, acting out of the bounds of logic by which hyper-rational beings are bound or by impressing the super being(s) with their potential to evolve.

Grenz (1996), a theologian writing about post-modernism, put this a slight-ly different way. He describes Spock as the personification of the Enlightenment ideal of rationality, that of the supremacy of reason. However, Grenz (1996:9) is quick to note:

In *The Next Generation*, Spock is replaced
by Data, an android. In a sense, Data is a
more fully realized version of the rational
thinker than Spock, capable of superhuman
intellectual feats. Nevertheless, despite his
seemingly perfect intellect, he is not the transcendent human ideal that Spock embodies,
because he is a machine. Unlike Spock, he
desires not only to understand what it means
to be human but in fact to become human.
He believes he is somehow incomplete
because he lacks such things as a sense of
humor, emotion, and the ability to dream.

These views of Spock and Data and the limits of rationality are not in con-flict. All the versions of *Star Trek* have the same basic characters. A highly rational being who has problems in understanding emotion (Spock, Data, Odo, Tuvok, Seven of Nine), a highly emotional or affective being (Dr. McCoy, Deanna Troi, B'Elanna Torres), and a human captain who must balance their often conflicting advice. With rare exception, the super-rational and hyper-emotional are portrayed by aliens and/or, perhaps prophetically, mixed human-alien beings. Almost always, it is the human captain, who combines the "best" of the extremes, who chooses the right response for the particular situation. Thus, in the *Star Trek* universe, intelligence is constantly defined within an idea of "freedom of choice" and those choices are constantly defined within human, most especially mid/late 20th century American, values.

Consider this. The reborn Spock in *The Voyage Home* finds the most important things are feelings and friendship; Data finds emotions, Odo understands love and is transformed, and Seven of Nine becomes human. The secret, unquenchable sides of many Borg hide out in Unimatrix Zero, and even the Borg, it turns out, are ultimately ruled by a hive-queen with free will. "Hard wired" by nature or "soft-wired" by nurture, all intelligent beings come to see, or experience, the basic superiority of humanity, usually a white, Americanized humanity.

Intelligence and Color

Benardi (1998:122-126) uses *ST:TNG* "Samaritan Snare" and "Transfigurations" among others to explain this curious intermix of assumptions and images about race and intelligence. In "Samaritan," the Pakled, a race of short, rotund beings with distinct Down's Syndrome features (associated with genetically caused mental retardation) kidnap LaForge and steal the *Enterprise* in an attempt to obtain a technological leap. Portrayed as slow moving and dim witted, they are foiled. Interestingly enough, the "minority characters" of the *Enterprise* who had been in the space station being repaired show little understanding of the Pakleds. Data states, "How they ever mastered the rudiments of space travel is a genuine curiosity" (quoted by Bernardi, 124). The female half-human, empath Troi states, "They're unwilling to wait for the timely evolution of their species' intellectual capacity" (quoted by Bernardi, 124). In response to the Pakled complaint, "You think we are not smart," Riker responds, "I think you need to continue to develop" (quoted by Benardi 124). The Federation, therefore, restricts the Pakled in their space travel. This is an old message well known to Blacks. Princeton professor Woodrow Wilson, before he became President and founded the League of Nations, wrote about Blacks, "Unpracticed in liberty ... excited by a freedom they did not understand ... were not ready for participation in American public life" (cited by Foner, 1998:132). In many ways it seems *Star Trek* carries on this idea.

In "Transfigurations" a white humanoid "evolves" into a superbeing portrayed by a white light in human shape. Indeed, as Benardi notes, the supernatural Q always appear in the guise of white humans. Similarly, it is always white humanoids who evolve into higher beings. The fresh-faced Wesley Crusher, who begins the next step of evolution could be from "middle" American suburbs, and even in _Voyager,_ the elfin Ocampa, Kes, who goes to the "next level," could have come from a Kansas farm. The only Black human who has an "association" with "gods" is Captain Sisko, yet he is often portrayed as more of a puppet than a participant. Would Kirk, Picard, or Janeway have been so tolerant of being used by the "gods?"

Still, this theme of whiteness is not wholly consistent; Whoopie Goldberg's Guinan character in _ST:TNG_ is godlike and chooses to serve drinks and offer counsel. Similarly, _ST:V_'s Tuvok is a "Black Vulcan." But a cynical person might say that Goldberg's character was a stereotypical "wise old black servant" who knew better than to directly interfere in the affairs of others, and that Tuvok, by being Vulcan, was not quite human. Of course, the better answer is that if a major movie star likes _Star Trek_ and wants a role, make one. Similarly, if the best actor for a role happens to be Black, race should not be a consideration, particularly if you need a Black to round out the cast.

COLOR AND MORALITY

If the nature of intelligence has a certain white, western bias, color also plays its role in the defining of moral behavior. It is tempting to argue that the multiracial crews of the _Star Trek_ universe portray a very humanistic vision of tolerance, a word seen and heard quite often in reference to _Star Trek_. But the word tolerance is itself loaded with overtones of superiority on a variety of levels. One tolerates differences, but that is not the same as embracing them as a strength, as is the ideal in the concept of diversity. Regarding intolerance in the 23rd century, Bernardi (1998:34) cites a statement by Gene Roddenberry circa 1968:

> Improbable! If man survives that long, he will have learned to take a delight in the essential differences between men and between cultures. He will learn that differences in ideas and attitudes are a delight, part of life's exciting variety, not something to fear. It's a manifestation of the greatness that God, or whatever it is, gave us. This is infi-

nite variation and delight, this part of the
optimism we build into *Star Trek.*

Notwithstanding Roddenberry's advocacy of diversity as a delight, the visual messages sent by the *Star Trek* universe are often different. Pounds (1999),
Bernardi (1998), and Paulsen (1995) have all commented on the racial stereotyping in *Star Trek*. Bernardi, in particular, points out that archetypes are in
truth just historical stereotypes. For example, in "Code of Honor" (*ST:TNG*),
there are the technologically sophisticated Ligonians whose leader covets a
white woman (Tasha Yar) while running around carrying a spear and wearing
an Ali Baba costume. Of course this advanced black humanoid race sports scars
from ritual combat. According to Bernardi (1998:109), this episode "… perpet-
uates a common racial stereotype: primitive, homogenous dark people ruled by
a self-serving, pompous chief who desires white women and is indifferent to
missions of galactic mercy." Along this line, Pounds (1999:170) relates that in
ST and *ST:TNG*, "[w]hether a loyal Starfleet officer or a maverick product of a
bygone world, ethnic and alien characters enjoy only provisional acceptance,
subject to revocation at any time."

It is this "suspect" status for nonwhite humans that is so ambiguous in the
Star Trek universe. While there have been "bad" white humans in the various
versions of *Star Trek*, there seems a general rule that the more "despicable" the
alien value structure or conduct, the more negatively archetypical the physical
imagery. Fascist, and/or dangerous races are usually dark, muscular, often
lizard-like (Klingons, Cardassians, Jem'Hadar); while sneaky, untrustworthy
races are usually small with extremely odd facial features or appendages
(Andorians, Ferengi). There are exceptions, but those exceptions seem, in turn,
to also have exceptions. Neelix, on *Voyager,* is small and odd, but open and
harmless looking. And, until near the end of the series, it seemed that his race,
the Talaxians, had been killed off by the Haakonians. They had been unable to
defend themselves. Over all, it seems that early 20th century "science" theories
about body types and behavior survived well into 24th century, or at least into
the late 20th century minds of directors and make-up artists.

Conclusion

On its face, the continuing, if not increasing, racial polarization in America
would seem to be at odds with the increasing heterogeneity of *Star Trek*. It
would seem that *Deep Space Nine* and *Voyager* especially became increasingly

science fiction/fantasy, as critically alien as Frank Herbert's *Dune* series rather than a hopeful future vision. Bernardi (1998), though, gives another perspective: beneath its multicolored face, *Star Trek* itself is becoming racially and intellectually homogenized. All are welcome, but in a Borg-like way assimilation is the cost.

Still, it must be remembered that it is a series, and, while there was substantial consistency, sometimes the plot just required a contrived ending. Or, if one wants an enlightened evolutionary view, it can be said that *Star Trek* evolved and matured in its understanding of the human condition. In *ST:TNG* "Elementary, Dear Data," the sentient holo-character Moriarty is saved as a program. A decade later, at the conclusion of *Voyager* the Emergency Medical Hologram would marry a flesh and blood being. Plot contrivance or evolution?

This writing began with *ST:TNG* "The Measure of a Man," an episode from 1989. From the admittedly limited review that followed, several important issues of conflict and discrimination can be said to still exist in the Federation of the 24th century:

- Sentience is defined within a context of individual autonomy and choice.
- Protected and respected life is biased toward the light skinned, humanoid, and organic.
- Sentience and life are legal issues, so who makes the laws remains critical.
- Creators of sentience and other life forms are superior to the created, and that superiority includes the right to end sentience and life.

But as *Star Trek* comes from 20th century minds with 20th century biases, so does this critique. If current demographic trends continue, many of these issues may simply disappear – the ideas underpinning the "faces" on bridges of the various *Enterprise*s may seem "quaint" a hundred years hence. Likely, intermarriage – blending – will make much of the polarity of race a meaningless concept. Recent advances in the understandings of quantum mechanics may render the technological utopia of *Star Trek* a humorous dead end. The future, as many have said, may be stranger than we can imagine, and *Star Trek* may look, even 50 years hence, as odd and technologically simplistic as the *Flash Gordon* of the 1930s.

Still, just because we have passed by Orwell's *1984* and there was no *Eugenics War* in 1993, does not mean these things cannot yet happen. A naïve sense of the past can produce an uncertain present, one open to defining a closed future in which every mistake must be made over and over again. As many others have said, those who do not remember history, and implicitly the history of fiction, are doomed to repeat it.

Bibliogaphy

Barad, Judith, with Ed Robertson (2000). *The Ethics of Star Trek*, New York: HarperCollins.

Bernardi, Daniel Leonard (1998). *Star Trek and History: Race-ing Toward A White Future*, New Brunswick, NJ: Rutgers University Press.

Foner, Eric (1998). *The Story of American Freedom,* New York: W.W. Norton & Co.

Frazer, Steven (1996). *The Bell Curve Wars: Race, Intelligence, and the Future of America*, New York: Basic Books.

Greenwald, Jeff (1998). *Future Perfect: How Star Trek Conquered Planet Earth*, New York: Viking.

Grenz, Stanley J. (1996). *A Primer on Postmodernism*, Grand Rapids, Michigan: William B. Eerdmans Pub.

Herrnstein, Richard J. and Charles Murray (1994). *The Bell Curve: Intelligence and Class Structure in American Life*, New York: Free Press.

Joseph, Paul and Sharon Carton (1992). "*The Law of the Federation*: Images of Law, Lawyers, and the Legal System in *Star Trek: The Next Generation*," 24 *U. of Toledo Rev.* 43

McCrone, John (1993). *The Myth of Irrationality: The Science of the Mind From Plato to Star Trek*. New York: Carroll & Graf Pub.

Pounds, Michael C. (1999). *Race In Space: The Representation of Ethnicity in Star Trek and Star Trek: The Next Generation.*

Section Three

STAR TREK AND THE FUTURE

Perhaps a better heading for this section would be "Applied *Star Trek*." We go beyond legal and social science disciplinary constraints to understand *Star Trek* issues through the interdisciplinary approaches of education, futuristics, information science, and phenomenology. It suggests an "applied *Star Trek*" that takes seriously the meanings we find within *Star Trek* as artifacts of our values and society, for both today and in the future. Thus, Professor Chaires' chapter on teaching *Star Trek* is more about its metaphorical assistance in developing critical thinking and writing than about how *Star Trek* addresses a specific law, social institution or problem. Within this perspective, *Star Trek* has become a <u>noun</u>, a <u>verb</u>, and an <u>adjective</u>, and each use brings different visions for future directions.

Star Trek as a <u>noun</u> is a registered trademark, a legally protected term, the title of the original 1960s series and generically descriptive of a host of television reincarnations, movies, and books. Much of the material in sections one and two of this book concern *Star Trek* as a <u>noun</u>, often comparing the world of *Star Trek* to laws, social institutions, or problems within our own. In this vein, *Star Trek* as noun, future directions would concern new presentations, television series, movies, and books, all of which would contain familiar characters and icons. As this work goes to press, the new series *Enterprise* is adding to *Star Trek*'s own copyrighted history of the future. This presents intriguing issues for the *Enterprise* producers and writers because much of the past that led to the *Star Trek*s of the 23rd and 24th centuries is already "historical fact" in the world of *Star Trek*.

Star Trek as a <u>verb</u> generates issues about a history according to *Star Trek*. As Professor Costanza points out, the *Star Trek* future is only one of several directions humanity may go, a future highly dependent on technological advances. It is, at least in the Federation, a largely utopian one. In this light, *Star Trek* is an action term, a question of how to do a *Star Trek* "future" without the steep learning curve of some sort of "genetic wars" or "WWIII." Ergo, there is an optimistic view that humanity can avoid actualization of the fears of today, the use of weapons of mass destruction, terrorist acts against innocent civilians, genocide, and ethnocide. Oops, we can't avoid that future history; it is already the past. Probably, along with being called the "Century of Technology," future historians will describe the 20th century as the "Age of Mass Terror," in which the hundreds of millions who were killed by weapons of mass destruction and acts of genocide, ethnocide, and terrorism will scream to the future, "No more!" But the dead do not scream or even talk. Only those living can speak for them, and *Star Trek* has been, and remains, a very loud and commanding voice.

Star *Trek* as an <u>adjective</u> is produced by this loud and widespread voice. Not only is there a more utopian future looming in that "undiscovered land" of the future, but the <u>noun</u> and <u>verb</u> of *Star Trek* have become, like Zen, a way of thought to make decisions toward it. At the utopian end of the current 24th century of the *Star Trek* future, technology in itself is not the panacea, a constant *Star Trek* message. As Professor Chilton points out, technology generates information overload. It is a common theme in *Star Trek* and the literature of information science that knowledge is no longer simply power; rather, it may overload all circuits and simply reinforce existing values (and problems) of our human condition. Other things, other conducts within the human equation and outside technology are required in the making of that better future. As there are *Star Trek* gadgets, *Star Trek* conventions, *Star Trek* classes, there is a *Star Trek* way or <u>adjective</u> to do life and reality. Implicit within this point is an idea similar to that of the limits of technological fixes: there are limits to the use of power that must be found by looking inward, not outward.

Just as Vulcans are portrayed in *Enterprise* as not being as far along the way of logic as they are in the 24th century, so the humans of *Enterprise* are portrayed as much closer to today than in, say, *Star Trek: The Next Generation*. But that is perhaps a great advantage of doing a prequel; you get to reshape the 'known history' by revising the past. No doubt, *Enterprise* will portray early warp drive humanity in a much more noble aspect than previous versions alluded. Still, that does not detract from *Star Trek* as a way to approach the future. Future directions in *Star Trek* are only limited by past imagination that has shaped the present. *Star Trek* is a way of transcending that imaginary line of historical continuity that so many believe shapes the future. As Professor Chaires concludes, perhaps the very act of imagining the visions of *Star Trek* will help make our future a better one.

Star Trek as a Pedagogical Vehicle for Teaching Law and Justice

ROBERT H. CHAIRES, JD, PHD

For more than 30 years, *Star Trek* in its many manifestations has entertained, intrigued – and educated. That *Star Trek* is entertaining cannot be doubted. While the original *Star Trek* (*ST*) of the '60s was relatively short lived (three years and 78 episodes), *Star Trek: The Next Generation* (*ST:TNG*), *Star Trek: Deep Space Nine* (*ST:DS9*) and *Star Trek: Voyager* (*ST:V*) each lasted many years. Indeed, *ST:V* will see its last episodes in the 21ˢᵗ century! Of note is that *ST:TNG*, *ST:DS9* and *ST:V* ended more because the actors became tired of the roles than because of a decline in popularity.

Of course, the numerous *Star Trek* movies and books continue the various visions and journeys of all the crews in other media. That *Star Trek* is intriguing is without doubt. *Star Trek* remains popular precisely because it continues to be both a mirror and a window into human nature and the human condition. *Star Trek* always has been a vehicle for displaying the darkest elements of humankind and the highest aspirations. That it is perhaps too intriguing for some has been a constant criticism. Over the years the term "Trekkie" has evolved, and that evolution has produced distinct connotations. For some it is just a healthy sharing of common interests, a kind of extended fan club. For others, the numerous clubs and conferences are indications of an unhealthy obsession, of a cult-like avoidance of reality.

That the *Star Trek* phenomenon also has an educational dimension is not so clear. The purpose of this writing is to present that *Star Trek*, in its many reincarnations and guises, is an extremely useful pedagogical tool with many curriculum applications. To convey this utility, the history, evolution, and current practice of a course that uses *Star Trek* as a central vehicle will be described. That description will include critical reflection on things that worked and things that did not. Finally, some suggestions on using *Star Trek* in more general courses will be presented.

Given the nature of the topic, this writing will deviate from the usual manner of scholarly writing. The theory surrounding curriculum and pedagogy is complex and contradictory, and numerous citations and critiques would contribute little. Apple (1991), for example, argues that curriculum is more ideologically than educationally driven. Indeed, it may be that there is *so much* theory about how to teach writing that we too often lose sight, as in the old Zen parable, of *the forest for the trees*. Harris (1997), for example, suggests that the American way of teaching writing at the college composition level may itself contribute to some of the antipathy it produces among students. He notes there are distinct American and British positions on the who and how of teaching writing. American writing faculty tend to see and define themselves as *scholars,* whereas British faculty tend to see and define themselves as *classroom teachers* (1997:4-5). Simply put, American educators strive to find out *why* something works – a teaching "science" – while the British are more concerned with what works – a teaching "art."

This writing is about teaching in the classroom, about a means of communicating complex ideas and generating meaningful classroom discourse. For this reason, what follows is in first person, a style that the writer is somewhat uncomfortable with. That itself may be a comment on the directions that being both scholar and teacher has taken many of us.

Some Context fro Teaching Star Trek

In 1994 the English Department of the University of Nevada-Reno (UN-R) developed and implemented the "English Seminar Program." The teaching/writing theory behind this program is beyond the scope of this writing. Still, like many things that involve implementing theory, arguably the underpinning theory is irrelevant to whether the practice works. In this instance the program was both popular and successful although not long lived. Basically, the English Seminar Program involves two distinct components: 1) Developing English 102 composition courses (part of UN-R's required "core") around themes, and 2) using regular faculty from disciplines outside English to teach them.

In developing the program, the English Department realized two things. The first was that while individual faculty might be interested in teaching such a course, few would be willing to take on an unpaid teaching overload and the budget was not there to pay faculty the going rate for such an overload. Secondly, few departments, if any, would be willing to let loose a faculty member from a regular teaching load to "work" in another department. The funding process that was worked out was politically and financially astute. For releasing a faculty member to teach an English Seminar course, the lending department would receive $1,500, which could be used for any purpose by the department. Given the short operations budgets of many departments, this was a significant carrot.

For an individual faculty member the rewards for teaching an English course are more subjective. For some it was a chance to do something different from the normal course load and to teach to a different group of students. For others, it was an opportunity to develop a course around a special area of interest, to explore "strange new worlds." At a practical level, for some faculty it was a "one shot" way to get away from teaching large, and very large classes, and do a real seminar. English 102 Seminar classes were held to a maximum enrollment of 18. Probably, there are as many reasons for teaching such courses as there are teachers. In any event, there was no shortage of faculty willing to teach in the Seminar series. Each semester during the three years the program was in operation, between 12 and 18 sections were offered.

WRITING TO THEMES

It is part of college student folklore that English composition courses are "boring," a necessary evil on the route to a degree. The roots of this folklore are multivariate. One root can be traced to wide variance in the quality of English classes in primary and secondary schools. Another root draws from stereotypes about who likes English courses and who teaches them. Finally, college-level faculty members themselves often are ambivalent about the whys and ways of student writing and may be the guiding root in directing student folklore about what English departments do. Like many kinds of sustained folklore, there are bits of continuing truth imbedded in the perpetuation.

Using faculty from other disciplines to teach thematic courses serves to pierce student folklore. The varieties of themes that have evolved in the English Seminar program reflect the wide variety of faculty that was involved. Environment, medicine, news media, politics, popular folklore, education, music, geography, feminism, and law are but a few of the thematic foci that have been developed and taught. Several of these themes have been adapted to, or specifically designed for, the UN-R Honors program. Students are attracted to these courses because they can "write" on subjects that may be of interest to them. Generally, the Seminar sections of English 102 filled-up long before the regular sections.

Using faculty from other disciplines serves several purposes. Primary among these is that the faculty members usually present a theme area they have disciplinary depth in. As such, they not only work with writing skills in the "form" dimension, they also can help develop the "substance" dimension. Simply put, the forte of English faculty is writing and literature. They are generally not qualified to comment on the substance of writing outside literature. For example, whether a paper is a "good" analysis of a novel is one thing. Whether it is a good presentation of an environmental issue is another.

WRITING, NOT "COMPOSITION"

A key point in the Seminar series is faculty concentration on "writing" rather than technical competence in composition. It is a given that the faculty who teach in the Seminar series have a strong and proven interest in student writing development. They, however, may have long forgotten the technical terms for the "rules" of writing. Within their discipline, most faculty, as a matter of routine, comment on mechanical writing problems and may severely grade down for same. Still, however, the primary role of disciplinary faculty is to examine the substance, the content, of writing.

In the Seminar series the focus is much more on students doing good writing than it is on students doing writing that looks good. This foundation for the course led me to consider and reconsider some issues about student writing about which I had long thought. For several years I had been using some episodes of *Star Trek* to accentuate critical thinking and writing points in my law and justice related courses. From this experience, the idea occurred to develop an entire writing course around *Star Trek*. The curriculum was developed, the syllabus submitted, and in 1994, as one of the first in the Seminar series, the course was offered. English 102: *Star Trek*: Visions of Justice is still being taught today. While the Seminar program ended because of funding programs, I took the course "on the road", so to speak, and have used the basic themes to teach writing at community colleges and in developmental English courses.

Star Trek in the Classroom

As a former police officer and civil rights lawyer, my specialty within the discipline of criminal justice centers on social justice issues. More specifically, as a Ph.D. in public administration, I study how criminal justice organizations interpret and apply law. Several of the courses I developed and teach are outgrowths of my particular interests and perspectives.[1] Over the years I have identified three distinct pedagogical problems in teaching courses with substantial social justice content. These are:

Student variables enter each and every classroom. They come with a wide variety of often strong preconceptions and experiences about particular aspects of social justice issues, i.e., race, gender, resource distribution, and state/individual relations.

Bridging the sometimes wide gap between theory and application in a way that generates critical inquiry and understanding, not simplistic polarization.

Generational context is always an issue. By the time the teacher becomes old enough to be the parent of the student, historical and social reference points can become confused. For example, the '60s were a major arena for social justice conflict. For a 50-year-old professor those times are "real." For a 21-year-old student, they are as historical as the "Great Depression" of the '30s was to that professor in the '60s.

Star Trek is a useful classroom vehicle for confronting these points. Some perspectives on this usefulness are condensed and displayed in **Table I**.

Table I Teaching Dimensions of *Star Trek*

Student Variables	*Star Trek* is a fictional vehicle. While many episodes directly address social justice issues, the fictional futuristic genre allows students to remove themselves from direct confrontation with things as they are "today."
Bridging	*Star Trek* has its own "social history" that suggests how conflicts were resolved in the past to produce the rather "utopian" future. Further, presentations of technology, social mores, etc., operate to generate discourse on what affects what.
Generational Context	*Star Trek* is transgenerational. It has been around so long that it is a cultural icon that is easily referenced. In addition, the evolution of the various series over decades lends a reference point for understanding social issues in a particular decade.

Table I is not exhaustive, nor is it in anyway intended to be, of the pedagogical uses of *Star Trek* in a variety of classes. It does begin to display, however, that *Star Trek* can be used as more than just a simple comparison/contrast discussion device. Okuda and Okuda (1996) give some indication of this in their *Star Trek Chronology: A History of the Future*. This monumental work, which develops a timeline for *Star Trek* until the late '90s, would play well as a discussion piece in many classes.

Some Examples

It is often said that in reading Shakespeare one will eventually encounter every kind of person. A similar statement can be made about *Star Trek*. There is an episode of *Star Trek* that centers on virtually every kind of human conflict or condition. In teaching my CJ320: Courts in Criminal Justice course, I was looking for a strong way to link the first half of the course, which deals with actors, lawyers, judges, juries, with the second half that concentrates on system process and structure. In an episode of *ST:DS9*, "Tribunal," I found the lynchpin.

Chief O'Brien, a carryover character from *ST:TNG*, is taking a long delayed vacation with his wife. The shuttle he is piloting is boarded by Cardassians (a thinly disguised neo-Nazi race of aliens), and O'Brien is arrested for unspecified charges. On Cardassia a trial takes place in which every aspect of a contemporary American criminal trial is weirdly perverted. The judge is there, the defense counsel and jury are there, and due process is there. Each, though, has but one role, to legitimate the verdict of guilty that is rendered before trial. In particular, the jury does nothing; it is a visual aid for the judge who acts as the prosecutor. In the trial remaining silent is an indication of guilt. The source of evidence is not discoverable because it is confidential. The defense counsel's job is to convince the defendant to plead guilty in order to maintain the legitimacy of the law. While at the end the "plot" to undermine the Federation by a political trial is exposed, the point is clear to students. Just having the form of constitutional adversarial due process means nothing. Judges, lawyers, and juries have distinct roles in the American system. Examining the court system often involves looking at the difference between the formal symbolic and law in practice.

In CJ420: Jurisprudence, explaining some of the major theoretical divisions in law is facilitated by using episode eight, "Justice," from *The Next Generation*. In that episode Wesley Crusher, a teenage member of the crew, is on shore leave on Rubicun III, an idyllic planet populated by the Edo, a human-like species who live in virtual perfect harmony. When Crusher is sentenced to death for accidentally breaking a garden green-house in a ball-game, the harmony takes on another dimension. The Edo get along so well because every violation of the law, no matter how minor, is punished by summary "trial" on the spot and immediate execution.

Of course, various members of the *Enterprise* crew have other ideas about the utility and justice of the Edoan criminal justice system. Captain Picard is in a special bind because the "Prime Directive" forbids interference in a planetary culture. In theory, he must let Edoan law prevail. What follows is a splendid example of argument about the differences and underpinnings of absolute equity and due process models of law and justice. The episode is especially relevant when it is juxtaposed against reading and discussing the classic *Case of the Speluncean Explorers* (Fuller, 1949). Based on a remotely similar issue, the application of an absolute law demanding the death penalty, the *Case*, which takes place in the "far" future, has been a staple of law and society courses at the undergraduate and graduate levels for over 50 years. While it evokes sometimes passionate arguments from students, it is also often dry and overly convoluted, as is the real case, *Regina v. Dudley (1886),* it was partially based on (see Simpson, 1984). Together, the academic depth of *Speluncean Explorers* and the immediate passion and compassion of "Justice" operate to bring the issues and dilemmas to a "real life" dimension.

In "Let That Be Your Last Battlefield," CJ427: Struggle for Justice students get a 1960s perspective on race conflict with this original *Star Trek* (1969) episode. The original *Star Trek* tended toward the obvious. Low budget and cheap special effects often accentuated this. Still, the idea, that of a law enforcement officer chasing a criminal endlessly through space and time, has impact in a *Les Miserables* imagery, especially when the crime is being different. While otherwise identical, the "cop" is black on the right side of his face and white on the other; the crime is being the reverse. The end of the episode leaves pursued and pursuer locked in eternal combat. For a class in the 21st century, the episode invokes some disturbing questions about how things have or have not changed.

Arguably, you could find and use other video vehicles that exposed the same issues and points as *Star Trek*. Movies, though, are too long. Television episodes fit nicely into short class periods and using one television series allows the students a reference framework. And, of course, as noted there are just so many episodes of *Star Trek* from which to draw.

Star Trek: *The Class*

Using an occasional episode of *Star Trek* to stress a particular idea or point is one thing; building an entire class around *Star Trek* is another. English 102 is still a writing class and the problem was, and remains, what to write about and how. A consideration of particular importance is that not all the students who take the class are familiar with *Star Trek*. While the majority of each class tends toward having some substantial exposure to *Star Trek*, and there are always a few hardcore Trekkies, a few students have no exposure at all.

From the beginning, the course was taught as if the students had no prior exposure to *Star Trek*. This served two purposes. First, it limited the ability of Trekkies to infuse too much *Star Trek* trivia into the format. Secondly, and most importantly, it allowed me to guide students into the social justice focus of the course. In the beginning, I also followed a fairly typical method of teaching a theme course by using theme readings, in this case, *Star Trek* novels. My first offering of the course was an eye opener for me. I did not need to guide the students into considering social justice issues. They were already there.

While it simply may be that the nature of the course just attracts students with broad, speculative minds, I think there is more. Within any English 102 class, the students represent a wide spectrum of backgrounds, educational experience, and writing competency. However, these backgrounds and prior educational experiences seemed to have little to do with their ability to generate and take part in discourse at some high levels of abstraction. In point, when I taught an honors program session of the course, I did not find any difference in the quality of student ability to hone in on issues and discuss them. The differences were in writing competency, the ability to translate an idea into written words. More particularly, I found wider disparities when it came to the process of reading-decoding-writing.

READING INTO WRITING

In a typical English course (and many others) students are required to read and then describe what that reading said (decode) and finally write about the reading (recode). When I had assignments that involved the reading-decode-recode process, they were markedly different in result than then assignments that only involved recode. In short, students were much better at translating *Star Trek* videos into issues and writing than *Star Trek* novels, a point I will discuss later.

For some context, it may be helpful to explain my grading method for writing. For several years in all classes, I have been breaking down the grading of writing into three distinct areas. The first is content. That portion of the grade (60%) involves the ideas and work that went into the particular writing. The second portion is structure and organization (20%), and concerns clarity of segments, flow, and transition between points. The final portion of the grade is mechanics (20%). This evaluates points such as grammar, typos, and proper citations. This method allows me to do a critical evaluation of student writing in a constructive way. Students know where their strong and weak points are. They know exactly what they have to work harder with. This works quite well in my upper division courses and even better in the *Star Trek* course where my teaching obligations specifically concern writing and I have more assignments to work from.

What I found was that the content and structure/organization dimensions of the writing were much better in the video-to-writing assignments. Mechanics did not appear to be affected by either. Perhaps, most importantly, I found that in reading/decoding/writing assignments, the honors students tended to do much better, but no better in video-to-writing assignments where content was concerned and only a little better in organization and structure. The honors class, understandably, tended to do much better in mechanics.

My speculation is that using the futurist genre of *Star Trek* allows students to approach complex and value-laden issues of today in a "value neutral" way. Simply put, the future is not personal. Rose (1999), in his observations about "writers block" in college students, notes that students get tied up in the do's and don'ts of writing, particularly in the mechanistic, but also in the cognitive "idea" stage. *Star Trek* videos do not require the decoding from writing; they go directly to the encoding of ideas into written words. Simply put, the visual stimuli make the writing process more direct. Recognizing at least part of this process, some English departments have adopted texts such as *Seeing & Writing* (McQuade and McQuade (2000), which are heavily into using visual cues, photographs of paintings, posters, and "scenes," to trigger and structure writing.

EARLY PROBLEMS AND EVOLVING DIRECTION

The writing assignments of my English 102 section are not much different overall than many other theme course writing assignments. A variety of specialized assignments exploring different styles and kinds of writing are required. For example, a "letter to the editor" of a "newspaper" circa 2400 about a major issue of the time is a routine assignment. Similarly, students write short essays on a variety of topics and conclude the course with a major paper on the "Prime Directive." Where my course may differ is in the use of "role playing" to teach certain aspects of writing. An example of this is involving them all in a "mock court martial." Using one of the videos as a "fact" situation, the students prosecute, defend, and judge an alleged violation of the Prime Directive. Students come to understand that a trial is an acted out form of expository writing and that, like a trial, writing often involves strategic and tactical considerations of what you are trying to say to which readers (jurors). From there, they write about what they learned about structure, organization, and argument.

Not all the things I have tried have worked. A few have been major flops. An assignment to write "policy and rules" for the use of the "holodeck," almost incited rebellion in the class. My idea was to use the vehicle as a way to work with writing precise sentences along with structure and organization. The concepts of policy and rule writing were just too advanced for many 19-year-olds.

Also, after the first three courses I tossed the *Star Trek* novels, except for one. Across the board, *Star Trek* novels tend to be poorly written and overly dependent on reader pre-knowledge about the *Star Trek* universe. While there may be good ones, I am unwilling to read through the hundred or so that exist to find them. The one I kept is used as an example of really bad writing.

Getting rid of the *Star Trek* novels allowed me to explore another direction for the course. I used some classic science fiction novels such as Arthur C. Clark's *Childhoods End* (1953) and Gordon R. Dickson's *Tactics of Mistake (1971)*, and similar different, sometimes darker, visions of the future of humanity. Students now get the largely utopian vision of *Star Trek* juxtaposed against alternative futures. What kinds of decisions and what kinds of actions would tend to send mankind in one direction or another is the focus of discussion and writing. So far this approach seems to work even better than *Star Trek* alone.

Conclusion

Using *Star Trek* as a teaching vehicle has not gone without criticism. Some faculty have expressed concern about using videos so extensively (about seven a course), and others question the propriety of *Star Trek* in the classroom, period. Overall, though, support for the course has been constant. The course has long passed from the stage of experiment to that of being a regular offering. My challenge for the future will be to keep it from becoming "routine" and to continue the effort to go where no course has gone before.

Bibliography

Fuller, Lon L. (1949). "The Case of the Speluncean Explorers," *Harvard Law Review*, v.62:617-645.

Gross, Edward and Mark A. Altman (1995). *Captains' Logs*, Boston: Little Brown.

Harris, Joseph (1997). *A Teaching Subject: Composition Since 1966*, Upper Saddle River, NJ: Prentice Hall.

McQuade Donald and Christine McQuade (2000). *Seeing & Writing*, Boston: Bedford/*ST.* Martin's.

Okuda, Michael and Denise Okuda (1996). *Star Trek Chronology: The History of the Future*, NY: Pocket Books.

Rose, Mike (1999). "Rigid Rules, Inflexible Plans, and the Stifling of Language: A Cognitivist Analysis of Writer's Block," in X. Kennedy, D. Kennedy and S. Holladay, eds, *Teaching With The Bedford Guide for College Writers: 2/ Background Reading*, 5 ed. Boston: Bedford/*ST.* Martin's (264-74).

Simpson, A.W. Brian (1984). *Cannibalism and the Common Law*, Chicago: U of Chicago Press.

Four Visions of the Century Ahead:
WILL IT BE STAR TREK, ECOTOPIA, BIG GOVERNMENT, OR MAD MAX?

ROBERT COSTANZA, PhD

Probably the most challenging task facing humanity today is the creation of a shared vision of a sustainable and desirable society, one that can provide permanent prosperity within the biophysical constraints of the real world in a way that is fair and equitable to all of humanity, to other species, and to future generations. This vision does not now exist, although the seeds are there. We all have our own private visions of the world we really want, and we need to overcome our fears and skepticism and begin to share these visions and build on them until we have built a vision of the world we want.

The most effective ingredient to move change in any particular direction is having a clear vision of the desired goal that is also truly shared by the members affected by it, whether an organization, a community, or a nation.

Social observer Daniel Yankelovich has described the need for governance to move from public opinion to public judgment. Public opinion is notoriously fickle and inconsistent on those issues for which people have not confronted the broader implications of their opinions. For example, many people are highly in favor of more effort to protect the environment, but at the same time they are opposed to any diversion of tax revenues to do so. Coming to public judgment is the process of resolving these conflicts.

To start the dialogue and move quickly to public judgment, we may consider issues in the form of "visions" or scenarios. This article lays out four such visions, each presented as a "future history" written from the vantage point of the year 2100. These visions include both positive and negative scenarios – hopes and fears – allowing us to fully explore what the future may hold and thus to make informed choices among complex alternatives with a range of implications.

While there are an infinite number of possible future visions, I believe these four visions embody the basic patterns within which much of this variation occurs. Each of the visions is based on some critical assumptions about the way the world works, which may or may not turn out to be true. This format allows one to clearly identify these assumptions, assess how critical they are to the relevant vision, and recognize the consequences of them being wrong.

Four Visions of the Future

The four visions derive from two basic world views that reflect one's faith in technological progress. The "technological optimist" world view is one of continued expansion of humans and their dominion over nature. This is the "default" vision in current Western society and represents the continuation of current trends into the indefinite future.

There are two versions of this vision, however: one in which the underlying assumptions are actually true in the real world and one in which those assumptions are false. The positive version of the "technological optimist" vision I'll call "Star Trek," named for the popular TV series that is its most articulate and vividly fleshed-out manifestation. The negative version of the "technological optimist" vision I'll call "Mad Max" after the popular, post-apocalyptic, Australian movie of 1979 that embodies many aspects of this vision gone bad.

The "technological skeptic" vision focuses much less on technological change and more on social and community development. The version of this vision that corresponds to the skeptics being right about the nature of the world I'll call "Ecotopia" after a book of the late 1970s. If the technological skeptics turn out to be wrong, and the optimists right, about the real state of the world, we see the version I'll call "Big Government" come to pass – a scenario of protective government policies overriding the free market.

Each of these future visions is described from the perspective of the year 2100. The visions are described as narratives with specific names and events, rather than as vague general conditions, in order to make them more real and vivid. They are, of course, only caricatures, but I hope they capture the essence of the visions they represent.

Star Trek: The Default Technological Optimist Vision

The turning point came in 2012, when population pressure was mounting and natural resources were being strained. The greenhouse effect caused by burning fossil fuel was beginning to cause some major disruptions. But the development of practical fusion energy allowed a rapid reduction of global fossil fuel burning to practically zero by the year 2050, eventually reversing the greenhouse effect. Fusion energy was infinitely better and cheaper than any alternative, and it was inexhaustible.

Air pollution was essentially eliminated between 2015 and 2050, as cars were converted to clean-burning hydrogen produced with energy from fusion reactors. Electricity for homes, factories, and other uses came increasingly from fusion, so the old, risky nuclear fission reactors were gradually decommissioned; even some hydro-power stations were eliminated to return some great rivers to their wild state. In particular, the dams along the Columbia River in Oregon were eliminated by 2050, allowing the wild salmon runs and spawning grounds to be reestablished.

While clean, unlimited energy significantly lowered the impact of humans on the environment, the world still was getting pretty crowded. The solution, of course, was space colonies, built with materials taken from the moon and asteroids and energy from the new fusion reactors. The initial space colonies were on Earth's moon, the moons of Jupiter, and in free space in the inner solar system. From there it was a relatively short step to launch some of the smaller space colonies off toward the closer stars.

By 2050, about one-tenth of the total population of 20 billion was living in space colonies. Currently (A.D. 2100), the total human population of 40 billion is split almost equally between Earth and extraterrestrial populations. The population of Earth is not expected to rise above about 20 billion, with almost all future growth coming in space-based populations. Since food production and manufacturing are mainly automated and powered by cheap fusion energy, only about one-tenth of the population actually needs to work for a living. Most are free to pursue whatever interests them. Often the biggest technological and social breakthroughs have come from this huge population of "leisure thinkers." People also have plenty of time to spend with family and friends, and the four-child family is the norm.

Mad Max: The Technological Skeptics Nightmare

The turning point came in 2012, when the world's oil production finally peaked and the long slide down started. The easy-to-get oil was simply exhausted, and prices started to rise rapidly. All the predictions about the rapidly rising price of oil causing new, cheaper alternatives to emerge just never came to pass. There were no cheaper alternatives – only more expensive ones. Oil was so important in the economy that the price of everything else was tied to it, and the alternatives just kept getting more expensive at the same rate. Solar energy continues to be the planet's major power source – through agriculture, fisheries, and forestry – but direct conversion using photo-voltaics never achieved the price/performance ratios to allow it to compete, even with coal.

Of course, it didn't really matter anyway because the greenhouse effect was kicking in, and the Earth's climate and ecological systems were in a shambles. Rising sea levels inundated most of the Netherlands, as well as big chunks of Bangladesh, Florida, Louisiana, and other low-lying coastal areas, by about 2050.

Once the financial markets figured out what was happening, the bubble really burst. During the stock market crash of 2016, the Dow Jones average dropped 87% in a little more than three days in December. Although there was a brief partial recovery, it has been downhill ever since.

Both the physical infrastructure and the social infrastructure have been gradually deteriorating, along with the natural environment. The human population has been on a long, downward spiral since the global *airbola* (airborne Ebola) virus epidemic killed almost a quarter of the human population in 2025-26. The population was already weakened by regional famines and wars over water and other natural resources, but the epidemic came as quite a shock. The world population peaked in 2020 at almost 10 billion. More than 2 billion died in the epidemic in the course of a year and a half. Since then, death rates have exceeded birth rates almost everywhere, and the current population of 4 billion is still decreasing by about 2% per year.

National governments have weakened, becoming mere symbolic relics. The world has been run for sometime by transnational corporations intent on cutthroat competition for the dwindling resources. The distribution of wealth has become more and more skewed. The dwindling few with marketable skills work for global corporations at good wages and lead comfortable and protected lives in highly fortified enclaves. These people devote their lives to their work, often working 90- or 100-hour weeks and taking no vacation at all.

The rest of the population survives in abandoned buildings or makeshift shelters built from scraps. There is no school, little food, and a constant struggle just to survive. The majority of the world's population lives in conditions that would make the favellas of 20th century Rio seem luxurious. The almost constant social upheavals and revolutions are put down with brutal efficiency by the corporate security forces (governments are too broke to maintain armies anymore).

Big Governmant: Public Interest Trumps Private Enterprise

The turning point came in 2012, when the corporate charter of General Motors was revoked by the U.S. federal government for failing to pursue the public interest. Even though GM had perfected the electric car, it had failed to make its breakthrough battery technology available to other car makers, even on a licensing basis. It preferred, instead, to retain a monopoly on electric cars, to produce them exclusively in China with cheap labor, and to gouge the public with high prices for them. After a series of negotiations broke down, government lawyers decided to invoke their almost forgotten power to revoke a corporation's charter and made the technology public property. This caused such a panic through corporate America that a complete rethinking of the corporate/public relationship took place, which left the government and the public with much more control over corporate behavior.

Strict government regulations had kept the development of fusion energy slow while safety issues were being fully explored. No one wanted a repeat of fission energy's problems: the Three Mile Island and Chernobyl accidents were nothing compared to the meltdown of one of France's fission breeder reactors in 2005, which left almost one-quarter of the French countryside uninhabitable, killing more than 100,000 people directly and causing untold premature cancer deaths throughout Europe.

Fusion energy therefore got a long and careful look. Government regulators also required the new fusion power plants to bear the full financial liability, causing a much more careful (albeit slightly slower) development of the industry.

High taxes on fossil energy counter-acted the greenhouse effect and stimulated renewable energy technologies. Global carbon-dioxide emissions were brought down to 1990 levels by 2005 and kept there through 2030 with concerted government effort and high taxes. Later, the new fusion reactors, along with new, cheaper photo-voltaics, gradually eliminated the need for fossil fuels, and the worst of the predicted climate change effects were thus averted.

Government population policies that emphasized female education, universal access to contraception, and family planning managed to stabilize the global human population at around 8 billion, where it remained (give or take a few hundred million) for almost the entire 21st century.

A stable population allowed many recalcitrant distributional issues to finally be resolved, and income distribution has become much more equitable worldwide. While in 1992, the richest fifth of the world's population received about 83% of the world's income and the poorest fifth received only a little more than 1%, by 2092, the richest fifth received 30%, and the poorest 10%. The income distribution "champagne glass" had become a much more stable and equitable "tumbler." Some libertarians have decried this situation, arguing that it does not provide enough incentive for risk-taking entrepreneurs to stimulate growth. But governments have explicitly advocated slow or no-growth policies, preferring to concentrate instead on assuring ecological sustainability and more equitable distribution of wealth.

Stable human population also took much of the pressure off other species. The total number of species on Earth declined during the 20th century from about 3 million to a low of about 2.2 million in 2010. But that number has stabilized and even recovered somewhat in the twenty- 21st century, as some species previously thought to be extinct were rediscovered and some natural speciation of fast-growing organisms had occurred. The current estimate of the number of species on Earth is about 2.5 million, and there are strict regulations in effect world-wide not only to prevent any further loss, but also to encourage natural speciation.

Ecotopia: The Low-Consumotion Sustainable Vision

The turning point came in 2012, when ecological tax reform was enacted almost simultaneously in the United States, the European Union, Japan, and Australia after long global discussions and debates, mostly over the Internet. In the same year, Herman Daly won the Nobel Prize for Human Stewardship (formerly the prize for economics) for his work on sustainable development.

A broadly participatory global dialogue had allowed an alternative vision of a sustainable world to emerge and gain very wide popular support. People finally realized that governments had to take the initiative back from transnational corporations and redefine the basic rules of the game if their carefully constructed vision was ever going to come to pass.

The public had formed a powerful judgment against the consumer lifestyle and for a sustainable lifestyle. The slogan for the new revolution became the now famous "sustainability, equity, efficiency."

All depletion of natural capital was taxed at the best estimate of the full social cost of that depletion, and taxes on labor and income were reduced for middle-income and lower-income people. A "negative income tax," or basic life support, was provided for those below the poverty level. Countries without eco-taxes were punished with ecological tariffs on goods they produced.

The QLI (Quality of Life Index) came to replace the GNP as the primary measure of national performance. The reforms were introduced gradually during the period from roughly 2012 to 2022 in the United States, the European Union, Japan, and Australia, giving businesses ample time to adjust. The rest of the world followed soon thereafter, with almost all countries completing the reforms by 2050. They had far-reaching effects.

Fossil fuels became much more expensive, both limiting travel and trans-port of goods and encouraging the use of renewable alternative energies. Mass transit, bicycles, and sharing the occasional need for a car became the norm. Human habitation came to be structured around small villages of roughly 200 people, whether these were in the countryside or inside urban concentrations. The village provided most of the necessities of life, including schools, clinics, and shopping, all within easy walking distance. It also allowed for a real sense of "community" missing from late-20th-century urban life. Such changes drasti-cally reduced the GNP of most countries, but drastically increased the QLI.

Because of the reduction in consumption and waste, there was only moder-ate need for paid labor and money income. By 2050, the work week had short-ened in most countries to 20 hours or fewer, and most full-time jobs became shared by two or three workers. People could devote much more of their time to leisure, but rather than consumption-oriented vacations taken far from home, they began to pursue more community activities (such as participatory music and sports) and public service (such as caring for children and the elder-ly).

Unemployment became an almost obsolete term, as did the distinction between work and leisure. People were able to do things they really liked much more of the time, and their quality of life soared (even as their money income plummeted). The distribution of income became an almost unnecessary statis-tic, since income was not equated with welfare or power and the quality of almost everyone's life was relatively high.

While physical travel decreased, people began to communicate electronical-ly over a much wider web. The truly global community could be maintained without the use of resource-consuming physical travel.

Judging the Four Visions

How should society decide among these four visions? A two-step process starts with forming and expressing values with the goal of finding a rational pol-icy for managing human activities. Social discourse and consensus is built around the broad goals and visions of the future and the nature of the world in which we live. When a consensus is formed, institutions and analytical methods are marshaled to help achieve the vision.

Three of the four visions are sustainable in the sense that they represent a continuation of the current society (only "Mad Max" is not), but we need to take a closer look at their underlying world views and critical assumptions, and the potential costs of those assumptions being wrong have already set up the four visions with this in mind. The worldview (and attendant policies) of the "Star Trek" vision is technological optimism and free competition, and its essential underlying assumption is unlimited resources, particularly cheap energy. If that assumption is wrong, the cost of pursuing this world view and its policies is something like the "Mad Max" vision. Likewise, the world view (and attendant policies) of the "Ecotopia" vision is technological skepticism and communitarianism (the community comes first), and its essential underlying assumptions are that resources are limited and that cooperation pays. If the assumption that resources are limited is wrong, the cost of pursuing this world view and its policies is the "Big Government" vision, where a "community first" policy slows down growth relative to the free market, "Star Trek" vision.

The next step toward coming to public judgment is to discuss the four visions with a broad range of participants and then have them evaluate each vision in terms of its overall desirability. Most of those I have already surveyed found the "Ecotopia" vision "very positive;" few expressed a negative reaction to such a world. "Star Trek" was the next most positive vision.

Questioning Technology

After discussing and evaluating these scenarios, we can choose between the two world views (technological optimism or skepticism) and their attendant policies, but we face pure and irreducible uncertainty. Who knows whether practical fusion or something equivalent will be invented? Should we choose the "Star Trek" vision (and the optimist policies) merely because it is the most popular or because it is the direction things seem to be heading in already?

From the perspective of game theory, this problem has a fairly clear answer; the game can only be played once, and the relative probabilities of each outcome are completely unknown. In addition, we can assume that society as a whole should be averse to risk in this situation.

For the optimistic policy set, "Mad Max" would be considered the worst case. For the skeptical policy set, "Big Government" would be the worst case. If "Big Government" is viewed as more positive (or less negative) than "Mad Max," then it would make sense to choose the skeptic's policy set, at least until more information is available.

In fact, the way I have set up the game, "Mad Max" is the one really negative outcome and the one really unsustainable outcome. We should develop policies that assure us of not ending up in "Mad Max," no matter what happens.

One also could argue that the probabilities of each state of the world in the scenario matrix are not completely unknown. If the prospects for cheap, unlimited, non-polluting energy were, in fact, known to be good, then the choices would have to be weighted with those probabilities.

But the complete dependence of the "Star Trek" vision on discovering a cheap, unlimited, non-polluting energy source argues for discounting the probability of its occurrence. By adopting the skeptic's policies, the possibility of this invention is preserved, but we don't have to be so utterly dependent on it.

It's like leaping off the Empire State Building and hoping to invent a parachute before you hit the ground. It's better to wait until you have the parachute (and have tested it extensively) before you jump.

FOUR VISIONS OF THE YEAR 2100

SCENARIO MATRIX		THE REAL STATE OF THE WORLD	
		Optimists Are Right: Resources are unlimited	**Skeptics Are Right:** Resources are limited.
WORLD VIEW AND POLICES	**Technological Optimism:** Resources are unlimited. Technical progress can deal with any challenge. Competition promotes progress: markets are the guiding principle	**STAR TREK** Fusion energy becomes practical solving many economic and environmental problems. Humans journey to the inner solar system, where population continues to expand.	**MAD MAX** Oil production declines and no affordable alternative emerges. Financial markets collapse and governments weaken, too broke to maintain armies and control desperate, impoverished population. The world is run by transnational corporations.
	Technological Skepticism: Resources are limited. Progress should depend less on technology and more on social and community development. Cooperation promotes progress. Markets are the servants of larger goals.	**BIG GOVERNMENT** Governments sanction companies that fail to pursue public interests. Fusion energy is slow to develop due to strict safety standards. Family-planning programs stabilize growth, and incomes equalize.	**ECOTOPIA** Tax reforms favor ecologically beneficent industries and punish polluters and resource depleters. Habitation patterns reduce need for transportation and energy. A shift away from consumerism reduces waste.

Star Trek and Stare Decisis:
LEGAL REASONING AND INFORMATION TECHNOLOGY

BRADLEY STEWART CHILTON, PHD, JD, M.L.S.

We are not far from a legal information parallel universe that once only the likes of Asimov and *Star Trek* writers could envision.[1]

CALR [computer assisted legal research] can impede the understanding of the legal process, which is reinforced by printed sources. Printed sources are designed in such a systematic and interconnected way that by using them the legal researcher not only will arrive at an answer to the issue being researched, but in doing so will reinforce his or her understanding of the legal process. To the extent that CALR allows the researcher to deviate from the system imposed by printed sources, some knowledge of the legal process itself may be sacrificed.[2]

Criminal justice practitioners are increasingly bombarded with new information technologies. From the Internet superhighway to computerized legal databases, information technologies grow and demand increasing time and money, not only of judges and lawyers in criminal courts, but also of police, corrections, and juvenile personnel in wide-ranging roles.[3] Compounding information overload are the uncertainties and criticisms of legal method, interpretation and impartiality in the use of the legal method. Like my previously published work,[4] this manuscript focuses on the confluence of emerging problems of information technology and legal reasoning. It uses the 1967 episode of *Star Trek* titled "Court Martial" as a launching pad to explore these issues as part of a growing literature on futuristics in criminal justice[5] and on *Star Trek's* general legal values[6] and social meaning.[7] This short manuscript overviews the history of the development of professional legal literature and the influence of three factors in the rise of the doctrine of *stare decisis*: (1) the invention of the printing press; (2) the development of court hierarchy by the 19th century; and (3) the efforts of entrepreneurial printers and publishers. The manuscript concludes that the rise of *stare decisis* was not simply due to the legal factors of court structure and hierarchy, but also because of the extra-legal influence of the printing press and the efforts of individual printers and publishers. The implication of this synergism is applied to contemporary developments of computer assisted legal research for criminal justice practitioners.

Star Trek

"Court Martial," Stardate 2947.3, episode 15 of the original 1967 *Star Trek* series, features the court-martial trial of Captain James Kirk of the *U.S.S. Enterprise* for negligent homicide. During an unscheduled layover at Starbase 11 for repairs to the *U.S.S. Enterprise* from ion storm damage, Captain Kirk is accused of the negligent homicide of Ben Finney. Finney had been taking readings of the ion storm from a pod attached to the *U.S.S. Enterprise* when Captain Kirk ordered it jettisoned to escape the storm. The computer records of the *Enterprise* indicate that Kirk negligently failed to follow standard procedures and notify Finney before jettisoning the pod. Kirk, who becomes the first starship captain to stand trial for a criminal homicide in the line of duty, is totally exonerated of all charges when it is revealed that Finney had tampered with the *Enterprise*'s computer records. In fact, Finney remained alive and was discovered aboard the *Enterprise*. After a dramatic fight with Kirk, Finney confessed to altering the computer records. In their Starfleet Academy days, Finney was an instructor and befriended midshipman-student Kirk (about Stardate 2086) and became so close that Ben named his daughter, Jamie, after Kirk. But aboard the *U.S.S. Republic, NCC-1371* (also about Stardate 2086), Kirk reported an error by Finney that may have caused Ben to be passed over for promotion and insanely blame Kirk for never attaining command of a starship. The story concluded with Jamie apologizing for her emotional outbursts against Kirk and helping her father off to his rehabilitation.[8]

The *Star Trek* writers of "Court Martial" (Don M. Mankiewicz and Stephen W. Carabatsos) also presented their vision of future legal information technology. Both Areel Shaw, the prosecutor, and Samuel T. Cogley, Kirk's defense lawyer, were placed in scenes demonstrating extraordinary legal databases and accessing a wide range of legal codes, cases and materials from several galaxies and over three millennia. And beyond the obvious falsification of the *Enterprise*'s computer records by Finney, these scenes dramatize uncertainty and criticisms of the legal method and interpretation in the use of computer assisted legal research. Defense lawyer Cogley, for example, is portrayed as a charming eccentric who still insists on using antiquated books in his legal method. He insists that the internal, historical narrative of law is found only in books, even dull old law books, and is lost in the sterile world of the computer. The computer legal database has none of the dog-eared pages, hand-scribbled notes and bookmarks, and well-thumbed versus untouched pages to cue the reader. And so he insists on stacks and stacks of books, even in the courtroom.[9]

Stare Decsis

Perhaps the most distinctive aspect of Anglo-American Common Law is the doctrine of *stare decisis*. According to the simple definition in *Black's Law Dictionary*, *stare decisis* is the:

> doctrine that, when court has once laid
> down a principle of law as applicable to a
> certain state of facts, it will adhere to that
> principle, and apply it to all future cases,
> where facts are substantially the same.[10]

Of course, this definition presents too simplistic a conception of *stare decisis*, which is in reality a complex endeavor, not the simple application of principles. This manuscript seeks to develop this more complex understanding of *stare decisis* in the following two sections.

For at least 100 years, Anglo-American courts have spoken of *stare decisis*, either in the "strict" or "latitudinarian" form,[11] and applied its precepts in the resolution of legal disputes. Various scholars of legal history allege the doctrine of *stare decisis* was brought into being by the influence of: (1) the invention of the printing press; (2) the development of court hierarchy by the 19th century; and (3) the efforts of entrepreneurial printers and publishers. Sir William Holdsworth, in his multi-volume treatise on the history of English law, claimed the invention and application of the printing press influenced the rise of *stare decisis*, arguing "it could be attributed to the fact that reports of judicial opinions were by that time not only officially reported in writing, but printed and published."[12] Others have repeated the claim that the technology of the printing press may have influenced the rise of *stare decisis*.[13] Traditional legal scholars have argued that the rise of *stare decisis* was due to the hierarchy of courts that emerged in the early 19th century.[14] Still others attribute the rise of *stare decisis* to the efforts of individual entrepreneurs in the printing and publishing world who stood to make profits from the requirements of large book purchases by lawyers across the country.[15]

English Legal Literature: 1066-1800

The professional legal literature of English Common Law had its origins in the conquest of England in 1066 A.D. by William the Conqueror. After his victory at the Battle of Hastings (1066) and the death of King Harold, William attempted to take the "treasure" of his conquered domain. For the collection of taxes, he spent most of his remaining life in a survey of property ownership in England called the *Domesday Book*, assembled in 1086. As the first official record of England, William did not impose a new set of statutes or code on the conquered peoples, as did the Romans and other European conquerors. Instead, laws were found in the common customs and traditions of the peoples in the small "shires" or villages of England.[16] Hence, the name "common law."

In spite of this departure from Roman civil code traditions, the early English legal literature was modeled after the Roman civil code legal encyclopedias, such as _Justinian's Institutes_. The earliest of the English legal treatises focused on property law, such as _Laws of Edward the Confessor_ (anonymous, 1118), and _Glanvill_ (justiciar Ranulf de Glanvill, 1187). These early works simply compiled legal documents (deeds, etc.) with commentary in Latin. A much larger treatise was written in the 1220-30s, attributed to Henry de Bracton (d. 1268). Bracton attempted to meld the two legal traditions together in this work, organizing in Roman encyclopedic fashion the many individual case decisions on the common law. But he only once referred to a specific case. Bracton's work was widely distributed in the 13th and 14th centuries, but its influence didn't last because it was written too early; the common law grew greatly in the centuries after.[17]

The common law was always in some sense "case law." Thus, it is no surprise that some of the earliest legal literature to appear in England were manuscript records of cases. Until about 1300, only the formal Latin phrases that service as the title of an action of law were recorded in the "plea rolls," a sort of court record. However, lawyers and their apprentices soon began taking notes of interesting judicial arguments in cases. As early as the 1280s there appeared specifically dated reports of legal arguments, usually in law French, attributed to named judges and lawyers in the English courts. By the 1300s, there was a regular chronological series of these summaries. As they were written anonymously, they were given the generic name "yearbooks," probably produced by apprentice-students who listened to the court proceedings and took notes.[18] These early yearbooks were produced by some sort of collective effort from 1300 to about 1550, informally and anonymously written in manuscripts, and often omitting details such as the names of the parties.[19]

With the advent of the printing press in England came the publication of the hand-written yearbooks found in London law libraries. The first printed law book, however, was a textbook titled _Littleton's Tenures_, printed starting 1481 and popular until the 1800s. As one scholar has observed, "within ten years of the introduction of printing into England in the 1470s, the London printers had found a market in the legal profession."[20] The last hand-written yearbook was dated in 1535 and called the _Michaelmas Term 27 Henry VIII_. By 1558, a complete set of yearbooks had been printed.

The rise of printed yearbooks correlated with the increased number of references to prior cases (or precedent) in judicial decision making. In summary of older legal historians, Robert Ruppin observed, "Jenks speaks of 'books of precedents which so rapidly appeared after the introduction of printing.' Published judicial decisions did undoubtedly influence the decisions of judges."[21] This correlation causes some scholars to conclude the advent of the printing press was the _first cause_ of the doctrine of _stare decisis_ in the use of precedent. However, other scholars point out the printing press was also in use on the continent, but no doctrine of _stare decisis_ or use of precedent was found in continental courts.[22] In fact, until the 20th century, the use of precedent in continental law was considered prejudice and unethical judicial conduct.[23] It would be a reckless generalization to argue the advent of the printing press alone caused the rise of the doctrine of *stare decisis*. However, there is no doubt that it was an important cause among others.

The rise of printed law books brought an extensive new source of business to printers. Scholars note that as the sale of printed yearbooks climbed, the attendance of apprentice lawyers at required court hearings and "moots" (simulations) declined. In fact, by the mid-1700s, attendance by apprentices *and their supervising trainers (attorneys)* was nil! And in spite of significant fines for nonattendance! Scholars speculate attendance waned as it became possible to cheaply acquire a printed book rather than write it all out manually.[24] Indeed, until the rise of university training in law in the 1700s, the apprenticeship lost its oral component and had become a matter of "reading the law," a phrase used to this day to describe legal education during this period. The effect of printed legal materials on legal education warrants even more commentary, but we must leave the history of legal research education for some other day and manuscript.

The demise of this oral transmission of information and the increased reliance on printed books appears to have synergized the development of a class of court reporters, printers, and booksellers to meet these needs. The modern case reports that were published after the 16th century incorporate the efforts of this service industry. Court reporters were sent to important courts to take down, word-for-word, what judges said in decisions. Printers worked closely with booksellers who were sensitive to the needs of lawyers and the law book market. Summaries were inserted by publishers for each case to meet the demand for speedy searching. Publishers also developed separate books, the "abridged" or indexed, the cases and their summaries for even faster searching. And they developed other treatises to assist the lawyer in learning or practicing the law.

American Legal Literature: 1750-Present

Erwin Surrency recounted the rise of similar changes in law book publishing in America from colonial times through the 1970s. He notes the close cooperation and responsiveness of the industry of law book publishing to the bar. For example, when lawyers complained there were too many cases being published, the printers responded with the beginnings of "case notes" or short outline summaries of the case (now standard).[25] Eventually, law book publishers developed complex indexing systems for retrieval, such as the "key number" system of West Publishing Company.[26] But Surrency neglects the obvious influence this change of information processing must have had on the bar. The staff at these publishing houses had taken on more and more of the tasks once reserved for the bar. And they had come to interpret, define, categorize, and index these cases! The bar had delegated these functions to the publishers to save money, but also placed in the hands of others the power of control over the legal information process.

Jenni Parrish develops more fully a thesis on the influence of early American law book printers and publishers in the development of common law in the U.S.[27] Early American lawyers had a surprisingly large number of law books. This great output of publishing was due to the prodigious efforts of individual printers and publishers who armed all of America with law books. Indeed, most early American lawyers learned their trade by "reading the law," from law books borrowed from a cooperative, practicing lawyer. Most popular among lawyers and laymen alike were *Blackstone's Commentaries*, first published in America by Robert Bell in 1771-72.[28]

Contemporary printer/publishers that dominate today's market arose in the 1870s. West Publishing Company was founded in 1879 with the promise to systematize legal information retrieval. By 1890, West had an extensive series of case reporters covering all sections of America, with extensive indexes to locate each legal issue in each case by its "key number." Other contemporary law book publishers include Commerce Clearing House (CCH), Bureau of National Affairs, and Lawyer's Co-operative. These publishers compete with one another, but essentially control all but a few official state and U.S. government printings of law books.

This perspective on the rise of *stare decisis* strongly implies the market demands for profit among law book printers and publishers led to the development of the doctrine of *stare decisis* by the 19th century. As lawyers and judges were required to follow prior cases under *stare decisis*, no longer to merely take the precedent under advisement, the bookseller stood to sell a great many more books. While compelling in its argument, this perspective lacks the empirical evidence of actual bookmakers, printers, sellers, etc. stating this intention in so many words. If it was the intent of booksellers to drive the lawyers to *stare decisis* to sell more books, wouldn't someone have said this at some time? A search of the literature reveals that no printer, publisher, bookseller, etc. is so quoted.

The traditional explanation given by lawyers to explain the rise of *stare decisis* in the 19th century (from its origins in use of precedent) is in court hierarchy. Frederick G. Kempin, Jr., argued that *stare decisis* was given birth in early 19th century America after the constitutionally dictated hierarchy of courts had settled in.[29] According to this interpretation, *stare decisis* arose only

after
the United States Supreme Court had convinced lower federal and state courts
that it was indeed the "Supreme Court of the land." After the Supreme Court
had established its power and legitimacy in the early 19th century, other courts
recognized this by strictly following the case decisions of the Supreme Court.
This hierarchy of authority flowed downward in pyramid fashion to lower
courts and maintained a classical bureaucratic information flow (in a Weberian
sense). Thus, it is argued, the bureaucratization of courts in hierarchy of
authority caused the development of the doctrine of *stare decisis*.[30]

Of course, the hierarchy of court structure in the 19th century made possible the enforcement of *stare decisis*. But so, too, did the advent of the printing
press and the efforts of individual printers and publishers. While the hierarchy
of courts may be said to be a most important factor in the development of *stare
decisis*, it is not the only causal factor. Indeed, the bureaucratization of courts in
a hierarchy of authority may be considered simply one link in a chain of events
from the advent of the printing press and commercialization of law book publishing that *synergistically* led to the development of the doctrine of *stare decisis*.

The Implications For Computers in Law

Computers came to the legal profession in the 1970s as devices for word
processing and data storage. However, since 1975, on-line data service for the
retrieval of entire legal documents, such as cases, has been available. On-line
computer retrieval systems were developed in the 1960s from experiments by
the Ohio Bar Foundation to produce Ohio Bar Automated Retrieval (OBAR),
later purchased by Mead Data Corporation. Mead developed and released
Lexis in 1972, making it on-line in 1975. Westlaw followed with a 1973 release
and was soon on-line, too. Westlaw and Lexis are now standard in most law
firms and law libraries, although Westlaw has come to dominate through its
market takeovers and introduction of "natural language" search engines in
1992.[31]

The printing and computer "revolutions" in legal literature are similar in
some respects.[32] First, both involve the incremental adaptation of existing, yet
unrelated, technologies by brilliant invention to solve problems of the transformation and retrieval of information. Just as Gutenberg used the metallurgist's
punch in rows under a wine press with a screw to "press" paper on the inked
rows of assembled works, so, too, was the computer born out of the inventive
application of the binary code from bi-plane machine guns and the jacquard
loom. Second, both were aesthetically imitative, designed to create products
that emulated existing information technology packages (the hand-written manuscript, or today, the printed book). Third, both were invented for a technologically more efficient answer to the problems of information control. Finally, in

their impact on society, both have <u>decentralized</u> the control of information transformation and retrieval.[33]

However, at a most basic level, the current approaches to computerized legal databases fail because of their high costs, ineffective "natural language systems" search engines, and lack of ergonomics and psychological fit. This critique is not simply the expression of computer technophobia or a romantic fondness for the printed word; it is a critique disciplined by the observations of technological success in imitation and efficiency. Legal databases are enormously expensive for criminal justice practitioners, not just in initial and monthly fees, but also with each new generation of hardware and software necessary to keep current.[34] The much-touted "natural word systems," such as those announced in 1992 by Westlaw,[35] are dismal failures in tests of their search capabilities.[36] And no current legal databases work like the "Superbook" developed by Bellcore, incorporating extensive ergonomic and psychological testing of users to more successfully imitate the hand-held book (although Microsoft Corporation's new generation of "notebooks" comes closer).[37] Thus, at this time, computer-assisted legal research is severely limited by the inability of the technology to adequately <u>imitate</u> the ergonomics of the printed book.

At a social level, the current approaches to computerized legal databases fail because of problems of access, authority, and the superficial legal method that often results. The impact of the high cost of legal databases includes a host of access problems for underfunded legal services and criminal justice agencies, particularly those dealing with the poor.[38] Further, as James Acker and Richard Irving suggested in the opening quote, legal authority and process is blurred by the lack of context and multiple sources of legal information.[39] And the sheer volume of law accessed by computer databases results in certain information overload and greater reliance on head notes, summaries, and other superficial and low-quality understanding of these codes, precedents and arguments.[40] Thus, at this time, computer-assisted legal research is severely limited by the inability of the technology to provide <u>efficiency</u> of access, authority, and information control when compared to the printed book.

At a phenomenological level, the current approaches to computerized legal databases fail for the reasons prophesied by Gene Roddenberry's eccentric *Star Trek* defense lawyer Samuel T. Cogley; the internal, historical narrative of law is found only in books, even dull old law books, and is lost in the sterile world of the computer that has no dog-eared pages, hand-scribbled notes and bookmarks, and well-thumbed versus untouched pages. The legal method is highly interpretive and extends beyond rule-based models of legal reasoning.[41] Legal information is interpreted according to socioeconomic,[42] gendered,[43] and aesthetically determined[44] phenomenological judgments.

Further, current legal information-retrieval systems are syntactic, or based on the structure of key words (even "natural language systems"). But lawyers think of legal concepts semantically, focused on the meaning of synonymous words or phrases. Access to information in Westlaw and Lexis cannot be found by semantic searching for concepts; only the correct key word will locate the case in point. Further, the current computer-retrieval technology will not allow the random access or systematic browsing traditionally employed by lawyers. Through systematic browsing, lawyers come up with analogies of law that can be used in cases with unrelated facts.[45] Finally, current legal information retrieval systems assume legal reasoning to be rule-driven logic, that lawyers simply find the appropriate legal prescription and apply it to the case for the single correct answer. But lawyers since the time of Cicero have acknowledged that the same rule has different meanings depending on one's concept of "justice." And justice is not rule-driven, but appears to be a somewhat emotional state of mind as to what is appropriate or "fair" in a given case. Thus, at this time, computer-assisted legal research is severely limited by the lack of <u>decentralization</u> of interpretation of information when compared to the printed book.

Conclusion

The information age has brought to criminal justice practitioners the problems of information overload compounded with the uncertainties and criticisms of legal method in the use of new information technologies. The 1967 episode of *Star Trek* titled "Court Martial" suggests, through science-fiction, that this dilemma may continue into the far future with the shortcomings of computer information technology. Thus, this manuscript discusses the implications of computer information technology for the legal method and the structure of a core doctrine of legal reasoning: *stare decisis*. First, based on an examination of the rise of the doctrine of *stare decisis* during the advent of the printing press, the paper concludes that the rise of *stare decisis* was not simply due to the legal factors of court structure and hierarchy, but also because of the extra-legal influence of the printing press and the efforts of individual printers and publishers. Second, the implication of this synergism leading to the rise of the doctrine of *stare decisis* is applied to an analysis of the contemporary information technology of computer assisted legal research for criminal justice practitioners. While the printing and computer "revolutions" in legal research are similar in some respects, the currently available computer information technology fails at a basic/ergonomic/psychological level, at a social level, and at a phenomenological level. Perhaps, in the end, we are left with the argument of the eccentric *Star Trek* defense lawyer in "Court Martial," Samuel T. Cogley, who argued against computer-assisted legal research and for books, saying:

"Do you want to know the law – the ancient concepts in their own language? Learn the intent of the men who wrote them? From Moses to the Tribunal of Alpha Three? Books!"

Endnotes

1. Donald J. Dunn, "Why Legal Research Skills Declines, or When Two Rights Make a Wrong," *Law Library Journal* 85 (1993): 49-61, at 60.

2. James R. Acker and Richard Irving, *Basic Legal Research for Criminal Justice and the Social Sciences* (Gaithersburg, MD: Aspen Publishers, 1998), 5.

3. Ibid., vii-viii.

4. Bradley S. Chilton, "Cliobernetics, Christianity, and the Common Law," *Law Library Journal* 83 (Spring 1991): 355-362.

5. E.g., John Klofas and Stan Stojkovic, eds., *Crime and Justice in the Year 2010* (Belmont, CA: Wadsworth Publishing, 1995).

6. Paul Joseph and Sharon Carton, "The Law of the Federation: Images of Law, Lawyers, and the Legal System In *Star Trek: The Next Generation*," *University of Toledo Law Review* 24 (Fall 1992): 43-85; Michael P. Scharf and Lawrence D. Roberts, "The Interstellar Relations of the Federation: International Law and *Star Trek: The Next Generation*," *University of Toledo Law Review* 25 (Spring 1994): 577-615.

7. Jeff Greenwald, *Future Perfect: How Star Trek Conquered Planet Earth* (New York: Viking Books, 1998). *See also*, www.startrek.com, the official Internet Web site of *Star Trek*, Trekkies, and other related information.

8. Star Trek. "Court Martial," episode 15 [videorecording, 51 minutes] (Hollywood, CA: Paramount Home Video, 1985 (1967 original). *See also*, Michael Okuda and Denise Okuda, *Star Trek Chronology: The History of the Future* (New York: Pocket Books, 1993).

9. Ibid.

10. *Black's Law Dictionary*, revised 4th ed., s.v. "stare decisis" (St. Paul, Minn.: West Publishing, 1968), 1577.

11. E.M. Wise, "The Doctrine of Stare Decisis," *Wayne Law Review* 21 (July 1975): 1043-60.

12. Sir William Holdsworth, *A History of English Law*, 2nd ed., Volume 9 (London: Sweet & Maxwell, 1937), 331.

13. E.g., David Mellinkoff, *The Language of the Law* (Boston: Little, Brown, 1963), 138-41.

14. John P. Dawson, *The Oracles of Law* (Greenwood, Conn.: Greenwood Press, 1968); Frederick G. Kempin, Jr., "Precedent and Stare Decisis: The Critical Years, 1800 to 1850," *American Journal of Legal History* 3 (January 1959): 28-54; E.M. Wise, *supra*, note 11.

15. E.g., Jenni Parrish, "Law Books and Legal Publishing in America, 1760-1840," *Law Library Journal* 72 (Summer 1979): 355-452; Thomas J. Young Jr., "A Look at American Law Reporting in the 19th Century," *Law Library Journal* 68 (1975): 294-306.

16. Theodore F.T. Plucknett, *A Concise History of the Common Law*, 5th ed. (Boston: Little, Brown, 1956), 11-14.

17. J.H. Baker, *An Introduction to English Legal History*, 2nd ed. (London: Butterworth's, 1979), 161-2, 171.

18. Edith G. Henderson, "Legal Literature and the Impact of Printing on the English Legal Profession," *Law Library Journal* 68 (1975): 288-93.

19. Ibid.

20. Baker, *supra* note 17, at 154.

21. Robert Ruppin, "The Legend of Stare Decisis," *The Alabama Lawyer* 41 (October 1980): 610-14, 602.

22. Dawson, *supra* note 14.

23. E.M. Wise, *supra* note 11.

24. Henderson, *supra* note 18.

25. Erwin C. Surrency, "Law Reports in the United States," *American Journal of Legal History* 25 (January 1981): 48-66, 62.

26. The key number system was the inspiration for numerous other indexing schemes that have appeared since for other professions and literatures.

27. Jenni Parrish, *supra* note 15.

> *See also,* Warren M. Billings, "Justice, Books, Laws, and Courts In Seventeenth Century Virginia," *Law Library Journal* 85 (Spring 1993): 277-296.

28. Kempin, *supra* note 14.

29. Ibid.

30. Ralph Allan, "Computerized Legal Research Pioneer: Mead Data Central and the LEXIS Service," *Law Librarian* 24 (September 1993): 131-133; Robert Berring, "On Not Throwing Out the Baby: Planning the Future of Legal Information," *California Law Review* 83 (March 1995): 615-635; William G. Harrington, "A Brief History of Computer-Assisted Legal Research," *Law Library Journal* 77 (1985): 543-56.

31. Nazareth A.M. Pantaloni, "Legal Databases, Legal Epistemology, and the Legal Order," *Law Library Journal* 86 (1994): 679-706. [Winner: 1994 AALL Call for Papers]

32. E.g., J. David Bolter, *Turing's Man: Western Culture In the Computer Age* (Chapel Hill: University of North Carolina Press, 1984); Svend Dahl, *History of the Book* (New York: Scarecrow Press, 1958).

33. E.g., Thomas K. Landauer, *The Trouble With Computers: Usefulness, Usability and Productivity* (Cambridge, MA: M.I.T. Press, 1995), 116-118.

34. E.g., M. Ethan Katsh, "Law In a Digital World: Computer Networks and Cyberspace," *Villanova Law Review* 38 (April 1993): 408-485; M. Ethan Katsh, "Digital Lawyers: Orienting the Legal Profession to Cyberspace," *University of Pittsburgh Law Review* 55 (Summer 1994): 1141-1175.

35. See, Landauer, *supra* note 34, at 215, 217.

36. Ibid., 247.

37. E.g., Robert Berring, "Chaos, Cyberspace, and Tradition: Legal Information Transmogrified," *Berkeley Technology Law Journal* 12 (Spring 1997): 189-212; Jean Stefancic and Richard Delgado, "Outsider Jurisprudence and the Electronic Revolution: Will Technology Help or Hinder the Cause of Legal Reform?" *Ohio State Law Journal* 52 (June 1991): 847-858.

38. E.g., Acker and Irving, *supra* note 2, at 5; Berring, *supra* note 38.

39. E.g., Sven Birkerts, *The Gutenberg Elegies: The Fate of Reading In an Electronic Age* (Boston: Faber and Faber, 1994), 159-160; Sven Birkerts, ed., *Tolstoy's Dictaphone: Technology and the Muse* (St. Paul, MN: Graywolf Press, 1996).

40. E.g., Lief Carter, *Reason In Law*, 5th edition (New York: Longman, 1998); Edward L. Rubin, "The Practice and Discourse of Legal Scholarship," *Michigan Law Review* 86 (August 1988): 1835-1905.

41. Susan Mann, "The Universe and the Library: A Critique of James Boyd White as Writer and Reader," *Stanford University Law Review* 41 (1989): 959.

42. Katharine T. Bartlett, "Feminist Legal Methods," *Harvard Law Review* 103 (February 1990): 829-888; Jill Anne Farmer, "A Poststructuralist Analysis of the Legal Research Process," *Law Library Journal* 85 (Spring 1993): 391-404. *But see,* Michael Duggan and David Isenbergh, "Poststructuralism And the Brave New World of Legal Research," *Law Library Journal* 86 (Fall 1994): 829-835 [response to Farmer].

43. E.g., Susan W. Brenner, "Of Publication and Precedent: An Inquiry Into the Ethnomethodology of Case Reporting In the American Legal System," *DePaul University Law Review* 39 (Spring 1990): 461-542; Richard Haigh, "What Shall I Wear to the Computer Revolution? Some Thoughts on Electronic Researching In Law," *Law Library Journal* 89 (Spring 1997): 245-264.

44. Philip Slayton, "Electronic Legal Retrieval: The Impact of Computer on a Profession," *Jurimetrics Journal* 14 (1973): 29-40.

Utopia vs. Dystopia:
THE QUANTUM MECHANICS OF STAR TREK

ROBERT H. CHAIRES, JD, PhD

Introduction

All the television recreations of *Star Trek* have had the same basic theme and the same basic characters. However, as the authors point out in previous chapters, the genius of *Star Trek* in its many reincarnations is that it has worked at so many levels. *Star Trek* at its worst is entertaining; *Star Trek* at its best can leave you with jaw dropped, stunned in wonder. Perhaps the key to *Star Trek* is that it can take the mundane and turn it into beauty and in the process inspire people to aspire to be better as human beings. It can trigger in people what could be called a *Quixote Complex*, a sometimes irrational desire to see things not as they are, but as they could be if we as humans were just a little better.

The question of seeing things not as they are but as they could be generates an intriguing way to examine *Star Trek* – a "what if," so to speak. We can look at this in two ways: *What if Star Trek*, individually or collectively, had never come into being and *What if* the existence of *Star Trek* has actually changed the future because it has changed the past and present? Considering that one question that quantum mechanics present concerns the effect of the observer on the observed, a question about the effect of observing *Star Trek* on the observer seems reasonable in light of the phenomena called *Star Trek.*

Simply put, the Federation of at least *The Next Generation*'s time presents a fairly utopian society. Physical wants have been largely banished via the vehicle of "replicators" and government prizes and protects individual autonomy and differences in a host of areas, not the least of which are sexuality and religion. Ergo, we can speculate that the collective effect of hundreds of millions of viewers watching *Star Trek* over decades has been to "sensitize" those hundreds of millions to the values of *Star Trek*. If *Star Trek* had never existed, then sensitivity in those "*Trek*" values might not exist in the breadth and depth they do today. This is not to say *Star Trek* is the only vehicle for learning tolerance and altruism. *Star Trek* does not have a monopoly on humanism, nor does it necessarily represent the "best possible future." Most of the issues confronted in

Star Trek are ones that have confounded humanity for millennia. It is just that never before have so many been exposed to thematic hope for so long.

Of course, one could argue that more millions have read the Christian Bible, the Koran, studied the Tao, sought comfort in the teachings of Buddha or Confucius, and that those enlightening pursuits have made little, if any, difference in the world. But how many have really read and studied these things? How many have just listened to another's interpretation or taken selected passages and used them to justify what they will? The Federation, more specifically Starfleet, does not allow these meanderings. There is physical comfort in the technology, but little easy comfort in the ethical requirements of living, and sometimes dying, as a member of Starfleet. As Barad (2000) continuously points out in *The Ethics of Star Trek*, the decisions and the choices made are remarkably consistent with much of the finest that had been written by philosophers of morality and ethics. In this vein, *Star Trek* is applied ethics for the human condition. And in this light, because it has been seen by those many for so long, it is not a stretch to imagine that many when confronted by hard decisions, hard choices, have thought, "What would Picard or Janeway or (choose your favorite) do?"

The point is the question of influence to date – and the ripples of that influence into the future. Is *Star Trek* a social mirror only representing current values in American society as some have suggested in their chapters, or is it in a quantum sense actually inspiring in some small or large way the aspiration for a more utopian society? Is it possible that *Star Trek* has already changed the future by generating a context for a series of "right" choices that extinguished a series of choices that would have led to a bleaker, more dystopian future? To examine these questions we will first look at some ideas about utopia and dystopia. From there, quantum theory and shaping the future will be explored.

Utopia vs. Dystopia

For many, if not most, an unreliable reality, past, present, or future is too chaotic if there is no commonality of goals, no linear thread to draw from that justifies the values of today and the hopes for tomorrow. Indeed, historians tend to be divided into two groups: traditionalists and critical. Traditional historians see history in a linear, progressive manner; for example, the history of education is one of gradual evolution toward an education for all children. Critical historians see another past, one in which "progressive" trends really operate to maintain a status quo of privilege for a few; thus, for example, "improvements" in education are really about producing a better work force, sharper tools for the manufacturing machine.

In the latter perspective, the inculcation of values is as important, if not more so, than the imparting of skills. An obedient workforce is maintained by generating an atmosphere in which the social and economic order is seen as natural. Part and parcel of making the social and economic order seem natural is to convince those who fail to achieve success in it that failure is their own fault; if you had just studied harder, if you had just worked harder, if you had just believed more fully in the values you were taught, you would have had more success. Of course, the other side of this is that the more you do succeed, the more likely it is you will believe in the rightness of the system. It is for this reason that commentators on education, such as Apple (1993), see schools as places in which curricula reflect indoctrination into believing one really had a choice about his place in society.

Of course, Apple's ideas have their limits – and their dark side. One limit is that individuals play small parts in overall historical trends. The dark side grows from this class-conflict perspective; reform just substitutes a "better" set of values to be inculcated. Real individual choice still plays a small part. But there is a direction here, a way of considering what is utopian and dystopian.

WHAT IS UTOPIA?

Star Trek represents a utopian future because it has met economic ideology with a simple answer; it does not attempt to divide a small pie in equal shares, but rather does away with the concept of one pie. All can have as much as they want. *Star Trek* also represents that once removed from economic need people will strive to better the condition of all. Unjealous of economic privilege and the social hierarchy it engenders, education becomes a vehicle for exploration of the self as much as the external; knowledge becomes an end within itself. One does not study to survive; one lives to study. And if some do not have any interest in studying or employment, well, it seems, while it is never mentioned, that in the *Star Trek* future there are no welfare parasites. People are so busy leading their own lives they have little interest in judging how others live theirs. At the very least, it appears that removing the economic cost from cost/benefit equations dramatically changes moral absolutes.

It is this ethical and moral dimension of living that seems to be the driving force in *Star Trek*. With rare exception, no one seems to care what anybody does in private. Indeed, it appears that invading the private life of another is a shocking idea, clearly a change from today. Further, there is integration among the economic, social, and political that serves to reinforce values in the *Star*

Trek future. **Table 1**, in a microcosm, displays that future directions, to utopia or dystopia, involve a series of societal choices about values and the political processes. Decisions that are dystopian tend to limit individual choice by constraining the environment in which choices are made.

Table 1: Values and Future Directions

FUTURE DIRECTIONS	UTOPIAN	DYSTOPIAN
VALUES	*Universal, free education to the highest level desired *Guarantees of food, shelter, and health care *Personal privacy is integral to a just society *Competitiveness as a means of self-improvement	*Pay as you go education *Formal and informal mechanisms that discriminate in educational access *No guarantees of food, shelter, and health care, market driven costs. *Personal privacy is a threat to public safety *Competitiveness as a means of producing winners and losers
POLITICAL PROCESSES	*Meaningful participation for all in making law and policy *Constant evaluation and revaluation of the status quo *Open system	*Participation in law and policy making based on privilege *Political process exists to maintain privilege *Closed system

To understand **Table 1**, consider the plight of the typical college student. They must make decisions about *where*, *when*, and *what*. Some of these choices and decisions already are directed by existing social policy and practice. For example, the decision to attend college often is constrained by birth. The best indicator of who goes to college is if one, or better both, parents graduated from college. Parental and peer values are also major variables. The choice of *where* is constrained by location and cost (the local community college or ...) and a more subtle and complex point of qualifications. Going to a top high school that prepares one for college as an expectation is often different from going to high school in some blighted, tax-starved, urban area. *When* is often determined by the sums of *where*. Similarly, *what* to study is too often the sum of all the *where*s and *when*s. The seven years or so to a doctorate and the enormous indebtedness incurred by many may be justified by a return of engaging in a high-paying (not a typical college professor) profession with substantial status. However, most cannot wait that long or see that far. Pressures of shelter, food, medical care and sometimes providing all of that for a family, create early 'outs.'

Few would argue that everyone should have a terminal doctorate. Indeed, few really want or need them. The point is individual choice. A utopian society fosters true choice; it removes as many of the environmental pressures that constrain *where*, *when*, and *what* as are reasonably possible. Further, a utopian society, in making decisions about what is reasonably possible, meaningfully engages as many as possible in making the policy decisions. Finally, a utopian society makes the "better" assumptions about human nature. Sure, removed of worry about basic necessities and provided virtually unlimited education, some might never leave school or do anything. But because the vast majority will use that education, no rules would be made to control the few who might restrain the choice of the many. A more enlightened societal self-interest view of this would be that if it takes a lifetime of study to produce one great thing – wait. Better to support a dozen never-weres than losing one would-have-been.

Besides the issues of fostering choice, **Table 1** displays one simple point about considering utopia; it is *not* a place in time or space. Rather, utopia is, like *Star Trek*, a way of doing the future. In *ST:TNG*'s "Justice," for example, the Edo are a healthy, beautiful, sensual race living in harmony amidst plenty. It is easy to overlook the minor subplot, the transporting and planting of a human colony and people who seek challenge, even hardship. It is doubtful the Edo and those colonists would get along for long, if at all.

Within this light, the idea of utopia as a way rather than an end should become clearer. To twist an old saying, "One person's utopia might be another's hell." Further, the sons and daughters, and their sons and daughters, or others if you choose, most probably will not have the same commitment to a particular vision of utopia. History is replete with groups that have separated themselves from the larger society to establish "the perfect" society. With rare exception, few last more than a couple generations, most no longer than a couple decades. Those that do survive a substantial length of time do so by adopting one of two techniques. The first is not allowing any contrary views; those who are different are banished from the community. The second is by changing, adapting and adopting while remaining true to fundamental values, integrating better ideas and throwing out those that do not work well.

The opening of a Pandora's Box of technology, especially communications technology, changed and continually changes many things. It is one thing to maintain the status quo in an agrarian world of illiterate peasants; it is quite another to do so in an industrialized world that requires literacy; and still another in a world of high technology that requires widespread advanced education. By the time even remote villages of illiterate farmers can see and hear the outside world, in their own language, with a satellite dish, the world, and the future, is irrevocably changed.

Once civilizations could exist for centuries. Great-grandparents and great-grandchildren, while they probably never knew each other given generally short life expectancies, would have the same ideas and lives, even lived in the same house. Today, while careers, another change, tend to disperse families widely, it is not uncommon for great-grandparents and great grandchildren to coexist in time. If they do not coexist in place, technology allows many forms of contact. Whether there is contact is, of course, another social issue. One choice that many people in the modern world have is to leave (not abandon, that is a different, much older thing) their family, their community, even their society. It always must be remembered that throughout most of human history it was a crime to be without master, without family. Industrialization and technology forced, and allowed, changes in family patterns. For many the choice was family or career. *The Next Generation* offered another choice: Not to be forced to make one. As the *Enterprise* went where "no one has gone before," some took the family along.

UTOPIA AS CHOICE

Choice is perhaps the operational word for utopia. Utopia cannot become a constant without becoming a horror. Therefore, utopia must be a place of great choice about differences: about *being* different; about *valuing* differences; about *maintaining* systems and processes, educational, social, and political, that go far beyond that tired old word "tolerance." While tolerance is a word often used in *Star Trek*, celebration of, as the Vulcans say, "infinite diversity in infinite combination" is not only an intellectual goal, it is a requirement for existence.

Tolerance and celebration do not have to mean infinite patience. The future world of *Star Trek* is intolerant of those who are intolerant. To reify *Star Trek*, probably some groups of colonists left Earth or Earth-dominated planets, just to get away from all that tolerance of what they deemed intolerable. Doubtless, much like some Puritan fleeing to America to avoid religious/political oppression of the Church of England, itself founded to avoid perceived oppressions of the Church of Rome, the thought, "finally free." For the Puritan, it was a freedom to oppress other religious groups in their new utopia. For many of those who metaphorically watched that particular group of Puritans leave, probably there were sighs of "good riddance."

As so many commentators have pointed out, the people of the *Star Trek* future are not perfect; they just aspire to be (see, for example, Barad, 2000; Joseph and Carton, 1992). Likely, in the colonial metaphor, many would say "good riddance" as some group left for the stars to find its own future or was denied entrance to the Federation. But there is an operational value that dominates, *all things to all*, not because they individually or collectively "deserve" them, but because no one or group does not deserve them.

The future is choice. It is not written in stone nor is it a product of the "basic" nature of humanity. It is not a war between good and evil. It is a potential that derives from choices, and that ability to make ethical choices is within us, all of us. We build the systems, we build the processes, and we choose to control, be controlled, or avoid the entire concept and actions of control by how we limit our imaginations about utopia and dystopia.

'Un'defining A Quantum Future'

Implicit in all the questions of the future as defined through the past is that, perhaps, we can choose the better one. Oops! A better one? That is an ideological statement out of the past that biases the future. Yet there are some futures, some ways, as **Table 1** attempts to outline, for humanity that are better than others. There are even some absolutes, at least in the near future. Costanza, in his "*Four Visions of the Century Ahead,*" gives *Star Trek* as only one possible future. But, as he relates, *Star Trek* is the "Default Technological Optimist Vision" of the future. It assumes we will develop all those neat technological gadgets, fusion power being the most important. Without that "free, clean" power, the other visions become more probable. Further, the great irony of technology is that it has fostered so much choice while at the same time, as so many have commented, alienating people from freedom of choice. In much of modern society, technology is so intertwined with day-to-day existence that one must master it just not to be left behind. For too many that is an extremely time-consuming enterprise. There are many choices of careers, but for many there is inbuilt obsolescence. People must rush faster and faster to keep in front of that obsolescence curve. In this light, Costanza's "Ecotopia" alternative (all nations of the Earth learn to conserve energy and play well with each other) sounds nice, but the benevolent "Big Government" scenario seems unlikely in the face of energy PACs and profit motives in producing new technology. The "Mad Max" scenario, unfortunately, seems most consistent with *Star Trek* history as seen from the past.

As *Star Trek* "history" suggests, we have to really "screw up," genetic wars,

WWIII, before we get our act as humans together (for example, Okuda and Okuda, 1996). As the early episodes of *Enterprise* indicate, it took a lot longer than a century beyond WWIII to develop the guidebook on *Really Serious Mistakes Not to Make Again,* also known as the law of the Federation.

It took the Borg to bring *Star Trek* visions of utopia and dystopia into focus. The Borg represented the ultimate interactive command structure, the ultimate rejection of all the values of the Federation and Starfleet – of the *Prime Directive.* They did not conquer; they did not desire political or social domi-nance; they did not even exterminate in the sense of genocide – they "assimilat-ed." Beyond all the obvious metaphors of communism and totalitarian govern-ment and fears about dehumanizing technology in general, the Borg were just plain nasty. They did not eat, drink, recreate, or consume beyond their immedi-ate need to do their job; worst of all, they did not excrete or bathe. If the Klingons, Romulans, and Cardassians were culturally and politically "different," they were at least understandable – convertible. The Borg were the ultimate dystopian future, a fate worse than death – a fate that was death in the minds of individuals and societies that value choice, but often do not think critically about what that word really means.

We came to find in the movie *Star Trek: First Contact* that they had their "hierarchy." As Gross and Altman writing in 1995 note, the Borg were needed to fill in an "enemy gap." Of course, the discovery of the "queen bee" in the *First Contact* hive ruined the whole image of the Borg. As a collective mind they were terrifying, a nightmare of totalitarianism; with a queen bee, they became just another enemy force driven by megalomaniacs, an extreme parody of Plato's *Noble Lie.*

At the very least, though, through *Star Trek*, mega-millions of viewers became more aware of one question of quantum mechanics – can we, do we, really affect what we observe? Can we really choose a utopian future above a dystopian one? Bleak deterministic views of human nature would hold – no. The optimistic view of human nature – that we do have free will and that when aware of choices we will choose the better one – would hold yes. *Star Trek* is always about choices. Sometimes those choices were bad in a dystopian sense; more often they were good in a utopian sense. Within *Star Trek*, the idea of utopia was not displayed within some narrow vision of paradise, but as con-stantly evolving, perhaps infinite in its possibilities. Again and again in *Star Trek,* the message is about searching for enlightenment, that just when you thought you were getting to the top of the hill, you found another higher one had been hidden behind it.

Simply put, the universe of *Star Trek* defies the logic of empiricism, a logical, in human eyes, universe. And each reincarnation of *Star Trek* has brought us closer to the quantum universe of infinite possibilities and to the idea expressed by the powerless Q in *ST:TNG*: "Deja Q," that the answer is simple: reverse the gravity constant of the universe. Of course, having been stripped of his powers by the Q, he could not "do it." Empiricists simply refuse to even envision the idea that Einstein, in his oft-quoted statement, "God does not play dice," might be wrong. In perspective, Stephen Hawkings has stated that eventually science will expose the face of god.

   Star Trek confounds, antagonizes, and even terrifies institutionally- or self-appointed holders of the Holy Grail of knowledge. Many of the adventures of *Star Trek* constantly have suggested, if not directly pushed, a Hawkings concept of the universe; it is understandable, but the understanding will transform us. The '60s *ST* version of man's transformation was personified in *ST:TOS*: "Where No Man has Gone Before" and the old idea that all power corrupts. Q's Loki-like portrayal of an omnipotent being that permeates the '90s *ST:TNG* was another version. Yet not all the omnipotent, or nearly so, beings of *Star Trek* were as corrupted or confused. The immortal Douwd disguising himself as a human in *ST:TNG*: "The Survivors" agonizes over his destruction of an entire species with a thought. Similarly, the escaped Q in *ST:V*: "Death Wish" shows that even a god might eventually desire to die.

STAR TREK AND QUANTUM MECHANICS

   Star Trek evolved in a time when the quantum mechanics science fiction of Arthur C. Clarke and Robert A. Heinlein, both Ph.D.-level physicists who wrote science fiction from the '40s through '90s, was well known. From the '60s, quantum alternate universes have been a popular mainstay of written fiction. In *ST*, they have become part of the utopian and dystopian visions of the future. For example, in *ST*: "Mirror, Mirror," 1967, Kirk, McCoy, Scotty and Uhura wind up in a parallel universe where Starfleet is essentially a pirate organization and they face some strange counter-parts, but an oddly similar Spock (see also *ST*: " The Alternative Factor," 1967). In one of the most classic quantum episodes, *ST:TNG*: "Parallels," 1993, the *Enterprise* hangs in space with hundreds of alternate universe *Enterprises*, some from universes where the Borg had prevailed (see also, *ST:TNG*: "Yesterday's Enterprise," 1990; "Remember Me", 1990). In *ST:DS9* the characters often shift to the alternate universe where the Cardassians rule and the alter egos live *very* different lives. In '90s television, the conflict between linear and quantum time and space theory was played out in another, quite popular series, *Sliders*. This show, an extrapolation of Heinlein's (1980) *The Number of the Beast,* played out the splitting perspective in alternating humor and terror. They never did, though, quite do justice to Heinlein's point that alternate manipulations of physical reality, like "magic," might exist.

Strangely, the one popular television series that did have "quantum" in its title, *Quantum Leap*, was not an alternate universe scenario. In it, one could go back and change the past and, thereby, mold the future. Again, this was not a new idea; it is in fact long pre-quantum, the old going back to kill your father before you were conceived dilemma. But *Quantum Leap* did approach the *Copenhagen Interpretation* of observer effect. What if we extinguish a particular reality by our intervention – a common theme in too many *Star Trek* episodes to mention. Indeed, Okuda and Okuda (1996) in their *Star Trek Chronology: The History of the Future* describe some 25 episodes and three *Star Trek* movies with such themes.

The point is *Star Trek* did not create the concept of alternate universes and time warps. Like many things in *Star Trek*, what is done is interpretations and extrapolations of current hard science. The original ideas came out of the minds of some of humanity's greatest scientists. But where *Quantum Leap, Sliders*, and, more recently, *7 Days* used the ideas as a vehicle for television series, *Star Trek*, on television, did it first. And *Star Trek* went beyond the popular to explore the ethical and moral implications and consequences of messing around in the "quantum" universe. But what does "messing around" really mean?

Zukov (1979:108), criticized by many as too "New Age" to be taken seriously by real scientists, gives perhaps the simplest explanation of quantum mechanics, the new physics and the difference between extinguishment and alternate theory. He utilizes the example of *Schrodinger's Cat* to explain the difference between the Copenhagen Interpretation and the Many Worlds Interpretation of observer effect.

Imagine a live cat, a poisonous gas pellet, and the trigger mechanism of a random decay isotope are placed in a container that shields the contents from outside view. Because a random decay isotope is used for the trigger, it could ignite the gas pellet in a second or in a thousand years. The question after the box is sealed is: Is the cat alive or dead? This is a "no brainer" for scientists and scientific method. "Open" the box and look. As Chaires and Stitt (1994:16) note, "Indeed, classical science demands that the box be opened." Of course, scientific method would demand a careful opening. One could not for example, pick the box up and shake it first to see if the cat screeched, that might set off the gas pellet and ruin the experiment. Some scientists might "open" the box by using some kind of electromagnetic device, a sophisticated x-ray machine or a device capable of hearing a whisper amidst a hurricane. Some might even wait for hours, even days to detect the slightest hint of movement, theorizing that if there is no movement in the time it takes a cat to die of starvation, it must be dead. All of this misses the point.

The *Copenhagen Interpretation* of reality presents the idea that the life or death of the cat exists in a kind of wave limbo as a potential to be alive or dead. No observer can approach the experiment without some bias; opening the box brings into existence the biased reality and extinguishes the other. In the *Many Worlds Interpretation,* the biased moment of opening the box splits realities. In one the cat is alive, in the other it is dead. Neither *alternate universe* is aware of the other. The key point here is that it is the bias of the observer, a bias that exists in all observers, a bias that exist in choosing a *Star Trek* future from among others, that influences either the extinguishment or splitting – one finds what they expect to find. As Zukov (1979:109) so aptly states: "Classical physics says there is one world, it is at it appears and this is it. Quantum physics allows us to entertain the possibility that this is not so."

Star Trek, by its sheer breadth of observations about the human condition, and humanity, presents a kind of Schrodinger's Cat experiment. Only the question is not if the cat is alive or dead, but if we are heading toward utopia or dystopia. In one scenario our biases about the fundamental nature of man or the limits of the political condition will send us one way or the other as we make decisions about our future direction(s); in the other, it will send us many ways as we split and re-split, sometimes making the "right" decisions and at others the "wrong." This latter image, that invoked by *ST:TNG*: "Parallels" of all the possible futures of the *Enterprise* hanging in space together, all that we were, and all that we might have been but never became, is the most terrifying vision because it offers no hope except the luck of being in the right decision stream. Or is it luck?

Conclusion

Whether we are lucky to be in this particular alternate universe is a question for philosophers to resolve. Or perhaps not. Some 80 years ago, long before current scientific controversy about quantum reality, W.T. Thomas made a statement that is still widely quoted by social scientists: *Things perceived as real are treated as real.* We do not have to go as far as quantum mechanics and the creation of literal alternate universes to understand that decisions and choices are too often based on things we perceive as real but only exist in our own mind or a few minds with the same biases. Still, while the things of the mind may not be real, the decisions and the choices are, as are the ripples in time and society that may flow outward.

In the context of increasing alternatives for the future, many deadly and dead-ended, perhaps it becomes an ethical duty to our children, to our great-great-grandchildren, to choose a better future – one in which we have not limited their decisions and choices because we have destroyed the past. Yes, the past. How many times have we cursed our ancestors, near and far, for their shortsightedness, for their greed, for their lack of vision in understanding that we would someday live and inherit not only their glories but also their dark, often knowing, deadly environmental mistakes that will last long beyond us? We accuse them of opening that metaphorical box too many times with too many deadly biases about what the future could or could not be – or of acting without any concern at all except for themselves. Barring some miracle of technology, we, every single person who is now alive and their children, even those yet to be conceived, are already the past to those who will be alive in 2202. A far time, yes. But 200 years ago someone sat on a hillside and wondered about those stars above, about what the future would bring, for themselves and for their children. Perhaps they planted a sapling oak outside their home and watched it grow as they lived their life. They loved, hopefully a lot, hated, hopefully very little. They felt joy and pain as they experienced the cycle of physical life around them. Eventually they died and became a memory, and, as for most of us, that memory eventually faded until it was as if they never were – except as a linkage in time. Those stars are still there and, perhaps still, that oak tree. But we have the potential for more. Technology allows us to "live" virtually forever in that our remote descendants will be able to "see" our faces, watch us sit on that hillside, and listen to our words as we plant our tree. In *Star Trek* it is not uncommon for a crew member of the *Enterprise* to have some memorabilia from the far past, a photo, a diary, and to look fondly and proudly at it. Whether our real descendants will look on us fondly or curse that we ever existed is in our hands.

Pragmatically, we must all become involved in deciding the directions of the future, or default to the decisions of the few. Not making decisions is a decision. That is a constant message of *Star Trek*. Yes, making decisions is often agony. Worse agony is doing things to carry them out. But *Star Trek* offers a template, that guidebook to *Really Serious Mistakes Never to Make Again*. That *Star Trek* is often about mistakes we have already made makes it "quantum historical" reinforcement on what not to envision in that "box." That *Star Trek* offers an alternative, often hopeful, albeit sometimes scary, vision of the future, offers the greatest thing we can choose for future generations – that they have choices about theirs.

Bibliography

Barad, Judith, with Ed Robertson (2000). *The Ethics of Star Trek*, New York: HarperCollins.

Chaires, Robert H. and B. Grant Stitt (1994). "Paradigmatic Concerns in Criminal Justice," *Journal of Crime & Justice*, Vol. 17, No. 2: 1-22.

Heinlein, Robert A. (1980). *The Number of the Beast*, New York: Fawcett Columbine.

Joseph, Paul and Sharon Carton (1992). "The Law of the Federation: Images of Law, Lawyers, and the Legal System in *Star Trek: The Next Generation*," 24 *U. Toledo Law. Rev.* 43.

Nemecek, Larry (1992). *The Star Trek The Next Generation Companion*, NY: Pocket Books.

Okuda, Michael and Denise Okuda (1996). *Star Trek Chronology: The History of the Future*, New York: Pocket Books.

Scharf, Michael P. and Lawrence D. Robert (1994). "The Interstellar Relations of the Federation: International Law and *Star Trek: The Next Generation*," 25 *U. Toledo Law Rev.* 577

About the Editors and Authors

ROBERT H. CHAIRES IS AN ASSISTANT PROFESSOR IN THE DEPARTMENT OF CRIMINAL
JUSTICE AT THE UNIVERSITY OF NEVADA-RENO. A FORMER DENVER POLICE OFFICER AND
LEGAL ACCESS ATTORNEY IN THE COLORADO DEPARTMENT OF CORRECTIONS, HE
RECEIVED HIS J.D. FROM THE UNIVERSITY OF DENVER AND PH.D. IN PUBLIC
ADMINISTRATION FROM THE UNIVERSITY OF COLORADO – DENVER. HIS PRIMARY ACA-
DEMIC INTERESTS ARE THE HISTORY OF LAW AND JUSTICE, CIVIL RIGHTS, AND FUTURISM.
WHEN NOT WRITING OR TEACHING, HE IS FIXING THE DAMAGE THE FAMILY DOGS HAVE
DONE OR SAILING HIS BOAT LOOKING FOR AN ISOLATED PLACE TO ANCHOR.

BRADLEY STEWART CHILTON IS AN ASSOCIATE PROFESSOR IN THE DEPARTMENT OF
CRIMINAL JUSTICE AT THE UNIVERSITY OF NORTH TEXAS, AND, PERHAPS BY A TRANS-
PORTER MALFUNCTION, ALSO HOLDS A COURTESY APPOINTMENT IN THE DEPARTMENT OF
POLITICAL SCIENCE AND IS A FELLOW IN THE TEXAS CENTER FOR DIGITAL KNOWLEDGE.
HE HAS PREVIOUSLY TAUGHT IN POLITICAL SCIENCE DEPARTMENTS AT WASHINGTON STATE
UNIVERSITY, THE UNIVERSITY OF TOLEDO, THE UNIVERSITY OF SOUTHERN MISSISSIPPI,
AND THE UNIVERSITY OF GEORGIA. WITH A J.D., PH.D. IN POLITICAL SCIENCE, AND
M.L.S. IN LIBRARY AND INFORMATION SCIENCE, HIS FOCUS IS ON THE INTERSECTION OF
LAW, PUBLIC ADMINISTRATION, INFORMATION SCIENCE, AND JUSTICE. FOR EXAMPLE, HIS
BOOK *PRISONS UNDER THE GAVEL* (OHIO STATE UNIVERSITY PRESS, 1991) ANALYZED
WHAT WORKS IN JUDICIAL PRISON REFORM AND WAS BASED ON HIS DISSERTATION, WINNER
OF THE 1988 ANNUAL DISSERTATION AWARD OF THE NATIONAL ASSOCIATION OF
SCHOOLS OF PUBLIC AFFAIRS AND ADMINISTRATION. HE HAS PUBLISHED BOOKS, ARTICLES,
CHAPTERS, AND PAPERS ON INFORMATION POLICY AND LAW, HATE CRIME AND DIVERSITY
ISSUES, ETHICS IN ADMINISTRATION, AND JUDICIAL PRISON REFORM. HE HAS ALSO BUILT
THREE HOMES FROM BLUEPRINTS HE CREATED, PLAYS DRUMS AND GUITAR IN A JAZZ COMBO,
AND IS A LAY LEADER FOR CHINN'S CHAPEL UNITED METHODIST CHURCH.

The Authors

SHARON F. CARTON IS A FORMER LAW PROFESSOR AND NOW A FREELANCE FICTION AND NONFICTION WRITER CURRENTLY RESIDING IN SEATTLE. HER FIRST MYSTERY NOVEL, *SOMETIMES YOU GET KILLED*, WAS RECENTLY PUBLISHED. SHE RECEIVED HER J.D. FROM HOFSTRA UNIVERSITY AND LL.M. IN INTERNATIONAL LAW FROM GEORGE WASHINGTON UNIVERSITY. OTHER THAN TEACHING, SHE HAS WORKED IN A SOUTH LONDON BAKERY, CLERKED FOR A MANHATTAN CRIMINAL COURT JUDGE, INTERNED WITH A BRITISH BARRISTER, AND SERVED AS A CIVILIAN ATTORNEY WITH THE UNITED STATES DEPARTMENT OF DEFENSE. SHE ALSO WONDERS "WHETHER THERE IS A FUTURE FOR THE LAW, WHETHER IT CAN KEEP PACE WITH SCIENCE, AND WHETHER THERE WILL BE ROOM FOR JUSTICE IN THE WORLD WE MAKE."

ROBERT COSTANZA IS PROFESSOR AND DIRECTOR OF THE UNIVERSITY OF MARYLAND INSTITUTE FOR ECOLOGICAL ECONOMICS. HIS RESEARCH GROUP IS CONCERNED WITH MODELING ECOLOGICAL SYSTEMS AT SCALES RANGING FROM MICROCOSMS TO LARGE REGIONAL LANDSCAPES. HE IS INVOLVED IN THE MULTISCALE EXPERIMENTAL ECOSYSTEM RESEARCH CENTER (MEERC) THAT EXAMINES TIME, SPACE, AND COMPLEXITY VARIABLES SUCH AS NUTRIENT INPUTS AND CONTAMINATE STRESSES ON AND IN ECOSYSTEMS.

PAUL R. JOSEPH IS ASSOCIATE DEAN, INTERNATIONAL AND EXTERNAL PROGRAMS AND PROFESSOR OF LAW AT THE SHEPARD BROAD LAW CENTER OF NOVA SOUTHEASTERN UNIVERSITY IN FORT LAUDERDALE, FLORIDA. HE RECEIVED HIS J.D. FROM THE UNIVERSITY OF CALIFORNIA – DAVIS AND LL.M. FROM TEMPLE UNIVERSITY. THE AUTHOR OF NUMEROUS ARTICLES ON LAW AND POPULAR CULTURE, HE IS ALSO THE MANAGING EDITOR OF *PICTURING JUSTICE,* AN AWARD WINING ON-LINE JOURNAL FOCUSING ON HOW TELEVISION AND MOVIES FICTIONALLY PORTRAY LAW AND LAWYERS.

SUSAN A. LENTZ IS AN ASSOCIATE PROFESSOR IN THE DEPARTMENT OF CRIMINAL JUSTICE AT THE UNIVERSITY OF NEVADA-RENO AND DIRECTS THE PRE-LAW PROGRAM IN THAT DEPARTMENT. PRIOR TO BECOMING AN ACADEMIC, SHE WAS A NAME PARTNER IN A LAW FIRM, A LEGAL EDITOR FOR A LARGE PUBLISHING COMPANY, AND SERVED AS A DEPUTY ATTORNEY GENERAL FOR THE STATE OF NEVADA. SHE RECEIVED HER J.D. FROM THE UNIVERSITY OF DENVER AND PH.D. IN HISTORY FROM THE UNIVERSITY OF WISCONSIN-MADISON. SHE HAS PUBLISHED EXTENSIVELY AS A FEMINIST SCHOLAR AND IN MORE GENERAL AREAS OF LAW AND CRIMINAL JUSTICE. WHEN NOT TEACHING OR WRITING, SHE SPENDS HER TIME TRYING TO KEEP HER TEENAGE SON, THREE DOGS, AND THREE CATS UNDER SOME SEMBLANCE OF CONTROL WHILE NOT MISSING ANY EPISODES OF *STAR TREK*.

MATTHEW LEONE IS AN ASSOCIATE PROFESSOR IN THE DEPARTMENT OF CRIMINAL JUSTICE AT THE UNIVERSITY OF NEVADA-RENO. BESIDES BEING THE ACKNOWLEDGED 'TECHNOLOGICAL WIZARD' OF THE DEPARTMENT AND AN EXCEPTIONALLY HIGH-RATED TEACHER, HE IS A CONSULTANT FOR NUMEROUS AGENCIES IN JUVENILE AND ADULT CORRECTIONS AND AN EXPERT IN 'COMMUNITY CORRECTIONS' ALONG WITH BEING COAUTHOR OF A TEXTBOOK WITH THAT TITLE. HE RECEIVED HIS M.A. AND PH.D. IN SOCIAL ECOLOGY FROM THE UNIVERSITY OF CALIFORNIA-IRVINE. WHEN HE IS NOT TEACHING AND WRITING ABOUT HIS SPECIAL INTERESTS: JAIL CROWDING, MEDICAL SOCIOLOGY, FACTORS WHICH AFFECT PUNISHMENT IN RAPE CASES, INMATE RIGHTS, AND CONJUGAL VISITATION, HE CAN BE FOUND FIXING CARS AND COMPUTERS FOR OTHERS.

MICHAEL STOKES PAULSEN IS BRIGGS AND MORTON PROFESSOR OF LAW AT THE UNIVERSITY OF MINNESOTA LAW SCHOOL. HE RECEIVED HIS M.A. IN RELIGION FROM YALE DIVINITY SCHOOL AND HIS J.D. FROM YALE LAW SCHOOL WHERE HE WAS EDITOR OF THE *YALE LAW JOURNAL*. BEFORE BECOMING A LAW PROFESSOR, HE SERVED IN THE UNITED STATES DEPARTMENT OF JUSTICE IN THE CRIMINAL DIVISION HONORS PROGRAM AS STAFF COUNSEL FOR THE CENTER FOR LAW & RELIGIOUS FREEDOM IN WASHINGTON, D.C., AND AGAIN IN THE DEPARTMENT OF JUSTICE IN THE OFFICE OF LEGAL COUNSEL. HE HAS PUBLISHED NUMEROUS ARTICLES AND TREATISES IN THE AREAS OF CONSTITUTIONAL LAW AND RELIGIOUS FREEDOM.

MICHAEL P. SCHARF IS PROFESSOR OF LAW AND DIRECTOR OF THE CENTER FOR INTERNATIONAL LAW AND POLICY AT THE NEW ENGLAND SCHOOL OF LAW. HE RECEIVED HIS A.B. AND J.D. FROM DUKE UNIVERSITY AND, PRIOR TO BECOMING AN ACADEMIC, SERVED IN THE U.S. DEPARTMENT OF STATE, OFFICE OF LEGAL ADVISOR. AMONG HIS ASSIGNMENTS, HE WAS COUNSEL TO THE COUNTER-TERRORISM BUREAU, ATTORNEY-ADVISOR FOR LAW ENFORCEMENT AND INTELLIGENCE, AND ATTORNEY-ADVISOR FOR UNITED NATIONS AFFAIRS. WHILE AT THE DEPARTMENT OF STATE, HE WAS ALSO A MEMBER OF THE UNITED STATES DELEGATIONS TO THE U.N. GENERAL ASSEMBLY AND TO THE U.N. HUMAN RIGHTS COMMISSION. HE IS THE AUTHOR OF DOZENS OF ARTICLES AND SEVERAL BOOKS, INCLUDING *BALKAN JUSTICE*, WHICH RECEIVED A NOMINATION FOR THE PULITZER PRIZE IN 1998. HIS WORK *THE INTERNATIONAL CRIMINAL TRIBUNAL FOR RWANDA* RECEIVED THE 1999 AMERICAN SOCIETY OF INTERNATIONAL LAW CERTIFICATE OF MERIT FOR OUTSTANDING BOOK IN INTERNATIONAL LAW.

B. GRANT STITT IS PROFESSOR AND CHAIR OF THE DEPARTMENT OF CRIMINAL JUSTICE AT THE UNIVERSITY OF NEVADA-RENO. AN ECLECTIC CRIMINOLOGIST, HIS RESEARCH INTERESTS INCLUDE THE EFFECTS OF LEGALIZED GAMBLING ON COMMUNITIES, VICTIMIZATION AND VICTIMLESS CRIME, AND ETHICAL DILEMMAS IN CRIMINAL JUSTICE, AS WELL AS THEO-

RETICAL AND ETIOLOGICAL ASPECTS OF CRIME. HE HAS PUBLISHED IN AN EXCEPTIONALLY WIDE VARIETY OF ACADEMIC JOURNALS RANGING FROM *LAW AND PHILOSOPHY* TO THE *JOURNAL OF CRIMINAL JUSTICE EDUCATION*. WHEN NOT TEACHING OR WRITING, HE SPENDS HIS TIME TRYING TO CONTROL AN EXCEPTIONALLY DIVERSE FACULTY WHO KEEP REELECTING HIM.

CHARLES M. VIVONA IS VISITING ASSISTANT PROFESSOR OF SOCIOLOGY AND CRIMINOLOGY AT THE SUNY COLLEGE AT OLD WESTBURY, WHERE HE TEACHES COURSES ON CRIMINOLOGY, JUVENILE DELINQUENCY, POLITICAL SOCIOLOGY, SOCIAL DEVIANCE, AND SOCIAL PSYCHOLOGY. FOR TWENTY YEARS HE WAS THE REPRESENTATIVE TO (NON-LAW SCHOOL) COLLEGE FACULTY NATIONWIDE FOR THE ACADEMIC LEGAL PUBLISHER, FOUNDATION PRESS – AND MORE RECENTLY FOR FOUNDATION PRESS AND WEST GROUP COMBINED. HE PREVIOUSLY TAUGHT FOR MANY YEARS AT THE SUNY COLLEGE AT CORTLAND AND RUTGERS UNIVERSITY IN CAMDEN. HE RECEIVED HIS M.A. AND PH.D. FROM SYRACUSE UNIVERSITY: HIS DOCTORAL DISSERTATION WAS TITLED "ACTORS/ACTING: THE THEATRICAL SELF AND THE CREATION AND CULTURING OF SOCIAL ORDER." HE HAS BEEN INVOLVED IN NUMEROUS ART WORLDS.

Further Reading

NOTE: This book comes on the cusp of many interesting new scholarly works analyzing *Star Trek* and *Star Trek* phenomena, from cooking to physics to social theory. We apologize in advance if we neglect to mention a book or any one of the many dozens of excellent scholarly journal articles. But it is important to get a sense of this academic activity with a list of some recent scholarly books on *Star Trek:*

Judith Barad, with Ed Robertson, *The Ethics of Star Trek* (New York: Harper Collins, 2000).

Michele Barrett and Duncan Barrett, *Star Trek: The Human Frontier* (Routledge, 2000).

William Cassidy, Susan Schwartz, and Ross Shepard Kraemer, *Religions of Star Trek* (Boulder, CO: Westview Press, 2002)

Joel Engel, *Gene Roddenberry: The Myth and the Man Behind Star Trek* (New York: Hyperion, 1994).

David Gerrold, *The World of Star Trek* (New York: Ballantine Books, 1979. 2nd ed., Chappaqua, NY: Bluejay Books, 1984).

Jeff Greenwald, *Future Perfect* (New York: Penguin, 1998).

Lois Gresh and Robert Weinberg, *The Computers of Star Trek* (New York: Basic Books, 1999).

Richard Hanley, *The Metaphysics of Star Trek* (New York: Basic Books, 1997).

Taylor Harrison, Sarah Projansky, Kent A. Ono, and Elyce Rae Helford, eds., *Enterprise Zones: Critical Positions on Star Trek* (Boulder, CO: Westview Press, 1996).

Mike Hertenstein, *The Double Vision of Star Trek: Half Humans, Evil Twins, and Science Fiction* (Chicago: Cornerstone Press, 1998).

Lawrence M. Krauss, *The Physics of Star Trek* (New York: Basic Books, 1995).

Michael Okuda and Denise Okuda, *The Star Trek Encyclopedia: A Reference Guide to the Future*, 2nd ed. (New York: Pocket Books, 1997).

Ethan Phillips and William J. Birnes, *Star Trek Cookbook* (New York: Pocket Books, 1999).

Jennifer E. Porter and Darcee L. McLaren, eds., Star Trek and Sacred Ground: Explorations of Star Trek, Religion, and American Culture (Albany, NY: SUNY Press, 2000).

Thomas Richards, *The Meaning of Star Trek* (New York: Doubleday, 1997).

Robin Roberts, *Sexual Generations: Star Trek-The Next Generation and Gender* (Champaign: University of Illinois Press, 1999).

Robert Sekuler, Blake Randolph and Randoph Blake, *Star Trek On the Brain: Alien Minds, Human Minds* (W.H. Freeman & Co., 1999).

Jon Wagner and Jan Lundeen, *Deep Space and Sacred Time: Star Trek in the American Mythos* (Westport, CN: Praeger, 1998).

Michael Wolff, Kelly Maloni, Ben Greenman, Kristen Miller, and Jeff Hearn, *Net Trek: Your Guide to Trek Life In Cyberspace* (New York: Michael Wolff, 1995).

Index